T0330625

Profitability and the Great Recession

From the mid-1980s, investors in the United States increasingly directed capital towards the financial sector at the expense of non-financial sectors, lured by the perception of higher profits. This flow of capital inflated asset prices, creating the stock market and housing bubbles that burst when the imbalance between stagnant incomes and rising debts triggered the banking meltdown. *Profitability and the Great Recession* analyzes these trends in profitability and capital accumulation, which the authors identify as the root cause of the financial crisis, in the context of the United States and other major Organisation for Economic Co-operation and Development countries.

Drawing on insights from Adam Smith, David Ricardo, John Stuart Mill, and Karl Marx, the authors interpret the relationship between capital accumulation and profitability trends through the conceptual lens of classical political economy. The book provides extensive empirical evidence of declining rates of US nonfinancial corporate accumulations from the mid-1960s and profitability trends in that sector falling from postwar highs. In contrast to this, it is shown that there was a vigorous rise of profitability in the financial sector from 1982 through to the early part of the twenty-first century, which led to the bloating of that sector. The authors conclude that the long-term falling accumulation trend in the non-financial corporate sector, highlighted by the bankruptcy of major automobile corporations, stands out as the underlying force that transformed the financial crisis into a full fledged Great Recession.

This book will be of interest to students and researchers in the areas of economics, political economy, business, and finance.

Ascension Mejorado is Master Teacher of Economics at New York University, USA.

Manuel Roman taught economics at New Jersey City University, USA for over 25 years, and is now retired.

Routledge Frontiers of Political Economy

Profitability and the Great Recession

The role of accumulation trends in the financial crisis

Ascension Mejorado and Manuel Roman

Routledge
Taylor & Francis Group

LONDON AND NEW YORK

First published 2014
by Routledge
4 Park Square, Milton Park, Abingdon, Oxon OX14 4RN
605 Third Avenue, New York, NY 10017

Routledge is an imprint of the Taylor & Francis Group, an informa business

British Library Cataloguing in Publication Data
A catalogue record for this book is available from the British Library

Library of Congress Cataloging in Publication Data
Mejorado, Ascension.
Profitability and the great recession: the role of accumulation trends
in the financial crisis/Ascension Mejorado and Manuel Roman.
    pages cm
    Includes bibliographical references and index.
    1. Profit–United States. 2. Capital movements–United States.
    3. Capital market–United States. 4. Global Financial Crisis, 2008–2009.
    I. Roman, Manuel. II. Title.
HC110.P7M38 2013
332'.04150973090511–dc23   2013015501

ISBN: 978-0-415-70993-4 (hbk)
ISBN: 978-1-315-88524-7 (ebk)

Typeset in Times New Roman
by Sunrise Setting Ltd, Paignton, UK

Contents

4 Mechanization and price/quality competition   61

5 Capital intensity and profitability: dissenting views   83

6 Heterodox models of technical change and profitability   105

Figures

Tables

1 Introduction

The path to the Great Recession

We present in this book an analysis of systemic trends in the US and other major OECD countries leading to the Great Recession, based on insights drawn from the conceptual framework of such classical economists as Adam Smith, David Ricardo, John Stuart Mill, and Karl Marx. We also provide extensive empirical evidence in support of the significance we attach to the structural determination of these trends. Thus, in line with the fundamental assumption of classical political economy, our approach highlights the link between profitability and capital accumulation trends. We argue that declining trends of US nonfinancial corporate capital accumulation from the mid-1960s to the present were caused by profit rates falling in that sector from their postwar highs to a 1982 trough, and, following a rebound extending to 1987, remaining lower and never recovering the high levels achieved in the postwar period. By contrast, the significant recovery of profitability in the financial sector from its 1982 trough outpaced the partial improvement of nonfinancial corporate profitability. We assume that businesses facing uncertain prospects regarding their new investments rely heavily on past profitability trends as a guide to the future. We argue that the bifurcation of financial from nonfinancial capital accumulation paths after the mid-1980s mirrored the growing gap between profitability paths in those two sectors. Rising profitability in financial sectors attracted growing capital flows into financial markets, including mortgage-backed securities. In the event, the formation of stock market and housing bubbles goaded the build-up of global investors' euphoria. Driven by competitive pressures and blinded by overconfidence in their chosen strategy, banks pushed the frontiers of profitable investments to perilous grounds that eventually triggered the system's crisis. In our view, however, weak accumulation trends in the nonfinancial corporate sector, the result of the inadequate restoration of profitability outside finance, transformed the financial crisis into a full-fledged Great Recession.

As the Great Recession gathered momentum, the illusions of sustained prosperity brought on by successive bubbles in the US economy since the early 1980s gave way to dark forebodings. Conventional economic theory failed to predict the slump, gauge its depth or offer a credible way out of it. Excluding the first half of the 1990s, financial euphoria did not trigger sustained accumulation upturns in nonfinancial industries: the investment boom of the early 1990s ended with a crash in 2001. Years after the onset of economic crisis, business confidence in the prospects for a speedy return to former levels of business activity remained low. The destructive force of the debacle has persisted long after its official ending. Despite the surge in corporate profits, investment spending since 2008 remained subdued. In a recent report on the state of household incomes and net worth published by the Federal Reserve, a bleak picture of the losses incurred since 2007 stands out. Median household income in the US fell 7.7 percent from its 2007 level and 6.3 percent since 2000. In the crisis aftermath, between 2007 and 2010, average family wealth declined by almost 40 percent. Household wealth in 2010 was 27.1 percent lower than the level attained in 2001 (Bricker *et al.*, 2012).

The business outlook conveyed by leading analysts in the financial media remained mired in uncertainty despite the strong performance of major Wall Street banks. Stunned by the scope of the crisis, and smarting from the failure of conventional economists to warn of the impending crash, daring financial commentators turned to sources generally treated with derision. Anxieties generated by the unending malaise surprisingly drew the attention of Wall Street gurus to Marx's views, although as Bronfenbrenner (1989, p. 22) cleverly noted, such interest usually reflects the needs of a "rich man's Karl Marx." In this context, going to Marx for counsel bore witness to the unease caused by the severity of the slump. The practice goes back over a decade before the financial crash in Wall Street challenged the belief in rational markets. Ten years earlier John Cassidy (1997) announced "The Return of Karl Marx" to skeptical *New Yorker* readers. That essay highlighted the views of an anonymous Englishman whose background, described as part of the "upper echelons" of the British civil service and the higher circles of a major Wall Street investment bank, presumably added weight to his opinions. "The longer I spend on Wall Street the more convinced I am that Karl Marx was right," he said (Cassidy, 1997).

The editorial director of the *Harvard Business Review*, Justin Fox, in a recent commentary on the apparent disconnect between the widely publicized rise in US corporate profits and low rates of growth in output and employment, rued the lack of "good explanations of secular shifts in profits" (Fox, 2010) and also turned to Marx wondering if "is it finally time to read *Das Kapital*." Fox emphasized that, contrary to widely held perceptions, "Pre-tax domestic nonfinancial corporate profits...are nowhere near record levels as a share of national income," down by more than half the percentage reached in the late 1940s, well below the ratios reached in the decades before 1980. Fox suggested that despite subpar nonfinancial corporate yields, the great ascent in "financial industry profits and 'rest of the world' profits" documented by the Bureau of Economic Analysis raised overall corporate profits. Recovery remained lackluster because "for much of the business community, profits are not that high by historical standards."

Raising the dreaded question, Nouriel Roubini (2011) wondered whether capitalism was "doomed" and settled on the possibility that "Karl Marx ... was partly right in arguing that globalization, financial intermediation run amok and redistribution of income and wealth from labor to capital could lead [c]apitalism to self-destruct." For his part, George Magnus (2011), senior economic adviser at UBS investment bank, suggested that lacking clear solutions to the persistent malaise in global markets, "Policy makers struggling to understand the barrage of financial panics, protests and other ills afflicting the world would do well to study the works of a long-dead economist: Karl Marx."

Most other influential commentators skipped Marx altogether, bringing up instead the unstoppable force of technological change. Thus, while acknowledging the gravity of "current woes" in the *Financial Times* series on "Capitalism in Crisis", Lawrence Summers called for "smart reinvention" of the economy in view of the fact that "few would confidently bet that the US or Europe will see a return to full employment, as previously defined, within the next five years. The economies of both are likely to be demand constrained for a long time." His diagnosis extended to China as well, finding the root cause of the depression "deep within the evolution of technology." (Summers, 2012).

Now well before Summers' technocratic view of historical evolution gained popularity, Ricardo and Marx singled out technological progress as a crucial force shaping profitability and capital accumulation trends. It is widely acknowledged that new technology in the 1930s led to the displacement of farm workers and more recently manufacturing labor. Such structural changes did not simply issue from advances in the technical conditions of production but rather from their impact on profitability and capital accumulation trends.

Profitability: the missing link in Stiglitz's view of structural change

Joseph Stiglitz's account of structural change in the US economy since the 1930s to the present provides a powerful historical framework in which to set our empirical findings. Evaluating developments from the heights of society's welfare, however, Stiglitz's story of structural change overlooks the decisive role played by business profitability in shaping the nature of growth and depression. In our view, glossing over the power of profit to direct capital flows in a capitalist economy weakens Stiglitz's ability to sort out the direction of structural change. We, on the contrary, identify profitability as the driving force behind the historical growth and stagnation of agriculture, manufacturing and (financial) services. In our view of structural change, periods of depression represent critical stages in the evolution of capital and profits. Irving Fisher's insight from 1932 – that "A depression is a condition in which business becomes unprofitable. It might well be called the Private Business Disease. Its worst consequences are business failures and wide-spread unemployment" (Fisher, 2011, p. 19) – captures our views of the significance of profits and the impact of their decline upon capital accumulation.

Stiglitz (2011) believes that in order to assess the nature of the financial crisis triggering the Great Recession "we have to understand the economy's problems *before* the crisis hit." In his view "the economy was very sick before the crisis...America and the world were victims of their own success," meaning that labor productivity in manufacturing had surpassed the growth in aggregate demand, "which meant that manufacturing employment decreased. Labor had to shift to services."

His argument provides a convenient setting to frame our own interpretation of the forces behind the financial excesses triggering the Great Recession: "the problem today is the so-called real economy. A crisis of the real economy lies behind the Long Slump just as it lay behind the Great Depression" (Stiglitz, 2012). In our view, the underlying cause of the current crisis was a declining rate of capital formation in the nonfinancial corporate sector compensated by the runaway growth of financial activities. Indeed, the long-term capital accumulation trend outside the financial sector fell after the mid-1960s, and, despite a cyclical but incomplete recovery of profitability in the 1980s, its level remained historically low.

Stiglitz has consistently refused to identify the financial sphere as causing the crisis, referring to the ensuing credit freeze as a mere pathology of the banking sector. He has repeatedly stressed that, while "the financial sector's inexcusable recklessness, given free rein in mindless deregulation, was the obvious precipitating factor of the crisis" (Stiglitz, 2011), the underlying cause should be found in the real economy. Stiglitz's view of the structural changes in the real economy behind the financial crisis provides an account of the accumulation crisis that transcends Minsky's narrow focus on the development of financial fragility due to overconfidence. In that light, Stiglitz's account will serve as a contrasting reference in our heterodox version of the crisis theory.

In Stiglitz's view structural changes in the US real economy, both in the 1930s and 2008, produced shortfalls in aggregate demand that only burgeoning debts were able to patch up for a time until financial defaults spread the slump throughout the entire system. From a Keynesian vantage, four years after the Great Recession of 2008 started, Stiglitz blames the lack of investment activity on a global-scale evidence for the persistent weakness in effective demand that blocks policy efforts to jumpstart the economy. While arguing that the "seeming golden age of 2007 was far from paradise," he decries the depth of the current malaise accounting for "6.6 million fewer jobs in the United States than there were four years ago." This is the first time since the 1930s Depression in the US that the unemployment rate exceeded 8 percent for over 4 years after the onset of an economic slump (Stiglitz, 2012).

Stiglitz's analysis stresses the similarities between the structural changes that prepared the grounds for the 1930s Great Depression and the more recent trends behind the Great Recession of 2008. As Stiglitz noted, since the 1930s to the present, the employment share of workers engaged in farm labor steadily declined from a peak of 20 percent to a 2 percent nadir. Between 1929 and 1932, farm incomes fell significantly, somewhere between one-third and two-thirds. This drastic reduction in employment and incomes happened because with "accelerating productivity, output was increasing faster than demand, and prices fell sharply" (Stiglitz, 2012). Stiglitz argues that in the 1930s, sustained growth in labor productivity in farming led to the massive displacement of labor from those sectors, along with the decline in prices and incomes; decades later, sustained growth in labor productivity in manufacturing had the same effect. In both cases, income losses led to excessive borrowing and caused the financial fragility that eventually crushed the financial system. The ensuing cascade of defaults triggered the financial crisis and the attendant credit cutoff aggravated the collapse of effective demand which had given rise to the financial excesses in the first place (Stiglitz, 2011, 2012).

In the 1930s, the economic malaise in farming spilled over into lower manufacturing sales, causing additional layoffs of manufacturing workers, and in a feedback loop a further contraction of demand for farming products. Confronted with the juggernaut of falling prices and diminishing incomes, while seeking to maintain their standard of living, farmers raised their bank borrowing. Unable to properly assess the extent of declining prices, incomes and employment, farmers and banks misjudged the risks of default, hence the growth of unsustainable debts. Then "The financial sector was swept into the vortex of declining farm incomes" (Stiglitz, 2012); today the implosion of the housing bubble triggered the financial meltdown. In both cases, the banking crisis precipitated the ensuing depression and extended its destructive power, but structural changes in the real economy caused it.

Stiglitz's valuable analysis: outside the mainstream, but not far off

We share Stiglitz's concern that the convenient assumption embedded in neoclassical theory "that markets are efficient and self-adjusting" lent credibility to deregulation of financial activities and contributed to the benign neglect of default risks involved in debt management (Stiglitz, 2010). Holding such assumptions explains why Martin Feldstein prefaced his presentation of an NBER volume dedicated to explore the *Risk of Economic Crisis* in 1991 with the observation that "the danger of a financial and economic crisis is more prominent in the thinking of policy officials and business leaders than in the research of professional economists."

Belief in the self-adjustment of financial markets allowed Feldstein to confidently predict that despite "the fear of an impending major economic crisis" among the uninitiated, brought on by the various financial mishaps encountered in the 1980s, "including the failure of most of the less developed debtor countries to service their debts, the deterioration of capital among money-center banks, the large numbers of bankruptcies of the thrift institutions, the wide swings of currency exchange rates, the increase of corporate debt, and the stock market crash of 1987," preventing a new financial crisis would simply require government policies designed to keep inflation low plus the implementation of asset diversification on the part of financial institutions (Feldstein, 1991, pp. 1–18).

Stiglitz readily recognizes that structural changes leading to systemic breakdowns are part of capitalist development, and he rejects Adam Smith's claim of an "invisible hand" carrying out the task of securing a macroeconomic balance (Stiglitz, 2010). In the real world, persistent waves of "irrational optimism and pessimism" buffet global markets and lead to instability and crisis. As an example, in the wake of the 1997–1998 East Asia financial crises, Stiglitz (2011) underscored the growth of bank reserves in developing countries seeking to shield their economies from IMF "mismanagement." In the event, this "precautionary" decision to channel export surpluses into bank reserves and thus stabilize their exchange rates led to excesses in the opposite direction. In Bernanke's (2005) view these practices generated a "savings glut," a growing gap, that is, between global savings and investment.

Stiglitz's analysis, however, sought to emphasize the other side of what Bernanke's concept implied, namely the emergence of a world-wide "investment dearth." Indeed, Stiglitz (2010) pointed out that such declines in investment opportunities played a central role in Keynes' theory of crises, arguing that his interpretation provided a better guide to understanding the underlying causes of the slump. Why did the housing bubble inflate so much, despite falling nonresidential capital accumulation and declining interest rates? For Stiglitz a meaningful parallel exists between the antecedents of the Great Depression and those of the Great Recession 80 years later. In the years leading to the 1930s Great Depression, high labor productivity growth in farming lowered prices, incomes and employment of farm labor. While the displaced labor then found employment in manufacturing, technical change today is creating similar labor redundancies in manufacturing. Stiglitz (2012) argues that systemic changes in the industrial structure before 1980 laid the grounds for the Great Recession: "Back then we were moving from agriculture to manufacturing. Today we are moving from manufacturing to a service economy."

The decline in the share of manufacturing employment today nearly approaches the contraction in farming jobs in the 1930s, from about one third sixty years ago to less than one tenth at present. Stiglitz finds the cause of the displacement of workers out of manufacturing in that sector's growth in labor productivity, the same cause that forced farm workers off the land and pushed them into manufacturing in the 1930s. But now the displacement of manufacturing labor is more extensive due to "globalization," the intensive search for "low-wage" countries to locate manufacturing activities, particularly countries with access to the latest technologies. The combined effect of pressures to raise labor productivity at home and outsource production to countries with cheaper production costs led to the same results that ushered in the Great Depression, namely high unemployment and income losses in the real US economy.

Stiglitz's probing of the structural antecedents of the Great Recession provides a convenient foundation for our alternative view. His critique reaches further than Paul Krugman's dismay at the economic policies enacted to cope with the current depression, because Krugman's approach rejects the possibility of systemic breakdowns in accumulation itself. On the contrary, Krugman remains sanguine that no structural maladjustment is discernible today or in the 1930s; for him the "economic engine" is fine: no structural change has impaired its ability to "roar back to life" (Krugman, 2012, p. 22).

Finally, the character of Stiglitz's policy preferences to overcome the slump allows us to raise crucial questions about the missing links of his structural analysis. For Stiglitz, emerging from the current global slump will require "a massive investment program – as we did, virtually by accident, 80 years ago – that will increase our productivity for years to come and will also increase employment now. This public investment and the resultant restoration in GDP increases the returns to private investment" (Stiglitz, 2012).

Competition, mechanization, and profitability

In Stiglitz's view structural changes brought on by technological progress caused the displacement of labor first from agriculture and then from manufacturing, both in 1929 and 2008. In whatever sector previously employing the majority of workers, agriculture in the 1930s or manufacturing in the post-war years, labor-saving technical progress allowed output to grow while employment declined faster than labor reabsorption increased in expanding sectors. In the 1930s, the gap between rising agricultural output and falling effective demand due to growing unemployment led to falling agricultural prices and lower incomes. Fifty years later, rising labor productivity in manufacturing and services reduced the demand for unskilled labor and led to a declining share of wages that hampered the growth of effective demand as well. Growing household debt filled the gap between rising aggregate supply and stagnant effective demand while interest rates fell. In both cases, in the 1930s Great Depression and 2008 Great Recession, rising credit propped up lagging effective demand, but not forever.

Stiglitz's outlines of structural transitions are largely devoid of references, data or analysis concerning three crucial factors: competitive wars, innovations as competitive weapons, and the impact on profitability. Abstracting from real competition separates the analysis of technical progress from business strategies to gain market share and competitive battle to increase profits. This concept of competition-as-war identifies innovations as weapons in business strategies to achieve market leadership. Baumol traced its source in Marx (Baumol, 2002) and found it operationally sound as a foundation for his more recent explorations:

> Our analysis starts with the hypothesis that the free-market mechanism creates remarkable pressures for innovation, and that these pressures are what more clearly distinguish the capitalist economy from all alternative economic systems...the adoption of new technologies, especially in the form of new products and new industrial processes has emerged as a prime competitive weapon for firms...The result is a kind of innovation "arms race" that can literally be a matter of life or death for the participants...the participants find themselves forced to keep running in order to stand still.
>
> (Baumol *et al.*, 2003, pp. 11–12)

In the context of competition-as-war, not only will undercapitalized firms unable to innovate be driven out of the industry, but even the winners in this competitive war will suffer the effects of larger capital outlays. In the US technical advances in agriculture delivered lower unit costs of production to larger farms through mechanization as a precondition to lower prices and higher market shares. In a setting of coercive competition, rising labor productivity or lower unit labor costs must be paid for with higher fixed unit capital costs, inevitably requiring reduction of unit variable costs more than proportionally. Stiglitz's emphasis on technical progress spurring labor productivity growth and the displacement of labor from agriculture and manufacturing ignores the competitive context and the regulating force of profits. In his account, the mechanization drive in farming and manufacturing appears only as an abstract drive lacking competitive determination. Abstracting from industrial competition, mechanization and the profits imperative deprives Stiglitz's account of structural change of the necessary linkages that underpin business behavior. As an NBER Report on *Technical Progress and Agricultural Depression* put it:

> Analyzing the recent depression...one feature stands out from the rest, namely, rapid mechanization and its consequences. The aim of mechanization, like that of any technical improvement, is to reduce cost...Once mechanization has been introduced on a large scale, the farmer has little choice in selecting the size of his farm and his equipment. Mechanization leads to an increase in output and a reduction in cost. Therefore, farmers not equally equipped with capital can no longer compete with the more progressive farmers.
>
> (Altschul and Strauss, 1957, p. 2)

The quotation highlights the cost-reducing effects of mechanization when used "on a large scale" and the fact that farmers unable to carry it through will be at a competitive disadvantage. Farm mechanization involves costly fixed capital outlays whose effectiveness in terms of profitability requires large economies of scale to lower total unit costs. The decline in competitive prices following the successful mechanization of farming in the larger farms may be accentuated by the displacement of farm labor as well as the disappearance of the least mechanized farms altogether, leading to temporary shortfalls in aggregate demand. That according to Stiglitz labor displaced from the farms was able to find employment in the postwar manufacturing sector attests to the fact that the rate of capital accumulation in manufacturing, also subject to the imperative of lowering costs through labor-saving technology, must have exceeded that in agriculture. Temporary profitability differentials guide the flows of capital in and out of the various sectors of the national and international economy. Accordingly, the divergent rates of accumulation should reflect equally divergent rates of profit in agriculture and manufacturing. In other words, the labor flows out of agriculture and into manufacturing paralleled the capital flows in similar direction.

Bifurcation of finance and nonfinancial corporate sectors

In the case of the Great Recession of 2008, we argue that the extraordinary rise in the share of financial profits in total corporate profits reflected not only great innovations in financial engineering but also the weakness of nonfinancial capital accumulation, particularly in manufacturing: "despite the dot.com investment boom of 1995 to 2000," internal funds were channeled into "'financial engineering' operations aimed to secure capital gains…share buybacks, private-equity purchases, mergers and acquisitions" (Dos Santos, 2009, p. 187).

We conceive our remit in this book to be marshaling evidence linking falling US nonfinancial corporate profitability trends prior to 1982 and their partial recovery in the 1980s with the structural turn to financialization, a more profitable sector for capital accumulation. In the event, of course, financialization excesses triggered the financial meltdown ushering in the global Great Recession of 2008. We explain its growth as being due to capital flows bypassing the declining prospects of nonfinancial industries. Like Stiglitz, we take a historical perspective on the causes behind the Great Recession. Throughout the Golden Age, falling profitability trends in the US nonfinancial corporate sector, punctuated by sharp cyclical movements, led to sharply lower profit rate levels culminating in the early 1980s trough. From the late 1940s to the mid-1960s, nonfinancial accumulation rates stayed high because while profitability trended downward it did so from an extraordinarily high level. Largely mirroring those cycles and trends since the mid-1960s, the capital accumulation rate in nonfinancial corporate industries experienced a long-term decline through the first decade of the twenty-first century. Between 1960 and 1984 the average share of nonfinancial corporate fixed investment in current profits rose to 23.7 percent, declining to 17.7 percent between 1984 and 2009.

Starting from a low point around 1982, business's grand strategy ("neocapitalism", "financialization") to lift profitability levels above the trough, focused upon increasing what the National Income and Product Accounts call corporate "net operating surplus": containing wage growth while raising productivity growth. Heterodox economists in the post Keynesian and Marxian tradition view wage stagnation and growing income inequality as supporting the financialization drive that eventually placed major banks in command. As household bank deposits declined and investment funds increased, the banks' traditional source of income based on (falling) interest-rate spreads diminished. Bank lending to nonfinancial businesses declined, but loans to households seeking finance for educational services, housing mortgages, health care, pensions, etc. expanded. As Robert Wade (2011, p. 25) puts it, banks

> created a large supply of securities… because they were responding to soaring demand for them. The demand came from those at the top… Meanwhile the great mass of the population received stagnant incomes and sought to raise consumption through borrowing… The two sides came together with the rich accumulating more and more assets backed by loans to the rest of the population.

Figure 1.1 shows a broad measure of profitability, net operating surplus of private nonfinancial corporations plus government enterprises over the corresponding current cost capital stock of both corporate entities. These estimates of the profit

US Nonfinancial Corporate Net Operating Surplus/Net
Nonfinancial Corporate Capital Stock and Fixed
Nonfinancial Corporate Capital Accumulation Rates

——— Nonfinancial corporate profit rate,
         private and government enterprises

-------- Nonfinancial corporate fixed capital
         accumulation rate

Figure 1.1 US nonfinancial corporate profitability and nonfinancial corporate capital
accumulation rate.

rate are gross of net interest payments. After 1982, the profit rate experienced four
cycles going into the Great Recession, with a trendless trajectory. Since 1988 we
appreciate a mildly declining trend. The link between the falling accumulation and
profitability trends is evident here. The stagnation of real wages and the declining
share of labor in net output that ensued, however, did not lead to a recovery in
nonfinancial corporate profitability comparable to what obtained in the halcyon
years of the "Golden Age." Basic tendencies associated with trends in technical change and intensified global competition contrived to prevent a significant
upturn in profitability. Actual capital–output trends in the nonfinancial corporate
sector, moreover, resumed their upward trajectory further contributing to the weak
recovery of corporate profitability. The rough parallelism between profitability

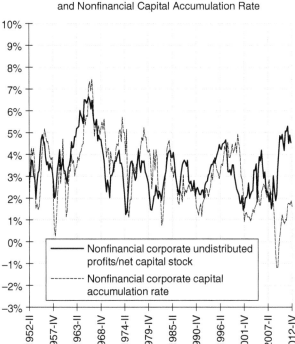

US Nonfinancial Corporate Undistributed
Profits/Nonfinancial Net Capital Stock
and Nonfinancial Capital Accumulation Rate

Figure 1.2 US nonfinancial corporate undistributed profit and nonfinancial corporate capital accumulation rate.

and accumulation trends obtaining since the 1950s finally unraveled after 2007 as accumulation collapsed and the Great Recession started.

In Figure 1.2 the rough correspondence between the nonfinancial corporate capital accumulation cycles and the fluctuations of undistributed profits divided by the nonfinancial corporate capital stock attests to the fact that, by and large, net corporate savings funded capital accumulation in that sector from the early 1950s through the onset of the Great Recession. After the collapse in accumulation that heralded the Great Recession, a total reversal of previous patterns developed. A sharp rise in retained profits did not elicit a corresponding increase in the rate of accumulation: an unprecedented gap appeared between them, portending the persistence of depressed expectations in future profitability. Indeed, undistributed profits relative to nonfinancial corporate value-added since the early 1950s reached an all-time high in 2011, but capital accumulation as a comparable share fell to an all-time low. Then what is the intended purpose and use for these retained funds?

Clearly nonfinancial corporations chose purchasing financial assets, including equity shares, as an alternative to investment in plant and equipment, hence the paradoxical boom in stock markets in the midst of lackluster growth in real sectors. This means that the pre-Recession dynamics behind capital flows flooding financial markets pursuing higher yields remained in place in the post-Recession recovery period and so the possibility of new excesses leading to similar breakdowns was preserved.

Looking ahead to Chapter 10, in Figure 10.4 our estimates show that the recovery of the profit rate in the financial sector (mainly comprised of banking and insurance companies) outpaced that of the nonfinancial industries. Figure 1.3 captures the significance we attach to the allocation of capital between financial and nonfinancial sectors. It shows the sharp divide between the accumulation of fixed capital and financial assets in the thirty-odd years before and after the early 1980s. The growth of the fixed capital stock and the net operating surplus remained moderate but the accumulation of financial assets accelerated after the mid-1980s. We argue that after 1987 the rebound of nonfinancial corporate profitability failed to achieve a consistently upward trend, and instead experienced sharp cyclical fluctuations characterized by lower values at the end of each successive cycle. As a result, the long-run trend of capital accumulation in the nonfinancial corporate sector, declining since the late 1960s, did not reverse course after the partial recovery of profitability in the early 1980s.

Our account of the crisis links profitability and falling capital accumulation trends in the nonfinancial corporate sector to the runaway expansion of finance, unsustainable speculation and the great crash. Rising asset prices created masses of paper wealth as well as unsustainable mountains of household debt. Pushing

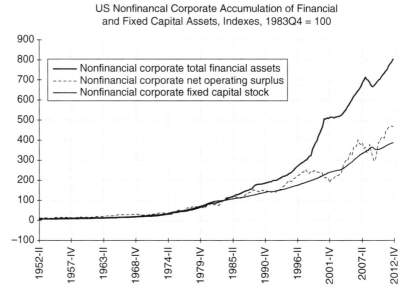

Figure 1.3 Growing bifurcation of US nonfinancial corporate stock of financial assets, fixed capital stock, and net operating surplus after 1983.

the frontiers of financial engineering to bridge the budget shortfalls caused by falling or at best stagnant household disposable incomes created immense opportunities for financial profits. Once the stock market and housing bubbles burst, however, the financial pyramid crumbled, credit stopped flowing to businesses and households, and effective demand collapsed. In the face of stagnant household income and falling capital accumulation rates, reflecting low or (mildly falling) nonfinancial corporate profitability, the banks' credit cutoff, triggered by the inevitable collapse of subprime mortgages, pushed major industries (automobiles) into bankruptcy. The financial crisis spilled into the real economy and the collapse reverberated across the globe.

Excesses, bubbles, and the financial crash

The excesses of financial engineering brought on by an intensified search for new markets in the banking sector triggered the financial collapse that ushered in the Great Recession. But the limited recovery of nonfinancial corporate profitability after 1982 eased the acceptance of risks inherent in speculative finance. In this regard, Paul Krugman (2010) has argued that "the very growth of the financial sector led to an upward trend in asset prices that masked the real risks – the way the housing bubble masked the true risks of subprime lending." Figure 1.4 shows the roughly parallel paths of rising financial profits and total debt. The connection reveals the downside of the financial bonanza. Both remained relatively subdued for the thirty-odd years preceding 1980 and both rose more or less in tandem for the next thirty-odd years. As we know, unsustainable debts built on the quicksand of stagnant household incomes eventually sank the mighty empire of finance.

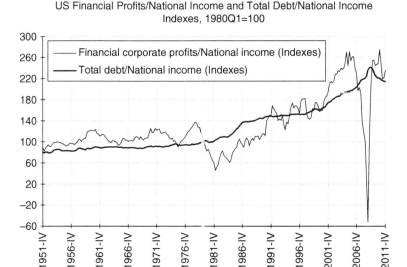

US Financial Profits/National Income and Total Debt/National Income Indexes, 1980Q1=100

Figure 1.4 US total debt/income and financial sector profits/income growth.

The path here simply involves the search for superior yields giving rise since 1982 to the bifurcation of capital flows between financial and nonfinancial corporate sectors. Falling interest rates after 1982, the "great moderation" in real wages, and the irrational exuberance aroused by bubbles in equity and housing markets laid the grounds for the subprime debacle. In the 1990s, efficient market theories denied the possibility of bubbles and the risk of financial collapse, thus abetting their timely occurrence. Spreading the risks of default among large "tranches" of securities throughout the world only ensured that the financial collapse spared no one. Speculation thrives and disaster looms when the profitability of nonfinancial sectors falters.

Through the lens of political economy

We examine in this book the secular link between profitability and accumulation trends leading to the Great Recession of 2008 in major OECD economies. We interpret that relationship through the conceptual lens of (classical) political economy, focusing on profitability as the driver of capital accumulation. The investigation proceeds sequentially, descending from a comparison of the conceptual foundations underlying classical and neoclassical growth models to the analysis of capitalist competition, technological change, and finally to the presentation of our empirical findings leading up to the crisis. Accordingly, the book's chapters reflect the progression from theoretical inquiry into empirical evidence necessary to bring out the significance of profitability-led structural change for a scientific understanding of the long road to the Great Recession.

We assess the contribution of Nicholas Kaldor to the critique of neoclassical growth models in Chapter 2, as well as his claims regarding historical constancies in capitalist development. In his model, technical progress is endogenous (generated through investment), but otherwise Kaldor's growth model furnishes the same conclusions regarding the stability of long-run growth paths as the neoclassical models do. Kaldor's claims underlying his growth model, however, went far beyond those made by his neoclassical counterparts. Along with his growth model, he wished to introduce a list of "stylized facts" that presumably characterized the actual historical path of capitalist development: full employment, constant wage shares, constant capital–output ratios, constant profit rates and neutral technical progress. Richard Goodwin did not endorse the claim of constant trends in full employment, wage shares and profit rates, advanced by neoclassical and post Keynesian economists such as Harrod and Kaldor, but assumed the long-run constancy of capital–output ratios as they did. It followed that, despite persistent cyclical fluctuations, the viability of capital accumulation around the long-run growth path remained unquestioned and therefore the system was crisis-free. Our views on this score depart from both, and that is the core of our book's message.

Chapters 3–6 explore the nature of real competition as opposed to perfect competition. These chapters identify the concept of competition-as-war (in contradistinction to notions of perfect competition) as the incubator of technical progress in capitalist firms. In Chapter 3, moving beyond the neoclassical concept of perfect competition, we see the direction taken by technological progress in connection with the competitive pressures constraining the decisions of real-world firms. In particular, we contrast the concept of competition-as-war developed by A. Shaikh (1978, 1980) with that of mere tension proposed by Baumol (2002) and Baumol *et al.* (2003).

Chapter 4 links mechanization to the competitive struggle and connects the drive to lower unit costs with the effort to improve product quality. For products of the same quality, lower unit costs enhance the competitiveness of the producer. For products sold at the same market price, higher quality enhances equally the competitiveness of producers. Both competitive improvements are commercially equivalent. We argue here that "Kaldor's paradox" claiming to prove that competitive improvements in market shares are compatible with rising "unit values" of exports conflates "unit values" (based on unit weight) with unit dollar costs, as is therefore artificial in character. We further show in this chapter how the application of scientific management principles led to the spread of automated systems, process innovations, and economies of scale, all of which strengthened competitive forces by lowering total unit costs.

Chapter 5 provides specific cases of growth models linking the competitive advantages derived from mechanization to profitability and larger market shares. Focusing on the pioneering efforts of Alain Barrère to challenge the structure of neoclassical growth models, we highlight his rationale for business's choosing capital intensive technical progress. We conclude this chapter discussing W. Eltis' views of the tradeoff between competitive gains and profitability in dynamic firms. In addition to the understanding of real competition advanced by Marx, Schumpeter, Baumol and Shaikh, Chapter 8 extends the discussion of the link between technological change and industrial competition, contrasting the views of Foley and Negishi with those of Marx and Shaikh.

Our empirical findings are highlighted in Chapters 6–11. In these chapters we lay out the evidence found by economic historians as well as our own research questioning the authenticity of the "stylized facts" advanced by Kaldor as canonical truths. Clearly, his claims on the historical reality of full-employment steady growth paths are not supported by the evidence. Reading our empirical findings through the lens of classical political economy allowed us to substantiate our challenge to his claims, followed by a consistent interpretation of profitability and accumulation trends leading to the Great Recession.

We start out by tracking the empirical evidence shedding light on the impact of competition-as-war on mechanization, its effect on profitability and accumulation trends of US nonfinancial corporations. Building on this evidence, we explain the growing turbulence of financial markets behind the Great Recession as originating in the global pressures to circumvent unsatisfactory profitability trends in the US and other OECD nonfinancial corporate sectors. We show how the decline in manufacturing profitability, strongly manifest since the second half of the 1960s, led to falling accumulation and then contraction in that sector extending into the 1980s and beyond. Similar developments lowered significantly the accumulation rate and hence the level of effective demand in the nonfinancial sector as a whole: as Stiglitz (2011) noted, "Without bubble-supported consumption, there would have been a massive shortfall in aggregate demand." Stiglitz's work suggests that the antecedents of structural change behind the Great Recession of 2008–2009 exhibited structural patterns similar to those found behind the Great Depression of 1929.

Chapter 7 highlights the empirical investigations on US capital–output ratios in the nineteenth century by Karl Snyder (1936), those of the economic historian Robert Gallman (1986), and, more recently, Robert Gordon (2004b) in direct contrast with Kaldor's stylized facts. At the end of the chapter, we show our own US output–capital ratio estimates since 1900. In Chapter 8, we review the estimates on US profitability produced by mainstream economists from 1948 to the late 1990s and compare them with the research findings of heterodox writers Robert Brenner (2006) and Fred Moseley (1992, 1999). Chapter 9 stresses the historical role of nonfinancial corporate investment for growth and highlights the significance of its downward trend as a share of national income. On the other hand, we show how the growth of US nonfinancial corporate acquisition of financial assets outstripped the accumulation rate of fixed capital. We interpret the falling trend in US nonfinancial corporate fixed capital accumulation after the mid-1960s as a reflection of the decline in retained corporate profits in that sector. The exception to the notable parallelism between the falling trends in accumulation and profitability, discernible in major OECD countries since the late 1960s, was found in Canada from 1992 to 2009. But in all nine OECD countries considered, estimates of incremental profitability conclusively predicted fixed investment growth fluctuations.

Chapter 10 provides the linchpin necessary to clinch the consistency of our argument's chief contention. We show our estimates of nonfinancial and financial corporate average profit rates diverging after the early 1980s when financial profitability recovered faster and rose higher than in the nonfinancial corporate sector. In addition, Chapter 12 introduces the question of capacity utilization capturing the effect of fluctuations in effective demand on profitability and capital–output ratios. Chapter 11 extends our view of financial excesses, linking the development of financial fragility in households balance sheets with the wage compression experienced since the early 1980s. Along with the accumulation of debts, the expansion of unsustainable bubbles in financial and housing sectors should have presaged impending collapse. Before Minsky developed his famous analysis of financial crises, John Stuart Mill's investigations established the link between low nonfinancial profitability yields and speculative euphoria leading to asset-price bubbles and finally a new crisis. Schumpeter blamed the investment collapse in the late 1920s precipitating the Great Depression on low industrial profitability and high debt.

As we see it, the growing capitalization of industry responds to business needs for lowering unit costs, as a preliminary of market strategies to reduce output prices. Prices decline after the introduction of process innovations because business leaders seek to expand their sales and gain competitiveness. From this perspective, the price reduction alluded by Stiglitz as simply reflecting the growth in labor productivity is the chief advantage sought in competitive wars. Rising profit margins as labor unit costs fall, however, encounter structural limits: the lower they get the less they can fall, but increasing fixed capital costs per unit output do not reach a ceiling. The economy-wide displacement of labor is not simply the natural consequence of labor-saving technology but the effect of falling aggregate accumulation rates when profitability falters. Rising unemployment trends is the dual of this competitive process.

It is our contention that capital accumulation in the real (nonfinancial) sectors proceeds along a path punctuated with barriers that, beyond mere business fluctuations, disrupt its normal course. The analytical structure of our approach derives from the classical view of capital flows driven by profitability differentials. Profit rates in nonfinancial sectors stubbornly declined in the postwar period before reaching a trough in the early 1980s. From then on they bounced back from their trough but failed to recover their previously higher levels. The perception of higher profit rates in one sector, such as the US financial sector after the mid-1980s, goaded investors to direct capital flows there well beyond the point where profit rate differentials warranted. No presumption of equilibrium outcomes applies, over- and undershooting of targets systematically occurs. Increases in asset prices generate stronger demands. Excesses build up, such as household and financial debts, and at some point imbalances trigger depression tendencies. The disconnect between stagnant incomes caused by low accumulation rates in real sectors and rising debts linked to unsustainable asset price bubbles triggered the banking meltdown.

2 Kaldor's "stylized facts": real or merely convenient?

Introduction

With the experience of the 1930s depression in mind, Kaldor's essays at the time denied the possibility of finding any theoretical grounds to conclude that capitalist development could reach a balanced growth path. As the postwar recovery unfolded, and memories of the depression waned, his outlook underwent drastic changes. In the late 1950s, while challenging the relevance of neoclassical growth models, Kaldor not only endorsed the search for such steady-state growth paths but also proclaimed a slew of "stylized facts," ostensibly characteristic of actual capitalist development. In fact, he now sought to refute the conceptual structure of neoclassical growth models precisely because they failed to support the reality of his "stylized facts." Kaldor's "stylized facts" of capitalist development included constancies of all the decisive ratios behind the system's growth: constant profit rates; constant capital–output ratios; constant share of profits; and full employment of labor. In addition, he saw steady technical progress leading to rising capital–labor and output–labor ratios. In the event, while at least one leading neoclassical economist questioned the reality of Kaldor's "stylized facts" (Solow, 1987, p. 2), mainstream followers soon realized his invaluable service to their research program.

Regardless of Kaldor's intentions, conceivably nothing could be more instrumental in strengthening the formal adequacy of neoclassical growth models than claims purporting to anchor their conclusions in reality. Now neoclassical assumptions of perfect knowledge would be substantiated in the historical record, for the structure of capitalist development in future would be the same as it was in the past. Despite technical change, past and future exhibited the same growth patterns. In retrospect, Kaldor's "stylized facts" provided neoclassical economics the scaffold needed to ignore endogenous breakdowns of the accumulation path. As David Gordon (1991) saw it, we have in "Kaldor's Macro System: Too Much Cumulation, Too Few Contradictions."

Exaggerated claims often lead to belated reversals. Disillusion with the practical results of his long-held views on equilibrium growth led Kaldor (1972) once again to announce "The Irrelevance of Equilibrium Economics." Further, in the aftermath of the 1980s slump Kaldor's confidence in the prospects for achieving steady growth in a world divided between developed and underdeveloped regions finally collapsed (Kaldor, 1986).

From capital deepening to balanced growth paths

In the 1930s, Kaldor followed Bohm-Bawerk's approach to capital theory. In his essay on "Capital Intensity and the Trade Cycle" he argued that capital–output ratios would likely rise due to technical progress (Kaldor, 1939). Kaldor argued that the concept of a capital–labor ratio required clarification. Capital was not a homogeneous entity but an aggregate of different kinds of things, including equipment of various vintages, plants of diverse age, and construction design, and therefore its size could not be measured directly. Kaldor believed, however, that indexes could be constructed that showed ordinal measures, indicating whether or not the whole stock grew larger or smaller. Thus, to measure the capital–labor ratio associated with a technical choice for producing a given output, Kaldor proposed the construction of indexes reflecting the difference between the "initial cost" and the yearly costs associated with that output. The ratio between the two costs could be taken as a proxy for the capital intensity of production.

At the time, Kaldor (1939, p. 45) was persuaded that automation embodied the characteristic form of technical progress under capitalism and gave rise to increasing capital intensity: "Greater economy of labor, per unit of output, can only be achieved, of course (given technical knowledge) by a greater expenditure of capital per unit of output." In a closed system, variable costs consist almost entirely of labor costs, although variable annual expenditures included raw materials also. Other than labor, all inputs are the outputs of other firms and thus in the aggregate cancel out each other. Believing that the rise in labor productivity resulted from the growth of capital intensity, Kaldor (1939) focused on ways to provide accurate measurements of the degree of that intensity.

A rise in capital intensity would be normally associated with the use of superior and more costly techniques, and in general the new technique would be labor-saving. The optimal degree of capital intensity would be an increasing function of the real wage rate but inversely related to the interest rate. Entrepreneurs would always choose the technique of production involving a superior and more costly capital outlay if the expected stream of profits more than exceeded the additional interest charges involved in purchasing the equipment:

> It is generally possible to reduce the size of the expenditure stream, per unit of receipts stream (i.e. per unit of output), by increasing the initial outlay (the size of the investment) per unit of output. Hence the relation between initial outlay and annual outlay can be regarded as a measure of the proportion in which "capital" and "other factors" are combined in a particular productive unit, i.e. of its "capital intensity" of production.
>
> (Kaldor, 1939)

Kaldor's advocacy of equilibrium growth paths in the 1950s undoubtedly reflected the boundless optimism of postwar reconstruction in Europe. In that context his earlier views tying the growth of labor productivity to capital deepening and the secular rise in capital–output ratios would not be compatible with the conceptual structural of mainstream growth models. Kaldor would now argue that such trends produced a secular decline in profitability that rendered long-term growth impossible to sustain. Kaldor then concluded that classical interpretations of mechanization as presented in the work of Ricardo and Marx had no empirical support at all.

The Corfu Round Table Conference

At various junctions in his long career as a critic of mainstream economics, Kaldor did not hesitate to advance claims that directly contradicted his previous convictions. By the late 1950s Kaldor found no use for the views articulated in the late 1930s. Thus, Kaldor first announced his celebrated claims on the historical constancies of capitalist development in the introduction of his new growth model to the Round Table Conference on the Theory of Capital, held on the Island of Corfu, September 4–11, 1957. While he had previously argued that investment decisions on new techniques involved continuous technical change and that the profitability of existing equipment had no relevance, since only expected profits applied, he now wished to assert that technical choices could not be classified as being more or less capital intensive. Despite endorsing all the historical assumptions behind neoclassical growth models, Kaldor rejected the possibility of measuring capital intensity as a token of neoclassical obfuscation.

In his Corfu growth model, "Capital Accumulation and Economic Growth," Kaldor (1965) denied any linkage between the growth of unit fixed capital costs and the reduction of unit variable cost as he had argued in the late 1930s. Now he required that all models should be grounded in actual historical trends, deeming unacceptable simply that the model's structure and the chain of causation among its variables be made explicit and internally consistent. Theoretical models should be able to account for the real "characteristic features" or trends in capitalist development.

Unfortunately, the results of empirical investigations on dynamic trends spanning long periods were not always conclusive and frequently the overall picture contained contradictory evidence. Kaldor then proposed that model builders should acknowledge the "stylized facts" of capitalist development as long as they were not falsified. Despite his brief for reality-based modeling, Kaldor introduced a caveat in his argument that absolved him of responsibility for the actual "historical accuracy" of his "stylized facts": he wished to propose taking them "as if" they really were good enough, even if empirical support was lacking.

Kaldor's (1965, pp. 178–179) list of "stylized facts" included six items that in his view typified the "process of economic change and development in capitalist societies," including:

1   The continued growth in the aggregate volume of production and in the productivity of labour at a steady trend rate; no recorded tendency for a falling rate of growth of productivity.

2   A continued increase in the amount of capital per worker, whatever statistical measure of "capital" is chosen in this connection.

3   A steady rate of profit on capital, at least in the "developed" capitalist societies...

4   Steady capital-output ratios over long periods; at least there are no clear long-term trends, either rising or falling, if differences in the degree of utilization of capacity are allowed for...

5   A high correlation between the share of profits in income and the share of investment in output...

6   Finally, there are appreciable differences in the rate of growth of labour productivity and of total output in different societies ....

At the 1957 Corfu Conference Kaldor's model of equilibrium growth met with considerable skepticism since it set itself apart from both the classical as well as the neoclassical traditions. While Kaldor sought to challenge the relevance of the classical economists, including Marx, he also wished to argue that neoclassical economics could not possibly account for the actual development of capitalist economies. Kaldor's audience, while predominantly neoclassical in persuasion, did not take well to his list of "stylized facts" as a reflection of historical trends.

At the Conference Kaldor argued that the assumption of diminishing returns built into the neoclassical growth models, as capital per worker rose, led economists to expect a "steady rise in the capital-output ratio *pari passu* with the rise in the capital-labour ratio." Such trends would produce a sustained fall in profitability, "not a steady rate of profit" as his reading of history presumably showed. Kaldor then rose to the occasion, battling the combined dragons conjured up in the old classical and neoclassical theories of growth, for "In this respect classical and neoclassical theory, arguing on different grounds, came to the same conclusion – Adam Smith, Ricardo, Marx, alike with Bohm-Bawerk and Wicksell, predicted a steady fall in the rate of profit with economic progress" (Kaldor, 1965, p. 179). Kaldor thought such views were unacceptable. The leading neoclassical economists gathered at the Corfu Conference found precious little evidence for his "stylized facts" in the historical record. But it was Kaldor's "discovery" of historical constancies that underpinned his determination to challenge the conceptual structure of current neoclassical theories of marginal productivity and to reject the older Bohm-Bawerk approach to capital theory. In Kaldor's view all of them failed to account for his canonical "stylized facts" of capitalist development and therefore they were all irrelevant. On the other hand, Kaldor believed his new growth model was fully consistent with the main trends of capitalist development in the West.

Despite his efforts to undermine the relevance of Ricardo and Marx to a modern understanding of capitalist development, Kaldor found it necessary to challenge the conventional view that the core dynamics developed by the classical economists, widely defined to include Marx, had nothing to contribute to modern growth theory. Surprisingly Kaldor conceded that his growth model had "more affinities with the classical approach of Ricardo and Marx" than with the mainstream theories of marginal factor productivity. In his view, however, too much should not be made of this affinity, for he also declared a strong relationship "with the general equilibrium model of von Neuman." Von Neuman's mathematical model of general equilibrium growth undoubtedly shared some of the fundamental postulates of classical economics, chiefly the connection between the accumulation and profit rates, the ratio of the surplus relative to necessary labor inputs. But Kaldor hoped that his heterodox references to Ricardo and Marx, properly sanitized and enlisted in support of his model's equilibrium paths, could be accepted by the neoclassical mainstream as somewhat eccentric but not beyond the pale.

Kaldor's model of capital accumulation

In his new growth model, Kaldor sought to combine elements taken from the classical approach with the Harrod–Domar dynamical equation. Given the capital coefficient (capital–output ratio) he believed that, as in the Ricardian or von Neumann models, the Harrod–Domar equation was a convenient way to show the relationship between the savings share in income and the rate of capital accumulation. In Harrod, the growth rate of output is given by

$$g_Y = \frac{\Delta Y}{Y} = \frac{\Delta K}{Y}\frac{\Delta Y}{\Delta K} = \frac{I}{Y}\frac{\Delta Y}{\Delta K} = \frac{S/Y}{\Delta K/\Delta Y} = \frac{s}{v} = g_K.$$

And since it is assumed that in equilibrium investment is internally financed out of savings and furthermore that all profits are saved (and all wages consumed), the propensity to save is

$$s = \frac{S}{Y} = \frac{I}{Y} = \frac{\Pi}{Y} = g_K v.$$

Therefore,

$$\frac{\Pi/Y}{v} = \frac{\Pi}{Y}\frac{Y}{K} = \frac{\Pi}{K} = g_K$$

links the rate of capital accumulation to the profit rate on capital and lends a measure of credibility to Kaldor's claim of preserving a key feature of the classical economics tradition.

Next, Kaldor tackled the issue of employment growth and its relation to capital accumulation. Defining employment growth as synonymous with the growth of labor supply,

$$g_N = L, \quad L = \frac{1}{L}\frac{\delta L}{\delta t},$$

Kaldor went on to point out, as he warned from the start, "the Ricardo-Marx-von Neumann model clearly does not work when $g_K > g_N$ since in that case the rate of growth of production cannot be determined by g_K alone." In fact Kaldor presented this imbalance as the central concept behind Marx's theory of crisis.

Kaldor's reading of Marx's crisis theory, translated into his own Keynesian framework, identified the potential inequality between fixed capital accumulation and population growth rates as the core of the dynamics. As Richard Goodwin (1972) pointed out in this connection, once the demand for labor grew faster than the labor supply growth rate, the reserve army of labor would be depleted and the competition of capitalists for the available workers would lead to wage increases, hence falling profits. Lower profit rates in turn led to falling accumulation rates and restoration of the system's balance, as pressures for rising wages weakened.

In reality Kaldor's version of the adjustment path does not necessarily lead to a crisis triggered by the collapse in accumulation, but rather to a lower accumulation rate and lower employment growth. Kaldor believed that with balanced growth, once equality between the capital accumulation and the population (labor) growth rates was achieved, full employment should prevail. But Goodwin demonstrated that equality between the growth rates of labor demand and supply did not mean that the levels of labor demand and supply coincided: the gap between the two could persist, preserving labor unemployment even in the absence of crisis.

In any event, the possibility of achieving balanced growth would recede in light of the fact that the effective growth of employment depended not only on population growth but also on the growth of labor productivity caused by technical progress:

$$g_{Nt} = L + t, \quad \text{where } t = \frac{1}{Y/L} \frac{\delta(Y/L)}{\delta t}.$$

Kaldor explored ways to bring the "natural" growth rate, enhanced by labor productivity growth, into line with the "warranted" rate, $g_K = g_{Nt}$ in order to achieve Harrod's "balanced growth equilibrium." His procedure simply required finding the right values for the savings ratio (out of profits), s, the capital-output ratio, v, the growth of labor supply, L, and the growth rate of labor productivity, t. As things stood, that configuration could only be achieved accidentally, since each of these variables was set independently from the others. Moreover, it was generally accepted that nontrivial discrepancies could lead to cumulative swings away from the balanced growth path. Long-term equilibrium growth was naturally and intrinsically unstable.

Kaldor's alternative to neoclassical methodology

Kaldor viewed the neoclassical alternative as another shot in the dark in the pursuit of a sound theory of equilibrium growth. Despite the fact that he shared with neoclassical economics common goals in the pursuit of equilibrium growth models, Kaldor clearly wished to differentiate his product from the mainstream version. He agreed with neoclassical economists that the variables that Harrod proposed as being independently determined should be considered as interrelated and malleable. A given output could be produced applying not just one but a whole spectrum of techniques involving varying proportions of capital and labor. Moving along a "homogeneous and linear production function" in the direction of points with higher capital per worker brought into play the "law" of variable proportions, leading to techniques with a falling marginal product of capital. Which technique was chosen depended on the relative prices of capital and labor.

In Kaldor's version, output per worker, O, depended on the capital–labor ratio:

$$O \equiv \frac{Y}{L} = f_1\left(\frac{K}{L}\right), \quad \text{and} \quad f_1' > 0, \ f_1'' < 0.$$

Given the fact that capital is scarce and costly, Kaldor assumed that entrepreneurs surely wished to adopt a technique of production requiring a capital–labor ratio that allowed them to maximize profitability. Moreover, the higher the wage rate, the higher the incentive to raise the capital–labor ratio, that is:

$$\frac{K}{L} = f_2(w), \quad \text{and} \quad f_2' > 0, \ f_2'' < 0.$$

Now higher wage rates leading to higher capital–labor ratios will also give rise to higher capital–output ratios:

$$V \equiv \frac{K}{Y} = f_3(w) \quad \text{and} \quad f_3' > 0, \ f_3'' < 0.$$

But higher capital–output ratios in turn will result in higher labor productivity:

$$O = f_4(v), \quad \text{and} \quad f_4' > 0, \ f_4'' < 0.$$

Kaldor's account of the false adjustment sequence proposed by neoclassical theory as a correction for the inevitable imbalance between capital accumulation and the labor supply growth rates started out with a rise in wage rates. As full employment came within sight, wage rates rose and the decline in profit shares slowed down accumulation. The increase in wage rates, however, would seem to call for the adoption of techniques with higher capital–labor and capital–output ratios. This shift required an increase of the investment share in output. Because the rise in investment would create excess demand and would lead to increased prices, the profits share could bounce back up especially if product wages fell following price hikes. But in the absence of technical progress, the presence of diminishing returns as investment expanded would dampen growth in the profit share, so that ultimately the accumulation rate would fall, dragged down by the combined impact of lower profit shares and higher capital–output ratios. In the final analysis equilibrium growth returned only when the rate of accumulation fell sufficiently to match the lower labor supply growth rate. Kaldor's interpretation rejected as unrealistic the pursuit of accumulation paths involving the adoption of capital deepening and labor-saving technology.

Kaldor's critique of neoclassical views on technical progress

Kaldor rejected the neoclassical explanation for the existence of neutral techniques compatible with equilibrium growth. Despite capital-deepening technical change causing labor productivity growth, neoclassical models contained the assumptions embedded in linear and homogeneous production functions. Such functions traced the boundary of possible maximum outputs for all quantities of "real" capital inputs. The resulting production frontier could then shift up or outwards in response to steady advances in technical knowledge. Moreover, progress in technical knowledge generated a spectrum of techniques whose unique characteristics preserved the constancy of the marginal product of capital (which neoclassical economics identifies as the profit rate on capital). This property of neoclassical technical change requires that all tangents of shifting production functions, such as f_t, f_{t+1}, f_{t+2}, at each point crossed by a ray from the origin drawn at a 45 degree angle, have the same slope. With the unbounded growth of capital–labor and capital–output ratios, sustaining a constant profit rate required the steady progress in applied knowledge issuing from a continuous flow of neutral technical change.

Kaldor found this argument to be a piece of purely circular reasoning. Relying upon the steady progress of technical knowledge to account for the upward shifts of production functions was equivalent to considering advances of technical knowledge as an argument in those functions, along with capital, land, and labor. But such functions could also shift due to increases in the labor supply with a constant state of technical knowledge. The fallacy involved, Kaldor argued, was that advance in technical knowledge could not be quantified directly in the same way that the amount of labor could. Comparing two different configurations of input–output alternatives, how could we distinguish a movement along the production function from a shift of the function itself?

It is a basic principle of the neoclassical theory of distribution that the sum of marginal productivities for all factors of production adds up to the total product. Knowledge, however, cannot be quantified as other factors of production can and therefore its growth cannot be matched with its putative marginal product. Endowing the function with the property of constant elasticities, the neoclassical argument sought to invert the order of causation. In the context of marginal productivity theory, the slope of the function expressed the profits share in income. But the inversion occurred when the actual profits share stood for the slope of the function and any outstanding residual became evidence of the alleged function shift. If progress in technical knowledge caused the shift of the function, marginal productivity theory ought to measure the quantity of such advance in order to impute its derived returns.

Kaldor's own technical progress function

It is clear that Kaldor's critique of the neoclassical growth model was not aimed at its conclusions but rather at the apparatus deployed to reach them. He was perfectly willing to accept the shifts of the neoclassical production function that preserved the constancy of capital–output ratios and profit rates, but not the alleged cause of those shifts. Kaldor proposed instead that the tempo of accumulation itself lied behind the shifting function, as technical progress advanced faster when the accumulation rate was higher. Thus movements along the curve representing the accumulation of higher capital per worker represented the introduction of more advanced techniques that raising labor productivity caused the function to shift. The shifts were not due to the passing of time but rather to the tempo of accumulation itself, defined as the speed with which the movements along the curve reflected the installation of new techniques.

To replace the ordinary linear and homogeneous production function of the neoclassical models, Kaldor proposed a "technical progress function" whose characteristics reflected both the effects of higher capital per worker and the steady advance of knowledge embodied in new plant and equipment. Ostensibly the advantage of Kaldor's new function was that, while combining configurations of higher labor productivity with higher capital per worker and superior technical knowledge, it avoided the pitfalls inherent in marginal productivity approaches, since it prevented fragmentation of its constituent elements. Kaldor argued against neoclassical theories of marginal productivities that any attempt to separate the contributions of the factors of production from each other or from technical progress was doomed to failure on purely logical – let alone practical – grounds.

For Kaldor the "technical dynamism" observed in some countries was essentially due to Keynesian "animal spirits." For him it would not suffice that entrepreneurs possessed the requisite finance to promote the adoption of new techniques if they lacked the necessary fortitude to accept the risks involved in their deployment. Achieving high accumulation rates requires both finance and foresight. Whenever both were present, growth would gain momentum propelled by the acceleration of technical progress. Technical progress as such did not flow separately from capital accumulation. Capital accumulation was not hampered by diminishing returns. Technical progress itself did not enter entrepreneurial plans like manna from heaven at appointed intervals. A vigorous tempo of capital accumulation, rather, was likely to usher in a strong dose of technical progress and if diminishing returns occurred, both components would jointly experience it.

Capital accumulation, k'/k, refers to techniques of production achieving higher growth rates of output, y'/y, than of fixed capital inputs. Beyond some point, however, further capital accumulation involved a growth of capital assets exceeding the output growth rate. In other words, the capital–output ratio while rising does not prevent profit rate increases, but beyond that point profit rates would fall. The equilibrium point, P, then represents the optimal condition for neutral technical progress, allowing the growth of capital to steadily match that of output, and as such identifies the essential conditions to preserve the constancy of profit rates and wage shares. For Kaldor the ineluctable link between capital accumulation and the introduction of superior technologies provides the theoretical basis justifying his claims on "historical" constancies: "It explains why there is no long-run tendency to a falling rate of profit, or for a continued increase in capital in relation to output, either in slow-growing or in fast-growing economies" (Kaldor, 1965, p. 209). Countries in which the entrepreneurial class is excessively risk-averse will experience low growth rates of output and weak advances in technical progress, but they will also reach steady growth paths with constant profit rates and (lower) capital–output ratios. At the other end of the enterprising spectrum, countries with high accumulation tempos and faster rates of technical change will also achieve their steady-state growth paths.

Finally, Kaldor wished to argue that such steady-state growth paths were not only a theoretical curiosity of his growth model, freed from the circular reasoning of his neoclassical critics, but also in fact a characteristic feature of the history in capitalist economies. He insisted that there were forces at large in the real world compelling entrepreneurs to move to the accumulation equilibrium growth path signified by his point P, if they were away from it. What he now needed to ground his theoretical claims in real-world evidence was for "statisticians" to collect data supporting his "stylized facts" showing long-term output growth, the capital–output ratio, relative shares, profitability, and by implication the rate of technical progress, as being constant.

Kaldor also introduced two qualifications that might prevent the system from reaching his equilibrium growth or at least explain why it did not attain it. One is of an empirical nature; his model might be correct in establishing the necessary outcome of the dynamic interplay among its core variables, but something external to it might interfere with its workings. He challenged the "statisticians" to gather evidence showing that a period of accelerating growth also evidenced a falling capital–output ratio. On the other hand, he argued, it would not be necessarily fatal to his model if the actual findings of the "statisticians" failed to confirm its predictions regarding the growth rates of output, capital–output ratios and the rest, it could simply mean that the effect of accumulation on the advancement of technical progress was temporarily weak, distorting the normal shifting of the curve. In this situation the growth rates of output and capital would not match.

Kaldor conceded, but only as an unlikely prospect, that, absent the empirical evidence for falling capital–output ratios in periods of rapid accumulation, confidence in the reliability of his model's projections regarding the attainment of equilibrium growth would be shattered, even if the relevance of his technical progress curve remained unquestioned.

His second caveat referred to the modeling of entrepreneurial behavior regarding capital accumulation. Kaldor assumed with Kalecki that the entrepreneurial perception of investment risks was an increasing function of the accumulation rate, and more specifically of the gap between the interest rate and the expected profitability of successive investments. The existence of such an investment function linking the investment propensity to the increasing perception of risk added one more uncertainty to the prospects for reaching the equilibrium growth point.

Depending on the subjective makeup of entrepreneurial behavior, as it shapes the assessment of risk prospects, the position of the investment risk function, I, might cut Kaldor's technical progress function, T, anywhere to the left or the right of the equilibrium growth point, P. Below such point, for instance, the growth rate of output would be consistent with entrepreneurial decisions regarding capital accumulation. Growth away from the equilibrium conditions balances the risk weight of the given accumulation rate against the expected profitability of output, and thus we have feasible growth paths: output growth consistent with the rate of capital accumulation entrepreneurs are willing to sustain.

On purely structural grounds, however, suboptimal growth rates ignore profit opportunities that would be available only if the growth of capital accumulation increased, requiring a shift towards the optimal growth path, P. Beyond that point the prospects for falling profitability will exclude further moves. Thus, investment decisions taken to the left of P involve output–capital ratios rising at a decreasing rate but falling beyond point P. Considering the lost profit opportunities neglected by lower accumulation rates, the excessively risk-averse behavior on the part of a country's entrepreneurs will lead to declining profit shares. Indeed, unwilling to raise investment spending to reach higher profits, entrepreneurs with weak animal spirits and high risk aversion to credit expansion demand in fear of rising interest rates and falling output–capital ratios would wind up with lower profit shares.

Despite the idiosyncratic shortcomings attributed to entrepreneurial behavior in countries where the spirit of capitalism had not yet thoroughly shaped the mentality of the investor class, Kaldor believed the strength of capital accumulation rates would reflect the growth or decline in profit opportunities. Emboldened by his firm belief that "statisticians" had actually provided empirical evidence for the underlying assumptions of his new growth model, Kaldor confidently dismissed all classical and neoclassical growth models as thoroughly incapable of explaining the boundless prospects for accumulation. Rejecting the existence of bias towards capital intensity in technical progress, Kaldor removed all standing barriers in the path of capital accumulation towards steady growth and full employment.

The primacy of investment over savings

In his 1957 new growth model, Kaldor argued that he was not just interested in adding one more abstract model to the existing literature on economic growth. His model structure actually reflected the ways in which the real world worked. Two things were crucial to succeed in this endeavor. The model required a theory of prices that allowed high price flexibility in product markets and relative rigidity in the determination of wages. This distinction allowed Kaldor to argue that if entrepreneurs decided to increase their rate of investment, the ensuing excess demand would raise prices while having a negligible effect on money wages. Hence, the profits share would rise and that of wages fall, lowering consumption and increasing savings. This proposition ensured, in the Keynesian tradition, the balance between investment and savings: firms' investment expansion induced a corresponding savings increase and brought both variables to their equilibrium level.

Kaldor assumed that a higher propensity to save out of profits, in comparison to wages, allowed business firms to finance their investment plans out of their accumulated reserves, and once their profit rate reached an acceptable level, sustained the chosen accumulation rate. In order to achieve steady-state profitability, firms' decisions should follow a simple operational rule: raise investment per man as long as there are available techniques that yield a higher increase in output per man. As investment per man rises, firms will select the best techniques according to the stated rule, and when no more are available, they will keep their existing methods. All firms in the industry faced the same spectrum of available techniques, and the famous Kaldor technical progress function, with its neat array of choices, achieved the desired optimal growth path. Eventually only one technique whose increased investment cost would just equal the increase in output per man would prevail, qualifying as a neutral innovation because factor shares remained unchanged. In Kaldor's equilibrium growth model constancies emerge spontaneously, and such constant profit and wage shares, capital–output ratios and profit rates are central to it. Kaldor's empirical underpinnings, unfortunately, are missing in the story.

Kaldor's model may be thought of as an early contribution to what nowadays is commonly known as the "endogenous" growth approach. While critical of the classical school and Marx, he faithfully retained their focus on profitability, accumulation, and technical progress. His "technical progress function" emerges from the accumulation of capital itself, not from external sources. But against the classical economists, Kaldor's entrepreneurs would have no way and no need to estimate the size of their accumulated capital stock, being satisfied to relate their estimates of expected profitability within a certain payoff period to the gross investment costs at current prices. Kregel (1971, p. 192) argued that this technical progress function played the role of a deus ex machina: "The only problem is to explain how and why the free enterprise system can (should), through its internal logic, produce neutral technical progress as a necessity."

Kaldor's "technical progress function" differentiates his model from the neoclassical perspective. Linking the flow of innovations to the accumulation tempo itself allowed him to circumvent the barriers to expansion erected by neoclassical diminishing returns, or classical falling profitability paths as in Ricardo and Marx. At the Corfu Conference, however, Solow expressed his support for Kaldor's approach with regard to technical change. In Solow's view entrepreneurial needs guided the direction taken by technical progress, although he was not ready to accept Kaldor's criteria for the selection of optimal growth paths. (Lutz and Hague, 1965, p. 393).

Further reflections on Kaldor's "stylized facts"

In our view, Kaldor's celebrated 1957 growth model based itself on questionable empirical trends not readily discerned in the historical experience of American capitalism. His "stylized facts," however, fitted the conclusions derived from neoclassical growth models. Kaldor just pressed into service his technical progress function in order to conveniently neutralize the neoclassical principle of diminishing returns. As Kregel (1971, Chapter 9) noted, Kaldor's use of a "technical progress function" allowed his growth model to achieve stability because, within the array of possible technical choices, only those that preserved the constancy of capital–labor and capital–output ratios (taking into account the rise in efficiency of both capital and labor), were deemed sustainable.

Kaldor (1965, p. 177) argued that "Any theory must necessarily be based on abstractions; but the type of abstraction chosen cannot be decided in a vacuum; it must be appropriate to the characteristic features of the economic process as recorded by experience." Although Kaldor himself did not produce any empirical support for his views on secular trends, he insisted that: "Theoretical analysis to be fruitful, must be closely related to, and firmly based on, empirically derived 'laws' or regularities" (Kaldor, 1978a, p. viii). What exactly those "laws" or the historical experience needing explanation were emerged as a contentious issue from the start, possibly because confirmation of the characteristic trends highlighted by Kaldor's model was not readily available.

The assertions made by Nicholas Kaldor at the Corfu Conference regarding the characteristic empirical facts underlying the evolution of capitalism initially seemed a little far-fetched until Solow and other participants showed their connection with standard neoclassical growth models. Once the theoretical structures were properly adjusted to neoclassical principles, Kaldor's stylized facts became truly canonical as far as mainstream economics was concerned. In turn, these alleged facts became the motivational foundation for what Bronfenbrenner (1971, pp. 421–426) called "magic constancy theories."

The participants at the Corfu Conference on capital theory, looking at available empirical evidence on capital–output ratios in the US, could not agree on the direction of their long-run trends. In fact, when Kaldor first proposed his "stylized facts," skeptical comments from the distinguished group of assembled economists challenged their credibility (Lutz and Hague, 1965). As the Conference roundtables evaluated the evidence, prominent economists voiced strong reservations regarding the Kaldorian claims. Thus, while acknowledging that "he had not been a close enough empirical student," Professor Solow made it clear that he "was less convinced of the stability of the capital–output ratio in the USA" than Kaldor appeared to be. (Lutz and Hague, 1965, p. 393). As an active participant in the discussion of Kaldor's paper, Haberler commented that "As far as empirical evidence was concerned, he could see no trace of constancy in the capital-output ratio, as it appeared in the statistics circulated by Dr. Goldsmith" (Lutz and Hague, 1965, p. 294).

Professor F. Lutz, editor of the Conference papers, "did not share Mr. Kaldor's impression that the average capital-output ratio was stable. If one looked at Table 5 in Professor Domar's paper and the figures supplied by Dr. Goldsmith, there was certainly no stable capital-output ratio there. What did participants mean when they talked of stability?" (Lutz and Hague, 1965, p. 343). In the exchanges following Professor E. Domar's presentation of his paper on capital–output ratios, Domar emphasized that, as far as he knew, and contrary to Kaldor's notion "that rapid growth was associated with a falling capital coefficient, American experience pointed in the opposite direction. During the last quarter of the nineteenth century the rate of growth of output was particularly rapid; yet the capital coefficient was rising not falling" (Lutz and Hague, 1965, p. 344).

In a generally positive appraisal of Kaldor's contributions to economic knowledge, Mark Blaug judged several items in Kaldor's list of patterns allegedly typical of capitalist development to be false: "Unfortunately," he wrote, "many of Kaldor's 'stylised facts' are not facts at all." Furthermore, a careful examination of the relationship between Kaldor's growth theory and his "stylised facts" led Blaug to conclude that:

> On balance we must conclude that if Kaldor's growth theory is interpreted as Kaldor would have us interpret it, namely, as an explanation of the common experience of the growth process in industrialized countries, the theory has in fact been explaining the wrong things. On the best evidence, even the aggregate features of long-run growth do not correspond to anything that can be described by a steady-state process.
>
> (Blaug, 1989, p. 80)

In defense of his stylized facts, Kaldor insisted, without the benefit of sound empirical evidence, that contrary to the classical view, long-run profit rate trends in advanced capitalist countries showed no trend whatsoever. Thus, historical research supporting Kaldor's "stylized facts" is conspicuously missing. Kaldor's proposed constancy of profit rates, profit and wage shares, as well as capital–output ratios, easily fitted into the neoclassical vision of a world without the turbulence of actual market economies wracked by periodic slumps. In neoclassical models, reaching the steady-state growth path was assured, and staying on it guaranteed, absent external shocks to the system. The world so constituted was set to enjoy the benefits of neutral, unbiased, technical progress leading to labor productivity rising uninterruptedly while maintaining a constant distribution of value-added.

Contrary to Kaldor's expressed intent, neoclassical economists immediately recognized the use of such "stylized facts" as empirical supports of the conceptual structure behind their own approach to economic growth and income distribution. Kaldor's growth model, conceptually outside the purview of neoclassical economics, exploited the existence of alleged "stylized facts" that in due course became welcome props of the neoclassical growth paradigm. Kaldor's canonical views of the late 1950s, built on his "stylized facts" shaped much of the discourse on long-run development by mainstream as well as some heterodox economists.

Presumably, Kaldor himself did not anticipate the cooption of his "stylized facts" by neoclassical economists, believing instead that they contributed an essential foundation for the theoretical construction of his alternate approach to the dominant neoclassical models of growth and distribution. It is ironic also that while Kaldor ostensibly proposed his "stylized facts" as a challenge to the theoretical foundations of neoclassical economics, actually neoclassical growth theorists easily recognized them as ideally suited for their own purpose and readily moved on to seek evidence for their historical presence (Blaug, 1989). Intimate knowledge of mainstream neoclassical economics allowed Mark Blaug to realize that Kaldor's alleged constancies would be used by neoclassical economists as welcome support for their growth models, noting that:

> Neoclassical growth theory is perfectly capable of accounting for Kaldor's stylized facts with appropriate assumptions about production functions, technical progress, population growth and saving propensities. Indeed, so elastic is the apparatus provided by neoclassical growth theory that it is capable of accounting *ex post* for any facts whatsoever.
>
> (Blaug, 1989, p. 78)

The controversy unleashed by Kaldor's claims of historical support for his "stylized facts" reemerged in the opening paragraph of an essay by Harcourt (1982). Harcourt evaluated Kaldor's unsubstantiated claims on the inability of neoclassical theory to support his stylized facts. He did not examine the historical evidence for Kaldor's "magic constancies" as such, because he wished to focus on the conceptual structure of Kaldor's growth models and for that purpose the "dispute is irrelevant to the present discussion." He could not avoid pointing out, however, that their historical authenticity as empirical facts was questionable, citing the skepticism with which the experts at Corfu judged them:

> Since 1956, Mr Kaldor has been developing a model of income distribution and economic growth in order to explain the observed constancies in the capital-output ratios, the distribution of income, and the rates of profit on capital of the United Kingdom and United States economies. Whether or not the three ratios are in fact constant is in dispute.
>
> (Harcourt, 1982, p. 67)

Coming from a leading economist outside the neoclassical mainstream, Harcourt's comment clearly conveyed the controversial nature of Kaldor's stylized facts. It is remarkable that while touching rather casually upon the empirical foundation for Kaldor's claims, presumably as characteristic features of capital accumulation trends, he raised instead questions about the scientific relevance of their theoretical foundation. A critical appraisal of Kaldor's growth models made it difficult to suppress the thought that if growth theories explained the wrong empirical trends, their scientific, as opposed to ideological import was questionable. What reality are such theories a guide to?

The presumed existence of such "magic constancies" (Bronfenbrenner, 1971, p. 421) undoubtedly spurred the use of Cobb–Douglas aggregate production functions as proper tools for the study of neoclassical growth and income distribution models. Assuming such constancies in these models delivered the expected results: free-enterprise systems moved into steady-state growth paths despite the disruptions associated with the unpredictable shocks that nature or misguided policy threw at them. The free-enterprise system was neither erratic nor endogenously prone to cyclical crashes. While short-term business fluctuations might be inevitable (chiefly short-term inventory cycles), their volatility was restricted by inherent forces and certainly did not block the natural tendency of capital accumulation to find its equilibrium path.

One of the issues raised by critics of the aggregate Cobb–Douglas production function pertains to the evidence found for the assumption of constant profit shares, a central aspect of the neoclassical theory of income distribution. Their criticism draws attention to the fact that from the identity of aggregate value-added and the sum of wages and profits one cannot derive the equality between wage rate and the marginal product of labor, or the correspondence between the profit rate and the marginal product of capital as a factor of production. In fact, Harrison (2005), Felipe and McCombie (2006), Lavoie (2008), Shaikh (2005), and others have shown empirically that profit and labor income shares are generally not constant in the long run and production functions do not explain their variability.

Evaluating the scientific worth of theories of accumulation and unemployment in Marx and other classical economists required, according to W. Eltis, deriving long-run empirical estimates of capital–output trends. According to Eltis, classical economists failed in this regard because he believed no such trends existed. Eltis argued that if one assumed biased technical progress, a secularly rising capital–output ratio should emerge, eventually producing a falling profit rate that in turn should usher in stagnation and the rise of unemployment. In his view, the empirical record provided no support for such views. Citing the work of Matthews *et al.* (1982) on British economic growth, Eltis believed that their research clearly showed the capital–output trend in the UK was roughly constant in the long run. In addition, the empirical estimates obtained by Klein and Kosobud (1961) appeared to support the same conclusion for the US. Altogether, Eltis (1985, p. 283) was satisfied that with regard to the link between profitability, capital accumulation and the growth of unemployment, earlier projections in Marx's work did not pan out:

> The difficulty with Marx's approach to the problem has proved to be his assumption that the capital-output ratio has an inevitable upward trend. The best evidence available indicates that the capital-output ratio has been relatively stable in the century since the publication of *Capital*.

Countering the Kaldorian constancies

Despite Eltis' critical comments questioning the historical reality of profitability trends embodying dynamic tendencies found in Ricardo and Marx, we have evidence in the encyclopedic research presented by Matthews *et al.* (1982) to challenge Kaldor's "stylized facts." Indeed Figures 6.3 and 6.4 in that book show the paths of profit shares, profit rates and capital–output ratios, both gross and net, and none are constant. In both figures, profit rates display an unambiguous downward trend from 1855 through 1975, although the overall rate of decline for the net profit rate is higher. Gross capital–output ratios fluctuate, reflecting capacity utilization, and in 1975 reach a level well above the initial value. (Matthews *et al.*, 1982, pp. 184–186).

Chapter 7 of this book presents substantial US evidence on long-run capital–output ratios derived mainly from mainstream sources. We believe that such estimates fail to confirm Kaldorian constancies.

In a comprehensive study of global trends in saving and investment published by the Brookings Institution, Barry Bosworth estimated that from 1965 to 1990 the capital–output ratio rose in 13 out of the 15 countries surveyed, including four non-European (US, Canada, Japan, and Australia) as well as four large European countries (France, Germany, Italy, and UK) and seven small European countries (Austria, Belgium, Denmark, Finland, Netherlands, Norway and Sweden). His data showed that the exceptions in his survey revealed no change in the US and a slight decline in Norway. For the group as a whole, Bosworth (1993, p. 61) found "a consistent increase in the estimated values" of the capital–output ratio after 1973.

Considering the exceptional position of Angus Maddison in the field of historical statistics, recognized by economic historians as well as other researchers on account of his empirical contributions to our understanding of global development trends, we share Andrew Sharpe's (2002, p. 20) view that Maddison could well rank "as the leading macroeconomic historian of his generation." His views on the constancy of capital–output ratios should be taken into account in the Kaldorian controversy. Maddison's experience after years studying the nature of dynamic forces in capitalist development led him to question the claims advanced by mainstream economists on the nature of actual growth patterns. In light of his empirical investigations of "long-run dynamic forces," Maddison (1991, p. 83) took exception to the fact that:

> In some of the theoretical literature on growth there has been a tendency to assume long-run stability of capital-output ratios: see N. Kaldor, "Capital Accumulation and Economic Growth" ... who took this proposition to be a "stylized fact". Gallman's estimates in S. L. Engerman and R. E. Gallman, *Long Term Factors in American Economic Growth*...suggest that the rise in the US capital-output...was the continuation of a process going back as far as 1840.

Relevant to the task of clarifying the reality of long-term capital–output trends, Maddison helped with crucial estimates of capital stocks and GDPs required for historical long-run capital–output trends in four countries (France, Germany, Japan and the UK). We take those four countries to represent development patterns characteristic of advanced capitalist economies. In this regard, Japan stands out as a new entrant in the group of advanced capitalist countries, with a vigorous history of development that replicates in a shorter period the experience of the older UK.

Figure 2.1 shows the gross capital–output ratios in those four countries, spanning over a century. The capital-output ratio rose in Japan through the early 1930s; then it fell in the 1930s depression. Growth resumed in Japan in the first half of

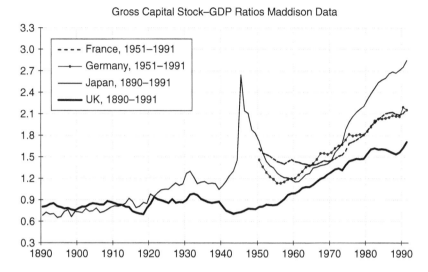

Figure 2.1 Capital–output ratios derived from Maddison data.

the 1940s, clearly following the collapse of its GDP in World War II. In the UK, the capital–output rose in the early 1940s and kept climbing for forty years.

Adjusting these fluctuations for capacity utilization reflecting changes in aggregate demand would reveal a smoother upward trend in both countries, obviously steeper in the case of Japan. The shorter time estimates for France and Germany overwhelmingly reveal a rising capital–output trend since the mid-1950s in the case of Germany and since the mid-1960s in the case of France. In any event, these trends do not conform to the historical patterns Kaldor claimed existed behind his "stylized facts."

Summary of main controversial points

Kaldor represented as empirical facts the stability of long-term profit shares, capital–output ratios and profitability trends, presumably derived from unspecified historical studies. Once neoclassical growth theorists brushed aside their initial reservations, Kaldor's "stylized facts" became accepted as largely indisputable. Perceptive followers of the neoclassical approach immediately recognized their convenient value and appropriated them as proof that their models reflected the real world as they conceived it. Regardless of his good intentions as a critic of neoclassical economics, Kaldor's alleged constancies propped up his opponents' research program.

There is no question that Kaldor's growth model builds on solid evidence of different saving propensities for capitalists and workers. But he went on to derive from this the inevitability of full employment and steady-state growth. If the capital–labor ratio deviated from its equilibrium path due to an excessive rate of fixed capital accumulation, the wage share in aggregate income would rise, squeezing profits. Since the savings rate out of wages was lower than out of profits and the wage share had expanded, total savings would fall and capitalist investment would weaken, lowering the accumulation rate. Such adjustment would push the capital–labor ratio towards its steady-state value. Once the system reached its steady-state growth path, full employment of labor was assured.

While acknowledging Kaldor's valuable insight linking growth and income distribution, some Keynesian economists noted the possible pitfalls of framing employment policy along Kaldorian lines. Smulders (2001) noted Kaldor's argument could be used to justify anti-labor policies seeking to bring about a reduction in the share of wages in order to increase employment:

> Kaldor's focus on income distribution attracted a lot of attention, perhaps because it shed new light not only on the Keynesian importance of spending and effective demand, but also on the older, classical and Marxian, role of social classes. By assuming that capitalists save more than workers, Kaldor showed that redistribution of income away from labour increases the rate of saving and hence may raise capital accumulation to absorb unemployment.

We survey in our book previous estimates of profitability and accumulation trends in order to contrast them with our own results. We do not question the existence of long-run "stylized facts," but we certainly deny that Kaldor's specifications reflect the actual path of development experienced by advanced capitalist countries. Kaldor's claims that his "stylized facts" were not only convenient assumptions for a short-term perspective on profitability and accumulation but also real patterns of long-run development in advanced capitalist countries cannot be validated.

Our findings challenge the conventional wisdom scripting the "stylized facts" advanced by Kaldor half a century ago into an unquestioned orthodoxy accepted by mainstream theorists of growth and distribution. The analysis of long-run trends requires combining the valuable empirical research of heterodox economists like Duménil and Lévy (1994) on the US profit rate with data derived from official sources such as the Bureau of Economic Analysis. Doing so reveals that most of Kaldor's "facts," but not all, are devoid of any general empirical support as far as advanced capitalist countries are concerned.

Ironically enough the endorsement of Kaldor's "stylized facts" by neoclassical economists eventually led Kaldor to abandon his search for equilibrium growth paths. After vigorously arguing for over a decade that his theoretical arguments for steady-state growth paths received support from the empirical constancies found in the development of capitalism, Kaldor announced in the early 1970s and in the pages of the *Economic Journal*, "The Irrelevance of Equilibrium Economics," thus reverting to his 1930s position. (Kaldor, 1972).

3 Innovations as competitive weapons

Beyond perfect competition

The crown jewel of neoclassical microeconomics, perfect competition, allows no space to deal with the actual behavior of real-world competition, no room for the concept of competition-as-war. In the conceptual structure of neoclassical microeconomics, the notion of firms acquiring competitive weapons, deploying technologies intended to lower costs in order to undersell rivals, makes no sense. Competitive firms have no need to employ such competitive weapons because they are too small to gain any advantage from so doing. Perfectly competitive firms are passive "price takers": they can sell all they can profitably produce for their size and their behavior cannot alter the industry's structure of market shares. Seeking to gain market share from rivals would bring no benefits, only losses, signaling the presence of combative oligopolies hell-bent on planting the seeds of their own destruction. As far as concerns neoclassical microeconomics in both extremes of market structures, perfectly competitive industries and pure monopoly, firms seek to maximize their profits. Focusing on producing output up to the level where marginal cost equals market price, perfectly competitive firms achieve efficient allocation of resources. While seeking to maximize profits, in perfectly competitive industries free entry brings in new firms that end up competing away all "pure" profits: profit rates fall to parity with the interest rate. Why business would carry on production activities when rewards are no higher than interest yields on no risk bank deposits is not considered. Monopolists obtain profits by lowering output relative to competitive levels, taking advantage of barriers to entry into the industry. But in all cases, neoclassical theory ignores business strategies to deploy innovations, preferably process innovations, as competitive weapons to gain market share at the expense of rivals (Tsoulfidis, 2010, 2011).

The brighter lights in the neoclassical field naturally detected the conceptual straitjacket constricting their view of competition. Expounding on the nature of universal economic laws, including the "law" of the competitive or atomistic market, Frank Knight (1946, p. 102) decried that:

> The "perfect" market, of theory at its highest level of generality, is conventionally described as perfectly or purely "competitive." But use of this word

is one of our worst misfortunes of terminology. There is no presumption of psychological competition, emulation, or rivalry.

In a critical essay elucidating the contradiction between the theoretical analysis offered by neoclassical economics regarding the structure of competitive industries and the real-world nature of competitive behavior, Paul McNulty (1968, p. 642) concluded that:

> Perfect competition, the only clearly and rigorously defined concept of competition to be found in the corpus of economic theory, which is free of all traces of business behavior associated with "monopolistic" elements, means simply the *existence* of an indefinitely large number of non-competing firms.

Neoclassical theory seeks to provide a rationale for its claims of market efficiency in economic systems where the invisible hand is assumed to deliver perfect outcomes. Reaching that goal then rules out acknowledgment of any purposeful behavior designed to gain advantage at the expense of rivals. In perfect competition, firms are too small to encroach on rivals and are not even aware of their rivals' behavior. The key objection should address the incompatibility of such conception with any semblance of real competitive behavior. In McNulty's view, paradoxically, neoclassical theory interprets all forms of competitive behavior as evidence of monopoly, while allowing no room either in perfect competition or perfect monopoly for competitive strategies. Aggressive price cutting is regarded as a sign of market imperfection, be it oligopoly or, if product differentiation is involved, "monopolistic" competition. After raising the notion of industrial competition to the rank of perfection, neoclassical economics proceeded to empty it of all real attributes.

McNulty stressed that while the unreality of perfect competition was frequently noted in the economic literature, the drastic transformation that the notion of competition had suffered since Adam Smith identified it as the control mechanism bringing order to an otherwise turbulent economic system, received insufficient attention. For Adam Smith competition ensured that market prices found their "natural" level and profit rates across industries tended to equality. It did not matter to his notion of competition whether the number of firms in the industry was large or small. Competition as a regulating force did not depend on a specific market structure. Smith's dynamical approach followed Newton's work on gravitation as the force that brought order in nature and allowed scientific understanding of its laws of motion. McNulty's interpretation failed to appreciate the full dimension of Smith's concept of competition, including process innovations.

For Adam Smith, viewing competition as a spur of the greater division of labor broadened the scope of competitive behavior beyond price cutting onto technical change. With technical change linked to progressive steps in the division of labor, the search for ways to lower production costs took center stage in competitive strategies. As a byproduct of the growing division of labor and technical change, Marx theorized the inevitable development of machinery to achieve the reduction of production unit costs by way of breaking down production activities into discrete mechanical tasks. Schumpeter followed up with his grand vision of entrepreneurial advances in product designs and process innovations. In both cases the scope and vigor of competitive patterns of behavior reached dimensions that evolved in tandem with the economic system itself (Clifton, 1977, 1983).

While neoclassical economics considered technical change, or innovation, as an exogenous determinant of accumulation and growth, other currents, building on the foundation laid out by Smith, Ricardo, Marx, and Schumpeter placed it at the center of their theoretical perspective. Classical economists were fully aware of the crucial role that innovations played in the development of capitalism. For classical economists, technical progress spurred the growth of productivity and regulated the formation of relative prices. Adam Smith understood that the economic forces pushing wages, profits, and rents to their natural level operated differently in the various phases traversed by the economy. In the opening paragraph of Chapter VII of *The Wealth of Nations*, Smith said:

> There is in every society or neighbourhood an ordinary or average rate both of wages and profit in every different employment of labour and stock. This rate is naturally regulated. . .partly by the general circumstances of the society, their riches or poverty, their advancing, stationary or declining condition.
>
> (Smith, 1965, Chapter VII, p. 55)

Free competition in Smith and Schumpeter

Classical economists anticipated several core ideas making up Schumpeter's theory of innovational investment. Both Smith and Schumpeter assumed the existence of full employment in the background setting preceding the introduction of process innovations. Smith argued that launching new activities would require drawing labor away from its current employment and hence push up wage rates. Assuming a full-employment economy as a starting point, Smith argued that the imbalance created during the gestation period in new lines of production, drawing capital and labor away from current employment, and thus lowering output, would spur transient inflation. Smith clearly adumbrated a theory of transitory inflation, tacitly tracing its roots to innovational activity.

In the long run Smith's dynamics led to a decline in profitability, as capitalism expanded and the supply of natural resources diminished, but contrary to Schumpeter's view, competition did not cause the erosion of industrial profits but rather their tendency to equalization across various sectors. The common assumption in classical economics was that retained savings out of profits financed business investment. The retained share of profits depended on perceived intensity of competitive pressures to expand the enterprise in order to achieve economies of scale. While Smith recognized the practice of occasional credit-financed investment, he typically assigned it marginal significance. Nonetheless, he certainly appreciated the connection between rising prices, thriving markets, competitive rivalries, and innovating activities:

> The increase of demand, besides, though in the beginning it may sometimes raise the price of goods never fails to lower it in the long run. It encourages production, and thereby increases the competition of the producers, who in order to undersell one another, have recourse to new divisions of labour and new improvements of art, which might never otherwise have been thought of.
> (Smith, 1965, Book V, Chap I, Part III, p. 706)

In contrast with Schumpeter's view of innovating investment, Smith saw it as a necessary, risky, and natural feature of the competitive struggle confronting all business enterprises. In Smith, competitive pressures created the need to sustain the flow of technical progress, whereas in Schumpeter the appearance of innovation swarms crucially depended on the flowering of entrepreneurial talents, the idiosyncratic expression of heroic personalities. Schumpeter's account shared with classical economics the innovating imperative, namely the search for higher profit opportunities on the part of entrepreneurs seeking to explore untested grounds. Successful innovations would remain exceptionally profitable only for a time, since the lure of higher gains drew imitators into the industry and the expanded supply lowered prices and reduced yields.

Classical economists did not postulate a state of zero profits as a systemic characteristic of balance tendencies brought on by competition, but rather equalization tendencies of profit rates among the various branches of the economy. In the case of Marx the disappearance of (marginal) profits due to over-accumulation signaled the collapse of accumulation and the unraveling of the system's growth dynamics, rather than a condition characteristic of the "circular flow."

Reflecting on the "overweening conceit which the greater part of men have of their own abilities" once driven by "Their absurd presumption in their own good fortune" (p. 107), Smith observed that:

> The establishment of any new manufacture, of any new branch of commerce, or of any new practice in agriculture, is always a speculation, from which the projector promises himself extraordinary profits. These profits sometimes are very great, and sometimes, more frequently perhaps, they are quite otherwise; but in general they bear no proportion to those of other old trades in the neighbourhood. If the project succeeds, they are commonly at first very high. When the trade or practice becomes thoroughly established and well known, the competition reduces them to the level of other trades.
> (Smith, 1965, Chapter X, p. 115)

In Smith's theory of industrial progress, development brought about the growth and improvement of machinery. He found it self-evident that "every body must be sensible how much labor is facilitated and abridged by the application of proper machinery" (Smith, 1965, Book I, Chapter I, p. 9). In the course of that development, the practical knowledge accumulated by machinery users should prove of limited value, and Smith anticipated the time when a new class of workers singularly engaged in drafting blueprints for new machinery would take their place:

> All the improvements in machinery, however, have by no means been the inventions of those who had occasion to use the machines. Many improvements have been made by the ingenuity of the makers of the machines, when to make them became the business of a peculiar trade; and some by that of those who are called philosophers or men of speculation, whose trade it is not to do anything, but to observe everything; and who, upon that account, are often capable of combining together the powers of the most distant and dissimilar objects. In the progress of society, philosophy or speculation becomes, like every other employment, the principal or sole trade and occupation of a particular class of citizens.
>
> (Smith, 1965, Book I, Chapter I, p. 10)

Schumpeter's innovators disrupted the synchronized structure of production found in his idealized "circular flow," a state of quasi-Walrasian general equilibrium in which profits had been competed away, carved out new development avenues propelled by their desire to exploit the potential benefits of superior technology and achieved drastic reductions in production costs that brought them high profits. Schumpeter's conception of circular flows allowed for growth due to population increases, but everything else such as the techniques of production, assortment of goods produced, marketing, and so on was repetitive. All production and exchange activities followed routine patterns. The chief and only motivation to sustain them was fulfillment of current consumption needs. The circular "is first, of course, no state of absence of motion, as it implies the ever changing flow of productive services and consumers' goods, although this flow is looked upon as going on under substantially unchanging conditions" (Schumpeter, 1928, p. 373). In the circular flow, no capitalists owning industrial assets as a class existed, no profits or interest collected. There were landlords possessing land which, despite yielding rent, absent interest rates, had no price (Samuelson, 1943). The characteristic features of the circular flow constituted nothing more than an "abstract construction," one in which, absent capitalists as a social class, everyone had "equal access to "capital" (Sweezy, 1943). In it, all income accrued to landlords and workers, for should an unexpected surplus appear in any branch of the economy, some workers would immediately seek bank credits to finance its growth and consequently is profitability would shrink. No obstacles to entry marred the perfect information available, due to the repetitive nature of all economic activity, and under perfect competition, bank credit was readily available.

Sweezy's view that "Schumpeter's theory bore certain striking resemblances to that of Marx" regarding the centrality of innovating investment for the dynamics of accumulation has some merit. But contrary to Sweezy's view, Schumpeter's notion that profit and interest would be absent from the circular flow would not be compatible with the conceptual structure of Marx's schemes of simple reproduction (Sweezy, 1943, p. 94). Whatever the merit of setting Schumpeter's circular flow as the launching platform for intermittent innovating activity on the part of entrepreneurs, it is clear that it was derived from assumptions very different from those underpinning Marx's schemes of simple reproduction.

Consumption, both productive and unproductive, defined the goal to which production and exchange relations were geared in Schumpeter's circular flow and Marx's simple reproduction. But in Marx's conception of simple reproduction the system yielded a surplus that capitalists, as the owners of the means of production, appropriated and actually consumed. In Schumpeter's circular flow no such surplus emerged since capitalists as a class did not exist, therefore only workers and landlords consumed, and the system's reproduction required only replacement of those resources that were actually used up. Without a "social surplus" to divide among property owners in the guise of profits, interest and rent, all net output accrued to labor (Kurz, 2006). Unequal levels in workers' consumption reflected differences in labor productivity across the various branches of the economy, not class differences.

Absent a capitalist class with claims to a surplus product, skills determined labor allocation and wages according to relative productivities. The presence of a landed aristocracy collecting rent on priceless (due to a zero interest rate) but obviously scarce land did highlight the artificiality of the scheme. A casual appraisal of the economic system sketched in Schumpeter's circular flow could lead to a false association with the dreaded socialist commonwealth which, he feared, the loss of the entrepreneurial spirit would usher in. Decades before the publication of his *Capitalism, Socialism and Democracy*, Schumpeter concluded that with capitalism maturing and entrepreneurial firms evolving into bureaucratic corporations:

> Capitalism, whilst economically stable, and even gaining in stability, creates, by rationalizing the human mind, a mentality and a style of life incompatible with its own fundamental conditions, motives and social institutions, and will be changed, although not by economic necessity and probably even at some sacrifice of economic welfare, into an order of things which it will be merely matter of taste and terminology to call Socialism or not.
>
> (Schumpeter, 1928, pp. 385–386)

Entrepreneurs emerge from the circular flow like mythical figures rising out of a primeval miasma, carrying their vision for a bright future of wealth and fame. In a world without profits, they reject complacency and are willing to risk fortune and fame in the pursuit of novelty: they are the leaders needed to overhaul the system and bring about progress to the world. Innovations alter consumption patterns, open new markets, implement cost-cutting management systems and introduce new labor-saving technologies:

> What we, unscientifically, call economic progress means essentially putting productive resources to uses hitherto untried in practice, and withdrawing them from the uses they have served so far. This is what we call "innovation."
>
> (Schumpeter, 1928, p. 378)

Attributing entrepreneurial talents to character traits of rare individuals, including vision and fortitude, ability to combine the advances of science with insights of creative thinking, and practical abilities to organize industry along new lines, Schumpeter saw them as essential for capitalist dynamics. For him innovators were not necessarily capitalists but visionaries who did not fear failure in their quest for success. Banks were there to provide the needed wherewithal:

> This process of innovation in industry by the agency of entrepreneurs supplies the key to all the phenomena of capital and credit. The role of credit would be a technical and a subordinate one in the sense that everything fundamental about the economic process could be explained in terms of goods, if industry grew by small steps along coherent curves. For in that case financing could and would be done substantially by means of the current gross revenue, and only small discrepancies would need to be smoothed.
>
> (Schumpeter, 1928, p. 381)

The credit provided by the banking system advancing the necessary credits enabled the completion of innovating projects. Potentially profitable projects requiring initial finance before reaching fruition were eligible. Entrepreneurs could not be expected to own the required capital, for none was available in the circular flow: they could not be expected to possess the means necessary to command producer goods and labor away from their current use and draw them into new ventures. Absent profits and innovating capital within the circular flow, their blueprints for new technical or commercial projects promising high returns were their chief marketable asset. The banking system played a key role in the dynamics of capitalist accumulation. This aspect of the Schumpeterian economics undoubtedly anticipated the Keynesian view of credit-financed investment, even though, as Hansen (1951) pointed out, Schumpeter neglected to acknowledge the existence of an income multiplier in his business cycles theory.

Schumpeter's theory of economic development merged with his theory of business cycles. The "circular flow" exhibited stationary equilibrium with full employment and zero profits. Breaking out of such mode required innovating activity underpinning the transition to a boom phase in the development path, typically initiated by inflation in product and resource markets. The boom phase facilitated the deployment of a superior productive structure. Inflation inevitably emerged out of the break-up in pre-existing product and resource networks as innovators, aided by the credit advanced by the banks, hired labor and capital resources away from their current employment. Once the projects of the innovating firms were completed, successful ventures yielded temporary high profits. Process innovations necessarily cheapened unit costs of production where applied, while price inflation in the boom phase raised revenues. Innovating profits, however, lasted only as long as the inevitable swarm of imitators failed to compete away the gains of the innovators.

Finally, Smith's interpretation of the quality of genius ran opposite to Schumpeter's. Schumpeter's gifted individuals transformed the channels that enabled economic reproduction and raised the level of technical complexity that sustained them. Smith, on the other hand, demurred at the notion of talent as a prime mover, unencumbered by the weight of the social division of labor, and argued that:

> The difference of natural talents in different men is, in reality, much less than we are aware of; and the very different genius which appears to distinguish men of different professions, when grown up to maturity, is not upon many occasions so much the cause, as the effect of the division of labor. The difference between the most dissimilar characters, between a philosopher and a common street porter, for example, seems to arise not so much from nature, as from habit, custom, and education.
>
> (Smith, 1965, Book I, Chapter I, p. 15)

Innovational cycles

The period extending from the initial steps in the implementation of the innovating blueprints to their completion, the gestation span, and the extent to which currently employed resources had to be pulled away from their current employment set the length and intensity of the inflationary phase, hence the strength of future profit growth. Schumpeter's innovational waves dissipated after cresting, declining at intervals of various lengths, before the system reached a new equilibrium at a higher level of output and technological complexity. Since these waves were initiated by the implementation of new projects conceived by the "entrepreneurial genius" available, the question remains why progress should be intermittent, wave-like rather than continuous. Why would innovating projects die down after successful breakthroughs? Why allow imitators to copy the new technology or product, avoiding the pioneers' overhead expenditures in research and development? Again, why would their innovating activity remain sporadic rather than continuous? As Kuznets (1940, p. 262) saw it:

> If imitators are ready to follow as soon as the entrepreneurial genius has proved that the innovation is successful, the disturbance of equilibrium at that time is certainly not sufficient to bar the genius from turning to new feats and thus initiating an uprush in another industry.

According to Kuznets, one possible answer was that the flow of technological knowledge from which the creative imagination of entrepreneurs drew inspiration might itself be discontinuous. This could be due to the uneven pace of developments in science and engineering. Kuznets (1940, p. 264) pointed out that the spread of electricity in industry was delayed until "the potentialities of steam power were exhausted by the economic system," which suggests that overhauling the industrial structure was not a viable alternative for as long as the old techniques remained profitable.

An alternative explanation for the bunching of innovations traces the intermittent character of innovational activity to the cyclically competitive pressures governing profitability itself. By their very nature, innovations will so disrupt the existing technical and economic structure of a given branch of production that not before the new readjustment is achieved could new breakthroughs be considered. Like any other profit-seeking activity, entrepreneurial endeavors are guided by the changing prospects for gain in the various branches of industry and commerce. As long as imitators are still at work and the deflationary phase not yet over, the incentive to innovate should be considerably weaker. Shifting focus to new branches might require time as potential entrepreneurs evaluated their prospects for success.

Echoing Smith's view on the progress of productivity caused by the introduction of machinery and the transient nature of the profits accruing to the innovator, Ricardo stressed that:

> He, indeed, who made the discovery of the machine, or who first usefully applied it, would enjoy an additional advantage, by making great profits for a time; but, in proportion as the machine came into general use, the price of the commodity produced, would, from the effects of competition, sink to its cost of production, when the capitalist would get the same money profits as before.
>
> (Ricardo, 1981, p. 387)

Because in Ricardo's terms the "application of machinery to any branch of production, as should have the effect of saving labour, was a general good" (p. 396), the time gap between the completion of the promising innovation and the unavoidable tide of imitators appropriating its benefits (free riding on the overhead costs of "research and development") played a crucial role in the competitive strategy chosen. Indeed, the competitive strategy pursued by innovators will determine which stance took precedence: the pursuit of extra profits by way of lowering unit costs, or lowering prices regardless of the profit consequences as a preemptive measure against rivals' actual or potential encroachment of market shares.

When the groundwork underlying process innovations relied on "speculation" conceived outside scientific or technological progress available as "a general good," and instead built upon insights of gifted individuals, imitation responses could be assumed to be slow and distant: competitive strategies could afford being somewhat less than outright aggressive. It would follow from Schumpeter's own account, however, that as the forces of production inherent in capitalism developed and the progress of science and technology accelerated, an increasing amount of innovation would emerge from their activities, thus reducing the importance of individual entrepreneurial genius.

As scientific advances and business R&D activities expanded, efforts to imitate successful innovations on the part of competitive business should intensify. The commercial advantage derived from such efforts would outweigh the expenses involved, let alone the risks involved in launching innovations. Seeking to expand market shares by any means necessary, leading corporations would be forced to alter their commercial and innovating strategies. In order to prevent potential imitators from threatening their market ranking strategies designed to dissuade imitators preemptive strikes against their commercial solvency were required. Lower prices and higher quality associated with technical progress would become weapons of choice in competitive strategies, even if losses threatened as a result. As Oscar Lange (1943, p. 25) saw it when evaluating the diversity of innovating strategies: "The type of competition and the entrepreneurial responses associated with innovations thus exercise an important selective influence upon them."

Innovating strategies of capitalist firms

While pre-capitalist societies, such as China, were capable of bringing forth major inventions early on, including printing, the compass, clocks, gunpowder, spinning machinery, a cotton gin, porcelain, matches, toothbrushes, etc., these technical breakthroughs did not by themselves transformed feudalism into a free-enterprise growth machine (Baumol, 2002). The systematic application of scientific knowledge to the development of productive forces rose to unprecedented heights with the growth of capitalism and the intensification of free competition that followed it.

In contrast with Schumpeter's focus on gifted individuals as being the ultimate source of innovations, Adam Smith and Marx in particular identified competition among capitalist firms as the major force behind the growing complexity of innovational activity. The competitive struggle among rival firms created the need to systematically transfer the fruits and insights of scientific research to productive methods lowering unit costs, forcing rivals to match the innovator's lower unit prices or risk being priced out of the market. Subjectively the relentless pressures of competition created the ideal social and psychological types ready to straddle the worlds of scientific research and business strategy, searching for the most effective innovations to gain larger market shares. Indeed, for classical economists, free competition "shapes people's aspirations, decisions and actions" (Kurz, 2006).

As capitalism developed, Schumpeter's romanticized entrepreneurial hero eventually lost his central role and largely faded away, replaced by R&D departments with engineering teams producing blueprints of potential innovations. Schumpeter himself pondered the difference between progress in earlier phases of entrepreneurial leadership and the new attitudes molded by corporate research teams whose goals were exclusively professional, not proprietary:

> Progress becomes "automatised," increasingly impersonal and decreasingly a matter of leadership and individual initiative. This amounts to a fundamental change in many respects, some of which reach far out of the sphere of things economic. It means the passing out of existence of a system of selection of leaders which had the unique characteristic that success in *rising* to a position and success in *filling* it were essentially the same thing – as were success of the firm and success of the man in charge.
>
> (Schumpeter, 1928, p. 385)

Developments in scientific and technical knowledge that could be used to launch new products were indispensable elements of successful business strategies. To the extent that advances in world science and technology were relatively accessible to all, successful innovating activity required specialization in the speedy adaptation of new ideas, lest rivals would move first. Because the frontiers of scientific and technical research reached beyond the purview of business interests, firms selected teams of experts devising ways to quickly convert the potential benefits of their work into successful commercial innovations. Possible alternatives to a single firm's efforts in launching new product or process innovations included purchasing licenses from other innovating firms, or combining efforts with outsiders carrying on complementary activities to achieve superior joint results. In order to choose between short- and long-term commercial strategies specific timetables to evaluate their success or failure were required.

Offensive vs. defensive innovations

Chris Freeman's contribution to our understanding of corporate innovating strategies is unsurpassed. Fundamentally, Freeman distinguishes between "offensive" and "defensive" innovating strategies. An offensive strategy is generally designed to push corporations into a position of market leadership, reaching that goal on the basis of technological prowess. If the firm maintains its own research and development facilities and utilizes the payoffs of its own scientific work, either the firm enjoys a privileged position in scientific research activities, or the firm excels in the ability to use potentially useful but not specific blueprints for designing new products or processes.

Such firms would have to be financially capable of maintaining their own R&D activities to reach their leadership goal, and therefore would necessarily be in the minority. Indeed, higher profits would just compensate them for the larger overhead expenses associated with the funding of costly R&D. Freeman (1982, p. 175) quotes estimates from the electronics and chemical industries indicating that about half of the total costs involved in producing new prototypes could be attributed to spending on such R&D.

Due to the high costs involved, firms driven by ambitions of global leadership were likely to be strong advocates of patent protection, since they rely on receiving exclusive rights in order to prevent imitators from reducing their initially higher profits. Firms aspiring to positions of market leadership in the absence of R&D departments of their own would have to employ staff capable of "monitoring" developments in scientific and technical institutions on a world scale, hiring consultants if necessary to keep abreast of the available knowledge elsewhere. Having access to the fruits of basic research facilities might provide firms with a distinct advantage relative to those that did not. More commonly, however, firms adopting offensive strategies in the race to bring new products to market simply enjoyed superior organizational flexibility. Their ability to marshal resources around design engineering projects or the layout of efficient plant facilities proved the decisive factor in that race.

On the other hand, firms without the resources necessary to support their aspirations to market leadership should adopt defensive strategies. Firms classified as imitators differed from those engaged in offensive strategies only in the scale of their R&D activities. In order to remain viable as market players, their R&D facilities should be extensive, not to produce original designs in product or process innovations, but to supply and market modified blueprints of the advances made by industry leaders. Their strategy required the ability to learn from the strengths and weaknesses of the industry leaders, aiming to benefit from their accomplishments while avoiding their mistakes. Their response policy involves introducing product improvements that allowed them to obtain patents without paying licensing fees. Not seeking positions of industry leadership, imitators should avoid the high-overhead R&D expenses and testing trials associated with innovating activities. In order to survive they should willingly accept a subordinate position that is cheaper to maintain and less hazardous, particularly if they also enjoy advantages in labor, materials or energy costs. The likelihood of success of imitators strongly depends on the speed with which innovators sustain the flow of technical progress.

Free competition in Freeman and Metcalfe

Freeman's neat classification of innovating strategies would be somewhat unintelligible if not placed in the context of free industrial competition, a concept far removed from the canons of perfect competition, and not explicitly developed in his analysis of technical progress. Without it the choices made hang loosely in the air of speculation. Why would firms choose either the travails of industry leadership, with all the risks attached, or a subordinate position as imitators? Are we back to Schumpeter's inborn talent account of personality differences, only this time transferred from gifted individuals to firms? Freeman's answer seems to involve force, not choice, but the nature of the compulsion is not explored. Freeman links firm survival with the profit drive, but as those two motivations ostensibly differ in kind, a connection between them needs be established: "The efforts of firms to survive, to make profits and to grow have led them to adopt one or more of the strategies" (Freeman, 1982, p. 183).

Freeman emphasized the enormous risks involved when firms accept the challenge of producing and marketing new products, given the high degree of uncertainty that typically permeates their own plans or the response reactions issuing from rivals. Freeman's outline of the major options facing firms when planning their innovating strategies accomplished two things: first, it dispensed with the fading choreography of the entrepreneur as portrayed by Schumpeter; and second, it cleared the grounds to appraise the significance of innovations as competitive weapons. Our view that Freeman laid the foundation for such an appraisal, without explicit acknowledgment of its far-reaching implications, takes into account his analysis of the consequences if firms recoiled from confronting the innovating challenge. His valuable perspective highlights the fact that for firms engaged in competitive battles, "not to innovate is to die" (p. 169). A thorough analysis of the dynamics of free competition was absent from Freeman's dramatic view of the consequences of passivity in firms facing competitive threats.

Metcalfe stressed the need to abandon notions of competition as a state, tied to an atomistic concept of market structure as in perfect competition, and bring in the concept of rivalry among firms struggling to gain market share while locked in a zero-sum game, but he also failed to draw the implications of his proposal. As Metcalfe sees it, entrepreneurial activity has no place in a setting of perfect knowledge, passivity with respect to market prices, product homogeneity, and the other features included in perfect competition. This is why Metcalfe advocated thinking of industrial competition "as a dynamic process of rivalry and struggle for shares of the market," warning that "This process is a competitive process in which old firms either adapt to the new competitive circumstances or decline and die" (Metcalfe, 2004, p. 164).

While acknowledging Schumpeter's pioneering role in the analysis of innovating activity, Metcalfe found his emphasis on individual personality traits outdated. The growing financial power of firms allows them to establish their own scientific and technical facilities, housing teams of experts devoted to the advancement of entrepreneurial strategies. These departments expand with the growth of large corporations and the global range of their business activities. But with the growth of corporations and their R&D programs, entrepreneurial activity lost much of its former link with the unique vision of gifted individuals. While radical changes in product design or production methods occasionally shake up the foundation of industrial activity, much of the advance in developed economies is incremental in nature: it is produced by R&D teams that could easily replicate the achievements of rival innovative firms. R&D expenditures are necessary to keep ahead of rivals, and such programs are an integral part of the market strategy adopted by all viable firms.

Much improvement in product and process technology could be derived from "learning by doing" practices on the part of firms, shortening the interval between invention and successful innovation. With the spread of R&D teams, the diffusion of technological advance grows and the number of firms engaged in innovating activities increases as the economy expands. Hence, as competition among firms intensifies, innovating firms need to consider not only the speed with which imitators circumvent their patents, but also the present danger of being outperformed by rivals.

As the market expands, firms contending for leadership positions become larger and their competitive battles more lethal. A firm's absolute advantage derives from its power to lower unit costs but not the quality of products relative to those offered by rival firms. But as the diffusion of innovations accelerates, absolute advantage weakens. The availability of finance provided by banks and other institutions raises not only the financial power of leading corporations but also the pace of diffusion for new innovations. In his comprehensive study of industrial competition Auerbach found evidence supporting the claim that "The movement to science-based innovation has clearly been a key aspect of the acceleration of the speed of diffusion of these innovations" (Auerbach, 1989, p. 269). As a result, the threat posed by rivals to cutting-edge advances achieved by temporary industry leaders looms larger. While achieving economies of scale proves effective in staving off unwanted market penetration by smaller firms, innovating strategies increasingly seek to fence off the encroaching efforts of other large firms. Auerbach also found that at present "it appears to be true that laggards within the world economy are likely to be punished more quickly and more severely than in earlier times" (p. 326).

Evolution of competitive objectives

Straddling conventional and heterodox economic theoretical perspectives, William Baumol recently proposed an effective alternative to Schumpeter's pessimistic forecast regarding the destiny of entrepreneurial activity. In Baumol's view, technical change will not be deterred by the growth of corporate bureaucratic structures because the spurs to innovate lie in the free-enterprise system itself, not in the psychological makeup of an elite class of individuals.

Outlining a "nonmathematical theory of entrepreneurship in general," Baumol (1990) wished to argue that throughout history "the supply of entrepreneurs *or the nature of their objectives*" did not undergo significant changes. What was subject to momentous transformations was "the set of rules" that governed their exertions, as they allowed for differential "pay-offs" in various endeavors. These rules included the "prevailing laws and legal procedures" outstanding at the time. Thus, distinct historical phases endowed with different sets of rules produced strikingly different innovating achievements, described by the essay's title as "productive, unproductive, and destructive." According to Baumol, it would not do to seek in the fading away of "the spirit of entrepreneurship" a valid reason for the dearth in "productive" innovations. Instead it would be right to consider the extent to which a change in "rules of the game" altered behavior in enterprising individuals.

Once the concept of entrepreneurship is extended to include "persons who are ingenious and creative in finding ways that add to their own wealth, power and prestige" (Baumol, 1990, p. 897), then we find the results of such activities may have little or nothing to do with the growth of output and in some cases may even bring about its decline. Furthermore, Baumol argued that entrepreneurial efforts may be concentrated around "unproductive" activities, such as creative schemes to circumvent legal impediments to rent-yielding pursuits.

As a historical illustration of the notion that wealth accumulation was not necessarily associated with productive activities, Baumol cited the case of ancient Roman society. In Roman society enterprising individuals chose careers yielding "power, prestige and wealth" but only if they did not involve exertions in "industry and commerce." The most coveted positions in Roman society included landholding, particularly if absentee management of the land was possible; usury, and offices allowing political payoffs stemming from "booty, indemnities, provincial taxes, loans and miscellaneous extractions." Industry and commerce were relegated to the purview of freed slaves, whose goal it was to amass enough wealth to buy land and mimic the aristocratic lifestyle. Persons retiring from financially successful occupations in industry and commerce and into "unproductive" occupations gained social prestige and thus reached the peak of their life achievements. Relying on research by leading historians, Baumol stressed the significance of records indicating that the development of science in Roman society was largely divorced from any consideration of its practical uses.

In medieval China, the king or emperor was the ultimate owner of his vassals' wealth and could confiscate any available assets belonging to his subjects if his own fortune declined. Such prerogative naturally discouraged the king's subjects from flaunting their wealth or exposing their property to the random hazards of royal greed. In China, the ladder of success leading to a post in the imperial bureaucracy as well as wealth and prestige required passing imperial examinations. Confucian philosophy and calligraphy were the core subjects in these tests, which were held every few years and reached such lofty levels of difficulty that only a few hundred scholars made it through. While the official salaries of the mandarin elite were modest, members generally achieved great wealth and social prestige, but not through any association with industry or commerce. Their revenues grew largely from corrupt practices reminiscent of those sustaining the aristocracy in ancient Rome: tribute extracted from those they were empowered to administer. How much it grew depended on the total debt, principal and interest, accumulated during their long period of preparation for the imperial examinations. The merchant class below the mandarins saw wealth accumulation as providing the necessary means to become a scholar-official or a landowner.

In Europe during the earlier Middle Ages, military adventures provided wealth for the nobility, mainly in the guise of castles and land. Innovating activity reflecting the exigencies of war among rival nobles proliferated: stone walls instead of wood structures strengthened castle defenses; towers were rounded to prevent collapsing corners; armor made more resistant to piercing; crossbows, longbows and artillery based on gunpowder expanded the arsenal of weaponry. In the conduct of war, sophisticated tactical and strategic plans guided their use. By the later Middle Ages the rules of the innovating imperative changed. The growing influence of the Church managed to restrain the turbulent behavior of warring nobles; the growth of towns led to successful efforts in curbing arbitrary levies on their residents; a new class of architects, designing and building castles, cathedrals, palaces, bridges, and other structures, attained great wealth and prestige while serving under the protection of kings and barons; the proliferation of Cistercian monasteries housing entrepreneurial monks became a powerful force behind the introduction of innovating technologies, chiefly water-driven mills.

Cistercian monks exhibited a strikingly high propensity to save in line with their ascetic way of life, allowing them to sustain remarkably high investment rates, expanding their vast landholdings and flocks of domesticated animals. Anticipating the Protestant ethic that in capitalist society lent fortitude to the behavioral patterns of wealth accumulation, the monks' puritanical lifestyle significantly aided their quest for expansion. The monks did not hold back when their competitors happened to be other religious institutions. Competitive wars drove financially powerful abbeys to encroach on property held by weaker rival monasteries and convents. The driving principles of entrepreneurial activities were not only different from those motivating the warring nobles of earlier medieval times, but the opposite of the behavioral guidelines setting the ground rules for wealth accumulation in Roman society.

Even after kings succeeded in implementing some semblance of law and order in society, no linear progression favoring productive enterprise as a source of wealth accumulation emerged in Europe between the fourteenth and eighteenth centuries. Instead, different forms of military exploits by the nobility were once again in ascendance, to be followed by rent-seeking schemes which "took a variety of forms, notably the quest for grants of land and patents of monopoly from the monarch" (Baumol, 1990, p. 907). Various systems of reward provided coveted riches for the ruling aristocracies, and therefore promoted different patterns of entrepreneurial behavior as circumstances changed.

Looking at Schumpeter's theory of the link between entrepreneurship and innovative activity from the historical perspective outlined by Baumol, it is evident that the nature of the innovations produced hinged on the socio-economic structure of capitalist society. Profit-seeking innovations did not take center stage before capital became dominant in society. Coerced by competitive pressures mounted by rival firms, capitalists seek expansion and market leadership through innovations. Innovating firms gain market leadership, securing higher profit shares and margins at the expense of rivals. Baumol stresses that innovations aimed at profit-making prevail only in capitalist society, for the simple reason that only in such society did profit-making become the supreme goal of creative enterprise. Baumol quoted the historian Eric Hobsbawm to the effect that:

> It is often assumed that an economy of private enterprise has an automatic bias towards innovation, but this is not so. It has a bias only towards profit.
>
> (Hobsbawm, 1969, p. 40)

Despite the dominant position reached by profit-making activities in capitalist society, what Baumol called "unproductive avenues for today's entrepreneur" did not disappear. On the contrary, Baumol (1990, p. 915) found that:

> Today, unproductive entrepreneurship takes many forms. Rent seeking, often via activities such as litigation and takeovers, and tax evasion and avoidance efforts seem now to constitute the prime threat to productive entrepreneurship... Corporate executives devote much of their time and energy to legal suit and countersuit, and litigation is used to blunt or prevent excessive vigor in competition by rivals. Huge awards by the courts, sometimes amounting to billions of dollars, can bring prosperity to the victor and threaten the loser with insolvency...It induces the entrepreneur to spend literally hundreds of millions of dollars for a single legal battle. It tempts the entrepreneur to be the first to sue others before those others can sue him.

The logic of competitive behavior necessarily reflects the assumed nature of competition. In perfect competition, the choreographed setting precludes antagonism among the participants, firms are not aware of each other's behavior, and equilibrium is the end-game. But in a competition-as-war setting, as Baumol's last two lines in his quotation suggest, it is rational to do unto others what others seek to do unto you, namely shrink your market share. In that setting, it is rational for potential victors to contemplate some losses even ahead of the fray. A costly technology capable of raising labor productivity beyond industry standards that allows the innovator to lower prices out of his rivals' reach is perfectly acceptable. Even if such a move lowers the innovator's profit rate, as long as rivals are worse off it makes sense: innovators gain since the threat of laggards falling behind is present at all times.

Celebrating the innovation machine

In his essay on the evolution of entrepreneurship, Baumol (1990) gathered historical evidence ranging widely from ancient Rome to Chinese society and modern-day capitalism in order to argue that changing social views of desirable paths to wealth accumulation governed the types of innovational activities undertaken. In a follow-up book years later seeking to demonstrate that "the growth miracle of capitalism" was due to the "free-market innovation machine," Baumol (2002) clinched his argument favoring entrepreneurship as the driving force behind the rise in living standards enjoyed by working people in capitalist society. While the general thrust of the analysis developed in Baumol's earlier essay, distinguishing "productive" entrepreneurship from other variants, could be found in his 2002 book, other themes went missing. Thus consideration of mounting evidence pointing to substantial diversion of entrepreneurial efforts into "unproductive" or, worse yet, "destructive" activities, duly emphasized in the 1990 essay, was largely absent in his later book. Baumol made a clean break away from Schumpeter's view of free-wheeling entrepreneurs, and instead linked the urge to innovate with the market threats unleashed by coercive forces of competitive wars for market supremacy.

With historical origins in the laboratories of nineteenth-century chemical firms in Germany, business funding for research facilities grew in proportion with corporate prominence. In a world where the preponderant industry structure allowed room for only a few giant corporations, innovational activities concentrated in R&D facilities ensuring steady outflows of new products and techniques. The routine character of such activities shifted focus from the psychological traits of industrial leadership to the efficient deployment of resources in corporate R&D departments aiming to spur technical change.

In Baumol's account, innovations are depicted as the most effective corporate weapons fending off rivals threatening market shares. For Baumol, despite his microeconomic background, the innovating urge springs from the turbulent nature of free competition, but the role played by unit costs and prices is not highlighted. In a recent book, Sheshinski *et al.* (2007) argue that technical change, promoted by oligopolistic firms subjected to relentless threats of losing market share, find investment on R&D a must to survive:

> This development is particularly evident in the rivalry among oligopolistic firms – those large firms in markets dominated by a small number of sellers. Particularly in the high-tech sectors of the economy, these enterprises increasingly rely upon *innovation* as their main battle weapon, with which they protect themselves from competitors and with which they seek to beat out those competitors. And much of this inventive activity is carried out within the firm.
>
> (Sheshinski *et al.*, 2007, p. 170)

Wishing to advance a "theory of the imperfect but, nevertheless, creditable efficiency of the capitalist growth process" (Baumol, 2002, p. 3) while crafting his paean for free competition, Baumol enlisted background support from two sources. First, Baumol found a kindred spirit in Joseph Schumpeter's *Capitalism, Socialism and Democracy*. Baumol (2002, p. 1) quotes Schumpeter extolling the virtues of free competition "which commands a decisive cost or quality advantage and which strikes not at the margins of the profits and the outputs of the existing firms but at their foundations and their very lives."

More daringly, perhaps, Baumol presses Marx and Engels into service with suitable quotes from their 1847 Manifesto, acknowledging that (1) "The bourgeoisie cannot exist without constantly revolutionizing the instruments of production"; (2) "Conservation of the old modes of production in unaltered form, was, on the contrary the first condition of existence for all earlier industrial classes"; (3) "The bourgeoisie, during its rule of scarce one hundred years, has created more massive and more colossal productive forces than have all preceding generations together." In the context of the book's main argument, these quotations provide Baumol with ecumenical support for his Schumpeterian views on the beneficent effects brought on by gales of "creative destruction." In this context, Marx and Engels' views are lined up purely in support of his Schumpeterian interpretation of historical progress. Baumol found it useful to recite selected snippets of Marx's historical observations taken out of context in order to dramatize the progressive nature of free-enterprise systems. By any criteria, extracting from Marx and Engels' early writings quotations suitable to prop up the Schumpeterian grand view of continuous economic and social progress requires innovational talent.

Baumol (2002) sought to rehabilitate an innovating theory of free competition that hitherto found support only in the writings of heterodox economists. But his textual sources seemed rather meager in this regard. While identifying the conceptual origins of his theory in Marx, Engels and Schumpeter, Baumol (2002, p. 4) regretted finding only "some four pages of Marx and Engels and ... six pages of Schumpeter's *Capitalism, Socialism and Democracy*" in support of his view linking innovational activity and free competition.

It must be said, however, that Baumol's research efforts were less than thorough, since he failed to acknowledge earlier contributions to the literature on the classical/Marxian theory of competition preceding his own writings. A. Shaikh challenged the relevance of perfect competition for the analysis of technical choices, laying out the conceptual structure of an alternative, Marx-based theory of competition in the late 1970s (Shaikh, 1978, 1980). After the appearance of Shaikh's theoretical reformulation of the classical/Marxian theory of competition, protracted exchanges in the *Cambridge Journal of Economics* found the leading heterodox economists struggling to break free from the shackles of neoclassical economics but still unable to shed the verities of perfect competition.

Baumol focused on the competitive pressures that "large, high-tech business firms" operating in "oligopolistic" sectors of the economy suffered, forcing them to innovate with new products or process innovations. Such innovations, labeled "primary weapons of competition" (2002, pp. 7, 30) or "the preferred competitive weapon" (p. 11) provided the arsenal to sustain an "arms race" (p. 26) among the oligopolists involved, but most tellingly did not trigger competitive wars. Indeed, Baumol refrained from converting his competitive strategy into an aggressive war for market shares. The notion of a competitive war, even the term itself, cannot be found in Baumol's writings on the competitive "arms race." The distinction would be crucial because in Baumol's "arms race" the motivation behind each firm's competitive behavior is defensive, that is, in response to the "threat of the firm's survival" (pp. 11, 41), not aggressive: each oligopolist just wished to avoid falling behind its rivals in innovating activity. Knowing that laggards in the competitive arms race lose market share if the quality of their products falls behind that of other rivals' or the price is higher for comparable quality, due to higher costs, they will innovate.

Hardly any signs of competitive-war strategies will be found in Baumol (2002) and Baumol *et al.* (2003). Despite its aggressive trappings, the outcome of Baumol's oligopolistic "arms race" could best be described as a cold war, an impasse among suspicious antagonists that will not likely escalate into a hot, competitive war. Firms are entirely safe pursuing research strategies allowing them to keep up with their rivals' programs of innovating R&D. Industry norms regarding spending on R&D emerge, ensuring attainment of "equilibrium" in the arms race, also described as a "truce" despite the persistence of "hostilities" among the contenders (pp. 45–46). A competitive firm will be satisfied to preserve its market share and therefore will do well complying with industry norms regarding R&D spending. Violating such norms will push it into perilous territory: falling behind its rivals in innovation spending leads to a shrinking market share and possibly to survival threats. Forging ahead and aggressively outspending them in R&D programs triggers retaliation in kind from threatened rivals. Once their own R&D program budgets are suitably enlarged, no advantage accrues to the aggressive "spoiler" firm. In that event, moreover, all firms in the industry would require higher R&D spending norms to maintain their relative market shares.

Baumol recognized that in the context of such arms race "firms will be tempted to exceed the equilibrium norm" in R&D spending. Aiming to forge ahead of rivals through innovating breakthroughs enabling them to lower prices or improve product quality, they would seek to circumvent the standing norms to reach a position of industry leadership. Labeling them "spoiler firms," Baumol argued that such strategies would only succeed if rivals failed to match the additional expenditures allocated to R&D program by the wayward oligopolist. But restraint on the part of firms threatened by such aggressive behavior could not be expected: once the norms regulating R&D investment for the entire industry were revised upward, the spoiler firm would not reach its intended goal.

Critically, the concept of industry equilibrium embedded in perfect competition reappeared in Baumol's theory of competition-driven innovations. Indeed despite his portrayal of oligopoly firms as "greedy producers" locked in "life-and-death" competition with a "multiplicity of rival and actively innovating firms," in the final analysis the industry's hierarchical structure remains frozen. While "each feels it necessary to be second to none in the weapons it has at its disposal" (p. 43), all fear the transformation of industrial rivalry into a competitive war, and general obeisance to the established norms regulating R&D spending leads to "equilibrium in the arms race" (pp. 45–46).

Profitability in Baumol's "arms race"

With regard to the profitability of innovational activity, Baumol's views differed markedly from Schumpeter's. Once such activities developed along the lines of routine operations carried out by firms locked in mutual rivalry, their actual payoff would fail to reach the high levels expected by Schumpeter's individual entrepreneur. Because the innovational output of corporate R&D departments was predictable, and all rival firms planned accordingly, its impact on industry profitability should be minimal. To illustrate the negligible profitability enhancement of routine innovations, Baumol cited "new automobile models" and "new spring clothing fashions" as "the most extreme cases." But examples like these would surely fall out of Schumpeter's grand vision of genuine product innovations. Raising such cosmetic modifications as these products habitually display to the rank of innovations effectively shattered Schumpeter's view of market breakthroughs.

Because many of the innovational practices of large corporations were routinely carried out with predictable results, as for example the new automobile models brought out every year, or the new clothing fashions announced every spring, Baumol questioned the extent to which many such activities classified as innovations raised industry's profitability at all. While firms achieving breakthroughs will attempt to retain full legal rights to their technology through secrecy patents, enforceable by litigation if necessary, Baumol thinks such privileges do not suffice to ensure them above average profitability.

In contrast with Schumpeter's view that innovators enjoy temporary monopoly profits, and that pursuit of extraordinary profits was their motivating drive, Baumol's firms could not expect such gains. Once firms accepted the necessity of innovating activities as a routine essential for their growth and survival, they had to forgo the lucrative spoils received in the past. This is because currently all competitive firms, seeking to avoid falling behind their rivals, push their innovating investment to the profit-maximizing limit. But since all rival oligopolists follow the same rules, the expected profitability of innovations will not normally exceed that of any other investment type, including humdrum expansion of plant and equipment. Unless firms owned unique talent, or secure access to cheaper or better-quality inputs than their those of their rivals, they had no grounds to expect above average returns from innovational investment. In fact Baumol (2002, p. 40) concluded that "routinized innovation" practices carried out by large oligopolists fostered "some tendency...for economic profits to be driven toward zero."

The enduring legacy of perfect competition

Baumol's extraordinary claims, side by side with his "equilibrium in the arms race" proposition, make it impossible to overlook the shared space between his concept of arms-race competition and the neoclassical theory of perfect competition. To see the connection, we need to closely follow the quaint choreography of perfectly competitive industries, and how, adjusting their output to maximize profits, they manage to wind up with no profits in the long run. Then it is appropriate to set aside the turbulent context in which Baumol's version of competition takes place: the arms race fought by corporations using innovations as weapons of choice. Finally, a portrait reminiscent of neoclassical tranquility emerges: as in perfect completion, an oligopolistic balance of market shares yields no long-run profits to the "warring" firms.

Other scenarios were possible but not likely to occur. Given the possibility that large "sunk costs" are essential to launch viable innovations, Baumol conceded that extraordinary profits occasionally would not be competed away: rival firms would lack sufficient funds to emulate the leading firm's research efforts. Once again, Baumol's arms race did not rise to the level of competitive warfare. This is so because, once protected from hostile entry by high "sunk costs," Baumol doubted the innovating firm would be inclined to lower prices aggressively. Given the cost advantages attained, it would keep prices high enough to enjoy a "substantial surplus" without preventing "at least the closest of the runners-up to operate profitably, though their profits will normally be more modest" (Baumol, 2002, p. 41).

These observations led Baumol to suggest that the dynamics of industrial competition were best modeled after Ricardo's analysis of differential rents, driven by the diminishing marginal fertility of land. In this light, the various degrees of innovational advances were analogous to the different qualities of cultivated lands. The most advanced innovation yielded the most profit, followed by others in a descending order of profitability according to their innovational success (Baumol, 2002, pp. 41–42).

Baumol's transfer of the Ricardian model of differential rents onto the field of industrial competition involves the question of price determination. In Ricardo's model, the expansion of land cultivation into progressively less fertile lands gives rise to diminishing yields, hence rising unit costs. Those farms located in best areas feel no competitive pressures to lower their unit costs relative to others operating in less fertile soil. The cost of production at the margin sets the price for the whole sector and the intra-marginal farms yield higher profits due to their lower costs. In Ricardo's model, the qualities inherent in fertile land are not reproducible, largely seen as gifts of nature.

Baumol's leading innovating oligopolists, on the other hand, are satisfied to preserve their leadership position without seeking to encroach any further upon their weaker competitors' market share. While enjoying the fruits of innovations yields them higher profit rates, they also shun strategies to gain a larger market share if they involve preemptive strikes against the remaining firms. Instead, Baumol sees leading innovator firms, even those temporarily enjoying a monopoly position, likely inclined to "renting" their superior technology to other firms, rather than using it to drive them off the industry. For Baumol, innovating technology, like anything else, will be available for renting at the right price, and if the price is high enough, this option he believes would be the most profitable.

The unintended outcome of such "live and let live" concept of competitive behavior overall would be wholly beneficent to society, Baumol believes, since an invisible hand ensures that this arms race will unleash "greed harnessed to work as efficiently and effectively as it can to serve the public interest in prosperity and growth" (2002, p. 15). The innovating arms race led to high rates of labor productivity growth and rising standards of living in such magnitude as to eclipse any possibly negative side effects. Echoing Schumpeter's dialectics contained in his notion of "creative destruction," Baumol acknowledged that indeed innovational activity could vanquish older products or productive methods whose worth or utility had not be impaired. At any rate, using GDP per capita as a gauge of progress, Baumol noted that "in the leading capitalist economies [it] is growing at a rate that apparently permits something like an eightfold multiplication in a century," thus confirming Keynes' own forecast on this issue made in 1932 (p. 20). The competitive arms race drove corporate firms to innovate, stimulated growth in the capitalist economy and raised the living standards of the population at large. From the perspective of society as a whole, "Each successful innovation contributes to the growth of the nation's GDP" (p. 289).

Technical progress and oligopolistic competition

The striking disjunction between innovative and price strategies introduced in Baumol's analysis of oligopolistic strategies to cope with the competitive arms race allowed him to use the concept of competitive weapons while excluding the notion of price wars. Even though the specter of aggressive competitive behavior was not conjured away since "a successful process innovation can be expected to expand output, reduce product price," the result is an impasse among rivals, not a war for market shares (Baumol, 2002, p. 154).

Baumol's views regarding the nature of "Oligopolistic competition among large, high-tech business firms" seeks to establish that Adam Smith's invisible hand, active as ever, leads to unintended consequences wholly beneficial to society. While powerful oligopolists are admittedly motivated by greed and bent on turning the innovation "arms race" into a profitable enterprise, Baumol concluded that "it is greed harnessed to work as efficiently and effectively as it can to serve the public interest in prosperity and growth." Winning market share, or simply avoiding losses, forces oligopolists to produce higher-quality products at "low prices," attracting consumers on "better terms than their rivals" (p. 15).

Baumol's development of this theme, however, led to one-sided emphases on the innovative or quality aspect central to the strategy of "large, high-tech firms," effectively downplaying their use of pricing strategy as a competitive weapon. In oligopolistic markets, the competitive arms race forced the contenders to adopt strategies in which "innovation has replaced price" (p. 4). Despite barriers to entry and exit erected by high levels of sunk costs underpinning their innovative efforts, Baumol stressed that innovative oligopolists typically ended up failing to secure "extraordinary" profits. Sharing authorship with two other writers, we find Baumol reporting that a typical individual entrepreneur in the United States "earns less monetary compensation than her employee counterpart" (Baumol *et al.*, 2007, p. 87).

Despite the long history of contributions made by classical economics from Smith to Marx, unraveling the linkage between capital accumulation, competition and technical change, Baumol *et al.* (2007) reached for antecedents of the connections no further than the work of Paul Romer in the 1980s. They noted that Romer "believed that the ideas that underpin technological advance are the unintended by-products of investment in new equipment" (Baumol *et al.*, 2007, p. 50). But this was the central point developed in Kaldor's 1957 "new model of economic growth" and a fundamental tenet of nineteenth-century growth theory.

Anchored in the traditions of neoclassical economics, and allowing for the fact that the notion of perfect competition sets conditions inimical to the realities of profit-seeking firms vying with each other for a commanding position in the global market, Baumol *et al.* found it necessary to invoke the structural characteristics of imperfect competition, requiring "extraordinary" profits to provide the necessary incentive to commit funds for risky innovative activities. Not unexpectedly, in Baumol's version of the neoclassical story the anticipated rewards would also be eroded in the long run as technical change proceeds unabated. A similar frustration plagued the fortunes of individual entrepreneurs. Baumol *et al.* (2007) argue vigorously that only capitalist economies motivate innovating entrepreneurs, people willing to sacrifice time and money to bring their dreams to fruition, doing so because they expect to be "handsomely rewarded and the rewards safely kept." Unfortunately, we need to conclude that typical entrepreneurs chased a will-o'-the wisp, because Baumol *et al.* tell us that entrepreneurial rewards normally sink below employees' salaries. Thus Baumol *et al.* end up sharing Schumpeter's romantic view of entrepreneurial personalities, those rugged individualists willing to risk it all, seeking "psychic rewards" beyond mere lucre for the sake of "being one's own boss, pride in self-accomplishment and so forth" (Baumol *et al.*, 2007, pp. 87–88).

In most industrial activities, rising innovational investments produce powerful technologies, raising the quality of products while lowering costs. These are the weapons of choice to win the competitive arms race. Having considered the motivation behind Schumpeter's entrepreneurs, or the goals pursued by R&D facilities engaged in designing blueprints for new products and process innovations, the link between quality improvements and cost reductions requires comment. Following Eltis, we assume that for a given production cost, the achieved quality improvement due to superior product design is equivalent to a commensurate reduction of cost. From this standpoint, innovational breakthroughs in new and better products are analogous to cost reductions of existing products, absent quality changes: both categories are examples of technical progress (Eltis, 1971, p. 505).

The firm using the most advanced technology and therefore operating at least cost lowers the competitive price for the industry as a whole while expanding its market share. Why would a competitive arms race devolve into a competitive war? As the tempo of innovating activity grows in scope and depth widely across industrial lines, competitive threats confronting firms escalate, reaching levels that justified the alarm expressed by Freeman, Metcalfe and Baumol concerning the survival of unresponsive firms. Confronted with such prospects, innovation or extinction, competitive strategies were bound to change. With mounting threats spreading globally, innovators will adopt strategies designed for a world where business survival and growth hinge on development of aggressive strategies. Fear of retaliation by rivals cannot deter the implementation of such plans. In the context of competition-as-war, preemptive strikes against rivals need to accept the inevitability of attendant costs for the victor. Innovations cannot be understood simply as methods shifting some abstract "production function" outward or disrupting a stationary economic structure as Schumpeter proposed. Technical progress and the growing mechanization of production produced an ever more powerful arsenal of weapons to fight in competitive wars. The acceleration of the mechanization drive, with larger masses of fixed capital replacing labor, strengthened the power of innovations to lower costs as effective weapons in competitive wars. The development of capitalism did not change the motivation behind innovating activity, achieving market leadership with its profitability advantage, but it shaped the technology appropriate for large corporations to win competitive wars.

4 Mechanization and price/quality competition

Two kinds of competition?

Having explored in Chapter 3 the Schumpeter–Baumol concept of innovations as competitive weapons, deployed to raise labor productivity and lower unit costs (Baumol, 2002; Baumol *et al.*, 2007), we now seek to connect their origin with the mechanization of production activities as first considered in Adam Smith and later on in management science. Once we complete the outline of the sequential stages comprising the mechanization drive and its significance for competitive strategies, we will consider as illustration the stagnation of the British economy in the post-war years, allegedly due to insufficient innovating progress. As a byproduct of this inquiry, we examine critically the suggestions made by neo-Schumpeterian theorists to replace models of price competition with models of quality competitiveness. We believe advocates of quality competeveness simply overlook the fact that price competitiveness refers only to goods of comparable or superior quality and therefore both kinds of competitive strategies cannot be separated.

Adam Smith on mechanization

In Adam Smith's theory of economic growth the growing division of labor, the extent of the market and the attendant improvement of industrial skills spurred mechanization. Before the Industrial Revolution skilled labor provided the bulk of manufactured products. One craftsman completed all the operations necessary to finish the product. His tools included hammers, forges, files, saws, etc. Handling of each required the acquisition of specialized skills, but their application sequence was never replicated in the assembly line. Not only did machinery speed up production beyond the limits of craft labor, but the acquisition of skills necessary to tend it significantly spurred the process of technological progress itself.

The momentous growth in labor productivity achieved by the division of labor in Adam Smith's celebrated analysis of the pin factory (Smith, 1965, Book 1, Chapter 1) could not have occurred in the absence of tools and machinery designed to perform specialized tasks with speed and dexterity previously unknown. In the second half of the eighteenth century, the output of pins per worker in a contemporary pin factory was 200 times larger than it would have been without the complex division of labor achieved (Meeks and Meeks, 2005, p. 512).

Examining the linkage between economies of scale and mechanization, Clifford Pratten (1980) tracked the development of labor productivity in United Kingdom pin-manufacturing and found in the early eighteenth century over 100 factories in the UK devoted to that task. By 1939 the number of manufacturing plants producing pins in the UK fell to about 12, and in the 1970s the total was reduced to 2. A rapid sequence of mergers, acquisitions and bankrupt firms exiting the industry pushed the concentration of pin production to very high levels indeed. Entry was significantly restricted by the high cost of new machinery, the cost of cutting-edge German equipment being the highest, due to its superior quality.

Economies of scale ranked high in the balance between benefits and costs involved in the purchase of materials and marketing. In two hundred years, labor productivity rose by a factor of 167 in one of the two firms operating in the 1970s, at the rate of 2.6 percent annually, rising from an estimated "four thousand eight hundred pins in a day," as reported by Adam Smith, to 800,000 per day in the late 1970s (Pratten, 1980). One of the two pin factories studied by Pratten in the 1970s showed the substitution of machines for hand labor enabled each worker tend a total of 24 machines. Due to mechanization, the speed of pin-making machines rose from 45 pins per minute in 1830 to 180 in 1900 and 500 in the late 1970s.

In the earlier handicraft phase of the labor process, skilled operatives employed their own tools and applied their skills to the task of transforming materials and bringing out the final product. The growing division of labor following the craft phase, however, spurred the growth of factories assembling large numbers of workers organized to perform discrete tasks with single-purpose tools. Once the Industrial Revolution of the eighteenth century swept away the bulk of craft labor, however, the stage was set for the replacement of skilled artisans by less skilled machine operators.

Mechanization changed the labor process through the progressive transfer of skills from workers to special-purpose equipment. Once the division of labor revealed the progressive power of specialization to achieve higher labor productivity, machinery capable of performing actions previously carried out by craft workers raised labor productivity to levels unattainable at earlier stages of development. As anticipated by Adam Smith, the high rate of labor productivity obtained issued from the specialization of tasks achieved through the division of labor and technical progress: "the invention of all those machines by which labour is so much facilitated and abridged seems to have been originally owing to the division of labour" (Smith, 1965, p. 9).

A characteristic example may illustrate the path leading from the division of labor to the advance of technical change. It involves an experiment starting out with technique A. One skilled worker performs three operations on three machines, each routine being restricted to one machine at a time. The individual machine displays two lights, one green and one red. When the green light turns on, the worker pulls a green lever letting one object enter the machine. Once the operation is finished, a red light comes on prompting the worker to pull a red lever that sends the object into the hopper of the next machine. Changing from technique A to technique B, three workers perform the tasks previously carried out by one, but this time each worker cares for just one machine.

Applying techniques A and B, each individual machine carries out one single operation. Now consider option C, a technique in which the three separate machines are merged into one, tended by one single operative. This worker now only needs pay attention to one set of green and red lights and is required to pull just one set of green and red levers, not three. Using techniques A and B involved each machine performing one task, and B and C required each worker carrying out one single routine operation. When using technique A, one worker alone was responsible for responding to separate prompts by three machines, but operating technique C, each machine completes three specific tasks all by itself. This example highlights the trend in technical change leading to adopting techniques of type C, that is, machines with a higher degree of performance capabilities, each able to complete three different tasks by itself.

Principles of scientific management

Between 1875 and 1925, Frederick Taylor and the scientific management movement sought to extend the productivity gains inherent in the division of labor promoted by Adam Smith in the eighteenth century. This project led the way for the spread of industrial automation and the overhaul of the structural design in American industry. Conceptually, the strategy pursued consisted first in breaking down production systems into four distinctive facets and then perfecting their connectivity. The initial step focused on the power source, that is, the energy source that powered the productive apparatus; then followed the processing technique, the machinery used to transform materials into finished products; next, the selection of techniques for moving materials from one stage of transformation to the next level; finally, attention centered on the control systems supervising the quantity and quality of the finished product.

Historically the first steps towards the mechanization of energy sources occurred in the eighteenth century with the use of water power, followed a century later by steam power and then in the twentieth century by electricity and the internal-combustion engine (Kaplinsky, 1985). Advances in processing materials occurred in tandem, including the development of high-speed steel production followed by the revamping of processing technology. As the nineteenth century ended, the progress achieved in speeding up the operation of transforming separate inputs into processed parts would have reached an impasse without the mechanization of transfer technology. The addition of conveyor belts, however, not only shortened the production time for finished products but also prompted the reorganization of the entire production system.

The transformation of the labor process occurred in two stages: first, mechanical devices replaced direct labor; and then improvements in the efficiency of the employed machinery followed. Most importantly, technical advances in any one of the separate phases of the mechanized system depended on complementary advances made in the others. Thus in order to raise the speed of special-purpose processing machinery, the power sources would need upgrading. This advance in turn could only yield benefits after the mechanization of materials transferring systems ranging from the processing stage to the next operation was completed, an issue solved by the development of conveyor belts matching the speed reached by the processing equipment. After achieving a higher speed of processing machinery and securing the steady flow of finished product, mechanical devices to monitor production volume and quality controls replaced labor previously engaged in such tasks (Faunce, 1965).

More recently, the development of flexible systems of transfer control received unprecedented support from advances in electronics, primarily by breakthroughs in microelectronic circuitry. Firms in such industries as automobiles and foods set up specialized departments linking knowledge-based product design, spelling out in detail the makeup of the product, with the actual processing units. Engineers, scientists, and technicians as well as their backup staffs provided the highly skilled labor involved in the performance of these tasks. Then attention focused on the problems posed by the actual transformation of materials and intermediate inputs into the designed final product. Finally, to achieve a successful operation management personnel stepped in to coordinate design and product-processing stages. By the end of the nineteenth century the production complex of leading firms in Europe and the US had reached a high level of technical sophistication. Scientific methods informed designing practices; the installation of automatic machinery accelerated the division and specialization of tasks; growing tiers of managers achieved high precision in coordinating all production phases; product supply chains expanded from local to national boundaries and then extended globally.

The advance of automation

The advance of mechanization, with the increasing substitution of machinery for labor, brought with it a radical change in the character of the labor process. Workers' jobs changed from tending a single machine to performing a single task. At the same time, the variety of tasks carried out by each machine increased. Technical progress promoted the diversification of mechanical functions in the assembly line, while their level of specialization diminished. On the other hand, workers tending sophisticated machinery increasingly performed single chores involving fewer skill-specific requirements. As Edward Ames and Nathan Rosenberg observed, designing superior technology embodying greater "skills" did not require replication of the labor tasks previously performed by less mechanized methods. The newly designed machinery gave rise to new production networks that did not necessarily conform to the patterns of the assembly line, hence: "an increase in the 'education' of machines increases their powers of discriminating, resulting in lower cost, for a given set of workers" (Ames and Rosenberg, 1965, p. 370).

Starting from machinery designed to handle a given activity within a given stage of production, automation extended to the intra-sphere networks linking various activities of the same production phase, and then to the inter-sphere of the production process integrating different such phases. As in the Ford assembly plant of the 1920s, intra-sphere automation required transfer mechanisms between different types of processing operations using lathes, drilling and boring equipment. In its more developed form, the so-called flexible manufacturing version, intra-sphere automation added close supervision of the transfer flow in each operation, including central controls able to readjust the flow of individual activities in order to enhance overall performance. More recently, inter-sphere automation introduced coordination controls linking the various phases of the labor process, from product design to automatic programming of machine parameters, allowing for changes in design parameters to be immediately implemented through programmed machine instructions (Kaplinsky, 1985).

The development of microelectronics made possible the establishment of control mechanisms integrating the separate spheres of specialized activities including design, processing, and management. From batch-oriented mainframe computers to interactive computer-aided design and drafting systems, the automation of design proceeded apace. Using electronic control systems, progress in automation systems sought to centralize the control of information flow linking the major spheres of production activity. Such control systems track the production process, measuring all its relevant characteristics involving timing, spacing, heating, and sounds. They even monitor the smooth functioning of the machinery involved, signaling the need to replace outworn parts while choosing alternative solutions. For students of automation like Kaplinsky, the irreversible trend emerging from the increasing mechanization of production activities unambiguously revealed the diminishing role of labor in modern industry: "best-practice production techniques are increasingly systemic in nature...there can be little doubt that the new technology is labor displacing" (Kaplinsky, 1985, pp. 436–437).

Process innovations and unit labor costs

With the quantity of direct labor necessary to operate automated plants sharply reduced, wage levels ceased to determine the location of industrial plants. Despite the high cost of automated equipment, manufacturing plants using it achieve such competitive advantages in the category of lower variable costs as to make its deployment necessary for commercial success. The quality controls imposed enabled manufacturing systems to reduce waste, increase processing speed and avoid unnecessary bottlenecks. At the same time automation technology made possible large reductions in inventories, production and office space, lighting and heating, per unit output. Automated equipment systems allowed firms to engage competitors not only in battles fought with lower costs and prices, but also higher product quality, thus extending the arsenal deployed in competitive battles (Moos, 1957).

A wide survey of "strategic and operational aspects of technological change" (Schoenberger, 1989) revealed the widest use of "computer-controlled machine-tools" in the largest US-based firm subsidiaries located in high-wage regions of Western Europe, those employing more than 500 people with an average yearly output exceeding 20,000 units, producing inputs for use in a diversified broad selection of industrial firms. The selected products included high-tech "computers, machine tools, semiconductors, electronic testing equipment, telecommunications equipment, scientific and medical instruments, office machinery, specialty chemicals, industrial and process controls, aviation and defense electronics." By contrast, smaller firms with an average yearly output of 200 units were the least automated, meeting their production needs with the use of "general-purpose" machinery.

Confirming Kaplinsky's finding, Schoenberger's field research revealed that one of the "fundamental" goals of managerial strategies regarding the use of all forms of automation, whether programmable or not, was the drastic reduction in the use of direct labor, and therefore a substantial decrease in labor costs relative to the total costs of production (Schoenberger, 1989). Managers testified that in many cases automated techniques achieved up to 80 percent saving of direct labor requirements. This significant reduction in labor costs virtually eliminated the obstacles to locate high-tech plants in high-wage regions of the US or Western Europe.

Moreover, Schoenberger's findings showed that the existence of low wages in a certain location did not necessarily stave off the deployment of highly capital-intensive automated plants, the implication being that rising wages was not the main force behind the spread of automation. Instead, managers insisted that automation systems were necessary to enhance product quality, due to the fact that only automated equipment could achieve the levels of precision and performance reliability required by their industrial customers (Schoenberger, 1989, p. 237). For high-tech firms selling machine-tools and other inputs to other industrial firms, whose own quality production depends on the excellence and reliability of their equipment, a competitive strategy simply based on selling low-price products led to failure. Success required steadily raising the quality of their product, as high-quality inputs allowed the purchasing firms to supply their own high-quality products at competitive prices. The buyers were willing to pay a higher price for superior-quality equipment as long as it enabled them to reduce their own operating costs and simultaneously improve their output quality.

Cost reductions through higher labor productivity and lower waste were major benefits associated with purchases of superior quality equipment. Finally, since cutting-edge technology is capital-intensive, capital outlays required to install a fully automated plant were high and profitability in the most technically advanced firms was extraordinarily sensitive to the phase changes of demand cycles. In this connection, the projected benefits in terms of falling unit costs very much depended on the economies of scale achieved and the degree of capacity utilization attained.

Because fixed costs are generally so high in industries ranging from petroleum refining to primary metals and electric power, scale economies were essential to lower total operating costs. Significant declines in construction costs per unit of output were found in oil refineries, steel and cement plants. In the computer chip industry also, unit costs of production are highly sensitive to economies of scale. In this industry as proficiency in management of large-scale integrated circuits improved and larger production runs established, unit costs of computer chips declined substantially. Meeks and Meeks (2005, p. 512) found that in plants capable of doubling the scale of output, unit production costs fell by 25–30 percent.

Earlier research by Haldi and Whitcomb (1967) found significant economies of scale in the engineering capacity of processing-type plants. Such studies typically assessed the effect of capacity expansion on costs, assuming constant factor prices, supply characteristics, product quality, and plant location. Substantial increases in plant capacity involved small expansion in the number of plant workers as well as a less than proportionate growth in managerial and supervisory staff. Despite the fact that engineering studies reported no substantial advantages due to economies of scale in the use of raw materials, the general view was that the expansion of plant capacity led to substantial reductions in overall processing and manufacturing unit costs.

Economies of scale

In many industries the initial fixed costs needed to set up the extensive R&D facilities necessary to generate new products are so high that only the largest firms possess the financial wherewithal to undertake these projects. Meeks and Meeks (2005) reported that in the pharmaceutical industry, on average, the cost of developing breakthrough drugs involving new technology rose to $250–350 million. In order to recover these costs, production runs in pharmaceuticals need to expand substantially. Moreover, significant economies of scale apply in the marketing of drugs: advertising requiring a very large threshold to achieve brand recognition. While larger firms did not necessarily achieve higher profitability, they unquestionably exhibited lower volatility in output, and higher survival rates than their smaller business rivals.

On the other hand, business longevity depends on the characteristics of the industry in which firms operate. The ability of large firms to survive in turbulent markets was found "exclusively" in industries requiring major innovational advances unavailable to smaller rivals, such as petroleum refineries and producers of electrical and chemical outputs. The cost advantages of running large production systems, however, soon brought on the need to upgrade management structures. The traditional system of hierarchical commands sending directives from control centers to the firms' operating units reduced transaction costs but failed to meet the challenges of scale economies. Increasingly, larger firms coped with the complexities of size regarding the allocation of funds only after establishing relations among their various units that replicated market principles. Each unit or department would compete for the funds available in the central office on the basis of its performance and its need for expansion. In this regard, trade among the firm's units would resemble transactions among autonomous entities (Meeks and Meeks, 2005, pp. 514–519).

From a neoclassical perspective, Brozen (1957) argued that the expansion of automated systems in manufacturing and process-type industries was directly linked to their growing capital stock. The growth of the capital stock led to growing wages, as the marginal product of labor rose. Automation simply carried mechanization to a higher level, interlinking the various machine-tools into a centrally controlled system enabling firms to reduce downtime and increase capacity utilization. Referring to the Ford Motor Company as one pioneer in automation systems, Brozen pointed out that initially the breakthrough consisted in providing a substantially larger stock of capital in conjunction with an unchanged labor force. Capacity utilization rose from 65 to 80 percent; capital outlays increased 25 percent in the Cleveland engine plant where the technology was first applied; and direct labor was reduced by 22 percent, while maintenance workers increased by 50 percent. In the end, employment as a whole expanded when output grew, not least because the new automated technology allowed for the production of a more sophisticated automobile requiring higher labor content (Brozen, 1957, p. 341).

Brozen argued that the experience of the Fairless Steel Works in this regard was typical. In this plant, the traditional technology called for capital outlays between $40,000 and $50,000 per worker producing on average of 160 tons of steel per worker per year. The automation system initially installed raised the capital outlays per worker to over $100,000 but allowed yearly output per worker to reach 300 tons of steel. Brozen stressed that in this case the increase in capital per worker was not motivated by the actual rise in wage rates but rather by the expectation that ten years after the new plant was installed wage rates would rise by 30 percent (Brozen, 1957, p. 343).

The literature on automation and market strategy presents industry leaders facing competitive pressures typically responding to the challenge through expansion. Achieving economies of scale allows them to lower production unit costs and reduce market prices below those of their rivals. In this choice, higher fixed capital costs are acceptable, seeking to reduce variable costs enough to achieve a lower total unit cost of production. Innovating strategies require business investment in R&D activities that, while raising fixed costs, improve product quality and lead to higher market shares. Such investments in quality improvements normally expand or enhance the set of attributes or services inherent in the product, and therefore, even if sold at the same price, gain a competitive edge.

Kaldor's "paradox" and quality competition

Fearing that the postwar boom experienced by advanced capitalist countries was losing momentum, Kaldor saw the slow growth of the British economy in the mid-1960s as an early sign of "economic maturity." He defined that condition as "a state of affairs where real income per head had reached broadly the same level in the different sectors of the economy" (Kaldor, 1968, p. 385). Such accomplishment meant the disappearance of the "dual economy" involving two sectors, one containing industrial activities and the other subsistence agriculture. In dual economies, industry and agriculture enormous differences in labor productivity levels and per capita incomes coexisted side by side.

As economic development proceeded and the scale of the industrial sector expanded, the abundant labor supply crowding agriculture, much of it trapped in "disguised unemployment," readily met the employment demands of industry at a constant wage. Labor productivity growth in industry rose with expansion due to the significant scale economies available. System-wide labor productivity growth also benefited from declining employment in low-productivity sectors. Depletion of the "surplus labor" previously confined to low-productivity agriculture led to "economic maturity" and then the growth potential for high-productivity industries depended on locating new sources of cheap labor willing to transfer there. In the late 1960s Kaldor suggested that the large mass of workers employed in Britain's "services" provided the alternative source necessary to avoid labor bottlenecks cramping the growth of British industry.

Contemporary critics of Kaldor's analysis voiced skepticism regarding evidence of scale economies available in manufacturing industries. Wolfe (1968) argued that even if productivity growth in manufacturing raised the productivity growth experienced by the economy as a whole, the extent of this improvement depended on the size of manufacturing relative to other sectors. The gain would be greatest in countries where manufacturing grew most rapidly and the share of manufacturing output and employment in the total economy was largest. Rowthorn (1975) disputed Kaldor's econometric procedures and the significance of his findings. He questioned the empirical evidence purporting to support Kaldor's claim that labor productivity growth increased as employment in manufacturing expanded. Rowthorn cited research conducted by Gomulka in 1971 surveying 39 countries and covering a decade, 1958–1968, showing that productivity growth in manufacturing bore no relation whatsoever with employment growth in that sector. In Rowthorn's account, only Japan's experience confirmed Kaldor's hypothesis.

Replying to his critics, Kaldor (1975) conceded he had abandoned his previous views regarding the slow growth of the British economy. His new thinking regarding causation of the slow growth of the British economy focused on its "poor market performance due to lack of international competitiveness" and as an effective remedy suggested devaluation. Three years later Kaldor changed again both his diagnosis of the ills and the means to palliate them. In his new interpretation, Kaldor (1978b) noted then that since the mid-1950s a group of countries, including Germany, Japan, and Italy, successfully raised their market share of world trade in manufacturing from 26 percent to 42 percent. In fact, he noted, the growth rate in their world market shares exceeded their manufacturing production growth rate. The expanding market share of world trade produced a surplus trade balance in Germany that persisted throughout the 1970s, leading to the accumulation of large dollar reserves rather than foreign investment.

On the other hand, the UK and the US suffered a loss in market shares of world trade from 44 to 26 percent. Kaldor attributed these trends in world trade market shares to bifurcating tendencies in competitiveness, with the UK and the US manufacturing sectors representing the losing side. Interpreting these gains and losses as deriving from changing degrees of competitiveness in the countries concerned, Kaldor first considered the behavior of unit labor costs or "efficiency wages" as the determining factor. In this connection, Kaldor pointed out that the growth of money wage rates in the UK and the US was in fact lower than in those economies gaining competitiveness. Moreover, Kaldor noted, in the post-Korean war period consumer prices rose also more slowly in the US than they did elsewhere. Therefore, RULC increases did not undermine the US international competitive position.

The degree of industrial competitiveness depends on the level and movement of real wage rates relative to labor productivity growth through time. Kaldor's empirical estimates did not explain why competiveness fell in the US, because while lower inflation rates compensated for lower money wages growth relative to other countries, he failed to take into account the decline in labor productivity growth in the US compared to other countries. In other words, RULC may deteriorate due to not only excessive increases in real wage rates but also lower growth of labor productivity.

At any rate, after examining the trade and "efficiency wages" data from the mid-1950s through the mid-1970s, Kaldor (1978b, p. 102) claimed to have made a paradoxical finding, "a 'perverse' relationship between changes in 'competitiveness' as measured by the relative change in labour costs per unit of output and changes in export performance." This discovery prompted Kaldor to question the notion that falling unit labor costs leading to falling prices would translate into a stronger competitive stance. He now argued that such belief had no empirical support, in fact the opposite was true and it should be abandoned. Instead Kaldor (1978b, p. 100) favored assessing the competitive strength of a country's exports on the basis of "unit labor costs in terms of dollars, as well as by the relative movement of export prices (or rather export unit values)." It is essential to note that Kaldor's "export unit values" refers to the amount of export dollars divided by the exports weight: dollars per kilo. Export prices, on the other hand, are indexes tied to cost indexes and not to product weights.

In Kaldor's estimates, measures indicating a steadily rising degree of competitiveness in the US, such as falling "unit labor costs," were strongly correlated with an equally sustained loss of manufacturing's market share in world trade. Kaldor's trade "paradox" vies with his "stylized facts" for uncontested acceptance among critics of neoclassical economics. It is celebrated as a momentous break with entrenched orthodoxy, despite Kaldor himself providing the key to its limited significance. Indeed, Kaldor (1978b, p. 106) insisted that examination of the relevant data made it absolutely clear that

> the customary statistical measures of "competitiveness" whether they be unit labor costs or export prices, are arbitrary and not an adequate indicator of a country's true competitive position. For "export prices" are no more than "export unit values" obtained by dividing the value of exports with the weight of commodities exported in particular categories; a rise in export unit values may therefore signify no more than that a country is trading "up-market",

i.e. selling machinery of higher quality, while the countries with falling export unit values are trading "down-market", selling machinery of the more primitive kind.

For Kaldor the trading successes of countries like Japan, Sweden, Switzerland, West Germany and so on is due to the fact that the quality of their manufacturing exports improved substantially, not that their export prices displayed a falling trend. On the other hand, UK exports appeared to contain increasing quantities of unsophisticated machines and equipment, thus accounting for their declining competitive position.

Clearly, Kaldor replaced quality competition for price competition without noting that price competition only applies to products of comparable quality. After relying on his aggregate trade data to point out that falling unit labor costs and lower export prices did not lead to higher market shares, Kaldor observed that official data on labor productivity available for the manufacturing sector as a whole, being an average, failed to distinguish between leading and lagging industries. Of course, growing market shares were likely to occur in markets where the growth in labor productivity was highest.

Kaldor's claims on finding contradictory evidence between alleged competitive gains in falling UK unit labor costs in manufacturing and declining market shares in UK foreign trade from 1960 through the mid-1970s did not pan out. Kaldor in fact did not reach his own conclusions comparing the evolution of the UK real unit labor costs (RULC) with those of Germany and Japan: he failed to deflate nominal wages in all these countries. We did so to obtain real product wages, and we found that indeed relative real unit costs between the UK, Germany and Japan declined through the 1960s, but rose in the 1970s, both in the UK/Germany and UK/Japan cases. In the decade of the 1970s the UK RULC relative to those two countries rose sharply, undermining the competitive position of UK manufacturing products in world trade. The big decline occurred from the early 1980s and through the mid-1990s. But an equally sharp reversal in the case of the UK/Japan competitive position and a milder one with respect to Germany wiped out the UK's competitive gains previously achieved.

Since manufacturing products predominate in international trade flows, we used US Bureau of Labor Statistics annual indexes for unit labor costs in manufacturing, estimated on a national currency basis, and producer price indexes from the IMF International Financial Statistics, to derive UK RULC relative to those in Germany and Japan from 1960 through 2009 (Figure 4.1). In any event, relative RULC indexes do not provide conclusive information about the absolute money unit costs of two countries, but only about the evolution from some base level. The UK initial money level might have been higher than it was in Germany and Japan in the early 1960s. So despite Kaldor's claim of its alleged decline through the mid-1970s, the UK's unit labor costs might not have reached a sufficient competitive level, one low enough to encroach on German and Japanese market shares.

That product quality improvements for a given price will enhance a product's market demand is not in doubt, it is the equivalent of a price decline for

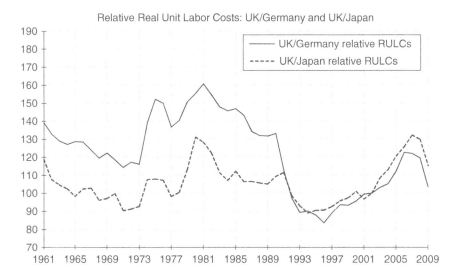

Figure 4.1 Measures of relative UK competitiveness.

comparable quality. As Metcalfe (1999, 2004) has argued, offering higher product quality in trade will not gainsay the competitive advantage derived from lower-cost production and cheaper prices. In competitive wars with industry rivals both things achieve similar results. Quality competition is one aspect of the real competitive wars fought by industry producers for larger market shares.

The decline in British industrial competitiveness

Explaining the relative decline in labor productivity growth of British industry motivated Pratten's (1972) study of postwar economic recovery, anticipating by six years Kaldor's observation regarding the loss of competitiveness registered by its exports. Indeed, Pratten set out to uncover the root "causes of the slow growth of labor productivity," and what he found led him to blame the relatively backward state of British industry on poor management and inadequate rates of innovation.

In the earlier postwar period, Pratten saw British industry endeavoring to catch up with American performance levels, but towards the end of the twenty-year period Pratten thought British entrepreneurs looked at German standards as benchmarks to emulate. But achieving high rates of labor productivity growth required the introduction of up-to-date technology. Writing in the early 1970s, he surmised that between 1950 and 1970 the direct labor required for a given level of output using state-of-the-art technology had been cut in half in the manufacturing industries. He pointed out, however, that this referred to production labor, since the employment of other kinds of labor engaged in R&D, marketing, distribution, and managerial tasks had expanded considerably. In his 1972 study, Pratten's estimates of productivity gains did not take into account the benefits of scale economies, being restricted to technical change alone.

But as his previous research demonstrated, Pratten (1971) was aware that embodied technical change, involving more capital-intensive technology, yielded economies of scale that unleashed the full potential of labor productivity growth. In order to achieve a new product mix and secure the full benefits in labor productivity growth after deploying new equipment, management systems needed reorganization. The wider use of computer networks in insurance and banking facilitated the enlargement of business operations and the attainment of economies of scale. Such economies of scale were applicable in commercial establishments ranging from retail stores to wholesalers, financial and transportation businesses.

Pratten ascribed the differences in labor productivity levels found in British industries to varying degrees of capital intensity. Therefore, he argued, attaining higher rates of productivity growth required higher expenditures on R&D to promote innovating designs and higher investment rates to implement their installation. The performance efficiency of plants operating with new machinery normally increased both due to scale economies attained with higher investment levels and the know-how stemming from larger production runs. All the benefits attained from new capital-intensive machinery, economies of scale, advanced management systems, and acquired know-how derived from higher investment strategies, as most advances in technology traced their roots to high levels of capital spending. Financing costly investment plans set a high budget constraint on the implementation of the equipment renewal plans.

But experience showed that profitability levels enjoyed by those businesses operating new, capital-intensive, large-scale plant and equipment fell significantly below profitability levels attained using older vintages. On the basis of his own fieldwork, Pratten questioned the professional competence of British industrial management in the 1960s. He noted, for example, the frequently found total disregard on the part of managers for detailed studies concerning the cost advantages inherent in scale economies. Poor management skills lowered the output range attainable from a given capacity and therefore pushed unit total costs higher.

Characteristically, the total capital costs of existing plants with a given capacity were generally lower than the costs of new plants with the same capacity level. On the other hand, labor costs in new vintage plants were significantly lower. Hence, improvements in managerial know-how and improving the ability to expand output from a given plant capacity could achieve scale economies that significantly lowered the total unit costs of production runs. Building his case on these premises, Pratten concluded that the underlying cause of Brittain's industrial decline with respect to Germany and Japan was the inability of British management to seize the advantages provided by technical progress and economies of scale. This deficiency explained the low growth achieved in labor productivity, particularly in the manufacturing industries.

Finally, he concluded, reluctance to face the challenges posed by investments in new plant and equipment explained British managers delays in deploying innovations. Such technological progress, despite requiring higher levels of capital intensity, delivered significant cost advantages. But fearing the likelihood of lower profitability associated with higher fixed capital expenditures, they prolonged the steady decline of British industrial competitiveness.

High and low roads to competitiveness

Twenty-four years after the publication of Pratten's fieldwork seeking to shed light on the causes of Britain's industrial decline, the problem persisted and the efforts to explain its nature and causation gathered momentum. Michael Kitson and Jonathan Michie's (1996) contribution in this regard acknowledged that in the previous twenty years manufacturing output had hardly increased in Britain. Between 1979 and 1989 manufacturing output grew by 15 percent, and by 1992 output had shrunk to the 1973 level.

While pointing out that the unprecedented economy-wide rise in unemployment rates over the same period all over Europe coincided with sharp declines in manufacturing employment, Kitson and Michie pointed out that in Britain the contraction was largest. As manufacturing lost 5.5 million jobs in the whole of Europe between 1976 and 1986, the employment cuts in UK manufacturing industries reached 2 million workers in the same period. The employment contraction in UK manufacturing happened at the same time that manufacturing trade deficits appeared and economy-wide unemployment continued rising. The fact that manufacturing output did not expand significantly showed that the productivity gains derived from staff reductions did not compensate for the job losses. Concerning the working conditions of the labor force that remained employed the acceleration of production lines, decreasing break times and other measures actually increased the amount of labor inputs used in manufacturing.

With the expansion of financial services and shopping malls, the British economy in the 1980s took a decisive turn towards deindustrialization. The gross investment–output ratio remained relatively stable because both variables declined in tandem. Between 1979 and 1989 Britain's manufacturing capital stock did not grow at all. Whatever productivity growth the drastic reductions in employment achieved, Kitson and Michie charged that managerial strategies aiming to leverage productivity gains into higher short-term profits, rather than improved competitiveness through lower prices, aggravated Britain's trade balance. This happened because the prospective growth in export shares was effectively blocked, leading to wider trade deficits, reduced employment and output. Recalling Kaldor's views on how to gain a competitive edge in world markets, Kitson and Michie blamed the neoclassical notion of competiveness for placing excessive emphasis on price to the neglect of quality, arguing that: "In reality…the key factors which contribute to competitive advantage are product quality and the characteristics of the customer-client relationship" (Kitson and Michie, 1996, p. 203).

The enduring legacy of Kaldor's "paradox"

Kaldor's "paradox," presumably overthrowing the classical conception of competitive success through lower unit costs and unit prices for comparable quality products (found in Smith, Ricardo, and Marx), continues to influence Keynesian economists searching for alternatives to what they believe to be the mainstream paradigm. Milberg's work on trade patterns is a case in point. Milberg (2005) found evidence confirming Kaldor's findings "that among OECD countries relative unit labor costs are often not statistically significant in explaining variations in international competitiveness over time." Not only did RULC not lead to competitive improvements in a country's industrial trade but, on the contrary, the relationship may be, paradoxically, a direct one. Assuming that economic policies providing relatively high levels of social services contributed to higher unit labor costs, and "cooperative" labor relations weakened competitive strategies, Milberg concluded that relative levels of unit costs and prices were largely irrelevant when explaining net trade flows.

Arguing that technological progress need not lower product prices of a given quality level, Milberg explicitly proposed to contrast "price competition" with "technological competition." In this light, he found that empirically his "results are consistent with Kaldor's (1978b) 'paradoxical' finding that countries with the most rapid growth in costs also had the most rapid growth in export shares" (Milberg, 2005, p. 142). While Milberg pointed out that Kaldor's alleged findings applied chiefly to high-income countries, he overlooked to mention that Kaldor himself gave away the secret of his paradox. Notably countries whose market shares went up despite higher unit costs were countries that "traded up-market," that is, countries whose exports rose in quality and hence fetched higher prices. Whether importers experienced shifts in demand due to higher incomes, or quality enhancements exceeded the price hikes, the trade gains achieved are no paradoxical anomaly.

Milberg's contention, similar to Fagerberg's, that two kinds of competition, cost and technological-gap competition, vie with each other for conceptual legitimacy, is problematical. Cost competition is based on the notion that lower (real) unit costs for comparable quality products afford producers a competitive advantage because they can outsell their rivals. The technological-gap alternative suggests that other variables such as innovational effort (R&D), technological progress, capital intensity, and higher mechanization are relevant factors of market-share gains.

But of course in the so-called technological-gap alternative, numerous factors will impinge on unit costs for a given quality product. By definition real unit labor cost measures the relation between real wage rates and labor productivity. Hence, lowering that ratio may be the result of falling wage rates for a given level of labor productivity, or raising labor productivity for a given level of wage rates. The latter increases generally follow innovational changes in technology, rising mechanization and economies of scale. Then the high road to competitiveness consists in undertaking all efforts to raise labor productivity through costly fixed investments, while the low-road alternative presumably simply requires containing wages growth or, better yet, battering down real wage rates. This dichotomy leads Milberg to expect that countries opting for the low-road path to competitiveness would specialize in cheap low-quality products, while richer countries will score big gains in higher-quality exports due to their innovational efforts.

Market share changes correlate with technological gaps between average producers located in a given region or country and leading firms. With superior management systems and higher levels of R&D expenditures, innovational leaders lead the race in quality exports because their production methods are more mechanized, their labor productivity higher, and their unit costs lower than those of potential competitors. A virtuous cycle of learning by doing and cost advantage derived from scale economies turns initial success into persistent gains at the expense of rivals. Efforts to redress the trade imbalances caused by innovational gaps by lowering the exchange rate of deficit partners fails to overcome the productivity advantage of innovators.

Global competition and lower unit costs

Challenging Kaldor's dismissal of price competitiveness as irrelevant, Milberg found that corporate concerns with quality enhancement did not preclude but in fact required cost reductions for maximum competitive effectiveness in global markets. Major corporations operating in "producer-driven" chains enjoyed economies of scale and benefited from outsourcing production of intermediate inputs to various countries, while retaining R&D and branding of final products at central decision centers. Examples of producer-driven industries included automobiles, computers, and aircraft, as well as consumer-driven products such as apparel, footwear, and toys. He found consumer-driven retailers like Wal-Mart, The Gap or Dell did not engage in production themselves and instead outsourced the whole array of products offered for sale. Along with scale economies, product branding and marketing provided a measure of consumer recognition effectively creating substantial entry barriers. Such firms have now become "manufacturers without factories," endeavoring to lower costs as much as possible. Milberg (2006, p. 3) reported that "U.S. firms have successfully used global production networks to reduce costs and raise markups without pushing up final goods and services prices." The oligopolistic power possessed by US world-class corporations enabled them to avoid price hikes to raise their profitability. Milberg attributed this change to a growing price elasticity of demand for consumer products. Oligopolistic firms were now able to achieve substantially more product differentiation than they did in the past, while maintaining their mass production capacity in order to benefit from scale economies.

Milberg argued that emphasizing lower costs rather than raising prices signified a major shift in oligopolistic strategies. Despite his Keynesian perspective on oligopolistic strategies, he keenly recognized the overwhelming competitive pressures to lower costs regardless of market structure. Indeed, whether product or process innovations were concerned, the emergence of global production networks in the past decade, providing the intermediate inputs of the final product in facilities scattered throughout various countries raised the significance of import prices.

Milberg noted that in the US manufacturing sector, imported inputs made up on average 30 percent of the total intermediate products used. Accordingly, the new oligopolistic strategy focused on lowering production costs by requiring suppliers to reduce prices. The grounds for the establishment of global production networks were laid by the development of "computer, telephone and transportation technology." Such technologies sharply diminished the costs of supervision and coordination of foreign production and marketing activities while increasing the effectiveness of managerial controls. Indeed, better supervision of assembly lines, just-in-time inventory flexibility along with the computerization of design activities contributed not only to unprecedented increases in labor productivity but also to broadening the variety of products supplied.

Under the rules dictated by the spread of "globalization," the typical behavior attributed to oligopolistic firms by neoclassical and post-Keynesian economics lacked credible evidence. Global corporations sought to expand their profits by means other than raising prices and restricting output. Instead corporations gained market shares by marketing greater varieties of product designs for various segments of consumer markets and promoting quality enhancements. But along with such strategies, the expansion of computer-driven automation and the growing sophistication of management systems allowed for better utilization of resources, resulting in new ways to improve product quality while lowering unit costs and also prices.

The key to profitability enhancement as practiced by global oligopolistic firms consisted in lowering input costs purchased from suppliers "at the low end of the global commodity chain" lacking market power to resist such pressures. Characteristic examples of such suppliers include the large producers of electronics and apparel located in China.

The dual structure of global manufacturing

Leading market players in highly concentrated industries, enjoying superior capacities for research, design, and product development, as well as access to finance, enjoy the benefits of economies of scale in marketing and purchasing of intermediate inputs. From Milberg's post-Keynesian perspective, such behavior demonstrated the presence of oligopolistic structures. These firms were not entirely competitive despite their sustained efforts to lower costs and gain market shares at each other's expense.

The strength of the argument in favor of the oligopolistic label for these global firms was somewhat diminished by the fact that Milberg saw them with weak market power to raise prices, and this handicap forced them to lower costs while searching for broader product diversification and higher product quality in order to retain or expand market shares. On the other hand, for Milberg the suppliers of intermediate goods to these industry leaders are a prime example of competitive sectors. They depend on the cost-reducing strategies of industry leaders since they could not survive on their own in the global economy.

Milberg argued that the markup over costs, $m = (p - c)/c$, set pricing norms in oligopolistic industries, with variable costs, c, varying with the prices paid for imported inputs, which in turn depend on the unit labor content, a, times the wage rate, w, in the supplying country, $c = wa$. Thus variable costs in the US consist of $c = rw^*a^* + (1 - r)wa$, the asterisk signifying foreign producers' wages and unit labor content and r representing the share of inputs supplied by the low-end producers abroad. Once you assume that wages abroad are lower than in the US, variable costs in the US will decline when using imported inputs, not only because they are cheaper but also because expanding such inputs will lower US wages. Milberg (2006, p. 13) found overwhelming evidence to support the fact that "the asymmetry of market structures found in many supply chains is not some natural outcome, but is the result of the competitive process itself."

The significant conclusion that Milberg drew from his analysis of asymmetric global production chains critically provided the insights necessary to overturn the staid interpretation of post-Keynesian market structures based on the exercise of market power. Winners of the free competition race moved to leading positions in the global division of market structures. But all such industry leaders confronted each other in the struggle for market shares. Hence, competitive battles among the winners decided new structures of supremacy, not preservation of the status quo. In other words, reasons why some horses win competitive races while others lag may range from having a stronger constitution, to being swifter, better trained or more adept at cutting corners or block competitors than others, possibly spurred by ruthless jockeys. Whether or not this is attainable by all, Schumpeter's view of dynamic competition encompassed all means to competitive success. According to marketing experts:

> Competition...consists of the constant struggle among firms for a comparative advantage in resources that will yield a market place position of competitive advantage and, thereby, superior financial performance. Once a firm's comparative advantage in resources enables it to achieve superior performance through a position of comparative advantage in some market segment or segments, competitors attempt to neutralize and/or leapfrog the advantaged firm through acquisition, imitation, substitution, or major innovation...Disequilibrium, not equilibrium, is the norm.
>
> (Hunt and Morgan, 1995, p. 8)

When consumers buy products they are really paying for the set of attributes or services provided by them. Let us refer to the services rendered by a product as S. The inverse demand for a product expressed as $p(S)$, and X being the quantity of products consumed, the cost of producing X is $c(X)$. Then $f(q)$ would be the quantity of services received per product, and the total services consumed, $S = f(q)X$, whose total cost of production, $TC = c(X)/f(q)$. Once R&D programs succeed in expanding $f(q)$, the production cost per unit of services will fall. Since

R&D expenditures are a fixed cost, firms achieving lower unit costs as a result of higher R&D spending are in effect reaping the benefits of higher fixed costs (Spence, 1984, p. 101).

Quality ladders in global competitiveness

Aiginger (1997) proposed a "quality ladder" theory of quality competition for markets supplying product or process innovations. Since unit labor costs were lower in less developed economies, advanced market economies should concentrate on up-market innovations, obviating the cost advantage of less developed economies and their ability to produce cheaper products. This will be an endless quality climb, however, as imitators operating in less advanced economies bid down prices and repeatedly force innovators to raise the quality content of their product. Despite finding that "roughly two-thirds of the 3-digit industries are dominated by price competition, and one-third by quality competition," Aiginger saw consumers willing to pay premium prices for desirable product variations judged to be superior in their innovative design or characteristic features (Aiginger, 1997, p. 586).

Jan Fagerberg (1996) decried the persistent habit "to equate international competitiveness solely with indicators of relative unit costs or prices," offering as a possible explanation that detailed information on "so-called non-price factors" was hard to find. Citing Kaldor's paradox, presumably finding a negative correlation between unit labor cost trends and market shares, Fagerberg inveighed against the neoclassical theory of competitive advantage for ignoring demand factors as determinants of growth trends, ruling out economies of scale and rejecting the notion of divergent paths of technical progress for trading countries.

Fagerberg denied that rising relative unit costs and prices in a given economy would have a negative impact on its sales, reducing its global market share. Instead of such a "simplistic" notion, he advanced the view that a country's market share gains depend on its ability to achieve high productivity growth through rapid technical progress. Hence, he wished to emphasize a country's capacity for technical progress or innovative effort as the leading factor defining its degree of competitiveness. The growth of a country's productive capacity, measured by the expansion rate of its capital stock, RULC trends and the changing structure of global demand, were relevant gauges of competitiveness but decidedly of secondary importance. Fagerberg contended that empirical evidence on trade from the early 1960s through the early 1980s supported his view that technological progress and capacity growth were the chief indicators of a country's competitive level and not cost reductions. Accordingly he found Kaldor's paradox vindicated and notions of price competition without merit: "The idea that in capitalist economies it is technological, rather than price competition that matters most, is not a new one. This thesis had been forcefully argued by Schumpeter...and by Marx before him" (Fagerberg, 1996, p. 43). It is unquestionable that Fagerberg's approach was rooted in Schumpeter's view of innovating activity and entrepreneurial creativity, but whether Marx shared that view is questionable. Critical assessment of the neoclassical theory of perfect competition does not require downplaying the role of market prices in the alternative concept of free competition such as Marx upheld.

Fagerberg himself admitted that "price competition" raged in low-tech industries such as textiles and garments. Even in markets served by the chemical industries, where technical progress was essential, price competition reached notable heights. Electrical instruments sales involving consumer products were also subject to price competition. On the other hand, price competition was less conspicuous in industrial machinery and transport equipment markets. As reported by Schoenberger, buyer firms of industrial machinery, especially high-tech equipment, rely on quality inputs enabling reduction of their production costs. Higher-quality machinery, of course, commands a higher price, but cost advantages are not obviated, they emerge once the machines are running and their full potential realized.

Deploying monthly data at the eight-digit industry level provided by the Eurostat COMEXT database from 1988 to 2001, for manufactured inputs supplied to the EU, Kaplinsky and Santos-Paulino (2006) suggested that "price competition" was less relevant in markets for high-tech products than it was in more traditional trades. According to their data analysis, Kaldor's alleged paradox of rising unit values (as proxies for export prices) giving rise to growing market shares was supported by data on high-tech EU imports. Acknowledging that price competition practiced by leading firms aiming to gain market share by lowering unit prices characterized two-thirds of EU import markets between 1988 and 2001, their research singled out high-tech markets as the relevant exception. The claim that high-tech product markets exhibited rising unit prices due to their high innovational content was certainly in line with Kaldor's own observation, explaining such "perverse" behavior as a result of trading "up-market." Kaldor's notion of trading up-market applies when a country upgrades its export product lines, discontinuing "unsophisticated" categories with a low market price and replacing them with more technologically advanced products at a higher price.

In a follow-up study linking "patterns of trade and technology," Kaplinsky and Santos-Paulino (2006, p. 591) proposed that rising export prices typically characterized the experience of high per-capita countries. Kaldor's "paradoxical" observation concerning the UK's loss of export market shares derived from the UK's inability to produce and export technically sophisticated products. They approvingly quoted the conclusion drawn by K. Pavitt's research indicating that UK exports through the 1970s were concentrated in "unsophisticated machinery and consumer durable goods, requiring relatively few innovative activities, and having relatively low unit values and value to weight ratios" (Pavitt, 1980, p. 7).

As an example of successful quality competition, marketing theorists Hunt and Morgan (1995, p. 7) pointed out how Japanese automobile companies secured a sharp competitive edge over their American rivals in the 1970s and 1980s due to their superior processing technology. Japanese companies produced cars consumers judged to be of better quality and also cheaper than those made by

American companies. By the 1990s, however, some American car manufacturers were able to lower their unit costs and thus regained their price competitiveness relative to Japanese car imports. Despite this price reversal, Japanese car sales continued to rise ahead of the American car brands because consumers continued to rate the quality of Japanese companies above that of the American makers.

Of course a higher-quality product will command a higher price because its attributes service consumer needs better or more fully. As world incomes rise, high-tech exporters will continue to gain market shares at the expense of low-quality products since the better quality of high-tech products affords to consumers benefits unattainable at a lower price. Advanced countries specializing in innovation-intensive exports will be safe from the onslaught of poorer countries enjoying lower costs of production, but lacking innovational capacity. Absent innovation, "price competition drives producers out of production, in a race to the bottom in living standards." Poorer countries will be relegated to engage in price competition within low-end product markets where entry barriers are universally low (Kaplinsky and Santos-Paulino, 2005, p. 334).

The false price/quality dilemma

In line with Schumpeter's evolutionary approach, Metcalfe (1981) argued against the notion that immanent forces pushed markets toward equilibrium. On the contrary, competitive firms constantly searched for ways to expand profits and means to encroach on the market shares of rival firms. Metcalfe took for granted that entrepreneurial decisions to introduce product and process innovations are driven by profit expectations. His neo-Schumpeterian provenance did not obviate the fact that whatever significance theories of quality and other non-price aspects of competition received, prices continued to play a central role in determining success or failure in business strategies to expand market shares. His view of competitive dynamics centered on rivalry among firms striving to expand their market shares on the basis of superior, cost-cutting process innovations and higher-quality products. Prospective innovators respond favorably to rising profit expectations. Successful firms enjoyed higher profitability than the rest, and higher profits enabled them to strengthen their competitive positions against rivals (Metcalfe, 1999).

In Metcalfe, quality improvements and price competition do not give rise to alternative market strategies. Both represent essential aspects of the two-pronged competitive struggle to achieve higher sales. Successful innovations should fulfill two basic conditions. On the demand side, conditions for success contained in the expression $g_d(t) = b[n(p_n, \alpha) - x_n(t)]$ include the potential market demand for process innovations given by their price, p_n, and the extent of their capacity to displace older technologies, the adoption index, α.

Metcalfe understood that innovational products of superior quality command a higher market price. Increases in the market price, $p_n(t)$, due to higher quality provide entrepreneurs the motivation to expand their output. Consumers' evaluation of the new characteristics or desirable features of the product may exceed its higher price, and they may respond as if confronted with a decline in price, p_n, by expanding demand.

Price and quality effects should work at cross purposes, giving rise to an unpredictable "adjustment gap" measuring the difference between the strength of market demand once the innovation reached its peak market diffusion, $n(p_n, \alpha)$ and its actual level at any point in between. The extent to which new process innovations, index α, either lower unit costs or improve output quality determines their maximum market demand, $x_n(t)$.

Expanding the supply side of innovations, on the other hand, requires increasing the demand for materials and machinery, and as a result, input prices will likely rise. The expression $g_{s(t)} = (p_{n(t)} - h_0 - h_1 x_{n(t)})/k$ captures the contradictory market forces involved in pursuit of innovational activities. While rising costs of fixed inputs, k, lower expected profitability, their deployment is required: in our conception of profitability-as-war, even the victors necessarily need to accept sacrifices. Their final market position would still be better than that of their rivals.

5 Capital intensity and profitability
Dissenting views

Barrère's heterodox stance

At the 1957 Corfu Conference where Kaldor first proposed his "stylized facts" as historical regularities, the French economist Alain Barrère presented a paper entitled "Capital Intensity and the Combination of Factors of Production" (see Barrère, 1965), challenging the conventional wisdom on firms' choice of technique. Barrère argued that when drafting their investment plans firms typically considered various indicators before selecting the appropriate technology. The technical designs were classified in a descending order of capital intensity. In his view, technical progress did not take place incrementally through minor changes in existing methods, but in lumpy replacements of older equipment with new vintage technology.

Barrère's basic factors weighing in on the firm's decision included the availability of finance to purchase new technology; interest rate levels; the supply of skilled labor in sufficient numbers to operate the new methods effectively; and projected wage and price trends. In general, operating costs depended on the degree of capital intensity. The most capital-intensive techniques employing the least amount of skilled labor ranked at the top of his list, and involved the lowest labor costs to compensate for the highest equipment costs.

For Barrère firms had to choose between techniques delivering the highest total profits and the highest profit rate. The most capital-intensive option delivered a given output at a lower total cost than the alternatives, allowed for the highest increase in labor productivity, and yielded the largest total profits. Less capital-intensive techniques, on the other hand, required higher operating costs but yielded higher profit rates. Barrère argued that the final choice depended on the extent to which initial capital funding was available. Large dynamic firms with means and the incentive to invest in superior techniques would likely opt to produce a given output at the lowest cost, while smaller, less affluent firms settled for less capital-intensive techniques and higher production costs but higher profitability. Starkly put, firms chose between a technique that minimizes costs and one that maximizes profitability.

Barrère's model of technical choice

Barrère's model, summarized in Figure 5.1, offered an alternative approach to neoclassical models of technical choice closer to the assumptions made by

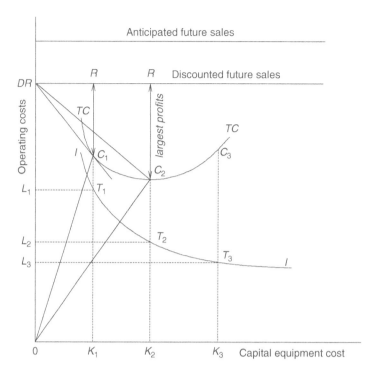

Figure 5.1 Barrère's model of technical choices.

late nineteenth-century classical economists regarding capital–output trends. His model assumed that technical progress occurred in discreet steps, not through marginal increments. Superior techniques were likely to be capital-intensive, requiring more capital and less labor, hence a larger capital expenditure on equipment, but given the wage rates of the complementary workforce, a smaller labor cost. Entrepreneurs seeking to lower their wage costs could not simply add additional equipment of the same kind expecting to retain their existing stock: they would have to buy new vintage technology. More advanced labor-saving technology was better but more costly than the equipment they currently used.

Along the horizontal axis, $0K_1$, $0K_2$, and $0K_3$ measure the amount of capital equipment necessary for each of the three techniques considered, estimated at current replacement money costs. Each of these techniques employs a specific number of required workers, $0L_1$, $0L_2$, and $0L_3$, with associated labor costs measured along the vertical axis. The three technical combinations of capital and labor inputs, at points T_1, T_2, and T_3, produce the same output. Adding the cost of capital equipment and the related labor cost for each technique, Barrère enhanced his diagram with a total cost curve, *TC*, showing the total costs for each of the three techniques under consideration.

Alternative profit-maximizing choices

Barrère's argument starts out assuming a given level of aggregate demand and a given distribution of supply among producers with different technologies. He then projects the expected future revenue derived from the output that these three techniques could realize. The horizontal line RR shows the present market value of those expected future revenues discounted at the prevailing interest rate.

Small and large firms make up the industry, divided into profit rate and total profits maximizers, respectively. Product prices, wage rates, and capital costs are either given or assumed to be stable. Barrère wished to examine the firm's behavior regarding the choice of technique and the alternative measures of profitability attached to them. Each technique of production offered a different kind of potential payoff. Before selecting any of the available techniques and their associated payoffs, however, entrepreneurs need to assess their financial situation, including the extent to which they have access to external credit sources.

After estimating the total revenues forthcoming from the discounted market value of future output, and the total costs associated with each of the available techniques capable of producing that output, firms decide to opt for techniques that maximize either the profit rate on the required capital stock or the total profits. In Figure 5.1, C_1 represents the combined cost of fixed capital and labor necessary to operate technique T_1, involving the use of capital $0K_1$ and labor $0L_1$. The slope of ray $0C_1$, given by ratio $0K_1/K_1C_1$, measures the degree of capital intensity for technique T_1. The lower slope of ray $0C_1$ compared to $0C_2$ shows that C_1 is less capital-intensive than C_2. In Barrère's model:

> In order to simplify, we shall assume that the most advanced techniques require most capital and least labor. There are of course exceptions, but the proposition seems plausible as the general rule, since in most cases technical progress leads to the appearance of more costly equipment operated at a lower labour cost.
>
> (Barrère, 1965, p. 146)

Barrère considered the profit maximizing rule of conventional microeconomics, requiring the equality of marginal cost with marginal revenue, as operationally unsound. Against it, he argued that following such a rule would force entrepreneurs to compare current costs with future revenues, only realized when the production process ended and goods were sold. While the cost estimates for each technique were readily available from current data on wages, interest rates, equipment prices, and so on, the expected market revenues depended on future market conditions. Due to the time lapse between completion of production and sale of the goods, future demand and prices could not be correctly estimated. The discounted value of those revenues introduced an uncertainty element impossible to overcome. With technical progress delivering ever more capital-intensive productive methods and lengthening the production circuit, the difficulty in assessing future market conditions rose to new heights. Equating marginal revenue with marginal cost to estimate equilibrium output offered no reliable guide to determining the best choice of technique.

The model's simplifying assumptions

To simplify the analysis of choices confronting different firms between maximizing either the profit rate or total profits, Barrère proceeded as if the practical problems associated with the calculus of future total revenues did not introduce insurmountable levels of uncertainty. Thus a technique identified with point T_1 on the isoquant requires $0K_1$ amount of capital and $0L_1$ of labor, which at the current capital and labor costs yields a total operating cost represented by point C_1. Given the discounted value of expected future revenue set by the horizontal line RR, the distance between RR and C_1 will be the corresponding level of total profits associated with use of technique $0K_1 - 0L_1$.

Drawing a ray from point DR, the slope of its tangent at point C_1, represents the profit rate on the money cost of capital equipment. Adding new rays from point DR, through the identified costs of different techniques, will show the slope of ray DR–C_1, tangent at point C_1, as the steepest of the lot. Therefore technique $0K_1 - 0L_1$ will be chosen if the firm wishes to achieve the highest profit rate.

Selecting this combination requires entrepreneurs to list all feasible techniques whose discounted profitability exceeds the current interest rate, according to their degree of capital intensity (the cost of the capital equipment, K, divided by the total operating costs, $K + L$). Such classification will place the combination yielding the highest profit rate, $0K_1 - 0L_1$, at the top of their list. Making this choice requires rejecting higher capital-intensive techniques of lower profitability, albeit capable of returning higher total profits. The exclusion covers options involving lower production total costs than the selected combination, including the lowest-cost technique. As Barrère's diagram shows, the technique yielding the highest profit rate, represented by the slope of ray DR–C_1, differs from the lowest total cost option at point C_2. Clearly the factor combination $0K_2 - 0L_2$, capable of yielding the largest total profits, $R_2 - C_2$, although a lower profit rate (represented by the slope of ray DR–C_2) than the alternative choice $0K_1 - 0L_1$, would be bypassed by firms seeking to maximize their profit rate.

For Barrère, choosing between techniques maximizing the profit rate or total profits depended on the financial wherewithal of the firm in question, that is, the extent to which entrepreneurs facing investment alternatives received a more or less favorable response from capital markets when seeking to raise capital. Facing this quandary when dealing with the banking system, Barrère argued, large established firms enjoyed a decisive advantage over smaller businesses. Despite the fact that those techniques that maximized total profits also require larger investments in fixed capital, larger firms need not be deterred from acquiring the necessary credits, because banks are generally well disposed to service their capital needs. With substantial amounts of internal funds at their disposal, borrowing to finance heavy capital investments will not derail the growth strategy of larger firms.

Barrère argued that, as a rule, following a long history of financial success, after achieving a leadership position in industry and gains in market share, a firm seeking a further expansion of its scale of production would likely choose the capital-intensive, cost-minimizing technique yielding the highest total profits from the available array of options. Barrère (1965, p. 155) concluded: "There seems to be a presumption that a deep capital structure tends to generate a yet deeper one." On the other hand, he was persuaded that smaller, less capitalized firms, lacking standing in the capital markets, would be barred from undertaking heavy fixed capital investments and hence would be forced to settle for techniques of lower capital intensity, choosing one whose profit rate was highest.

Expanding revenues

Dropping the assumption of a given level of aggregate demand and allowing for the expansion of sales, estimates of potential profitability rise in complexity and lose predictive value. Technical progress delivers increasingly more capital-intensive methods of production that allow firms to reach unprecedented levels of labor productivity. But the introduction of increasingly capital-intensive techniques itself contributes to the degree of uncertainty involved in making estimates of future revenue as the period of production lengthens. Responding to the perceived growth in future demand, those entrepreneurs who decide to expand adopting expensive capital-intensive techniques need to evaluate the impact of growing supply upon prospective sales.

Because the productivity gains achieved with technical developments, however, will more likely exceed the projected growth in demand, entrepreneurs are likely to find that future growth in revenues, R_a, R_b, R_c, fails to match their output growth: future prices are likely to fall as growth in supply surpasses growth in demand. On the assumption that productivity growth attained through capital-intensive innovations is higher than aggregate demand growth, it follows that prices would fall relative to capital costs. Total profits might rise because the scale of production expanded while costs and prices fell, but not necessarily profitability.

Barrère draws three ranking isoquants, I_a-I_a, I_b-I_b and I_c-I_c rising in a northeastern direction, illustrating the decisive trend in technological progress towards more capital-intensive factor combinations. The U-shaped total cost curves corresponding to each one of them, and the horizontal lines setting the present value of the expected total revenues associated with the expanding output, identify the optimum combinations for either maximum profit rates or maximum total profits.

Barrère's model reveals some striking outcomes. First, even if the ratio of capital to physical output remained stable, the maximum profit rate would fall as the capital–revenues ratio rose with increasingly more capital-intensive techniques deployed. Second, the paths linking maximum profit rates and largest total profits would tend to converge through time and merge at some point where the "profit of enterprise" disappeared, as the business profit rate equaled the rate of interest, and total costs equaled total revenues. Barrère did not believe that private firms would ever reach such a state:

> There is a presumption that the capitalistic firm will never reach this degree of capital intensity, because the entrepreneur will wish to keep a high average rate of profit per unit of capital. But there is a type of firm which may reach this point and stay there. It is the public enterprise which... tends towards the highest degree of capital intensity... The ultra-modern and very costly equipment of the French National Railways is a case in point.
>
> (Barrère, 1965, p. 159)

Meek and Richardson's objections

Contrary to the conclusions found Barrère's model, Ronald Meek (1964) argued that the self-interest filter used by firms to sort out the pros and cons attached to the "right" choice of investment between two techniques contained "a bias against the choice of capital-intensive techniques" and favored low capital-intensive projects.

The "right" choice from the standpoint of "social welfare" would be the method that allowed firms to produce a given output at the lowest total cost, one requiring high capital but low total operating costs rather than low initial capital but high operating costs. Meek believed, however, that business expediency would likely direct them to adopt lower capital-intensive techniques yielding a higher profit rate. Business logic would surely favor giving up the extra profits flowing from the discarded lowest-cost option if the additional capital finance thereby saved could be used to finance any alternative investment of higher profitability. Meek's representative businessman would not approve, even if the necessary finance for capital-intensive techniques was readily available and such investments enabled the firm to rake in the largest profits in future. Doing so would be sound business, thereby preserving the finance needed to tackle future opportunities that might spring up yielding a higher profit rate.

Meek acknowledged a common foundation with Barrère's model. Both presented an ideal option between a capital-intensive technique of production yielding the lowest total cost, and given the present value of total revenues, the highest total profits, and a less capital-intensive option with higher total operating costs but the highest rate of profit. His objection applied to Barrère's explanation regarding technical choices in a competitive setting: small firms seeking to maximize their profit rate opting for less capital-intensive techniques, and large firms opting for the largest total profits using more capital-intensive alternatives.

The decisive factor in Meek's rejection of Barrère's technical choices derived from Meek's belief that businessmen generally preferred maximizing their "rate of profits on investment" rather than their total profits, and consequently they avoided capital-intensive options. Such conviction led him to argue counter-intuitively "that capitalism has an inherent bias against the use of capitalistic methods," a conclusion that set him squarely at odds with Barrère's basic position (Meek, 1964, p. 353). Meek charged that Barrère "appears to think that he has proved that the less capital-intensive method is bound in all cases to show the higher rate of profits, and that the more capital-intensive method is bound in all cases to show the higher amount of profits (i.e. the lower total annual costs)" (Meek, 1964, p. 337).

But in his paper Barrère did not argue his case as a matter of abstract choices. He simply identified factor combinations for three increasingly more capital-intensive techniques, indicating that in reality no continuum of techniques existed (linking the three by isoquants nevertheless) and coupled them with their respective total costs curves. He then identified one of the factor combinations with the lowest total cost option (due to lower operating costs). Barrère argued that "as a general rule" entrepreneurs preferred labor-saving techniques that lowered total wages proportionately more than the increase in fixed capital equipment, because they made it possible to produce a given output at the lowest total cost. Such techniques allowed the highest levels of labor productivity growth and produced the best results from the business standpoint.

Concerned with the possibility that Meek's argument in favor of investment projects that maximized profit rates rather than total profits had missed relevant points, G. B. Richardson (1965) denied the likelihood that capital-intensive techniques would be adopted even if their projected profitability initially exceeded the current market rate of interest. Regarding the choice of investment in capital-intensive techniques, Richardson expressed two objections. He joined Barrère in rejecting the assumption of a perfectly elastic supply of finance. In his view additional finance borrowing would lead to interest rate hikes as risk considerations mounted. In addition, Richardson argued that any considerable expansion of a firm's productive capacity would run up against managerial limitations that would unravel the firm's projected plans to lower production costs. Richardson's analysis relied heavily on projections of marginal profitability, defined as the change in projected total profits following the firm's incremental planned investment, *pm*.

His conclusions did not apply to any investment spending taken by itself but to the profitability expectations of changes in the aggregate investment of the firm. But profitability changes in any other activities carried out by the firm should impact the marginal profitability of investment, the change that management expects to take place in a firm's total profits from a marginal increase in the level of investment, *mp*. For example, managerial limitations associated with the completion of enlarged capital-intensive projects will likely lower the marginal profitability of the firm's combined investments below the profitability of its marginal investment. Moreover, the incremental cost of finance, *mcf*, should grow as the incremental level of investment increased. Richardson argued that to the degree that the scale of capital-intensive techniques grew in size and the marginal cost of the associated borrowing rose, the marginal profitability of the aggregate activities undertaken by firm would likely fall.

Richardson agreed with Barrère that while in a world of certainties the equality between the marginal profitability of investment, *mp*, and the incremental cost of finance, *mcf*, would determine the profit maximizing scale of investment, in the real world uncertainty ruled. In the absence of reliable estimates of future revenues, managers would simply acknowledge the fact that expansion beyond some point undermined profitability, either by handicapping management's ability to work efficiently or raising financing costs beyond acceptable levels. Consequently, Richardson thought uncertainty about future profitability and strong expectations of rising finance costs and growing managerial constraints would deter firms from committing significant amount of resources to large capital-intensive projects.

An alternative strategy for lowest-cost firms

Suppose now some of the initially small firms which had opted for Barrère's profit rate maximizing technique, T_1 in Figure 5.2, requiring $0K_1$ equipment costs and $0L_1$ operating labor costs, with expected sales of αS, and total costs c_1, managed to raise the funds necessary to expand and adopted a more capital-intensive technique, T_2. According to Barrère's choices, as their total costs declined with the enlarged scale of production, their outlook should change, trading off lower profit rates in exchange for larger total profits. The adopted new technique would lower their total costs to c_2, and if they chose to maintain their price unchanged,

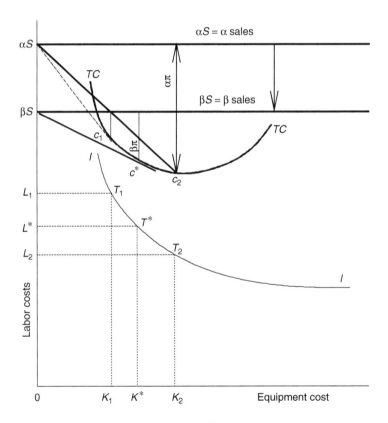

Figure 5.2 Alternative investment strategies.

the widened gap between sales and costs would raise their profits significantly, as shown by $\alpha\pi$. This would be the likely outcome were the larger firms not concerned with the threat of retaliation from their industry rivals.

Fearing that other firms would seek to deploy advanced technology in order to challenge their market leadership should play a decisive role in their strategy. Accordingly, they could pursue a policy designed to prevent such threats, lowering their sales price enough to force some of their smaller rivals away from their previously optimal, profit-rate-maximizing technical choices. Losing market shares would force the smaller profit-rate-maximizing firms to adopt more capital-intensive, lower-cost techniques. The number of rival firms in the industry would be reduced, as those firms unable to finance the more capital-intensive technique, T^*, necessary for a profit-maximizing strategy, would disappear. A technique such as T^* would be feasible only to the most successful firms surviving, since its capital requirements are larger.

The profit rate for the firms adopting technique T_2 would be lower than it was before they expanded. But industry rivals using technique T^* faced even lower profitability prospects. While the industry leaders lowered the market price, and unit revenues fell, as long as their total costs of production fell proportionately more than their revenues and their market share rose, their total profits would be larger as well. Hence, the aggressive strategy of the largest and most efficient firms would wipe out some rival firms, decrease the profit rate in the industry as a whole and possibly enlarge their own profits mass. Barrère's concept of passive, not aggressive, competition deprived his otherwise suggestive model of profitability and technical change of real-world and credible strategies.

Operating leverage and competitive advantage

In their acclaimed textbook on managerial finance, *Essentials of Managerial Finance*, Weston and Brigham (1993, pp. 331–334) subscribe to the argument that competitive forces drive the selection of viable technical change. Weston and Brigham define the presence of a "high degree of operating leverage" when a "high percentage of a firm's total costs are fixed."

For illustrative purposes, they construct hypothetical tables for an industry made up of three firms, A, B, and C, showing production levels and their corresponding sales revenues, total operating costs and operating profits. Firms A, B and C find themselves initially producing and selling 200,000 products each at $2 per unit. It would appear that the total market sales for this product amount to $1,200,000. Now the fact that these three firms differ in their degree of operating leverage, hence their productive capacity, might suggest that setting the individual output for A, B and C at 200,000 units each, exactly one third of the total output, might seem contrived, but the authors ignore this point.

Firm A has the least operating leverage, using a minimum of automated equipment, hence its fixed costs, $20,000 are the lowest. With the lowest fixed capital–labor ratio, A's marginal and average variable costs, at $1.50, are the highest of the three firms. At a 40,000 output, total costs including $20,000 fixed plus

$60,000 variable equal total revenues. Beyond that output, firm's A profits rise to a maximum of $80,000 as sales reach 200,000 units.

Firm B enjoys a normal operating leverage since it operates with a normal degree of mechanization, with fixed costs rising to $40,000, 100 percent higher than A. The higher fixed costs push B's marginal and average variable costs, at $1.20, 20 percent lower than A's. Combining its higher fixed capital stock and lower unit costs raises B's breakeven point, at 50,000 units, above A's. With sales of 200,000 units B's total profits of $120,000 are 50 percent higher than A's.

Firm C, as a highly automated firm "using expensive, high speed machines that require very little labor per unit produced," has the highest level of operating leverage. Its fixed costs rise to $60,000, 200 percent higher than A's. Firm C's marginal and average variable costs, at $1, are the lowest of the three, 33.3 percent lower than A's. Operating with the highest fixed costs, C's breakeven point reaches the highest level as well, 60,000 units. With sales of 20,000 units C's total profits climb to $140,000, the highest returns for the three firms, exceeding A's by 75 percent.

Price-cutting in competitive wars

Firm C's total unit costs, at $1.30, attained with fixed costs of $60,000 and a production scale of 200,000 units, are 18.75 percent below A's at the same level of output, allowing C a competitive edge over A and B as well. Weston and Brigham's account of a sound competitive strategy for C goes no further than to suggest that since C enjoys a significant unit cost advantage over A and B, cutting its sales price by 25 percent, from $2 to $1.50, C would become the industry's market leader. In that position C would still enjoy a $0.20 margin over its unit cost at a production scale of 200,000 units, a substantial 13.3 percent profit margin versus 6.7 percent for B. Of course, lowering the price from $2 to $1.50 would shut A's operations sooner or later, its revenues just covering variable costs but falling short of total costs by $20,000 at all levels of output.

While Weston and Brigham make an impressive case for the competitive advantage derived from high operating leverage, we believe that as presented in their textbook the story contains unsupportable assumptions. Firm C's decision to lower the sales price must weigh the cost of aggressive price-cutting against the lure of expected market gains.

Once A is driven out we may assume that B and C will split the total market sales between themselves. This would provide a likely motivation for C's lowering its price. The new division of sales may well be determined by the degree of operational leverage deployed in each firm, that is, by the stock of fixed capital behind their respective fixed costs. We may assume that the firms produce at their capacity levels. Firm C's fixed costs being 50 percent higher than B's would mean that its productive capacity is 50 percent higher than B's. After putting A out of business the total market sales of $1.2 million are divided between B and C according to their capacity potential, so C would produce and sell 50 percent more than B. Firm C's capacity output would be 480,000 units, valued at $720,000, while

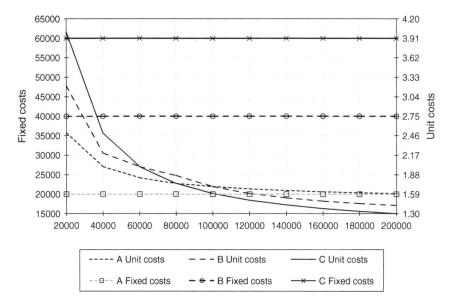

Figure 5.3 Operating leverage and competitive cost structures.

B produced 320,000 units with sales of $480,000. Now we can better appreciate the motivation behind C's decision to lower the unit price from $2 to $1.50. This price-cut of 25 percent will allow C to expand its market share from an initial 33.3 percent, when three firms were in business, to 60 percent, when only two remain. But we may also surmise that C's initial motivation to raise its operating leverage sought to lower its unit costs of production precisely for the purpose of achieving market dominance. In other words, C chose a sound strategy to support its expansion and bring about A's business failure.

Figure 5.3 simply illustrates the advantages obtained by firms using high levels of operating leverage to lower their unit costs, reduce prices, and gain market share away from their rivals.

Eltis on technical progress and profitability: Britain's case

As we saw in the previous chapter, what is missing in Barrère and his critics is a sense of the turbulence and rivalry among firms brought forth by forces identified by Marx, Schumpeter, and Baumol as fundamental to capitalist development (Vickers, 1995). Sorting out the evidence supporting the accepted belief that competition should force costs down and promote innovational activity, Nickell (1996, p. 741) concluded that "Perhaps competition works not by forcing efficiency on individual firms but by letting many flowers bloom and ensuring that only the best survive."

Jovanovic succinctly brought out the chief trait possessed by firms enjoying success and enhanced prospects for survival. In his view, achieving low costs was the crucial test of their efficiency and only those firms capable of doing so survived: "Efficient firms grow and survive; inefficient firms decline and fail. Firms differ in size not because of the fixity of capital, but because some discover that they are more efficient than others" (Jovanovic, 1982, p. 650).

Stoneman and Kwon (1996) argued that innovations should allow firms to improve performance, lower costs, and improve product quality, but how their individual profitability fared would depend on early adoption of superior technology and the extent to which other firms followed suit. If Barrère's firms anticipated the potential threats stemming from aggressive rivals leveraging their higher profit rates into expansion plans, their passivity would be suicidal.

Baumol's notion of innovations as competitive weapons, despite its limitations, provided the conceptual framework to render such passive conceptions of competition untenable. Why would the capital-intensive firms not take advantage of their lower costs to reduce the market price sufficiently and so render smaller rivals (supposedly enjoying a higher profit rate) unprofitable, thus incapable of borrowing sufficient finance to mount hostile actions against them? Absent real competitive threats, of course, live-and-let-live modeling of strategies among firms with diverse technologies and profit rates is conceivable.

Eltis (1971) advanced two suggestions to construct a sound technical progress function. Taking as his point of departure Kaldor's hypothesis that the rate of technical progress hinged on the level of investment spending, specifically linking the growth in labor productivity with the growth in capital per worker, Eltis proposed that technical improvements achieved in the production of capital goods depended on their sales volume, linked to the share of investment in output. He also suggested that design imperfections affecting quality would be more easily detected and rectified the larger their scale of production. Thus higher rates of investment should strengthen the incentive to improve profitability while raising the technical proficiency of the means of production.

Eltis' technical progress function, labeled RR, showed the annual expenditures for research and development, X, necessary to bring about corresponding annual reductions in unit costs of production for existing equipment, m (Figure 5.4). The RR schedule is drawn cutting the vertical axis at a given level on the assumption that inevitably some R&D expenditures will be required in advance of any forthcoming positive results. The slope of the RR function rises because achieving higher rates of annual cost reductions, m, requires higher annual expenditures on R&D.

Eltis argued that as R&D departments expand, the flow of innovational results did not run into diminishing returns and hence their profitability did not decline. On the contrary, successful breakthroughs prepared the grounds for further discoveries. Attempts to raise the rate of annual cost reductions, however, ran into increasing annual R&D costs. In other words, speeding up the achieved rate of cost reductions raised R&D expenditures. Cutting in half the time normally necessary to attain a given cost reduction would more than double the required R&D

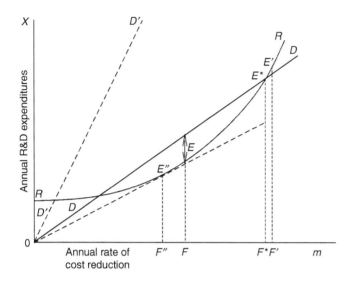

Figure 5.4 Eltis' (1971) growth model.

expenditures. Algebraically, the shape of the *RR* function, showing the functional relationship between the rising annual R&D cost, *X*, necessary in raising the annual rate of cost reduction, *m*, implies that $\frac{dX}{dm} > 0$, but crucially $\frac{d^2X}{dm^2} > 0$.

Technical progress covered both cost reductions and quality improvements. The fact that results achieved by research departments often involved new equipment of higher quality did not raise insurmountable problems in Eltis' model. Eltis considered the quality improvement of an existing product with no change in production cost as an increase in its market value, *m*. A cost reduction, alternatively, improved the marketability of a qualitatively unchanged product. Both aspects of the R&D program expanded firms' profits and therefore entered into entrepreneurial calculations regarding optimal research funding.

After achieving a given percentage of cost reduction or quality improvement in some product, Eltis argued, a firm could sell it at a price bringing in higher profits than before the change occurred. The extra profit accruing to the firm would be proportional to the rate of technical progress attained and the sales thereby generated. In Eltis's model, the extra profits that such a firm could realize from the marketable advances in annual cost reductions flowing from its research department is labeled *DD*.

Thus, "a profit-maximizing firm" would raise its R&D expenditures to a level where the difference between the annual extra profits derived from the sale of a superior product and the incremental costs incurred in its design were greatest. That desirable outcome would be found where the gap between *RR* and *DD* schedules is largest, a condition satisfied where the slope of a tangent to *RR* equals that of *DD*, showing a certain percentage of annual cost reduction. For firms doubling their product sales, following a certain percentage reduction in production costs, earnings would increase. Consequently their extra profits schedule, labeled $D'D'$, would be steeper than the previous one, DD, since each point on the new schedule would be higher than before the change occurred. The point where the slope of the new schedule $D'D'$ equals that of a tangent to the technical progress function, RR, defines the higher percentage of annual cost reduction needed to bring about the sales expansion.

The struggle for market shares

Eltis' argument ignored the impact of an innovating firm's behavior on other firms in the industry. It limited itself to showing how far R&D expenditures would have to grow relative to the expected extra profits to achieve maximum profits, absent competitive wars among rival firms.

Bringing a measure of realism to the story, however, required adopting arguments familiar to Schumpeter's dynamics. Eltis pondered the fact that firms coupling the fruits of technical progress with price hikes, seeking to realize what he called "abnormal" profits, would face undesirable setbacks. Outsiders might seek to partake of the profits bounty and attempt entry into the industry in question. Firms would be able to enter the industry whenever their DD schedule rose above the RR progress function. Once they did so, using additional equipment of a superior kind to enlarge their sales would reduce prices, revenues, and profits, lowering the slope of the DD schedule for each firm. Entry of new firms would go on until their DD schedules were no longer above their RR functions but just tangent to it, that is, at any point located to the left of the profits-maximizing position, labeled E.

In view of this likely outcome threatening firms that chose to follow the mirage of short-run maximum profits, disregarding the impact of such behavior upon potential rivals, Eltis endowed his innovating firms with the power of foresight. Firms that exercised such defensive strategies would be well advised to avoid R&D programs of the scope identified by the optimal E option, thus avoiding unwelcome consequences from rival firms. Innovating firms could avoid the loss of profits and market shares as long as they expanded their annual R&D expenditures to the financially sustainable limit found at point E^*, located at the intersection of their RR and DD schedules, as previously defined. Such growth paths would allow them to realize normal profits while attaining the highest rate of technical progress compatible with their profit-seeking goals.

Flaws in Barrère's and Eltis' models

Because the perspective shared by nineteenth-century economists clashes so sharply with the assumptions built into mainstream neoclassical growth models, we wish to include here a few quotations highlighting the paradigm shifts dividing them. We believe that they shed invaluable light on important features of the pre-neoclassical paradigm. Sidgwick (1883, p. 158), for instance, built his theory of accumulation on the assumption that "Inventions have generally had the effect of complicating and prolonging the processes of industry, while at the same time increasing the ultimate productiveness of labor." David (2004, p. 43) quoted from Sidgwick's 1887 edition of his *Principles of Political Economy* as follows:

> Though the progress of Invention–including the developments of the great system of cooperation through exchange–does not necessarily increase the need of capital, it has, on the whole, tended continuously and decidedly in this direction: the increase in the amount of consumable commodities obtainable by a given amount of civilized labor has been attended by a continual increase in the amount of real capital required to furnish these commodities to the consumer.

Clearly what Barrère's model lacks is the element of "coercion" present in Sidgwick's view of competition. But in our view, despite neglecting the coercive effects of real ("free") competition (totally different from "perfect" competition), Barrère's contribution should not be ignored.

In contrast with the neoclassical notion of free-of-cost technical change, the classical view of late nineteenth-century economists such as Henry Sidgwick (1883), F. W. Taussig (1896), as well as Marx, was that technological progress raised the degree of mechanization and intensified the displacement of labor, generally resulting in higher fixed capital costs per unit of output. The business strategy characteristically pursued sought to reduce unit variable costs proportionately more than unit fixed capital costs increased, hence lowering total unit costs. Such business strategy sheds light on the question why competitive wars favor financially stronger corporations over weaker firms. It makes sense because in order to maintain competitive leadership heavy capital investments are required as well as levels of investment finance not available to less powerful firms.

In the late nineteenth century, Sidgwick saw clearly that competitive pressures on firms "forced" upon successful innovators a path requiring the installation of labor-saving equipment intended to lower total unit costs. For market leaders the initial reduction in unit cost allowed them to lower prices to levels beyond the reach of competitive laggards with an unfavorable cost structure. The coercive element was necessary because carrying out investment plans designed to maintain industry leadership involved willingness on the part of cutting-edge firms to accept lower profitability, although their weaker rivals fared worse. These innovators sought to expand their market share at the cost of lower profitability:

> we can see without refined analysis that so far as producers using better machinery are forced by competition to reduce the price of their products below what was required to remunerate the less efficient producers which they have now superseded, the gain of the improvement goes to the consumers of these products and not to the owners of the capital as such.
>
> (Sidgwick, 1883, p. 165)

Barrère offered no evidence supporting his claim that larger, more capital-intensive firms employing the latest technology were less profitable than smaller, less-capital using businesses. In addition, Barrère allowed these capital-intensive firms *peacefully* to share the market with less capital-intensive but more profitable businesses. But empirical evidence gathered by Amato and Wilder (1985) showed that "there is no relationship between firm size and profit rate." While Amato and Wilder acknowledged that other studies found a positive relationship between market share and profitability, their own interpretation led them to conclude that "absolute firm size" was not a relevant factor in that relationship.

Ghemawat and Caves (1986) distinguished between "ongoing and sunk costs" and, in the context of dynamic competition favored by the "new industrial economics," set out to unravel the relationship between sunk costs and firm profitability. They found two opposing trends. From the standpoint of entry theory, the presence of large sunk costs appeared to deter entry, conferring on established firms a distinct advantage in the protection of their profitability. On the other hand, supergames theory, investigating how incumbents' pursuit of different sunk costs strategies impacts each other's profitability, brought out the increasing risk of failure attached to them. While recognizing that market-share growth brought about by growing capital intensity and product differentiation would "increase profitability," they ended up cautiously conceding that their approach "might not suffice to detect complex interactions among variables" (Ghemawat and Caves, 1986, p. 110).

Eltis and Kaldor on Britain's industrial decline

Thirty years after Nicholas Kaldor first sought to pinpoint the cause of British industrial decline, the persistence of the problem continued to motivate fresh inquiries into its roots. Thus, while noting that between 1979 and 1996 the growth rate of Britain's GDP kept pace with Germany's as well as France's, Walter Eltis (1996) questioned the reasons why British manufacturing growth did not keep pace with the expansion of commercial and service companies.

Contending, moreover, that after 1970 profitability in UK manufacturing remained lower than in other commercial sectors, Eltis traced the uneven growth dynamics of industrial and commercial sectors to their profitability differentials. As Eltis pointed out, between 1962 and 1973 employment in the UK services sector grew faster than in "any other leading economy," exceeding the employment growth in manufacturing, due to the higher profitability achieved by service corporations relative to those in manufacturing.

Following the neo-Schumpeterian perspective, Eltis suggested British industry suffered from a paucity of innovational breakthroughs in producing and marketing new products. In order to succeed in world trade, countries needed to transform their production lines into "research-intensive" activities. Failure to do this in the UK stemmed from investment plans not designed to keep up with the range of product innovations that other countries supplied since the 1980s. Countries gaining competitiveness were those whose high-tech industries delivered growing masses of new products. Despite their sustained efforts to increase labor productivity on the basis of employment reductions and lower labor costs, UK manufacturing failed to achieve world-class competitiveness.

Eltis argued that in order to take market shares away from the leading producers in Germany and Japan, additional funding for R&D programs designed to promote innovational activities were needed. Moreover, increasing gains in market shares involved raising R&D expenditures. Such extra spending shared the characteristics of fixed costs and was likely to lower profitability in the firms involved. Pratten (1972, p. 196) had previously noted that "conventional accounting practices" deducted R&D expenditures from current profits, hence tended to reduce net profitability for innovating firms. But drawing on Marx's distinction between "technical composition of capital" and "value composition," Eltis hoped the information technology sweeping the foundations of advanced economies would cheapen the elements of capital equipment to such an extent that whole new industrial plants could be built without additional spending beyond depreciation allowances.

For Eltis, Kaldor's technical progress function ignored the linkage between the investment propensity and technical progress. In Kaldor's version, the growth rate of labor productivity depended on the growth rate of capital per worker. Kaldor's technical progress function cut the vertical axis because even in the absence of growth in the capital–labor ratio some growth in labor productivity will occur, for reasons unconnected with capital accumulation. In his growth model, Kaldor drew a 45° line showing the equilibrium path between labor productivity growth and the growth of capital per worker.

Assuming a nonlinear technical progress function, steady growth occurred at the intersection with the growth of capital per worker function. Therefore steady growth required specific growth rates of capital per worker and labor productivity, no other solutions being possible. According to Kaldor's model, two economies endowed with similar technical progress functions, *PP*, but divergent saving and investment ratios, would nonetheless wind up settling at equilibrium points with the same growth rates of labor productivity and capital per worker. This outcome entirely depended on the assumed concavity of Kaldor's technical progress function. That only one point fulfilled the conditions for steady growth marred Kaldor's claim that his technical progress function was endogenously linked with the accumulation of capital and the strength of investment activity.

Kaldor's technical progress function specified that the growth rate of output, g, minus the growth rate of the labor employed, n, depended on the growth rate of the capital stock, k, minus the growth rate of the labor employed:

$$g - n = A_1 + A_2(k - n).$$

In this expression A_1 and A_2 are constants, and therefore Kaldor's technical progress function should be a straight line. Translating these terms into Eltis' algebra, $g - n = m$, and since the model's solution required that g should equal k, it followed that:

$$m = A_1 + A_2(k - n)$$
$$= A_1 + A_2 m$$
$$= \frac{A_1}{1 - A_2}.$$

Eltis' expression for his technical progress function, on the other hand, linked the growth rate in labor productivity (the achieved cost reduction derived from it) to the investment propensity, S, promoting technical advance, so that $m = A + B \cdot S$. With that modification, Eltis concluded that in fact Kaldor's formulation was equivalent to postulating an exogenously determined rate of technical progress. But, for Eltis, whether the growth rate of labor productivity was related to the growth rate of the stock of capital per worker, or instead to the propensities to save and invest, made a world of difference. On the basis of his formulation of the technical progress function,

$$m = A + B \cdot S,$$
$$g = A - n + B \cdot S,$$

Eltis concluded that economies with different investment propensities, other things being equal, should give rise to different growth rates in labor productivity and output. Expanding R&D ran into increasing costs and led to falling profit rates. The *PP* schedule in Eltis's diagram (Figure 5.5) showed the decline in profitability associated with market shares gains at a given level of R&D expenditures. The *PP'* schedule tracks the change in profitability associated with a rising level of R&D spending. The *FF* line shows the real interest rate level. Additional R&D spending would allow firms to expand market shares, moving to point g, for example, as long as the marginal profits were higher than the real interest rate, but doing so required accepting a lower profit rate on total capital.

Eltis acknowledged that incremental expansion and renewal of existing plant and equipment contributed somewhat to higher profitability, but not as much as upgrading the whole plant and equipment with the latest technology. Unfortunately, Eltis recognized that manufacturing investment plans in the UK typically did not undertake the construction of whole new plants equipped with the latest technology, but rather incremental expansion of existing facilities. Adding new plant and equipment to older installations raised the growth of labor productivity by cutting employment and consequently lowering labor costs. But the benefits so gained did not match those obtained by replacing the whole plant with a new vintage technology as in Germany and Japan.

Eltis concluded that since the real cost of financing R&D was generally the same in all the advanced countries comprising the OECD, a country like the UK enjoying lower profitability in manufacturing (a lower *PP* schedule) would also

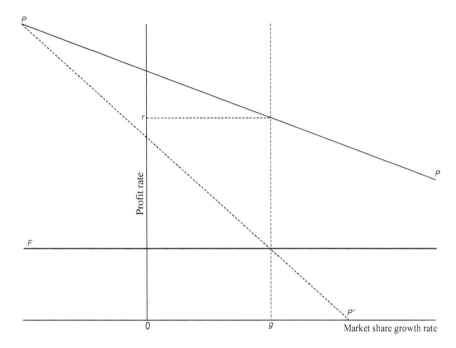

Figure 5.5 Relationship between market share and profit rate.

have lower market shares than its industrial competitors. With lower profitability and reduced prospects for market share gains, firms' incentives to embark on costly R&D programs faded and their prospects for export gains linked to marketing new products diminished. In this light, Eltis related the poor performance of output growth and employment in British manufacturing from the late 1950s through the early 1980s to the fact that manufacturing profitability in the UK remained below other corporate levels in that period. His calculations showed that profitability in UK manufacturing, defined as the net operating surplus over the net capital stock, fell below the levels attained in France, Germany and the US. Because profitability trends in British manufacturing did not match the level attained by its chief competitors, the UK lacked the wherewithal to finance growth in research-intensive activities, and consequently UK exports remained mired in low value-added markets without growth prospects. Our own estimates, shown in Figure 5.6, confirm the sharp decline in profitability for UK manufacturing and the nonfinancial corporate sector up to the early 1980s, but also a significant rebound thereafter.

Eltis' view of the problem in 1996 did not stray far from Kaldor's in 1978, emphasizing the inadequacy of quality exports and loss of world market shares. Eltis, however, reached beyond these symptoms of lackluster performance on the part of British manufacturing to bring out its record of low profitability. In

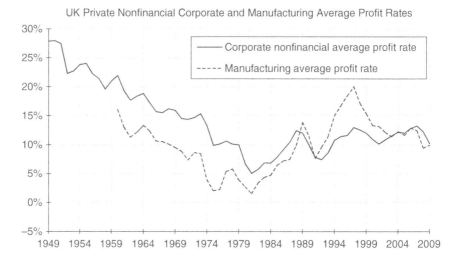

Figure 5.6 UK profit rates: corporate and manufacturing industries.

addition, Eltis blamed the highly volatile nature of British macroeconomic policy and its effects on GDP growth and inflation. Such policy produced successive periods of over-expansion and recession and created unnecessary turbulence in business expectations. Raising investment risks discouraged capital accumulation as well as R&D by raising the necessary rate of return that would compensate for the uncertainties involved. While real wages in Britain remained close to those in France or Germany, labor productivity levels were lower. Such a discrepancy existed, Eltis thought, due to inadequate skills training programs for workers and (echoing Pratten's and Richardson's views) inadequate management.

Showing the power of rising profitability to straighten up stagnant markets, the various deficiencies previously noted in the competitive performance of British manufacturing in the 1970s disappeared the following decade, for, as Eltis (1996, p. 194) saw it, "While wages increased, profits grew still more, and widened the share of profits in manufacturing industry to reduce one of the United Kingdom's greatest weaknesses."

Manufacturing profit rates in Germany, Japan, the UK, and US

As noted, the UK profitability trends shown in Figure 5.6 support Eltis' observations regarding the lower levels of British manufacturing industry from the early 1960s through 1980, compared to yields in the overall nonfinancial corporate sector. They also add weight to his appreciation of the remarkable profitability recovery evidenced from the early 1980s through that decade's end. After the mid-1990s, however, the manufacturing profitability trend reversed quite as sharply as it had previously risen.

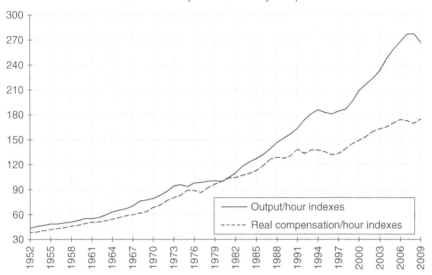

UK Manufacturing: Post-1980 Widening Gap Between Hourly
Labor Productivity and Real Hourly Compensation

—— Output/hour indexes

- - - - Real compensation/hour indexes

Figure 5.7 Behind the reversal in UK manufacturing profitability.

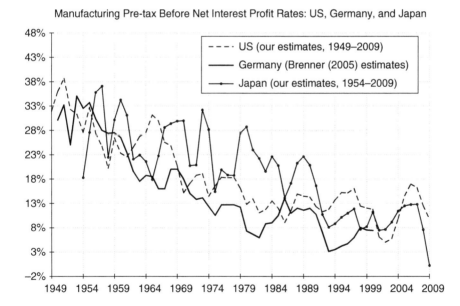

Manufacturing Pre-tax Before Net Interest Profit Rates: US, Germany, and Japan

- - - - US (our estimates, 1949–2009)

—— Germany (Brenner (2005) estimates)

—•— Japan (our estimates, 1954–2009)

Figure 5.8 Manufacturing profitability trends in Germany, Japan and the US.

The post-1980 reversal of previously downward profitability trends reflects the equally striking change in the relationship between labor productivity growth and real labor compensation from that year on, shown in Figure 5.7. While both time series rose more or less in tandem for thirty years after 1950, from 1980 on the gap between them grew persistently larger. The rise in manufacturing profitability derives from the growth of the "operating surplus" in that sector since labor productivity growth outpaced real labor compensation. This would explain why manufacturing profit rates in the UK not only reversed course after 1980 but rose above the average yielded by UK nonfinancial corporations in the 1990s. After reaching a peak in 1997, however, their sharp descent in the twenty-first century brought them below the performance of other corporate sectors. After a few years of stable yields, manufacturing profit rates fell below the average level of nonfinancial corporations again.

After 1980, the profitability trend reversal not only achieved success in the UK but also brought the profitability levels of British manufacturing within the international range enjoyed by the big international players, Germany, Japan and the US. Thus, UK manufacturing profitability managed to catch up and briefly surpass the average profitability level of the three major industry leaders after 1989 because they were all facing a long-run downward trend. As Figure 5.8 shows, noting the rise of UK manufacturing profitability to ranges comparable with the average levels enjoyed by these countries in the 1990s, one should not overlook the fact that, in these leading countries, profitability trends were much lower in that decade than in any other since the 1950s.

6 Heterodox models of technical change and profitability

Introduction

In this chapter we explore the views of three heterodox economists on how competition shapes the direction of technical change; that is to say, why competitive pressures force firms to choose increasingly capital-intensive techniques. A comparison of alternative heterodox theories of competition should help to frame the relevant issues surrounding the direction of technical change. We selected three representative accounts of this process, including those by D. Foley, T. Negishi, and A. Shaikh, each reflecting a different reading of classical political economy. They provide seminal interpretations of the rationale for the introduction of biased technical change in competitive industries, and of the available empirical evidence detailing its impact on labor productivity, wages, and prices. We specifically examine the impact of technical change on profitability trends from these three perspectives.

While individual firms, including industry leaders, wish to raise labor productivity, x, the nature of classical/Marxian technical progress reflects the competitive pressures stacked against them in their struggle to expand market shares. Surrounded by aggressive rivals, each individual unit of capital seeks to lower its unit costs by raising labor productivity as much as possible. But raising output per unit of labor time worked will generally require the expansion and modernization of fixed plant and equipment. The extra cost in fixed capital necessary will be compensated by a proportionally larger reductions in variable (that is, labor) costs, since the amount of raw and intermediate materials inputs processed should likely increase with output. Hence, it is argued, the rising capitalization of production should consist of capital-using, labor-saving techniques giving rise to falling output–capital ratios. Then even if wages lagged behind productivity growth, the relentless drive to raise the level of mechanization, to advance the capitalization of production, will, under normal conditions of capacity utilization, give rise to falling trends in average profitability as an unintended development.

The Foley–Marquetti–Michl efficiency schedule

In the Foley–Marquetti–Michl view of the dynamics underlying long-run classical/Marxian profitability trends, the rising capital intensity of production methods played a central role. Rising capital per worker, k, provides a measure of the progress achieved in transforming the labor process into a progressively more effective system. In a paper entitled "Economic Growth from a Classical Perspective," Foley and Marquetti (1997) constructed a simple diagram labeled "the efficiency schedule" which subsequently provided Foley and Michl the basic analytical platform for their textbook, *Growth and Distribution* (1999). After the original version of the wage–profit rate schedule appeared in the seminal book by Sraffa (1963), Foley and Marquetti expanded its analytical range. Profitability trends depend on the distribution of income between wages and profits and technological change. This efficiency schedule illustrates the logical structure behind the classical notion that wage and profit rates are inversely related.

In the extended interpretation of the efficiency schedule by these writers, the treatment of income distribution between profits and wages and the dynamics of technical change are inseparable: rising wage rates inevitably cause a falling profitability trend despite proportional increases in labor productivity. Marquetti's empirical work shows that technical progress in competitive industries is such that steady gains in labor productivity growth are generally associated with falling "capital productivity" trends (Marquetti, 2003; Marquetti and Mendoza, 2010). In other words, increasing capital–labor ratios are concomitant with the rising capitalization of production.

The efficiency schedule tracks patterns of income distribution between wages and profit rates. The real wage–profit rate relationship depicted shows the inverse relationship between wage rates and profit rates for a given output–capital ratio and labor-productivity level, that is, given the degree of capital intensity attained by the technology deployed. The diagram in Figure 6.1 shows the intersection of the efficiency schedule with the vertical axis setting the level of labor productivity, x, corresponding to a given technique of production at a certain stage of development. Its intersection with the horizontal axis denotes the capital intensity of production, as measured by the output–capital ratio, ρ. The slope of the schedule represents the degree of mechanization achieved with the technology employed, as measured by the capital–labor ratio:

$$\frac{x}{\rho} = \frac{X/N}{X/K} = \frac{K}{N} = -k.$$

The symbols used to represent the relevant variables comprising the efficiency schedule diagram necessary to derive the relationship between the relevant ratios are: $X = \text{GDP} = W + Z$; $W = \text{wages}$; $Z = \text{gross profits}$; $K = \text{capital stock}$; $D = \text{depreciation}$; $Y = \text{net output} = X - D$; $R = \text{net profits} = Z - D$.

The efficiency schedule is a powerful device to bring out the structural relationships among the following ratios and the direction in which technical change will push them: gross profit rate, $v = Z/K = (X - W)/K$; net profit rate, $r = R/K$; output per worker (labor productivity) $x = X/N$; capital intensity, $k = K/N$, a dollar measure of capital per worker; output–capital ratio,

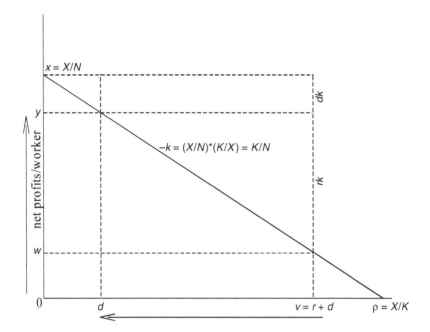

Figure 6.1 Foley's efficiency schedule.

$\rho = X/K = \frac{X/N}{K/N} = x/k$; depreciation rate, $\delta = D/K$; and net output–capital stock ratio, $y = Y/K = (X - D)/K = \rho - \delta$.

The nexus between profitability and the accumulation rate

In a regime of internally financed accumulation, the growth rate of the capital stock, $a = I/K$, defined as the ratio of investment per worker to the capital–labor ratio, is a function of profits per worker minus the overall consumption, C, of workers and capitalists per capita, relative to the capital–labor ratio:

$$a = \frac{I}{K} = \frac{I/N}{K/N} = \frac{Z/N - C/N^*}{K/N}.$$

The accumulation rate will rise as the gross operating surplus increases and consumption per capita is held unchanged. Conversely, as Figure 6.2 illustrates, a change in distribution caused by higher wages or expanded capitalist consumption will lower the profits per worker necessary to sustain the current rate of capital accumulation.

The real wage–profit rate efficiency schedule cuts the vertical axis at the point where the wage rate, w, equals output per worker, x, and hence the operating surplus disappears. Such contingency would yield a profit rate, r, which due to the

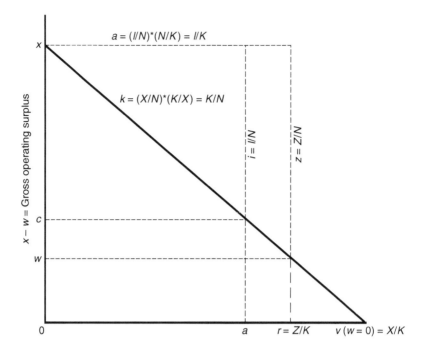

Figure 6.2 The transformed efficiency schedule.

absence of surplus should impose a negative rate of depreciation per worker, $-d$, bringing on the erosion of the capital stock. At the opposite end, wage rates falling to zero, $w = 0$, the distribution pattern yields the maximum profit rate, $v = Z/K = (X - W)/K = \rho$, which defines the output–capital ratio. Treating the wage rate as a residual in the income accounts, whether its components are taken as gross or net values of the output and profit variables per worker, yields

$$w = \frac{W}{N} = \frac{X}{N} - \frac{Z}{N} = \frac{X}{N} - \frac{D}{N} - \frac{R}{N}.$$

Thus, carrying the derivation from the gross values, the wage rate equals gross output per worker minus gross profits per worker, $w = x - vk$. In net terms, $w = y - rk = (x - \delta k) - rk$, the wage rate equals net output per worker minus net profits per worker (after subtracting depreciation). In any case, for a given technique of production with a given capital–labor ratio, represented by the slope, $-k$, of the linear schedule, wages per worker are the residual when profits per worker are subtracted from output per worker, that is, $w = x - z$. Alternatively, additional insight into the structure of the efficiency schedule emerges looking at the diagram from the standpoint of the output–capital ratio, ρ, instead of the wage rate. Thus the expression $w = x - z$ may be written as

$$w = x - x\frac{z}{k}\frac{k}{x} = x - x\frac{z/k}{x/k} = x - x\frac{v}{\rho} = x\left(1 - \frac{v}{\rho}\right).$$

And some manipulation of the expression yields

$$x\left(\frac{v}{\rho}\right) = x - w$$

$$xv = (x - w)\rho = (x - w)\frac{x}{k}$$

$$v = \frac{(x - w)x/k}{x} = \frac{x - w}{k} = \frac{x}{k} - \frac{w}{x}\frac{x}{k} = \left(1 - \frac{w}{x}\right)\rho.$$

Neoclassical and Marxian concepts of technical change

Changes to the efficiency schedule brought about by technical progress, as conceived in different economic paradigms, provide a convenient framework for comparing the contrasting assumptions behind them, regarding its effect on labor productivity, x, and output–capital ratios, ρ. Different pairs of x and ρ represent various types of technical progress. When x and ρ rise simultaneously, the new technique allows firms to save both capital and labor per unit of output. An increasing x/ρ ratio represents a higher capital–labor ratio, k, per unit of output.

Marx's views of the characteristic traits of technical progress, linked to the social production relations binding capital and labor in capitalist economies, differ from those held by neoclassical economics. Marx saw mechanization as an intrinsic force of capitalist development, gaining momentum and transforming the labor process as it advanced. Its purpose was to achieve an operation ever more capable of flawless production runs and less prone to conflictive disruptions: "it is the most powerful weapon for suppressing strikes, those periodic revolts of the working class against the autocracy of capital." (Marx, 1976, p. 562).

Mechanization involved the development of capital-intensive, labor-saving technologies that progressively grew into fully automated systems of production. In Marx's view of technological progress, more advanced methods led to increases in labor productivity precisely because automated systems allowed for increasing masses of raw materials to be processed by each worker. Such technical progress, however, lowered the maximum profit rate (the output–capital ratio), ρ, as it raised output per worker, x. On Marxian assumptions, given any level of the wage rate, a falling output–capital ratio, (the capital coefficient) ρ, will lower the gross profit rate, v.

Figure 6.3 illustrates the conceptual differences underlying the views of technical change held by neoclassical and Marxian economics. In parts (a)–(c), the changes brought about by technical change bring about increases in profitability.

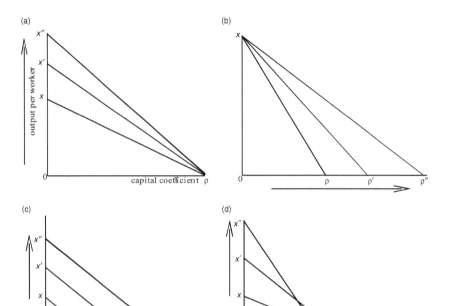

Figure 6.3 Alternative classifications of technical change: (a) Harrod-neutral; (b) capital-
saving; (c) Hicks-neutral; (d) Marxian.

Figure 6.3(a) reflects Harrod-neutral technical progress raising labor productivity without changing the capital coefficient. Figure 6.3(b) represents the case of
capital-saving or purely capital-augmenting technical change yielding the same
level of labor productivity but higher output–capital ratios. Figure 6.3(c) illustrates Hicks-neutral technical change meant to increase both labor productivity
and output–capital ratios. Finally, Figure 6.3(d) shows the effects of Marxian
technical change raising labor productivity but lowering output–capital ratios, the
structural dynamics underlying falling profitability trends.

Foley on technical change and profitability

Foley's account of the classical/Marxian argument concerning the introduction
of technical progress and its effect on falling profitability was comprehensively
worked out in his book *Understanding Capital* (1986). In that book Foley crit-
icized Okishio for denying that the entrepreneurial decision to introduce new

techniques of production could ever result in lower profitability for the innovator. The question remained, however, why any capitalist would choose to invest on new technology if the change produced a fall in profitability.

More recently, the issue has been addressed in a very clear and straightforward manner by Foley and Marquetti (1997) and Foley and Michl (1999). Both contributions worked out a model showing how a falling profitability trend could possibly emerge from the stream of technical progress most characteristic of capitalist development. Their argument grants that individual firms in the vanguard of innovation strategies will invest in technologies capable of raising their profitability. For such firms higher profitability is not only desirable as a general goal of business but also necessary to finance their expansion through higher rates of accumulation. The structural presence of such imperative actually defines the progressive nature of capital.

Capital-using techniques that increase labor productivity and lower unit costs relative to current wages and prices are "viable." Innovating firms consider three different profit rates to assess the viability of their innovating strategy. The starting point will be their current profit rate prior to the introduction of the innovation. Secondly, such firms should consider the "transient" profit rate they may expect to receive right after deploying their technical innovation but before the diffusion of such technology across the industry had an impact on prices and wages. Finally, they must evaluate the emerging profit rate, after all firms in the industry have matched their technical changes and the new lower product prices raised real wages.

Assuming a constant wage rate w, the profit rate will depend on the change in labor productivity x_t, and the output–capital ratio x_t/k_t, previously labeled ρ:

$$r_t = \frac{Q_t - w_t L_t}{K_t} = \frac{x_t - w_t}{k_t}.$$

The growth rate of labor productivity, γ_t, will be

$$\gamma_t = \frac{x_t - x_{t-1}}{x_{t-1}}$$

$$x_t = \gamma_t x_{t-1} + x_{t-1} = x_{t-1}(1 + \gamma_t).$$

The growth rate of the output–capital ratio, ρ, is given by

$$\chi_t = \frac{\rho_t - \rho_{t-1}}{\rho_{t-1}}$$

$$\rho_t = \chi_t \rho_{t-1} + \rho_{t-1} = x_{t-1}(1 + \chi_t).$$

Consequently, the derivation of the rate of profits in terms of the growth rates of both variables would involve two expressions, r and k:

$$r_t = \frac{Q_t - w_t L_t}{K_t} = \frac{x_t - w_t}{k_t} = \frac{x_{t-1}(1 + \gamma_t) - w_t}{k_t},$$

$$k_t = \frac{x_t}{\rho_t} = \frac{x_{t-1}(1 + \gamma_t)}{\rho_{t-1}(1 + \chi_t)}.$$

Hence, the profit rate is

$$r_t = \frac{x_{t-1}(1 + \gamma_t) - w_t}{k_t} = \frac{x_{t-1}(1 + \gamma_t) - w_t}{(x_{t-1}(1 + \gamma_t))/(\rho_{t-1}(1 + \chi_t))}.$$

As we know, movements of the profit rate reflect variations in income distribution in addition to changes in the output–capital ratio. The growth rate of the profit rate is given by

$$r'_t = \frac{dr_t}{dt} = \frac{x_{t-1} - w_{t-1}}{k_{t-1}}.$$

Defining the profit share, θ, as

$$\theta = \frac{x_{t-1} - w_{t-1}}{x_{t-1}},$$

and with lagged output–capital ratio

$$\frac{x_{t-1}}{k_{t-1}} = \rho_{t-1},$$

we obtain the expression for the Marxian profit rate as a function of the output–capital ratio, ρ, and the profits share, θ:

$$r_{t-1} = \frac{dr_t}{dt} = \frac{x_{t-1} - w_{t-1}}{k_{t-1}} = \frac{x_{t-1}}{k_{t-1}} \frac{x_{t-1} - w_{t-1}}{x_{t-1}} = \rho_{t-1}\theta.$$

Constant wage rates

Assume that the wage rate, $\bar{w}$, is held constant, rather than rising. The expression for the profit rate would show that its movement depends on the positive growth rate of labor productivity, γ_t, combined with the falling output–capital ratio. Because γ_t has a positive value in the numerator, $x_{t-1}(1 + \gamma_t)$, the profit rate should increase. The denominator of the expression, however, is set to grow faster. Since the denominator includes the rising labor productivity growth, $x_{t-1}(1 + \gamma_t)$, relative to the decreasing output–capital ratio, $\rho_{t-1}(1 + \chi_t)$, it should increase faster than the numerator in the profit rate expression. Hence, under the combined assumptions of rising labor productivity and a falling output–capital ratio, the profit rate should be falling even if wage rates failed to rise:

$$r_t = \frac{x_{t-1}(1+\gamma_t) - \bar{w}_t}{k_t} = \frac{x_{t-1}(1+\gamma_t) - \bar{w}_t}{x_{t-1}(1+\gamma_t)/(x_{t-1}(1+\gamma_t))}$$

$$= x_{t-1}(1+\gamma_t)\left[\frac{\rho_{t-1}(1+\chi_t)}{x_{t-1}(1+\gamma_t)}\right] = \rho_{t-1}(1+\chi_t).$$

Okishio assumed that money wages would not change after the introduction of superior techniques, despite the rise in labor productivity. He also assumed that the decline in unit costs would not prompt innovating firms to lower prices in order to gain market share. For the innovating firm achieving lower unit costs without a price change, technical progress must raise its profit rate, not lower it. Absent a rise in wage rates, innovators would not be motivated to adopt new productive methods unless they experienced a rise in profitability. As the innovator's profitability rose without that of the laggards falling, the average profitability of the industry would certainly rise as well. Diffusion of the new technology across the competitive industry, however, leads to lower prices and higher wages, as the bargaining position of labor is strengthened in tandem with the growth of labor productivity.

Foley's rejection of Okishio's argument relies on the observation that typically money wages rise along with technical progress. His chief objection to Okishio's denial of the claim that capital-using, labor-saving technical change leads to falling profitability centered on the rejection of Okishio's assumption that increases in labor productivity were possible without triggering pressures for wage increases. Foley argued that innovating firms need to stay ahead of their competitive rivals in order to gain market share. Since they can only enjoy above normal profits temporarily, their innovating activity must be sustained, as single innovations sooner or later lose their profit advantage once laggards catch up with them.

Foley argued that, once completed, the new realignment of costs and revenues would belie the initial judgment of technological viability. As the wage share recovers its previous level, the higher capital–output ratio brought about by the capital-using bias of innovations will depress the hitherto above normal profit rate of the innovators, leading to a decline in profitability across the industry as a whole. Foley accepts the "conventional wage share assumption" taken to be that "wages increase proportionately with labor productivity," so that evidence for rising wages in any period would likely follow the spread of technical progress beyond the control of individual capitalists.

While the Foley–Michl interpretation supports the Marxian notion of technical change exhibiting a distinct bias for capital-using, labor-saving characteristics, the cause of falling profitability is the rise in wages, a perspective previously advanced in the influential work of Maurice Dobb (Shaikh, 1978): "The fate of the average profit rate for the whole economy, however, depends on what happens to wages as labor productivity rises" (Foley and Michl, 1999, p. 121). In the Foley–Michl interpretation, falling profitability trends occur only if wages rise as much as labor productivity. In their view of labor history, which they share with Baumol, the working class appropriated the full benefits of technical progress. Innovating entrepreneurs, as the Foley–Michl text pointed out, time and again succumb to the "fallacy of composition," failing to appreciate that "actions that appear to be advantageous to individual capitalists are not always advantageous when all capitalists take them" (Foley and Michl, 1999, p. 121). Somehow individual entrepreneurs either fail to realize this fact or simply aim to collect whatever above normal profits come their way while the industry realignment following technological diffusion proceeds apace.

Figure 6.4 shows two efficiency schedules from the perspective of Marxian technical change. Initially, schedule $y\rho$ depicts net output per worker, y, and its associated net output–capital ratio, ρ. The second schedule, $y'\rho'$, tracks the changes brought about by the introduction of a superior technology. Net output per worker and the capital–labor ratio are higher, but the output–capital ratio is much lower: $y' > y$; $\rho' < \rho$; and $k' > k$. In Figure 6.4, the wage rate, w, remains unchanged and so does the consumption component of nonworkers, hence a constant consumption per capita, c. The net operating surplus increases from z to z'. Assuming that this surplus, after subtracting total consumption per capita, is the

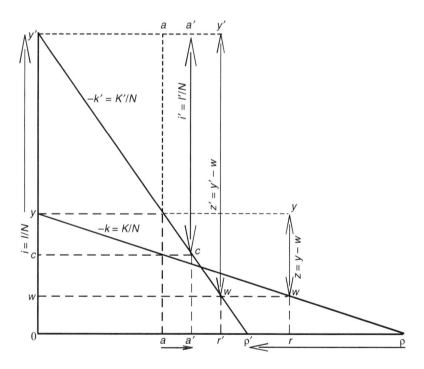

Figure 6.4 Marxian technical change.

source of accumulation funds, investment per worker, i', will rise from its previous level. The rise of investment per worker, i, can be predicted because the new output per worker, y', is so much higher than it was before the technical change occurred, although consumption per capita remained the same, c. Precisely because the capital–labor ratio of the new technique is higher, the accumulation rate, I/K, should increase from 0a to 0a$'$, and the net profit rate fall from r to r'.

Negishi's model of technical change

A central proposition found in models exploring the linkage between competitive forces and technical change holds that technical change of the kind postulated by Marx (capital-using, labor-saving) is viable only if its adoption raises the profitability of the innovating capitals. If it does not, entrepreneurs would not consider it, regardless of any advances of its technical design. Negishi accepted the validity of what he called the Shibata–Okishio theorem (Negishi, 1998) claiming that adopting biased technical change that led to a profit rate decline would invalidate the notion of rational entrepreneurial behavior (Negishi, 1989, pp. 222–223). Innovating firms, however, could enjoy higher profitability than their rivals after deploying cost-cutting techniques while accepting a profitability decline compensated by larger market shares.

Since the neoclassical model of perfect competition allows firms no control over market prices, the viability of new techniques gauged by their positive impact on profitability hinges on falling unit costs without a change in prices. Searching for a way out of this conundrum, Negishi considered the two prongs of the proposition that a decline in profitability given a "perfectly competitive equilibrium environment with a constant real wage" was impossible. On the one hand, Negishi argued that the notion of rising wages violated the core of classical/Marxian economic theory. Hence, he wished to preserve his belief that a "constant real wage (subsistence wage)" was a postulate of the Marxian theory of wages. In his model, wage rates remain constant at subsistence levels, on the assumption that such specification agreed with Marx's approach on the matter. In addition, Negishi rejected perfect competition as a suitable concept to evaluate the effects of technical change on profitability trends. Despite his sympathetic efforts to interpret Marx's views on competition, Negishi's search for a relevant competitive model, however, did not transgress the conceptual borders of neoclassical economics.

Negishi stressed that competition in Marx unleashed forces that led to declining profitability even when real wages remained unchanged. The ever-present drive for firms to expand derived from the declining cost of production associated with scale economies and the growing mass of profits that such expansion brought on. Negishi noted that growing firms faced declining, not infinitely elastic demand schedules. Hence, he suggested that, in order to properly understand the issues surrounding the effect of Marxian technical progress on profitability, "the Walrasian model of constant returns and perfect competition" should be set aside. In its place, Negishi endorsed Chamberlain's model of monopolistic competition, arguing that its relevance derived from the fact that in that model economies of scale and falling

unit costs received their due consideration. In a model of monopolistic competition, not unlike that of perfect competition, relatively large numbers of firms
carry on unconcerned with the behavior of other rival firms in the industry. Each
monopoly shares a portion of total demand and faces a downward-sloping demand
schedule, the steepness of which depends on its prices relative to the prices of its
competitors. Negishi accepted the view that technical progress characteristically
took the form of rising fixed capital costs compensated by declining total unit
costs. Generally increasing fixed capital costs would lower the profit rate calculated on the fixed capital stock, but in his view not if the decline in unit variable
costs far exceeded the rise in unit fixed costs.

Negishi distinguised between the effects of economies of scale with unchanged
techniques on the costs of production and the impact of innovations on the firm's
cost schedule. He noted that unit variable costs, reduced to unit labor costs, would
not change with the scale of production, but unit fixed costs would fall as output
expanded. While the level of fixed costs of production determined the depreciation
flow, the frequency and strength of technical progress established the depreciation
rate, not the physical wear and tear of plant and equipment.

Negishi on monopolistic competition

Negishi (1989, p. 227) shows how in the absence of technical change the representative firm under monopolistic competition attains its equilibrium position. The
equilibrium point, E, identifies the tangency between its current demand schedule, dd, and its average cost function, AA, drawn to reflect a normal average profit
derived from the general rate of profit.

Introducing a new technique of production having a higher capital–output ratio
involved higher fixed capital spending per unit of output but lower variable unit
costs. The firm's average cost schedule would change position, from AA to a
steeper schedule BB, reflecting lower unit costs at a higher level of output. After
deployment of the new technology, the firm could not maintain its current output, $0Q$, because at that level the new average cost would be higher than current
demand conditions justified. A higher output would be feasible if the expansion
did not require an excessive price reduction. As long as the new technique is not
widely adopted the pioneer firm will benefit from the advantages of lower unit
costs, receiving above normal profits.

In Negishi's version, the overall elasticity of the demand schedules facing each
firm would fall following the spread of new techniques across the industry. When
all firms raise their output in order to benefit from the cost reductions yielded
by technological change, the overall elasticity of their demand schedules would
decline. Once the individual demand schedules rotated to a position such as ED,
the demand line would be steeper than before the technology spread throughout
the industry, and the decline in price confronting each individual firm would likely
exceed the anticipated change *ex ante*.

The extent to which economies of scale materialized played a decisive role in
the final outcome. With unit costs falling rapidly, the average cost function would

be steeper than it was before the introduction of technical change, and the average cost schedule, *BB*, would remain above the post-diffusion demand schedule, *ED*, for a considerable range of output. Firms would be forced to expand output, and prices would fall substantially before reaching the new equilibrium point, *E'*. At the new equilibrium level of output the general profit rate associated with the average cost schedules would fall: "A falling rate of profit is possible if and only if the economies of scale achieved by each firm is rather less than expected when all the firms adopted the new technique" (Negishi, 1989, p. 229). Even if firms chose to consider the negative consequences of capital-using, labor-saving technical progress, they would have to weigh the disadvantages of discounted future lower profitability with the benefits of short-term above normal profit rates. Hence, they could well decide to carry through the changes repeatedly, believing it worthwhile to trade off higher current profit rates for likely lower profitability in future. Negishi's (1998, p. 254) final conclusion regarding technical choice was that "The falling rate of profit is a good example of the fallacy of composition in an irreversible process of technical innovation in a capitalist economy." Alternatively, firms failing to carry out the technical advances introduced by their more aggressive rivals could opt to enter other industries not yet affected by a fall in the normal level of profitability. But raising the accumulation growth rate in such industries would lower their market prices and pull their profit rates below pre-entry levels.

Baumol's nonaggressive innovations

Despite Baumol's claim that his theory of technical innovations sprung out of Marx and Schumpeter's concept of free competition and not from the neoclassical model of perfect competition, his own interpretation left out a key aspect of the classical approach. We may recall that Baumol's "oligopolists" are said to use their innovations as "competitive weapons," but these arsenals are not intended for offensive purposes but rather as means to preserve the peace, that is, the existing market shares. Fear of falling behind the industry leaders motivates each participant to finance R&D programs that result in technical blueprints preserving the ranking order of market shares in each industry. Efforts by aggressive firms to break up or reverse that order met with effective retaliation from the rest, thus nullifying the potential benefits derived from R&D expenditures by any maverick firm.

The distinction between innovations introduced by firms as "competitive weapons" but deployed in the pursuit of stable market shares and the same innovations deployed as weapons in competitive wars to gain market share is crucial to understand the price dynamics behind profitability trends. The spirit, if not the letter, of this seemingly passive-aggressive strategy of innovations is not inimical to neoclassical theories of equilibrium: innovations as "competitive weapons" are conceived as enforcers of equilibrium rather than armaments in the battle for larger market shares. The development of ever more powerful "competitive weapons" would lead to the impasse associated with a cold war, not a hot one.

In Baumol's interpretation of the nature of Marxian competition, his oligopolists are reluctant to engage in aggressive strategies designed to increase their market share. Indeed, firms seeking to break out of the existing competitive hierarchy would face additional spending on innovational R&D to achieve lower unit costs of production or (equivalently) higher product quality. But since other rivals would immediately match the expenditure, acquiring the same results, the decline in unit costs would not lead to any market share advantage for any one firm and the overhead costs would be higher for all. From this perspective, it would be foolhardy for a firm to trigger the escalation of overhead expenditures on R&D knowing that its strategy would inevitably fail.

Baumol's point here is that since innovations as competitive weapons lead to stability of shares even in a growing industry, a break in the discipline would lower profitability and would generally be avoided. While market strategy remains each firm's choice, allocating expenditures to prevent falling behind would be all that the development of "competitive weapons" requires. Excluding from his interpretation of Marxian competition the aggressive aspect of business strategy, Baumol's account effectively blocks the turbulent dynamics of profitability derived from understanding competition-as-war and its attendant coercive logic.

Competition-as-war and the cost of winning in Marx

The losses in market shares inflicted upon laggards by competitively successful firms cannot obviate the fact that such wars carry a cost for the winners. Moreover, the state of permanent hostilities sustained by increasingly more powerful contenders for market leadership, technologically and financially endowed with massive resources, precludes the chance of competitive battles raging with winners unscathed, suffering no losses. Adopting competitive techniques involves an extra cost to innovators, for, as Marx put it, "the increase in the productive powers [of labor] must be paid for" (Marx, 1993, p. 776).

Marx argued that mechanization provided the most sustainable form of technical change under capitalism to boost labor productivity and (even if wage rates remained unchanged) to lower real labor costs, the real wage, w, relative to labor productivity, y. It is important to stress that the force driving technical change ranging from tool-making to the most sophisticated systems of automated machinery springs from the class division at the core of capitalist enterprises, not from the rise in real wages. The penetration of technology throughout industry allows the growth in labor productivity to extend equally throughout sectors producing means of production and means of consumption. Hence, the unit labor values in Marx's Sector I for means of production, λ_k, as well as the unit labor values in Sector II for means of consumption, λ_L, should exhibit a falling trend, but the long-term ratio between the two, λ_k/λ_L, would remain roughly constant.

Now because the complex machinery processing the growing mass of material inputs transformed into a final product expands relative to the size of the labor force employed, Marx argued that the "technical composition of capital,"

K/L, will increase. The "value composition of capital" on the other hand, C/V, representing the labor value materialized in the stock of fixed capital, $\lambda_K K$, relative to the labor value equivalent of variable capital, consists of the product of unit labor values for consumption goods, the wage rate, and the number of workers employed, $\lambda_L wL$, that is,

$$\frac{C}{V} = \frac{\lambda_K K}{\lambda_L wL}.$$

As a precondition for rising labor productivity, such transformation implied that an increasing quantity of machinery and other intermediate inputs, K, would be involved in producing the finished output per unit of labor time: the mass of means of production would rise relative to the employed labor, L.

Marx's "organic composition of capital" reflects the impact of the rising mass of machinery upon the value composition. Since the relative unit labor values remain roughly constant or trendless while the mass of machinery relative to the employed labor rises, Marx argues that the organic composition of capital would tend to increase. In conventional national income accounting terms, the average profit rate, r, measuring realized profits in relation to the total capital advanced, may be written as

$$r = \frac{\Pi}{K} = \frac{Y - W}{K}$$
$$= \frac{\Pi/Y}{K/Y} = \frac{1 - W/Y}{K/Y} = \frac{1 - wL/Y}{K/Y}.$$

A rising profits share, Π/Y, that is profits, $1 - wL$, rising relative to the net output, Y, increases profitability but it does so at a diminishing rate. In the limit, as wages fall to zero and the whole conventional net value-added reverts to profits, the profit rate approaches its maximum value: the evolution of profitability would depend on the extent of mechanization and the rising capital–output ratio, K/Y.

The development of machinery reflected the competitive pressures confronting business firms on two fronts. Technological innovations as effective weapons in the arsenal of industry leaders intensified the lethal character of competition. Raising labor productivity allowed firms to extract more output per unit of labor time, thus reducing total unit costs. On that basis, they could lower their product price, undersell their competitors and gain market share. The increasing level of mechanization could conceivably raise the capital–output ratio beyond any intrinsic limit. The larger the share of the net product appropriated by capital as surplus profits, however, the more directly will falling output–capital ratios lower the (maximum) profit rate. In other words, the higher the achieved level of profits shares, the more strongly profitability trends would be affected by rising capital–output ratios and the weaker the impact on profitability of further expansion in profit shares.

Shaikh's theory of competition

In classical political economy, from the perspective of Smith, Ricardo, and Marx, competing capitalist firms rely on technological progress to increase their labor productivity, lower unit costs, increase market shares, and achieve higher profit rates than their rivals. After Adam Smith, the direction of technical progress pointed towards the introduction of methods raising the degree of mechanization and labor displacement. Marx argued that in the fullness of time, automated production systems would spread to all branches of the economy. Free competition would impose its coercive rules and set off storms of creative destruction that would alter market structures, bringing about higher concentration and centralization of capitals. Hayek and the Austrians shared with Marx the notion that the rising capitalization of production came at a cost for capitalist firms: their outlays for fixed capital would increase as the system of production lengthened and became more "roundabout." The mass of fixed capital per unit output would tend to rise as automation systems spread and labor productivity rose.

Marx defined competition as "the action of the many capitals upon one another" (Marx, 1982, p. 97). Competitive forces directed capital flows into industries with higher profitability and out of those with lower returns, hence sustaining the tendency for profit rate equalization in the various branches of the economy. In order to win competitive battles capitalists require technical methods capable of the "cheapening of commodities" (Marx, 1976, p. 777).

In the Marxian perspective, competition is a distinctly coercive force that forces leading firms to innovate and laggards out of business. Innovations are not just "competitive weapons" to maintain the hierarchy in market shares existing at any given time, but weapons to overhaul it. The development of science, technical change, and competitive wars occurred

> through the action of the immanent laws of capitalist production itself, through the centralization of capitals. One capitalist always strikes down many others. Hand in hand with this centralization, or this expropriation of many capitalists by a few, other developments take place on an ever-increasing scale, such as...the conscious technical application of science.
>
> (Marx, 1976, p. 929)

Competition forces firms in all sectors of the system to mechanize in order to remain competitive and profitable. The need to increase labor productivity applies to industries producing capital goods as well as consumer goods. While unit labor costs fall in both sectors, the growing technical composition of capital associated with mechanization involves a rising (though at a slower pace) capital–(net) output ratio.

Two path-breaking articles by A. Shaikh (1978, 1980) preceded Baumol's (2002) belated "discovery" of Marx's comments on the role of technical innovations in capitalist development. Drawing on Marx's mature views concerning differential rents in capital, Shaikh laid out a far richer micro-foundation of the dynamics governing the development of automated technologies as the characteristic form of technical change in advanced capitalism. He showed how the competitive struggle forced firms to adopt innovations in order to survive pressures to lower unit costs. Shaikh views competition as a struggle for market shares involving capitalist firms of diverse technological characteristics. Industry leaders use the best available technology, operate with the lowest unit costs and set the industry price at a level affording them the highest profitability. The other firms in the industry share less advanced techniques and therefore are saddled with higher unit costs. Facing a market price that tends to converge with the level set by leading firms with a cost advantage, technologically lagging firms enjoy lower profitability.

With the development of capitalism, the reduction of throughput time per unit of output achieved by leading firms due to technical change and the related expansion of their scale of production set the stage for falling unit costs and lower prices. The growing productive capacity of business enterprise fostered by the division of labor depended on increasingly discreet, specialized activities performed by workers aided by machinery in all facets of their work. As the division of labor advanced and new repetitive labor tasks proliferated, the grounds for accelerated mechanization of production activities requiring sequential coordination expanded. Indeed, for each working day stretching for a given number of hours, employers sought to extract the maximum output out of their labor force. The most effective way to accomplish this objective involved transformation of the productive methods themselves.

With Ricardo, classical political economy had anticipated the relentless progress of labor-saving mechanization and in Chapter XV of *Capital*, Volume I, Marx sought to systematize its impact on profitability, labor employment and wages. Shaikh's contributions built on the idea that complex machinery incorporates in its structural design the skills previously possessed by workers: "Any given level of mechanization presents the capitalist with the same problem all over again: the machine represents the ideal worker; the actual worker merely an imperfect machine" (Shaikh, 1978).

The most suitable conceptual framework for Marxian competition is that of war among the "many capitals" vying with "one another" for market leadership. Launching preemptive attacks on potential rivals threatening to achieve industry leadership and raising the capitalization of production is the most effective way to achieve it. Success requires better technological means than are generally available and effective strategies to deploy them effectively. Access to superior technology provides the weaponry to overrun established market positions, lower unit costs and prices. In this context, freedom of choice applied to technology adoption is constricted by the warlike context of industrial competition. A superior technique needs to prove itself in the field of competitive strategies. Only those methods that lower production costs merit consideration. Gaining market share at the expense of rival firms proves a firm's effectiveness, and driving them out of business proves its efficacy.

Shaikh's critique of Okishio's competitive model

To obtain a measure of profitability, firms may assess their profits, Π, relative to the flow of capital used up, k, that is, the "cost price" of production, and thus estimate their profit margins, m. Alternatively, profits, Π, relative to the stock of capital advanced, K, provide firms with estimates of their profit rate, r.

Okishio had shown that free competition promotes those firms that managed best to lower their "cost price" of production to positions of industrial leadership. Shaikh pointed out that while Okishio's argument regarding the profitability of innovations shared Marx's assumption that only techniques capable of lowering the unit cost price were viable, his neglect of fixed capital stocks merely proved that, holding wage rates constant, profit margins will rise. In other words, Okishio had not accounted for the impact of mechanization upon the growth of fixed capital per unit of output as a precondition for the reduction in the "cost price" of production.

Considering the tradeoffs between real wage rates and profit margins as well as profit rates for two methods of production, Shaikh represents one of them as handicraft methods, whose capital composition excludes fixed stocks, hence offers no distinction between profit margins and profit rates. The second method involving mechanization requires distinguishing between profit margins and profit rates. Adoption of the mechanized technique will raise the profit margin above the initial yield obtained with handicraft methods, but the corresponding profit rate for the mechanized technique will fall relative to that of handicrafts.

Shaikh's model of technical change

Shaikh (1998) developed a fresh analysis of technical choice and competition in connection with Robert Brenner's original and influential book on *The Economics of Global Turbulence*, published the same year. (The 2006 Verso edition of this book, listed in our Bibliography, extends Brenner's time horizons from 1945 to 2005.) Shaikh's argument focused on sorting out the causes behind the falling profit rates in US manufacturing from the 1960s to the mid-1980s. To that end Shaikh drew a diagram depicting the range of choices confronting innovators facing competitive battles. Initially, the innovating firm, despite being poised at the cutting edge of technical progress, is still operating with an "old technique" of production represented by the "Old" schedule. At the current product price, this yields the firm a certain profit rate. Then two new methods come under consideration, both better than (superior to) the "Old" one currently used, labeled New (A) and New (B).

If the choice between superior techniques hinged on estimates of higher profitability made by innovators neglecting the impact of technological diffusion on the current price, method New (A) would be preferred. But once such technique replaced older methods throughout the industry, the innovating firm and the imitators would find that lower prices depress their profit rate to the level yielded by the Old method.

On the other hand, if the technique labeled New (B), requiring a higher investment per unit of output, is introduced, allowing innovating firms to achieve unit costs of production well below the range of other firms using New (A) methods, they will acquire an absolute competitive advantage. Such change enables firms deploying New (B) technology to push their price low enough to encroach on the market share of all their rivals and thus emerge from the turmoil with the highest profit rate in the industry. Major reductions in price should wipe out the profitability of firms unable to replace the Old technology with New (B) methods. With lower prices encroaching on the market shares of laggards and innovators operating with the lowest unit costs, they will receive the highest profit rates in the industry.

Higher capital outlays per unit output, however, will lower the innovators' profit rate compared to previous stages of competitive growth. The magnitude of the initial price reductions will depend on the technological power of the New (B) method to reduce unit costs, and the intensity with which rival firms can retaliate in kind.

Measuring profitability: gross versus net capital stock

As Shaikh (1999a) pointed out in his critique of Brenner's 1998 account of the *Economics of Global Turbulence* (see Brenner, 2006), profitability estimates crucially depend on the specific method adopted to measure the fixed capital stock. Using the perpetual inventory method, national income accounting traditionally distinguished between current cost, gross and net capital stocks. Gross estimates of the capital stock at year-end, GCS_t, refer to the current replacement cost of all fixed assets in use, that is, their full undepreciated capital values at any time, by new ones of similar type and matching quality:

$$GCS_t = GCS_{t-1} + GCF_t - R_t.$$

The gross capital stock, GCS_t equals the gross capital value in the previous period, GCS_{t-1}, plus current gross capital formation spending, GCF_t, minus current capital assets retirements, R_t. This measure acknowledges the fact that with proper maintenance and repairs the contribution of all assets to the final output may not change appreciably before retirement. On the other hand, their effectiveness is terminated suddenly once their service life is ended (Hill, 1998). Net capital stock, NCS_t, at year-end, on the other hand, represents the current replacement cost of the existing fixed assets, calculated as the net capital stock in the previous year, NCS_{t-1} plus the current gross capital formation spending, GCF_t, after subtracting current depreciation, D_t:

$$NCS_t = NCS_{t-1} + GCF_t - D_t$$

In the initial year, gross and net capital stocks are identical. As time passes, subtracting the accumulated depreciation incurred throughout their service life lowers

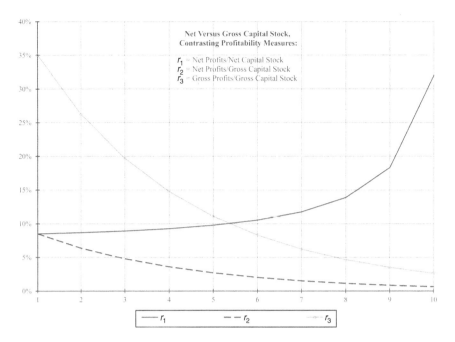

Figure 6.5 Net versus gross capital stock: impact on profitability.

the replacement costs of net capital stocks relative to the gross measure. Using this accounting method, total depreciation charges are deducted even if the asset's efficiency did not necessarily diminish with time.

Figure 6.5 and Tables 6.1–6.3 show the evolution of the relevant variables behind profitability trends using gross and net measures for a fixed capital asset (a piece of equipment) with a purchase price of $2000. It is assumed that this asset will have a service life of 10 years, at the conclusion of which it will be retired. Columns 1 and 2 in Table 6.1 show declining annual depreciation charges for this asset and their corresponding accumulation for 10 years before its retirement. Columns 3 and 4 list the resulting changes in the net and gross capital stock measures: the net values falling sharply and the gross remaining constant at $2000.

Assuming declining asset effectiveness and depreciation during its service life, falling estimates of gross and net value-added during the asset's service life will have divergent impacts on profitability, depending on the measure of capital value used. Output–capital ratios will fall throughout the 10 years of the assumed life service for gross stocks, but such ratios will rise if net capital measures are used. The practical significance of this difference for our empirical estimates derives from the fact that the US Bureau of Economic Analysis discontinued issuing gross capital stock estimates after 1994, publishing from then on only data on net capital stocks.

Table 6.1 Alternative measures of the capital stock (10 years): net and gross of depreciation

	Annual depreciation $Dep(t) = Dep(t-1) * (1-0.25)$	Accumulated depreciation $AcDep(t) = Dep(t-1) + Dep(t)$	Net capital stock $NK(t) = NK(t-1) - Dep(t-1)$	Gross capital stock $GK(t) = NK(t) + AcDep(t-1)$
1	530	530	2000	2000
2	397	927	1470	2000
3	298	1225	1073	2000
4	224	1449	775	2000
5	168	1616	551	2000
6	126	1742	384	2000
7	94	1836	258	2000
8	71	1907	164	2000
9	53	1960	93	2000
10	40	2000	40	2000

Table 6.2 Gross and net measures of value-added and profits (percent)

	Gross Value-Added $GVA(t) = GVA(t-1) * (1-0.25)$	Net Value-Added $NVA(t) = GVA(t) - Dep(t)$	Gross Profits $GP(t) = GP(t-1) * (1-0.25)$	Net Profits $NP(t) = GP(t) - Dep(t)$
1	1600	1070	700	170
2	1200	803	525	128
3	900	602	394	96
4	675	451	295	72
5	506	339	221	54
6	380	254	166	40
7	285	190	125	30
8	214	143	93	23
9	160	107	70	17
10	120	80	53	13

Table 6.3 Alternative output–capital ratios and average profit rates

	Net Output/Gross K NVA(t)/GK(t)	Net Output/Net K NVA(t)/NK(t)	Net Profits/Net K GP(t)/GK(t)	Net Profits/Gross K NP(t)/GK(t)	Gross Profits/Gross K NP(t)/NK(t)
1	53.5	53.5	8.5	8.5	35.0
2	40.1	54.6	8.7	6.4	26.3
3	30.1	56.1	8.9	4.8	19.7
4	22.6	58.3	9.3	3.6	14.8
5	16.9	61.4	9.8	2.7	11.1
6	12.7	66.2	10.5	2.0	8.3
7	9.5	72.8	11.7	1.5	6.2
8	7.1	87.3	13.9	1.1	4.7
9	5.4	115.3	18.3	0.9	3.5
10	4.0	201.3	32.0	0.6	2.6

7   Capital–output ratios in retrospect

Introduction

Because long-term capital–output ratios play such a central role in the assessment of profitability trends, and conventional wisdom in mainstream as well as heterodox economics assumes them constant or falling, in this chapter a fresh look at the historical record proved unavoidable. We found the widely accepted assumptions underpinning the foundations of growth models not confirmed by the findings of leading economic historians. Angus Maddison (1991, p. 83), for instance, warned that the presumption of constant long-term capital–output ratios commonly found in neoclassical and post-Keynesian growth models was unsubstantiated. But despite his widely recognized contributions to the study of long-run trends in capitalist development, Maddison's counsel remained largely ignored. Our criticism of the conventional view derived from evidence uncovered by Maddison's own investigations, as well as the findings of ground-breaking studies by Abramovitz and David (1973), Gallman (1986), and Atack *et al.* (2003) challenging conventional views on capital–output trends in the US economy from the nineteenth to the earlier part of the twentieth century.

The perception that technical progress behind labor productivity growth involved capital deepening or "more roundabout modes of production" was shared by leading economists in the late nineteenth century. Despite different theoretical outlooks, their research showed that capitalist industrialization proceeded on the basis of rising capital–output trends. As Abramovitz and David saw it, recognizing the crucial role played by Harrodian labor-saving, capital-deepening technological change in the economic development of Western capitalism was essential to gain a good understanding of its real underpinnings. Looking back at the changes brought about by triumphant industrialization, late nineteenth-century economists of very different persuasions shared this view of economic development. On the whole, they were quite ready to recognize the large rise of capital–output ratios as a necessary characteristic of the growth in productive capacity.

Capitalist expansion and the secular rise of capital–output trends received recognition as intrinsically connected not only by Marx, but also Sidgwick (1883), Taussig (1896), and Bohm-Bawerk (1896), among others. While this group of late nineteenth-century economists reached this conclusion theoretically, they were undoubtedly impressed by direct observation of the emerging industrial economy, even though their conceptual presuppositions obviously differed substantially in many other respects.

In his "Survey of the Theory of Process-Innovations", the historian of economic thought Mark Blaug (1963) pointed out that from the late nineteenth century through the 1930s leading economists, regardless of their orientation, shared the belief that capital–output ratios rose due to the increasing mechanization of production:

> None of them doubted that technical change had been overwhelmingly labor-saving in the past. The growing influence of the Austrian theory of capital around the turn of the century, emphasizing as it did capital formation which increases the durability of plant and equipment further encouraged the belief that economic development, even when technical change is allowed for, typically entails not only an increase in capital per man but also a steady rise in capital requirements per unit of output.
>
> (Blaug, 1963, p. 23)

Paul David's research emphasized that Sidgwick and Taussig acknowledged the fact that rising capital–output trends emerged as an intrinsic characteristic of industrialization in the modern world:

> Contemporary observers understood what was happening during the closing quarter of the nineteenth century in terms that were closely related to this. They spoke of technological progress as achieving gains in the productivity of labor by increasing the "roundaboutness" of production; innovations could be incorporated into production, on this view, only by the agency of raising the economy's stock of tangible capital goods in relation to the real flow of final goods and services. Or, putting the point slightly differently in the terminology of those times, "the progress of invention" was tending to raise the physical capital-output ratio that producers would choose at any given level of the real rate of interest.
>
> (David, 2004, p. 38)

Indeed, Sidgwick (1883, p. 158) was persuaded that "Hitherto, Inventions have generally had the effect of complicating and prolonging the processes of industry, while at the same time increasing the ultimate productiveness of labor," and Taussig (1896, pp. 10–11) argued that "Hence it has been laid down as a general proposition...that every increase in the efficiency of labor brings with it an extension in time of the process of production," while for Bohm-Bawerk (1896, p. 128) "the rule that a larger product is secured by the more roundabout process" was a given in capitalist economies.

The momentous impact that technological progress had on the expansion and scale of fixed capital clearly led these economists to appreciate the role of rising capital–output trends in bringing about increasing levels of labor productivity and growing shares of property income. Late nineteenth-century economists directly observed the increasing scale of capital investments fueled by growing masses of profits: these were the hallmarks of a fast expanding, progressive industrial capitalism. Once the first three decades of capital accumulation in the twentieth century ended in depression, however, the notion that rising capital–output ratios were a sign of industrialization and an expression of the rising capitalization of production lost its conceptual appeal. The perspective on capital–output trends held by the earlier economists gave way to revisionist views involving the nature of technological progress and the development path.

Abramovitz and David: nineteenth-century US capital–output trends

In their 1973 essay aiming to identify the driving forces of American economic growth, Abramovitz and David sought to dispel the notion fostered by neoclassical growth theory that achieving a "modern" rate of output per capita required a "balanced growth path." They denied that historical records confirmed that real economic growth required all the characteristics propounded by neoclassical models, including the equality between the rate of capital accumulation and output growth, as well as constant savings rate and Harrod-neutral technical progress. They also questioned the assumption of steady growth in the capital–labor ratio capable of raising labor productivity at just the rate needed to maintain a constant profit rate on capital.

Against this conceptual framework, Abramovitz and David proposed that the actual growth path of the American economy exhibited a "sequence of technologically induced traverses": a number of growth stages periodically lifting the overall development path to higher levels of output per capita. In their view rising capital accumulation and wealth–output ratios were the critical forces responsible for the achievement of rising output per capita, not the "growth rate of total factor productivity" which in the nineteenth century remained strikingly small compared to the 4 percent growth rate in real GDP. Labor productivity, on the other hand, rose significantly, increasing between 1835 and 1890 by 0.75 percent annually, largely sustained, Abramovitz and David indicated, by the "near doubling of the reproducible capital-gross product ratio." Such an increase in accumulation required the savings ratio to rise, as they put it, "dramatically from about 10 percent before 1840 to 16 to 20 percent in the decades immediately preceding the Civil War," to top the 25 to 30 percent level in the last three decades of the century. This impressive expansion of savings was possible by the increase in the profits share between the first thirty-odd years of the nineteenth century and its last decade, from 23 percent to 37 percent (1973, p. 437).

Gallman's nineteenth-century capital–output trends

Gallman's (1986) findings, calculated in current and constant prices, confirmed the Abramovitz–David estimates showing that the nineteenth century's capital stock grew faster than the GNP. His data drew from the six "reasonably comprehensive" federal Census surveys on national wealth carried out between 1850 and 1900. For the earlier period of the nineteenth century, from 1805 to 1840, Gallman relied on the information collected by "able and informed contemporaries," but the main body of his findings concerned the years after 1840.

Gallman interpreted the available Census data on plant and equipment as referring generally to current cost replacement, not book values. He also concluded that the Census surveys sought to ascertain the net, not the gross capital values, because the figures published either closely matched or fell below calculations made on the basis of the perpetual inventory method. Between 1840 and 1850, leaving out farm structures, three fifths of the agricultural capital stock consisted of land improvements, such as clearing, fencing, draining and irrigating farm projects. This proportion fell below 50 percent by 1900. In constant prices, improvements to farmland made up two thirds of the national capital stock in 1840 but declined to one third in 1900. On the other hand, the proportion of machinery and equipment rose in constant prices from one twentieth in 1840 to over one fourth in 1900 (Gallman, 1986, p. 193).

Gallman's reading of the evidence for the ninetieth century's record of growth and mechanization in the US economy reveals a picture of development consistent with earlier economic perceptions regarding capital–output trends. Gallman calculated the growth rates for the national capital stock using two categories, A and B. Category A included investments to improve farming, such as "fencing and the construction of drainage and irrigation ditches," and category B ignored all such improvements to agricultural lands other than construction. The anomalous trend found in the period 1860–1880 showing a falling capital–output ratio did not happen due to the slowdown in the growth rate of equipment stocks or inventories. In fact Gallman noted that inventories rose moderately if calculated in current or constant prices, while the growth in equipment stocks did not fall in current prices and sharply increased when measured in constant ones. What declined drastically was the part of the capital stock pertaining to "farm improvements" in relation to the GNP, and Gallman attributed this trend reversal to the disruptive effects of the Civil War.

As a whole, interpreting the development path of the US economy in the nineteenth century led Gallman (1986, p. 198) to conclude: "It would be fair to say, then, that the upward movement of the national capital/output ratio ... represents a fairly pervasive movement, affecting the chief industrial sectors." One decisive factor that Gallman found responsible for the long-term rise in the capital–output ratio after the Civil War was the persistent decline in interest rates, both nominal and real.

Carl Snyder on US capital–output trends, 1880–1930

We do not have detailed empirical studies of secular trends in capital–output ratios until the 1930s. In that decade, though, Keynes' *General Theory* challenged the theoretical structure of neoclassical economics, stressing the importance of profit expectations and uncertainty to explain the volatility of effective demand, chiefly the rate of investment. Neoclassical economics could not account for the 1930s depression since it denied or excluded the possibility of prolonged slumps, and posited full employment equilibrium as the natural tendency for unregulated markets. On the contrary, Keynes rejected Say's law as well as the assumption of full-employment equilibrium tendencies. In a growth context, Harrod's transformation of the Keynesian short-term model into a dynamic one expressing the conditions for balanced growth required the assumption of a constant capital–output ratio to sustain the balanced growth path.

In the midst of the 1930s depression, however, Carl Snyder's (1936) article "The Capital Supply and National Well-Being" outlined an alternative argument, shared by leading economists of the late nineteenth century that totally bypassed the Keynesian approach. Snyder built his own dynamical approach upon two basic premises: first, capital accumulation over the past century had taken the form of growing mechanization of production, leading to sharply increasing labor productivity and significantly reduced average costs; and second, industrial profits funded capital accumulation and technical progress, hence they should not be excessively taxed. In this work, moreover, Carl Snyder broke new ground in collecting data on capital–output ratios in US manufacturing from 1880 to 1930. Snyder's views coincided with the earlier writings of Sidgwick, Taussig, and Bohm-Bawerk, while ignoring the Keynesian contribution as well as the nascent neoclassical approach: its theoretical thrust remained consistent with the legacy of classical political economy. All these economists were staunch supporters of capitalism. Carl Snyder's work in the mid-1930s uncritically advanced an unabashed paean of corporate profits, for him the crucial element to preserve capitalism mired in mass unemployment. Yet his orientation did not lead him to adopt neoclassical visions of how capitalism achieved steady-state growth in the absence of external shocks. While not able to explain the depression juggernaut, these writers could not ignore the changing relationship between capital accumulation and the growth rate of output. Snyder recognized the turbulence of historical trends in capital accumulation, rejecting neoclassical growth theories and their vaunted equilibrium growth paths.

As a pioneer in statistical analysis of industrial development, Snyder focused on the long sweep of economic history, spanning a century of industrialization, and emphasized that unit costs had drastically fallen with the passing of time in every sector of industrial production, including agriculture. Snyder estimated that, while in the first 30 years of the twentieth century the annual growth rate of manufacturing industry output in the US averaged about 4 percent, the growth of capital investment exceeded it, at 5–5.5 percent. The 1930s depression interrupted this secular path of progress and between 1930 and 1935 no net gain in national wealth was recorded, hence no profits and no capital accumulation. In his 1940 book *Capitalism the Creator*, Snyder concluded that:

> For every dollar of additional value added per annum in manufacturing, as far back at least as 1850, something more than an additional dollar of new capital has apparently been required. The ratio of capital to annual value of product

has been rising slowly in the eighty years from 1850 to 1930, so that it now requires nearly twice as much capital to produce a given value of output.

(Quoted in Stern, 1945, p. 169)

Snyder reported that, for instance, wheat production had experienced a sharp reduction in cost per bushel, not because the quality of the soil had improved but rather due to the massive introduction of labor-saving machinery. Thus, whether the chosen sector was agriculture or automobile production, the kind of technical change underlying industrial progress reduced the labor time required per unit to a fraction of the original count. Snyder's (1936) paper clearly followed on the steps of late nineteenth-century classical economists, when theories had not yet hardened into neoclassical or Keynesian frameworks, selecting only those features of the private enterprise economy deemed historically progressive. His paper abstract reads:

Discovery and computation of new data as to the value and volume of manufactures, horse-power and capital employed seem to reveal the precise mechanism by which the wondrous industrial advance of the United States in the last century and more has been achieved. The essential of this prodigious advance has been a corresponding supply of new capital, and this capital appears to have been derived almost wholly and directly from the industries themselves, from high profits, and not from imaginary "national savings." It is this capital, invested in machinery and the development of new processes, which alone has made possible the increase in product per worker, and the resulting gain in real wages and in general well-being.

(Snyder, 1936)

At the outset Snyder reflected on the "amazing decline" that the labor cost of producing a bushel of wheat had experienced in the past 100 years, which he hazards at 80 percent of the original. He attributed this feat to the use of machinery. In the previous 100 years, he argued, the growth of fixed capital reduced the "field time" in the production of a bushel of wheat from 60-odd hours to one or two "on a highly mechanized Kansas wheat farm."

The same transformation occurred in every other industry. Snyder estimated that in the last 100 years, the use of machinery in the automobile industry had cut the cost per car by 80 percent. In fact, Snyder managed to produce "an index of primary mechanical power" measuring the "horse power" potential in all industry, showing a clear parallelism with manufacturing output. Massive doses of machinery simultaneously absorbed monumental quantities of capital investments. The capital invested in manufacturing, however, "increased at a somewhat higher rate due, as may be surmised, largely to the steady rise in the cost of machinery, owing to the growing complexity and intricacy of these mechanical miracles." The point that Snyder wished to stress, repeatedly, was that the progress achieved in raising labor productivity, or lowering unit labor costs, inevitably involved an expansion of fixed capital and therefore a growth of fixed costs per unit output. Increasing unit fixed capital costs was the dual of lowering not only unit labor costs but necessarily total unit costs. For that to happen the reduction in variable costs, largely wages, due to lower labor requirements, exceeded the rise in fixed capital costs. Drawing from his empirical work, Snyder forcefully argued that the growing need for capital to maintain output precluded any serious consideration of policy proposals limiting profit growth through taxation.

The centrality of profits in Snyder's view

The other side of Snyder's argument was that rising investments in fixed capital required a correspondingly expanding flow of funds to implement them. He derided the notion that "national savings" could ever be a suitable source for industrial investment funding, for in his view the savings undertaken by people outside corporate business were both too small and not usually available for capital accumulation. Household savings, large or small as they may be, were typically channeled into the purchase of houses or fixed-income assets like bonds. For Snyder, corporate profits were the chief source of funding for fixed capital assets. Corporate savings, the profits retained after payment of taxes and dividends, provided the lion's share of corporate capital needs: "a dollar for dividends and a dollar for betterments."

Since the growth of industrial plant and equipment was essential to sustain the growth in labor productivity, which was the basis for the impressive reductions in unit costs of production, Snyder rejected any calls for increases in social welfare programs financed by taxing corporate profits. He argued that the stagnation and collapse of corporate profits preceded the massive growth in unemployment during the depression. Snyder himself had no plausible explanation for the profits collapse that preceded the depression, limiting himself to point out the lack of evidence to indict the usual suspects: sector imbalances, overproduction or underconsumption maladjustments. Instead, Snyder suggested, excesses in credit growth throughout the 1920s caused the financial speculation and stock market volatility that totally unraveled financial markets and triggered the collapse of the real economy.

Snyder further argued that improving the standard of living in the depression years required increasing labor productivity, but such increases could not depend on costless improvements in workers' "efficiency": he did not think that the average worker in the 1930s was more efficient, skillful or industrious than his predecessors 100 years earlier. Increases in labor productivity since the Industrial Revolution required costly investments in improved machinery. Therefore in order to bring about the fruits of technical progress, this "expensive and complicated new machinery," a certain percentage of the labor force needed to work in activities that produced it. That proportion typically grew along with the wealth of nations, which in this context referred to the mass of profits available to fund "exploration, research, new machinery, and the development of new processes."

On the basis of Snyder's long-term estimates of capital–output ratios in US industry, Ernest Stern (1945) set out to assess "the order of magnitude of the capital requirements with which the various countries will be faced once they have repaired the damage wrought by the war." While Snyder had limited himself to examining the historical record regarding capital–output ratios, Stern wished to use those estimates as benchmarks for future capital needs. He was concerned to find how the rising incremental capital–net output ratio, as it applied to producers' equipment, structures and inventories, would affect the necessary balance between aggregate supply and demand. Summarizing his findings, Stern concluded that in future "the expansion of economic activity" in the major industrial countries would require a rate of investment spending high enough to increase the "stock of capital at the average rate of, say, between 2 and 3.5 times" the growth of net output. For the US Stern found that with an incremental capital–output ratio of 3.3 "the net capital requirements per unit increase in net output" would rise to around 10% of the net product. Thus, Stern joined Snyder in cautioning that Keynesian policies such as state funding of employment programs that did not expand productive capacity, would fail to achieve the desired results. Conservative economists were not alone in acknowledging the likelihood of a secular rise in capital–output ratios. Before the War, two progressive Keynesians temporarily accepted the likelihood of rising capital–output trends. As we saw in Chapter 4, Kaldor himself supported this view and Joan Robinson also subscribed to it in the 1930s. Statements by Robinson (1937) and Kaldor (1939) unambiguously expressed their support at the end of a depression decade characterized by minimal investment. Following Hicks in his *Theory of Wages* (1963, pp. 125–126) on the nature of technical progress, Kaldor (1939, pp. 56–66) argued then:

> It is sometimes suggested that while capital saving inventions do occur, the majority of inventions is more likely to be labour-saving than capital-saving. If this is so, then technical progress has the effect of creating a secular (or trend) increase in the capital intensity of production... Unless additional machines are increasingly labour-saving there will sooner or later be a deficiency of labour to work with them and their product (and value) will fall.

That the growth in labor productivity owed its astounding ascendancy to the increasing capitalization of production, Joan Robinson (1937) readily accepted:

> It appears obvious that the development of human methods of production, from the purely hand-to-mouth technique of the ape, has been mainly in the direction of increasing "round-aboutness," and the discovery of short cuts, such as wireless, are exceptions to the general line of advance.
>
> (Quoted in Blaug, 1963, p. 22)

Both of them, of course, reversed themselves once the postwar recovery gained momentum and the economic upswing strengthened the sway of neoclassical economics. In the event, Kaldor's traverse on this issue went furthest, taking him to propose several variants of a growth model which, along with Solow's, inevitably achieved equilibrium paths via all sorts of constancies, including profitability, capital–output ratios, and others.

Capital deepening in nineteenth-century US manufacturing

In a paper devoted to studying the direction of capital–output trends in nineteenth-century manufacturing, Atack *et al.* (2003) examined direct data collected by Census surveys and used it to assess the degree of capital deepening in American establishments. For purposes of measuring the changes experienced in capital–output ratios, the authors focused on the evolution of capital-deepening trends. They chose the years 1850–1880 because that period witnessed great technological advances in manufacturing techniques, involving the widespread introduction of steam power in the factories, replacing artisans and waterpower. The increase in labor productivity so achieved was decisive in the transition, and as long as such gains "were proportionately smaller than any increase in the capital–labor ratio, the capital–output ratio will be higher in the factory than in the artisan shop" (Atack *et al.*, 2003, p. 15).

Atack *et al.* found that "the aggregate capital–output ratio was about thirty percent higher in 1880 than in 1950," calculated in nominal terms. Deflating the manufacturing capital stock by an index that declined faster than the output's, Atack *et al.* estimated that "real capital per (constant dollar) of output was between seventy and one hundred percent higher on average in 1880 than in 1850." Despite the decline in the relative price of capital goods, the authors were satisfied that "Virtually all of the increase in the real ratio during the 1870s, however, occurred because of pure capital deepening" and was not caused by the movement of relative prices. They found evidence supporting the view that by and large the establishment size was positively correlated with the capital–output ratio. In fact, it was the largest manufacturing establishments that pioneered in the use of the new technology and it was in such factories where the sharpest increases in capital deepening (i.e. capital–output ratio) took place.

Regarding the data collected in these Census surveys on capital values, Atack *et al.* shared the view expressed by Robert Gallman, "the leading authority" on empirical history of the nineteenth century, that in the surveys "the capital figures refer typically to market value or net reproduction cost." Fixed capital consisted of equipment and structures, while so-called working capital referred largely to inventories and raw materials. A question that remained unsettled, despite all efforts, was the extent to which Census figures on capital stocks included working capital. To account for this quandary, Atack *et al.* estimated two sets of index numbers for the capital–output ratio in nineteenth-century American manufacturing.

Atack *et al.* calculated their "real" indexes for capital–value-added ratios, multiplying their nominal values by the output deflator–capital stock deflator ratio. These indexes fell from 1 in 1849 to 0.76 in 1879. In their data tables, columns designated as A refer to index numbers assuming that the Census surveys data reported both fixed and working capital stocks. Indexes in columns labeled B reflect a reading of the Census data measuring exclusively fixed capital stocks, requiring Atack *et al.* to produce their own estimates of working capital stocks to augment the fixed capital data. They did so taking the 1890 Census data which explicitly included working capital estimates as benchmark ratios for the surveys preceding it. This procedure assumed that working capital from 1850 to 1890 was used in the same fixed proportion relative to gross output as in the 1890 report.

Rising manufacturing capital–output ratios and profit rates

Obviously such sizable increases in capital–output ratios would lower manufacturing rates of return. Atack *et al.* found that, surprisingly, those establishments whose size and technological superiority qualified them to assume industry leadership appeared to enjoy lower profit rates than the smaller factories employing less advanced methods. Their calculation of sector-wide profit rates involved subtracting from value-added wages plus depreciation charges; such measure of profits was then divided by the survey data on capital, with the assumption that it referred to total capital stock (at replacement value). Alternatively, where the surveys excluded working capital, their own measure of total capital stock added estimates for working capital stocks.

Relating factory size, capital–output ratios, and rates of return, Atack *et al.* came up with "the most intriguing finding": namely, that the largest establishments, those deploying the most advanced technologies (and reaching the highest capital–output ratios), enjoyed lower profit rates than the smaller establishments. It is noteworthy, however, as Atack *et al.* pointed out, that smaller manufacturing shops were only sporadically active, while their closing rate was much higher than it was for larger factories operating all year round.

Taking into account this divergence between the operating resilience and survival rates of large and small factories, we can suggest a plausible explanation for the disconcerting incongruity of their findings. Capital-deepening technological change drove the expansion of factory capacity, allowing progressive firms to undertake year-round operations to achieve economies of scale. They thus contributed to the marginalization of smaller firms. While consolidating their industry leadership position, their higher capital–output ratios lowered their profit rate, but allowed them to maintain stable operations all year round, yielding larger total profits.

The historical evidence behind capital–output trends

In the early 1960s, empirical work by Klein and Kosobud (1961) questioned the evidence for rising capital–output trends in American manufacturing. In their paper, Klein and Kosobud sought a compromise between two different positions in the controversy over the historical capital–output trends characteristic of American economic development. On the one hand, they praised Kuznets and Goldsmith as "two of the principal investigators of the statistical capital–output ratio," and acknowledged that "Kuznets' decade capital–output estimates rose from 2.83 to 3.19 between 1879 and 1944." While acknowledging that Goldsmith's more detailed annual values confirmed these findings, Klein and Kosobud (1961) advanced the opposite claim instead, namely that in the long run the capital–output ratio ("the accelerator coefficient"), "is likely to fall in advanced industrial economies as a result of technical progress." The controversy, however, did not end there.

The debate continued beyond the 1960s. Leading economic historians from the 1970s onward confirmed the evidence for rising capital–output ratios in the nineteenth-century American economy, particularly in the manufacturing sector where the rise was substantial. As previously indicated, Atack *et al.* (2003) found "capital deepening" in American manufacturing, stressing the strong rise in the capital–output ratio between 1850 and 1880. The exhaustive research by Robert Gallman into nineteenth-century factors behind American economic growth showed that, from 1840 to 1900, "the capital stock increased faster than the national product... This means that the capital/output ratio was rising; the economy was engaged in capital deepening" (Gallman, 1986, p. 191).

Seeking to counter the contemporary efforts to revise the findings of previous historical investigations regarding capital–output trends, Paul Anderson (1961) and Vernon Smith (1962) carried out a careful examination of the methodological underpinnings informing measurements by Goldsmith, Creamer, and Kuznets of the capital stock in manufacturing and the whole economy. Anderson subjected the statistical procedure for the collection of the raw data to critical scrutiny, unraveling in some detail the confusions contained in the standard measurements of capital–output ratios. It is likely that Anderson's analysis of the pitfalls facing researchers in this field broke the ground for the later comprehensive reconstruction of capital measures at the hands of Robert Gordon (1990).

Anderson's critique of the revisionist literature advancing claims of falling real capital–output ratios as characteristic features of American industrialization was two-pronged. First, he questioned the accuracy of price deflators used to calculate the evolution of fixed capital goods in constant prices. Anderson's paper noted that Goldsmith's capital–output ratios, estimated in current dollars for the whole economy, remained relatively stable from 1880 to 1937, declining only 9 percent in that period, and in a more extended period, only 7 percent up to 1955. On the other hand, Goldsmith's data in constant 1929 dollars showed that capital–output ratios declined 32 percent from 1897 to 1949.

In light of this discrepancy, Anderson focused on the accuracy of the deflators used to explain the divergence between nominal and real values of fixed capital stocks. He doubted that capital-goods deflators, said to rise faster than those for general output, caused the greater decline in the constant dollar capital–output estimates. In fact, Goldsmith capital-goods deflators rose from an initial index of 41 in 1897 to 175 in 1949, relative to a base of 100 in 1929, while the GNP deflator for the same period and the same base in 1929 rose only from 45 to 149. Anderson questioned the legitimacy of that discrepancy. Why would the prices of capital goods rise so much faster than the general index for the GNP?

In Anderson's judgment Goldsmith's method for the construction of capital goods price indexes was flawed. Because the physical structure of capital goods changed considerably more than most other goods and comparisons between capital goods of different vintages are difficult to make ("the steam or diesel-electric shovel as compared with the hand shovel"), Goldsmith's procedure to estimate capital–goods price indexes reflected the price indexes of the labor and raw material inputs used up in the production of capital goods. Hence, such a price index procedure overlooked productivity gains in the capital-goods industry: "A current capital good is treated as a unit identical to its predecessor if the same quantity of inputs is used in its manufacture even though is twice as productive."

Next, Anderson turned his attention to the evident inconsistency found when comparing Daniel Creamer's (1958) volatile estimates for capital–output ratios in manufacturing with Goldsmith's (1952) relatively stable estimates (in current prices) for the whole economy. Creamer's estimates, elaborated from Census and Internal Revenue Service data, showed capital–output ratios in manufacturing rising sharply from 1880 to 1919 but falling precipitously from 1919 through the depression years and beyond, up to 1948. Now Anderson focused on the reported depreciation measures, pointing out that depreciation accounting was not crucial prior to the introduction of the corporate income tax in 1909.

Initially the corporate income tax was as low as 2 percent, but it grew substantially over the years, while additional excess profits taxes introduced in the wake of World War I raised the combined corporate tax burden up to 40 percent. Hence depreciation charges in the post-1919 years not only introduced a powerful incentive for manufacturing firms to account for actual depreciation, but even exaggerated it as the years passed. Manufacturing firms especially relied heavily on growing depreciation allowances to lower their income and excess profits tax payments. Anderson pointed out that reported depreciation allowances in manufacturing grew substantially, reaching as high as 50 percent of the gross cost of the capital stock. After 1919 such practices were bound to substantially lower Creamer's estimates of the net capital stock.

The net-to-gross capital stock declined annually 0.8 percent from 1934 to 1939. Projecting this rate of decline back to 1919, the net capital stock would fall to only 72 percent of the gross value. Thus, Anderson concluded, "depreciation accounting" practices were responsible for much of the falling capital–output ratios from 1919 to 1937 in the standard data. Anderson went on to show that correcting for these flaws, instead of falling, the evidence pointed to a rising capital–output ratio all the way from the late nineteenth century to the 1930s depression.

Furthermore, he was able to produce estimates of a rising capital output ratio by plugging Goldsmith's and Kuznets' data into Harrod's growth equation, $s/c = y_g$. Goldsmith's findings showed that, from 1897 to 1929, the saving (s) and investment (i) ratios exhibited stability throughout at 13.68 percent of annual net income, or 12 percent of GNP. Anderson took his GNP growth data, y_g, from Kuznets' (1952) study. According to Kuznets, GNP growth from the years

1869–1878 to 1889–1898 averaged 4.7 percent annually; 4.4 percent from 1889–1898 to 1904–1913; and 3.1 percent from 1904–1913 to 1919–1928. Dividing the 12 percent saving ratio by the 4.7 percent annual average GNP growth rate from 1870 to 1890, Anderson estimated an average capital–output ratio of 2.55 in the earliest decade under consideration: in 1890–1910 it rose to 2.73, finally reaching 3.87 in 1910–1930.

Anderson concluded that his data indicated "a substantial rise in the incremental capital–output ratio during the forty years before the big depression," and suggested that most likely the discrepancy between Goldsmith's capital–output estimates and his derived from Goldsmith's overvaluation of fixed assets at the beginning of the century, suggesting that this mistake reduced Goldsmith's capital stock growth in the following years. As evidence for this claim, Anderson carried out a comprehensive analysis of Goldsmith's long-term debt data for American industry, including bonds, notes and mortgages, relating it to fixed assets flows. Mindful of the shocks jolting this relationship during the World War I and the 1930s depression, Anderson limited his inquiry to the first 29 years of the twentieth century. Comparing the results from 1900 to 1929, Anderson pointed out that the 3.7 ratio in 1922 could be attributed to the asymmetry between inflated asset prices, reflecting the 50 percent rise in the price level right after World War I when compared with the immediately preceding years, and the growth of long-term debt most likely linked to the lower prewar price levels.

Assuming the inflation effect amounted to 23 percent would suffice to account for the discrepancy in the asset ratio of 1922 with the estimates for 1912 and 1929. No such inflation boost existed in 1900, and debt was high in the railroad industry, which alone represented almost half of all industry debt. At any rate, lowering Goldsmith's valuation of fixed assets in 1900 by a mere 13 percent would bring down the ratio to 3, pulling down Goldsmith's capital–output ratio from 3.3 to 2.9 and closely in line with Anderson's estimate of the capital–output ratio derived when dividing the savings ratio by the GDP growth rate. The corrections introduced led Anderson (1961) to expect that:

> A secularly rising capital-output ratio signifies an appreciably larger amount of investment in, say, the next decade than a secularly falling ratio. If the long-term trend is actually a rising one, the postwar business and consumer investment boom is not surprising.

The new orthodoxy advanced different versions of dynamic economies requiring constant capital–output ratios. One variant (Solow's), that eventually dominated the discussion, elaborated models built on the necessary marginal productivity adjustments of capital and labor that presumably led to steady-state growth paths. Other options (Kaldor's), preferred by Keynesians, dispensed with the engine of marginal movements while buttressing the consensus view on the necessity of constant if not falling capital–output ratios in the long run. Both versions proclaimed the inevitable convergence of all relevant variables into values suitable for steady-state growth.

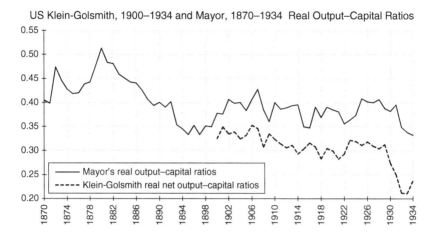

Figure 7.1 US alternative real output–capital ratios, 1870–1934.

Kaldor's own dogged defense of his "stylized facts" as real facts (albeit not actually generated by his own empirical research) did initially run into skepticism from his neoclassical colleagues at the time and was never accepted by economic historians. Marc Blaug (1989, p. 79) acknowledged that, despite repeated claims by Kaldor and others, "There is actually little evidence in the data to suggest the notion that there is some 'steady trend' or 'normal' relationship between capital and output."

Figure 7.1 shows a composite of two sets of output–capital ratio estimates: one reported in Mayor's (1968) and the other combining the data of Klein and Kosobud (1961) and Goldsmith (1952). While the full period considered by Mayor extended from 1870 through 1958, we chose to exclude the years after the Depression and after World War II because of the special circumstances surrounding the trends of capital accumulation and output in those years. Both events unraveled the normal workings of the economy, so that analysis of the recovery phase in accumulation and output should be carried out separately. In our view, the 1930s depression created a historic divide, a clear demarcation between two phases in the evolution of output–capital trends.

We calculated the second set of output–capital ratios using Goldsmith's capital stock data and Klein's estimates of the US net national product for the first 34 years of the twentieth century, both deflated in 1929 dollars. We applied Domar's rule to the data behind these output–capital estimates: "In defining capital and output," Domar (1965, p. 96) argued, "I would place the emphasis on the expression 'pro-duced by it', in the sense that the stock of capital should include all capital needed to produce a given output, while the latter should contain all output produced by a given stock of capital." Accordingly, Goldsmith's measures of the capital values net of depreciation were matched with estimates of output net of depreciation as well, in the period 1900–1934.

Objections to standard estimates of US capital stocks

Robert Gordon's efforts to refine the measurement of US capital stocks across the historical divide separating the 1930s Depression from the post-World War II period sprang from his determination to resolve the conundrum presented by the alleged historical jump of the output–capital ratio ("capital productivity") in the 1950s. From the standpoint of neoclassical economics, the evolution of "capital productivity" deriving from technical progress has major implications for the achievement of steady-state growth and the viability of capital accumulation. Gordon (1969) prepared the grounds for a sustained research program designed to uncover the flaws underlying the standard accounts of capital–output ratios. These efforts culminated in a major book entitled *The Measurement of Durable Goods Prices* (1990) where Gordon developed new methods for measuring quality-adjusted capital inputs, and eventually led the Bureau of Economic Analysis to revise its own calculation procedures.

As Robert Gordon recalled in his path-breaking essay "Interpreting the 'One Big Wave' in US Long-term Productivity Growth" (2004b), studies published by Kendrick (1961) and Kuznets (1961) had revealed what he called "the puzzling behavior of the output-capital ratio" once the 1930s Depression came to an end. While paying tribute to these pioneering efforts in measuring the "great ratios" of American economic history (Klein and Kosobud, 1961), Gordon repeatedly expressed his dissatisfaction with their findings.

Concern with the clarification of issues underlying the long-run behavior of the output–capital ratio played a major role in Robert Gordon's research output for over 30 years. Shortly after completing his dissertation, Gordon (1969, p. 221) identified the puzzle created by the studies that deployed the standard data: "The long-term behavior of the capital-output ratio is an unsolved mystery in the annals of U. S. economic growth." Thirty years later he felt closer to its resolution:

> The jump in the output-capital ratio intrigued me sufficiently to devote my Ph.D. dissertation (Gordon, 1967) to explaining it. This paper represents a return to several themes that remained unresolved at that time. My attention to the big wave was drawn by Duménil and [Lévy] (1990), who call attention to this "rupture" in technical change without decomposing it by sector nor providing any link to the several aspects of capital input mismeasurement that in substantial part are responsible for it.
>
> (Gordon, 2004b, p. 54)

The unprecedented leap of the output–capital ratio which standard empirical studies revealed in the aftermath of the 1930s depression awakened Gordon's earlier concerns with the quality of data used in the standard measurements of the capital stock. Indeed, looking at the overall trend for the output–capital ratios derived from the standard data revealed a striking picture of two distinct phases. Such procedure involves the notion that a ratio of "real" not nominal variables is the proper gauge for capital–output ratios and requires mixing deflators for output and capital goods.

The bifurcation occurred in the midst of the 1930s depression, as the output–capital ratio (the "productivity of capital") suddenly jumped to an unprecedented level almost twice as high as that experienced in the pre-1930s depression phase. Having reached such lofty heights, the output–capital ratio remained perched at levels towering over the pre-depression phase despite its more or less pro-nounced (depending on the deflators used) forward downward trend. Despite the puzzling bifurcation of levels before and after the 1930s depression, standard estimates showed the US output–capital ratio trending downwards from the late 1960s on, reaching lower values in the late 1970s than those registered in the 1940s. Nonetheless, its level remained far higher even at its trough in the early 1980s compared to any peaks attained in the pre-depression phase.

Gordon's corrections to the data making up the capital stock showed that the level of the output–capital ratio obtained in the standard procedure resulted in fact from measuring errors in the assessment of capital inputs in the US economy from 1870 on, and especially during and after the Great Depression of the 1930s. Correcting for the flawed methodology employed when the standard estimates of capital inputs were used uncritically, Gordon's new estimates, stretching all the way from 1879 to 1996, revealed that the output–capital ratios before World War II were nearly as high as those following it. His research thoroughly undermined the credibility of the standard measures of capital–output ratios in the US economy. In addition, the impact of capacity utilization is totally ignored. We may bear in mind that from the 1940s to the present capacity utilization rates rose steadily compared with such ratios in the previous phase, and this rise can be mistaken for a fall in capital–output ratios (Foss, 1963; 1985). Separating these structural changes in capacity utilization from the growth of capital stocks would narrow considerably the gap between the two development phases.

Looking back at his pioneering efforts to develop new measures of capital stocks, Gordon (1993, p. 104) recalled his determination to provide "quantita-tive estimates of quality and price changes for a wide variety of durable goods." Using two characteristic cases, computers and trucking, to illustrate the general approach, Gordon's new methodology for measuring real capital inputs required taking into account the number of calculations computers delivered per second rather than the number of computers used for a given project or the amount of ton-miles trucks ran per day instead of the number of trucks in service. The new procedure next called for adding the costs associated with the employment of the necessary computer operators or truck drivers plus the energy expenditures involved.

The gist of Gordon's (1990) argument stressed the need to measure the quan-tity of capital used by the volume of the specific properties intrinsic to various capital inputs, x, that actually served to produce the given output, y, not by the number of capital units deployed. Gordon (1990) proposed to evaluate capital goods according to their ability to yield real net revenue, n, the difference between real gross output, y, and the real costs of variable inputs, calculated as their real price, w, times their quantity, q, plus a measure of the efficiency achieved using those inputs, σ:

$$y = y(x, q), \quad y_x > 0; \; y_q > 0,$$
$$n = y(x, q) - wq(x, \sigma).$$

Real net revenue, n, is defined as nominal revenue divided by the output price, p, and consequently nominal net revenue, N, will be:

$$N = py(x, q) - wq(x, \sigma).$$

The demand for variable inputs is related to the size of the total capital input plus a measure of technological change reflecting new proportions between fixed and variable inputs needed, such as "fuel-saving" innovations in the transport industry. The cost of production for a capital good, c, will vary with its physical properties, z, since they embody those characteristics that enable firms to produce net revenue, plus "a shift parameter," λ, representing changing relations between the physical properties of capital inputs and their ability to produce net revenue for their users:

$$c = c[z(n), \lambda], \quad c_z > 0; \; c_\lambda > 0; \; z_n > 0.$$

Gordon argued that, taking as a pertinent example the computer industry, at any moment in time purchasing a more powerful computer, for example a machine endowed with faster speed, more memory or greater storage, involves a higher cost as well as higher net revenues, n. As time passes, however, the price of such powerful computers declines relative to their ability to produce net revenues because of technological progress reflected in the parameter λ. A similar development occurs in the field of fuel efficiency. Systems delivering higher fuel efficiency cost more at any given date, but technical progress generally results in equipment that requires less fuel and performs better than older vintage models of the same cost. This dichotomy between the rise in equipment prices and net revenues associated with higher-quality capital inputs would explain why firms managed to increase net revenues by a multiple with only relatively small increases in their costs.

Gordon's neoclassical persuasion induced him to develop a method capable of measuring "real" capital inputs, and as previous efforts in that direction showed, appropriate deflators were needed to transform the nominal investment expenditures carried out by firms into real ones. He first rejected the fixed-base approach representing two capital goods as exactly the same if they sold at the same price in the base year. Gordon also turned down the claim that two capital goods embodied the same capital input if they were capable of producing the same output, on the grounds that this would obviate the distinction between capital and output. He preferred to equate the real size of two capital inputs if, given the prices of variable inputs, w, and output, y, they produced equal net revenues, n. Then estimating the relevant implicit deflator for two capital inputs (0) and (1) in a given year required dividing the ratio of their market prices by the ratio of their expected net revenues:

$$p = \frac{c_1/c_0}{n_1/n_0} = \frac{c[z(n_1), \lambda_1]/c[z(n_0), \lambda_0]}{[y(x_1, q_1) - w_0 q(x_1, \sigma_1)]/[y(x_0, q_0) - w_0 q(x_0, \sigma_0)]}.$$

Moreover, citing evidence that two vintages of jet planes with the same characteristics of speed and passenger seats fetched a different market price supported the view that net rather than gross marginal revenue was the relevant criterion for selection. The model with the higher price used fewer pilots and required lower fuel consumption.

In the absence of technical change lowering production costs, λ, or a higher degree of efficiency achieved when combining variable inputs, σ, the price deflator would remain constant when real net revenues rose proportionally with the prices of capital inputs due to higher capacity equipment alone. At the other end, the relevant price deflator for a capital good whose market price rose by a factor of 2 while its real net revenue remained constant, would double. Had the real net revenue risen as much as the market price the relevant deflator would remain unchanged.

Setting aside these anomalies, Gordon pointed out the characteristic product of technical change delivered increases in real net revenues that exceeded the rise in market prices. As a case in point, while the market price of the first jet planes produced doubled, the net revenues received by the companies that purchased them increased tenfold due to increased speed and lower fuel consumption. Consequently the effective deflator index for jet planes fell from 1 to 0.2 and this pattern occurred in various proportions throughout the industrial sectors of developed economies.

Despite the fact that neoclassical economics conceives of measuring real investment spending by the assumed sacrifice of consumption goods, Gordon spurned Denison's (1993) proposal to measure real capital inputs by deflating nominal investment with the consumption goods deflator instead of using the conventional investment deflators. In fact switching deflators, Gordon pointed out in his reply to Denison, without correcting for quality improvements, would produce minor differences in the official estimates that he found inadequate:

> We note that the distinction is of little practical importance. The 1929–91 annual growth rates of the official deflators were 3.45 percent for consumption, 3.64 percent for fixed nonresidential investment, and 3.29 percent for producers' durable equipment (PDE). These differences are trivial compared to the three percent annual difference between the official PDE deflator and that developed for my book for 1947–83.
>
> (Gordon, 1993a, p. 109)

Gordon's (1990) new quality-adjusted methodology for the measurement of capital inputs brought to light the extent to which the official estimates overstated the price inflation of capital goods and consequently underestimated the growth of the capital–output ratio. As he noted, the capital–output ratio derived from the official data barely rose by 5 percent from 1947 to 1983 (the years covered by his 1990 study). The ratio displayed a sharp fall from 1947 to 1967 and a mild rise from 1967 to 1983. In contrast, Gordon's estimates for 1947–1983 revealed a significant increase of 406 percent in the capital–output ratio for equipment, and even without the absence of quality adjustment data for structures, a 44 percent rise of the aggregate capital–output ratio (Gordon, 1990, p. 25).

Gordon's revision of US capital stocks, 1870–1996

Gordon's research efforts to correct the standard measures of the US capital stock culminated in his paper entitled "Interpreting the 'One Big Wave' in US Long-term Productivity Growth" (Gordon, 2004b), which first appeared in 2001. This essay provided comprehensive corrections to the standard data effectively under-mining the conventional accounts on the anomalous behavior of the output–capital ratio after the 1930s depression. While Gordon's scientific achievements extend into many fields, his persistent efforts to solve this historic puzzle provided a main-stream perspective in support of our own assessments of capital–output trends. On the whole, Gordon's (2004b) findings seriously undermined the traditional assumptions upon which the conventional view of secular capital–output trends rested.

After the 1930s the disproportionate output increase recorded, relative to the standard measures of capital stock, awakened Gordon's original interest in search-ing for flaws in the standard methodology used to assess the real size of the capital stock. He found three areas of concern in that regard: the changing composition of capital goods between equipment and structures, the standard assumptions con-cerning the retirement of capital goods, and the unaccounted quantities of capital goods provided to private industry by government (GOPO) absent from standard measures of the capital stock.

Estimates of the service price of equipment carried out in official or standard measures of the capital stock used the formula p^E $(r + \delta^E)$, meaning the product of its relative price times the interest rate plus its depreciation rate. Using service prices as relative weights therefore raised the growth rate of equipment as well as its share in the capital stock, since depreciation rates for equipment are generally four times higher than for structures. Gordon noted that in the early period of American economic development, from 1870 to 1913, the equipment–structures ratio in the capital stock averaged 0.18, and the unabated growth of that ratio after the 1930s depression pushed it to 0.62 in the 1990s.

Gordon's corrected index for the capital stock reflected the secular rise in equip-ment investment relative to structures. Such index increased sharply from the mid-1930s up to 1950 while losing some of its former tempo in the following decades: new factors were required to complete the search for corrective measures of the standard estimates. Gordon's correction of the standard measures of the non-residential capital stock involved first reweighting the equipment–structures ratio as 3 : 1, instead of the standard ratio that evenly weighed equipment and structures dollar-for-dollar on a "1 : 1" basis, and then extending it back to 1870.

Gordon questioned the realism of using constant service lives and retirement schedules to calculate the growth of capital stocks. Citing findings by Feldstein and Foot (1971) and Feldstein and Rothschild (1974), Gordon argued that retirement schedules are intimately tied to the cash flow and investment patterns of firms responding to market fluctuations. Equipment and structures are replaced not on a fixed schedule but only when gross investment is on the rise. Gordon observed that despite the fact that business investment spending fell drastically in the 1930s and 1940s, firms did not engage in wholesale demolition of their standing structures according to a prearranged schedule. Gordon expected that with variable retirement plans replacing fixed ones, the downward bias in the estimates of capital stocks in years of economic depressions or wars would be corrected. When he applied the variable retirement assumption to track the changing equipment–structures ratio, he found it rising from 0.2 in 1929 to 0.248 in 1945. On the other hand, using a constant schedule to assess the service lives of capital goods, the 1929 ratio of 0.2 would instead fall to 0.199 in 1945.

Variable schedules of capital retirements

Gordon's linear function for the rate of capital replacements, R, relative to the capital stock, K, included measures of the cash flow ratio, F/K, and the net capital accumulation rate, N/K, plus the unemployment rate, U:

$$\frac{R}{K} = \beta_0 + \beta_1 \left(\frac{F}{K}\right) + \beta_2 \left(\frac{N}{K}\right) + \beta_3 U.$$

He then took the cash flow ratio and unemployment rate to vary with the gross rate of accumulation, G/K, as follows:

$$\frac{F}{K} = \alpha_0 + \alpha_1 \left(\frac{G}{K}\right), \quad U = \gamma_0 + \gamma_1 \left(\frac{G}{K}\right).$$

Since

$$\frac{N}{K} \equiv \frac{G}{K} - \frac{R}{K}.$$

it follows that

$$\frac{R}{K} = A_0 + A_1 \left(\frac{G}{K}\right).$$

Starting out with the official data on retirements, as well as gross investment and capital stocks from 1925 to 1988 issued by the Bureau of Economic Research, Gordon went on to estimate his adjusted retirement rate, $(R/K)^*$. The procedure consisted in multiplying the official rate by the ratio of the annual rate to the sample average over the period 1925–1996:

$$\left(\frac{R}{K}\right)^* = \frac{R}{K}\frac{(G/K)_t}{G/K}.$$

The corrected measures revealed changing growth rates for the capital stock. The capital stock grew faster between 1928 and 1950 than it did between 1950 and 1979. The growth of equipment and structures over the period 1929–1965 exceeded the official estimates and in the case of structures the higher growth extended to 1970. On the other hand, because the build-up of capital since 1929 exceeded the official rates, the adjusted growth of the capital stock, including equipment and structures from 1975 to 1996, turned out to be lower than the standard estimates showed. Gordon's conclusion was that adopting his variable schedules for the retirement of capital goods would raise the estimates for the accumulated stock of equipment and structures substantially, particularly from 1928 to 1950.

Finally, Gordon argued that the unprecedented leap of the output–capital ratio between 1940 and 1945 was also partially due to the fact that GOPO for the production of goods and services was not included in the standard estimates of the capital stock. Setting aside the capital composition effect and just dropping the assumption of fixed retirement schedules in favor of variable ones plus counting GOPO capital inputs would considerably raise capital input growth between 1930 and 1944: the capital stock did not fall by 7.4 percent as in the standard estimates, on the contrary it rose by 28 percent. Gordon's corrections showed that the changing composition of the capital stock, with the share of equipment rising relative to structures, had its major impact on the growth of capital input between 1964 and 1988 and as a result "The output-capital ratio that takes account of capital composition change (Y/J) declines at about one percent per year after 1964" (Gordon, 2004b, p. 60).

Gordon (2004b) went further than anyone else in solving the puzzle of the historic jump in output–capital ratios that standard research made so puzzling. After making the necessary adjustments to the conventional data for nonfarm capital stocks, Gordon's estimates revealed a secular trend in output–capital ratios significantly different from that of standard accounts. As he put it:

> Indeed, when both output and capital input are expressed in 1992 prices, the output-capital ratio is lower in 1996 (0.64), than in 1870 (0.71), in contrast to the doubling that occurs with the standard capital input data (0.37 to 0.74).
>
> (Gordon, 2004b, p. 78)

Coming from a leading mainstream macroeconomist, Gordon's findings regarding the secular trend of the capital–output ratio in the US economy effectively deprived one of Kaldor's notorious "stylized facts" of relevant content. As such

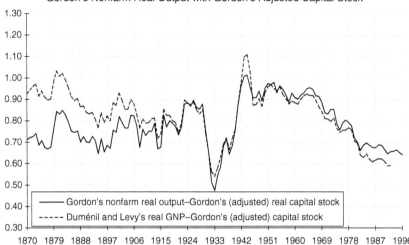

Alternative Measures of Real Output–Capital Ratios: Duménil/Levy's Real GNP versus Gordon's Nonfarm Real Output with Gordon's Adjusted Capital Stock

Figure 7.2 US alternative real output–capital ratios, 1870–1996.

it played a central role in our perception of the long-run trends in profitability shaping capital accumulation in the US.

Recalling the intensity with which Duménil and Lévy's (1990) claim of historic "ruptures" between the pre- and post-depression output–capital ratios motivated Gordon's doctoral dissertation and subsequent research, the relevance of Gordon's results can hardly be exaggerated. After carrying out his adjustments to the capital stock, the "rupture" claim indeed lost much of its credibility. As Figure 7.2 shows, superimposing the output–capital trends resulting from Gordon's research upon those derived from combining Duménil and Lévy's (1994) real GNP with Gordon's adjusted capital stock (adjusted) estimates (Gordon, 2004b, Figure 2.7, p. 76) produces very similar results, that is a highly diminished jump in levels between the 1930s and the 1950s (Foss, 1963, 1985).

Following the methodology created by Shaikh (1987) and applied by Shaikh and Moudud (2004) to estimate capacity utilization in major OECD economies, we derived our measures of capacity utilization in the US economy from 1880 to 2010. We show in Chapter 10 capacity utilization estimates in manufacturing, non-financial, and business sectors derived from the cointegrating relationship between nominal capital stock and net output, expressed in logarithmic scales as suggested in Shaikh and Moudud's work. Applying this methodology to the US business sector since 1900, we show in Figure 7.3 our capacity utilization estimates for the US business sector, revealing significant medium as well as long-term cycles, superimposed upon the narrower movements of the official estimates around an assumed normal level not very different from those produced by Duménil and Lévy (1994) applying the Hodrick–Prescott filter. Our sharper fluctuations capture

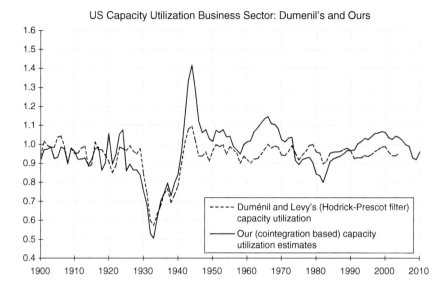

Figure 7.3 US alternative capacity utilization measures, 1900–2010.

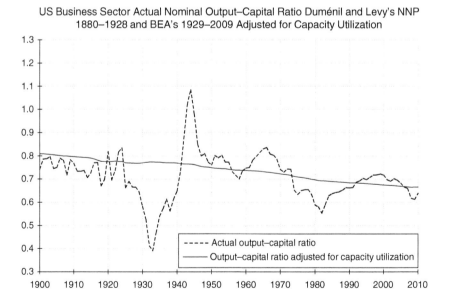

Figure 7.4 US output–capital ratios, 1900–2010.

the equally strong variations in the level of aggregate demand typically generated in major business cycles by changing policies, war spending contingencies, and so on, reflected in capacity utilization levels and business activity.

After adjusting actual output–capital ratios for capacity utilization, however, whatever differences existed in output–capital levels at both ends of the depression divide disappear. Figure 7.4 displays a long-run trend in output–capital ratios exhibiting continuity rather than structural breaks between the pre- and post-World War II periods. In addition, it shows that, adjusting the actual output–capital values for capacity utilization, a remarkably mild but steady downward trend emerges cutting across the sharp fluctuations of the unadjusted values. This trend applies to the business sector as a whole, hence a wider context than the traditional manufacturing industries as conventionally covered in accounts of technical progress. We attribute great significance to this finding in our account of the gravitational force exerting downward pressure upon the long-run profitability trend issuing from the "Golden Age."

8   Profitability trends after the "golden age"

Mainstream debates on US profitability trends

In the wake of the 1930s depression and the World War that followed, the leading capitalist economies enjoyed a "golden age of economic performance" (Glyn *et al.*, 1991) extending from the late 1940s to the mid-1960s. From the late 1960s to the early 1980s, however, the conditions that produced such prosperity unraveled, torn asunder by the rising inflation and unemployment rates experienced in most OECD countries through the mid-1980s:

> After 1973 there was a deterioration in the performance of the world economy and the industrial countries within it. Whilst investment in capital stock held up reasonably well to 1979 ... output, productivity, and export growth all fell sharply, instability in export volumes and GDP increased, and unemployment and inflation both rose. Even so, performance during the period 1973–79 still looks comparatively good in long term historical perspective. The position deteriorated radically after 1979.
>
> (Glyn et al., 1991, p. 45)

Indeed, the growth forces that sustained the recovery from depression for a quarter century weakened, replaced by stagnation-cum-inflation trends, something notoriously absent in the postwar "golden age." Then, spurred by the unexpected change in the system's behavior, a rising component of the research program carried out by mainstream economists in the US from the early 1970s through the next two decades concerned itself with two issues connected with the reversal of growth prospects: why did the rapid growth following World War II end so abruptly after 1973, and what structural breakdowns blocked the return of prosperity?

Assessing the postwar period as a whole, the answer to this question, succinctly given by two neoclassical economists, saw profitability trends as decisive: "One striking aspect of the US economy's performance during the last decade is the decline in the rate of return on corporate capital" (Holland and Myers, 1978). Despite substantial boosts to aggregate demand associated with war expenditures in the late 1960s, the overall decline went on unabated. A decade of declining capital accumulation within the context of seemingly unending stagflation characterized the 1970s trends preceding the deep slump of the early 1980s.

Understanding the impact of profitability trends on the growth prospects of the US economy motivated orthodox as well as unorthodox economists to gather and evaluate the available empirical evidence. Thus the decade of the 1980s witnessed the publication of major contributions not only in the heterodox literature but also in mainstream studies of profitability trends. Such effort testifies to the significance attached by researchers in the 1970s and 1980s to the causes and consequences of falling profitability trends.

Findings by neoclassical economists provide an unequivocal picture of overall declining profitability for US nonfinancial corporations in the postwar years extending through the early 1980s. In this regard, the leading neoclassical economists undertaking these studies, such as Martin Feldstein, Larry Summers, James Poterba, and Michael Bruno, persistently sought in their work to wrap their conclusions in caveats designed to soften the dire effects of falling profitability trends. To this end they included concepts of corporate profits (like after-tax profits, subject to policy changes) showing greater resilience and used capital stock measures adding nonproduced inputs like land or non-fixed assets like inventories. Their efforts notwithstanding, their findings clearly showed the US average profit rate in 1980 falling in all sectors of the economy to about half the average level of the 1950s and 1960s. Chronologically tracking these findings provided the foundation for a comprehensive evaluation of the postwar period leading up to the 1980s watershed. In our view, this is the background that led to the growth of "financialization" that triggered the banking crisis of 2007.

Okun and Perry's profit-squeeze hypothesis

One of the earliest findings in the field of profitability studies by Okun and Perry (1970) focused on the declining share of corporate profits in GNP, leading the authors to single out its impact on accumulation and growth prospects. In line with the essay's title, "Notes and Numbers on the Profit Squeeze," Okun and Perry pointed out that profit shares in the US had fallen since the mid-1960s, reaching a low of 9.2 percent in 1969, down from a high of 11 percent of GNP in 1966. Furthermore, in 1970 the share fell again to 8 percent, a level lower than the 8.7 percent recorded in the 1958 recession and 9.1 percent in 1961, also a recession year. Since profitability trends reflect the changes of profit shares and capital–output ratios, a falling profit share would lower the average profit rate even if capital–output ratios held steady.

While it was clear that in boom years overhead costs spread over rising outputs and labor productivity grew faster leading to expanding profits shares, recession periods worked in reverse, raising both average fixed and unit labor costs, hence falling profits shares. Okun and Perry argued that for most of the postwar period up to 1966, average nominal wage growth surpassed the increase in the nonfinancial corporate goods deflator by 3 percent. Every year until 1966, however, labor productivity gains also reached 3 percent, thus ensuring the constancy of wages shares. For Okun and Perry the falling trend in profit shares from 1966 on indicated that either prices in the corporate sector did not rise as much as in earlier years or labor productivity growth slowed down more than in previous periods.

While acknowledging that the cyclical growth of the GNP caused some volatility in the profit share, Okun and Perry doubted, or at least could not confidently predict, that the recent profitability trends would be transient, or that the rising trend of the wages share in the national income of the late 1960s could be treated as an anomaly likely to disappear soon. While the authors did not spell out the negative consequences attached to the reversal of the previous profit-share trend, the thrust of their argument stressed their concern that persistently falling profits shares reduced investment and weakened the foundations of future productivity growth.

Okun and Perry, however, provided data on corporate profits gross of net interest that cast a shadow over their central argument regarding trends. Their own data showed that gross profit shares exhibited fluctuations without a discernible long-term trend. The fall in the gross profit share from 1966 to 1970 followed a comparable rise from 1958 to 1966, although it took 6 years for the gross profit share to rise from its lowest level to its highest, and only 4 years to fall back to its previous trough.

Responding to the claims advanced in their paper when delivered at the Brookings Institution, Robert Gordon took exception to interpreting the recent reversal of the profits share as an unusual development, pointing out that "even before the First World War," Wesley Mitchell noted as a stylized feature of business cycle dynamics the inevitable contraction of profit margins occurring in the last stages of a sustained bout of growth, precisely as happened in the late 1960s (Okun and Perry, 1970, p. 473).

It does not diminish Mitchell's valuable contributions to empirical research on business cycles to point out that his findings regarding the impact of the distinct stages of boom and recession on profits and wages shares only confirmed the validity of earlier formulations drawn out by economists outside the orthodox fold. As we showed in Chapter 3, Goodwin's growth models, building on Marx's cycle outline in Chapter 25 of *Capital*, Volume I, formally demonstrated how changes in the rate of accumulation affecting the demand for labor would impact the "reserve army of labor" and thereby wages and profitability cycles in the absence of technical change.

Adding a linear trend to Okun and Perry's data on corporate profits plus net interest shares in GNP, jointly with our nonfinancial corporate sectors shares of net operating surplus in GDP, as plotted in Figure 8.1, shows that despite sharp fluctuations in both profit shares, the linear trends running through them provide no basis for a profit-squeeze hypothesis. We carried out our own calculations of the nonfinancial corporate shares because Okun and Perry failed to fill in their estimates for every year between 1954 and 1966. Because Okun and Perry's calculations of nonfinancial corporate shares related profits plus net interest to a nonfinancial corporate gross product varying between 55.1 percent and 54.4 percent of GDP, their estimates are higher than ours. Graphically, however, dividing both corporate

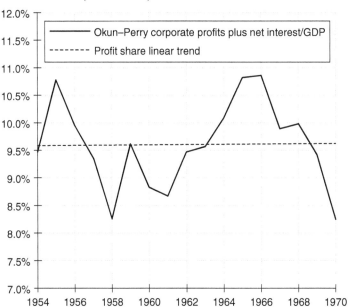

Figure 8.1 Okun–Perry profit-share data.

profit measures by GDP delivers a clear picture of the similar paths in profit shares between the mid-1950s and 1970.

Nordhaus' falling share of profits

Four years after the appearance of Okun and Perry's essay highlighting the sharp decline in profit shares, Nordhaus' (1974) paper on "The Falling Share of Profits," also delivered at the Brookings Institution, sought to ground the weak evidence on declining profit shares advanced by these writers in a firmer theoretical and empirical foundation. The evidence gathered in the US extending the period for four more years, and the inclusion of other countries undergoing similar changes, provided Nordhaus a broader perspective in this matter. Indeed, Nordhaus confirmed that profits of US nonfinancial corporate businesses with inventory valuation adjustment (IVA) and net of interest payments as a share of GNP fell from 11 percent in 1966 to 7.1 percent in 1970. In 1973 that share rose to 8.5 percent, a year in which profits reached a peak. But despite the spectacular rise in profits accruing to oil companies in 1974, Nordhaus expected the share to fall back to just 8.1 percent.

Nordhaus pointed out that the average profit share in the years 1971–1973 fell to 57 percent of the level reached in 1948–1950. The profits share descent occurred in two stages, first in 1948–1954 and then in the most recent 1966–1970 period. Furthermore, Nordhaus noted, the decline in profits share extended to the advanced capitalist countries located in "most of Western Europe." In light of such ominous declines in profit margins, Nordhaus wondered whether the strengthening bargaining position of labor in the wake of a prolonged economic expansion caused the increase in labor's share. Assuming that this was no statistical mirage, Nordhaus proceeded to seriously ponder the deeper implications of the declining shares in the grand historical sweep of postwar capitalism: "does the declining share of profits portend the euthanasia of the capitalist class, and indeed of capitalism itself?" (Nordhaus, 1974, p. 170).

Two key findings framed Nordhaus' answer to his provocative question. From 1948 to 1973 Nordhaus estimated corporations averaged a 7.1 percent after-tax rate of return on capital. Defining the cost of capital as the interest rate on debt and equity that corporations were willing to pay, Nordhaus pointed out that throughout the period under consideration the cost of capital averaged 6.5 percent. Thus the gap between average returns and costs, net profitability, remained below 1 percent. Despite average net profitability rising to 1.9 percent after 1958, Nordhaus concluded that throughout the entire postwar period corporate business enjoyed negligible net profitability. In his view, "the declining share was probably a *result* of the declining rate of profit rather than its *cause*" (Nordhaus, 1974, p. 215).

Nordhaus wished to stress, however, that the absence of net profits did not foretell the decline of capitalism. Vanishing concerns with bankruptcies, falling taxation of corporate capital and rental prices (the dollar cost of capital, given by the price of capital goods and the falling cost of capital) spurred the growth of debt-financed corporate investment. Nordhaus wished to argue that the postwar period the corporate profits share as well as the share of investment financed by corporate retained earnings fell because the average return on capital declined. The falling net profitability trend, however, merely reflected lenders' and investors' gains in confidence regarding the stability of future prospects, as fears of the Great Depression faded.

Feldstein and Summers' "inconclusive" results

Dissatisfied with the results of Nordhaus' paper on profitability, Feldstein and Summers (1977) returned to the troubling question three years later: was the profitability trend in the postwar US economy really falling? As Feldstein and Summers saw it, Nordhaus' conclusions regarding falling profitability derived from his contention that capital intensity in the corporate sector rose inexorably once "investors" lost their risk aversion to financing high levels of investment in that sector. Feldstein and Summers for their part sought to calculate the pre-tax rate of return for nonfinancial corporations in the postwar years, defined as the ratio of domestic "profits plus interest payments" to "the total value of real capital including fixed capital, inventories, and land."

In their empirical estimates, summarized in Figure 8.2, Feldstein and Summers carefully stressed the marked fluctuations the profit rate experienced from 1948 to 1958, pointing out the deep decline from its high levels in 1948–1951, the bottom

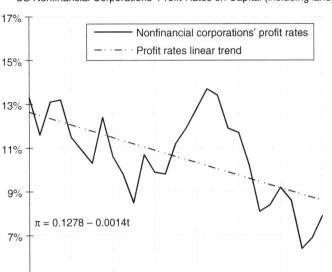

Figure 8.2 Feldstein–Summers profit-rate data.

reached in 1957–1958 and the upturn leading to the peak between 1965 and 1966. While the upward movement fostered optimistic expectations of a sustained boom, the downward drift starting in the late 1960s undermined such confidence. Indeed, the decline from 1966 only reached a new trough in the early 1970s.

An alternative reading of the evidence presented by Feldstein and Summers would look at the 1960–1965 increase in profit rates as the rising first half of a whole cycle that after reaching its crest in 1965 reversed course. The profit rate continued falling for another four years through 1970 and, after a brief recovery, plunged to the lowest level in 1974. Despite such definitive evidence, indicating that "the 1970s have seen unusually low rates of return," Feldstein and Summers (1977, p. 217) expressed confidence that "there is no reason to believe that this fall is more than temporary."

In Feldstein and Summers' (1977) estimates the nonfinancial corporate profit rate in 1974 fell to a level less than half the value recorded in 1948. Further investigations carried out by Feldstein and Poterba (1981) in fact showed that the downward trend continued beyond 1974 into the late 1970s. Despite the statistical effort to downplay the overall tendency for corporate profitability to fall, the simple fact remains that the linear trend running through the intermediate cycles from 1948 through 1976, $\pi = 0.1278 - 0.0014t$ (see Figure 8.2), is unambiguously falling and Feldstein and Summers' optimistic forecasts of profitability returning to the lofty levels of the postwar era did not materialize.

Confirming Nordhaus' findings

As the 1970s approached its conclusion, Lovel (1978, p. 787) showed that in the nonfinancial corporate sector of the US, "by all measures, the profitability of non-financial corporations declined gradually over most of the period since World War II" – but, again, he expressed confidence in the coming reversal of the trend. In his work Lovel argued that explaining profitability trends chiefly on the basis of cyclical changes in the variables involved in that sector failed to account for the nature of long-run trends in the whole economy. Accordingly, he could not advance a theory for the long-run trend as derived by Nordhaus. Weisskopf (1992) confirmed the existence of a long-run falling profit rate in the US economy. Using calculation criteria identical to Nordhaus' earlier study, Weisskopf argued that the nonfinancial corporate sector was a significant and dynamic component of the US economy, representing about 60 percent of its GDP at the end of the 1970s. Thus, focusing on the nonfinancial corporate business (NFCB) sector of the US economy was a legitimate research strategy, because the profitability prospects of finance and unincorporated businesses depended on the performance of the NFCB sector, where Weisskopf (1979, p. 372) found that:

> The (before-tax) rate of profit in the NFCB sector of the US economy displayed a long-run downward trend from 1949 to 1975: it fell from cycle I (1949–1954) to cycle II (1954–1958) and from cycle II to cycle III (1958–1960); it rose from cycle III to cycle IV (1960–1970); and it fell again from cycle IV to cycle V (1970–1975). Within each cycle the rate of profit rose during the early stage of the expansion, then fell during the late stage of the expansion as well as in the contraction.

Weisskopf's (1979, p. 372) explanation for the falling trend in NFCB profitability supported Okun and Perry's (1970) contention that falling profit shares caused the postwar profitability trend, driven by "a rise in the strength of labor *vis-à-vis* capital – as reflected in a suitably adjusted wage-share of income." As a "radical" economist, Weisskopf contended that alleged gains in bargaining power on the part of labor, and hence rising wages, were decisive in bringing about long-term falling profitability trends in the manufacturing sectors of six leading OECD economies from the early 1950s into the mid-1980s (Figure 8.3).

Liebling's (1980) findings confirmed the strength and duration of the profitability decline affecting the NFCB sector in the postwar years. According to Liebling (1980, p. 58), in fact the fall in profitability experienced in the 1970s "registers more than cyclical influence" and reflected the intensification of international competition. The following year, Munley (1981) added his empirical findings to the growing body of research on profitability trends, supporting Weisskopf's (1979) as well as Boddy and Crotty's (1974) claims that falling profit shares were responsible for dragging down the profitability trend of nonfinancial corporations.

In a Brookings Institution (1982) research project on profitability trends, Bosworth *et al.* (1982), while acknowledging the "very sharp decline that began in

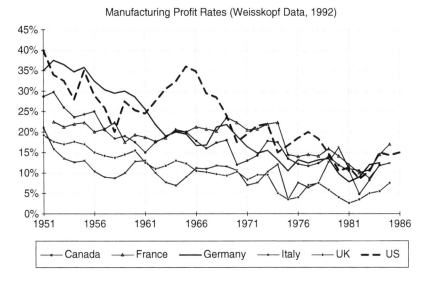

Figure 8.3 Manufacturing profit rates in six OECD countries, 1951–1986.

the late 1960s and that has persisted to the present – lowering the before-tax rate of return from 11 percent in 1967 to 8 percent in 1980," contradicted the conclusions of previous studies regarding their fundamental cause. Rather than the shrinking profit share, they found that the ratio of "business tangible assets" to output "rose substantially throughout the 1970s." In their view the decline in business profitability reflected the increasing capital–output ratio associated with the postwar investment boom, sustained by rising business confidence.

New evidence from Feldstein and Poterba

After Feldstein and Summers (1977) found "inconclusive" evidence supporting a falling profitability long-term trend and Lovel (1978) argued that "by all measures, the profitability of nonfinancial corporations declined gradually over most of the period since World War II," mainstream research on profitability trends continued. A new article on corporate profitability trends by Feldstein and Poterba (1981), possibly seeking to clear the ominous cloud surrounding the earlier paper by Feldstein and Summers, confirmed that "average return between 1970 and 1976 was some 1 to 2 percent lower than would have been predicted on the basis of fluctuations in capacity utilization alone." With their new paper, they sought to reach a comprehensible explanation for the unanticipated persistence of the declining trend.

While recalling that in their earlier work Feldstein and Summers believed the "factors that contributed to the lower rate of return in the 1970s were likely to be transitory so that the fall in the return might also be temporary," now they were not so sure. Their quest for emerging factors that could be expected to reverse the current trend remained hopelessly blocked once they admitted that "Changes in productivity growth, in inflation, in relative unit labor costs, and in other variables are all associated with changes in profitability. None of these variables, however, can explain the difference in profitability between the 1950s, 1960s and 1970s." Could some other transient factor, yet undetected, explain the fall in profitability? The extension of the falling trend to the late 1970s led Feldstein and Poterba (1981, p. 23) to raise once again the question that motivated Nordhaus's paper in 1974: "Does the lower rate of return in recent years reflect a fundamental fall in the rate of profit or has it just been a cyclical or temporary change?"

We would suggest that correcting the actual profitability estimates for changes in capacity utilization will help to locate the underlying long-term trend in profitability. Dividing the actual profitability ratios produced by Feldstein and Poterba by our own estimates of manufacturing capacity utilization in fact yields a smoother profitability trend falling throughout the period 1948–1979. The sharper fluctuations of the Feldstein–Poterba estimates actually hide the underlying long-term trend brought out by the capacity utilization adjustment. In any event, Feldstein and Poterba, bound by their neoclassical perspective in steady growth paths, reaffirmed their confidence that "Only the experience of the future will provide a definite answer."

Focusing on the US manufacturing sector, Coen (1980) expressed absolute confidence that despite the substantial decline of profitability from 1948 to 1974, the evidence did not justify concluding that a "secular decline in the rate of return" was underway (Coen, 1980, p. 146). Coen's suspension of judgment, along the lines expressed by Feldstein and Poterba, reflected his hope that "if the economy can once again attain high real growth" manufacturing profitability would likely rise to the lofty levels of the immediate postwar years.

Aschauer's fundamental hypothesis

Confirmation of the falling profitability trend that Feldstein and Poterba (1981) left to future research on the persistence of corporate profitability cycles after 1948 appeared in 1988. Delivered in a neoclassical context by David Aschauer of the Federal Bank of Chicago (Aschauer, 1988) the new study extended the calculations through 1985 using the same data sources and assumptions made in earlier research efforts. Aschauer showed that linear profitability trends in the nonfinancial corporate sector indeed remained negative all the way through the early 1980s. His work revealed that the linear trend between 1953 and 1985 showed "a strong negative movement in the net return." Moreover, Aschauer advanced a perfectly neoclassical theory of the decline for the years 1953–1985 providing "a clue to the mystery of the downward trend in the profit rate over the sample period."

His "fundamental hypothesis" contends that public sector capital expenditures complement private sector investment and raise the marginal product of capital in the corporate sector: "New highways, airports and modern power plants – components of a general economic infrastructure – are likely to heighten the productivity

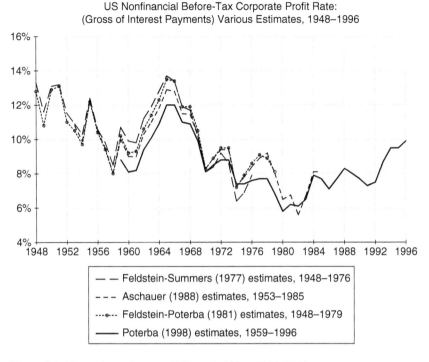

Figure 8.4 Alternative estimates of US profitability, 1948–1996.

of private capital and spur expenditure on new plant and equipment" (Aschauer, 1988, p. 11). According to Aschauer, the persistent decline in corporate profitability occurred because the ratio of public to private fixed capital stocks fell from a high 0.84 in 1964 to a low 0.564 in 1985, and consequently the marginal product of corporate capital fell throughout the period. The cyclical upturn in profitability after 1983 reduced the negative value of the linear trend from −0.0014 per year to −0.0012, but the profit rate in the mid-1980s, at about 8.1 percent, remained over 30 percent below the level achieved in the mid-1950s. As Figure 8.4 shows, the empirical evidence assembled by mainstream economists concerning US corporate profitability trends since the late 1940s reveals a significant downward trend, punctuated by sharp fluctuations, not reversed before the early 1980s.

Duca and Poterba on trend reversals

In the 1990s, profitability appeared poised for a sustained trend reversal and optimistic expectations survived the 1987 stock market crash. But Duca (1997), focusing on the prospects for long-run nonfinancial corporate profitability trends, strongly dissented from the gathering consensus. Aware that corporate profitability trends shaped the prospects for future investment spending plans, Duca sought to clarify the nature of the apparent upturn in profitability, while separating the cyclical fluctuations from the underlying trend. His research led him to conclude that "Contrary to popular perception, virtually all of the resurgence in corporate profitability during the 1990s reflects a cyclical increase in profits and a decline in net interest expense associated with deleveraging and lower interest rates" (Duca, 1997, p. 2).

Duca attributed the "cyclical increase in profits" to rising capacity utilization because "the profit ratio should rise as real fixed costs ... shrink as a share of output." While he acknowledged that rates of return on capital provided a better gauge of profitability trends, he argued that practical difficulties gathering capital stock data made the profit-share approach preferable. His estimates tracked the evolution of the profit share rather than the rate of return on capital because in his view the official measures of the net capital stock underestimated its magnitude. As an example, Duca cited the sharp fall in prices for nonfinancial corporate structures recorded by official statistics in the early 1990s, "even though vacancy rates in the early 1990s and 1980s were similar." As a result of this writeoff in corporate buildings prices:

> Because profits are measured contemporaneously, whereas the capital stock reflects previous investment and depreciation, the measured return on capital in the mid-1990s looks high largely because the measured rate of return jumped after the stock of office buildings was largely written off
>
> (Duca, 1997, p. 5).

Thus for Duca "virtually all of the run-up in the unadjusted profit rate is due to swings in the business cycle and net interest," while the falling long-run profit-share trend reflected the rising pressure on domestic prices exerted by global competitive forces. In his view competitive pressures rose not only in industries trading goods in international markets but also in all activities experiencing deregulation since the early 1980s.

One year after Duca's study was published and 15 years after the average "accounting" profit rate for nonfinancial corporations reached an unprecedented trough (excluding the 1930s depression), Poterba (1998) sought to quantify the extent of its recovery. His estimates focused on the "pretax return on nonfinancial corporate capital" because in his view that measure provided the best gauge to evaluate future investment activity. Poterba's tangible assets, as in previous studies carried out by mainstream economists, included land. Conflating such definition of tangible assets and capital stock (fixed reproducible means of production) allowed the tangible assets–income ratio to reflect speculative fluctuations in land prices, which according to Poterba largely explained the profit rate recovery of the 1990s because:

> The decline in the tangible-asset to national-income ratio over this period, from 1.664 to 1.441, is ... almost completely the result of a decline in the ratio of land values to national income. The land-to-national-income ratio

falls from 0.306 in 1990 to 0.138 in 1994. This decline, in turn, is due to the fall in the estimated market value of commercial real estate relative to national income during this period. The [balance sheets] compute land values as a residual after subtracting the Commerce Department's estimate of the replacement cost of corporate residential real estate from a market-value estimate for commercial real estate.

(Poterba, 1998, pp. 227–228)

Uctum and Viana on accumulation trends

Ricardo had argued that profitability and accumulation should be considered as two moments of the self-expansion of capital circuits, and that the tempo of accumulation reflected the evolution of profitability: "Without a motive there could be no accumulation... The farmer and manufacturer can no more live without profit, than the labourer without wages. Their motive for accumulation will diminish with every diminution of profit" (Ricardo, 1981, p. 122). The empirical evidence confirms Ricardo's view that the capital circuit linking the rate of accumulation to the dynamics of profitability expands via a feedback loop from accumulation to profitability itself. Ricardo (1981, p. 292) believed that "There is only one case, and that will be temporary, in which the accumulation of capital with a low price of food may be attended with a fall in profits; and that is, when the funds for the maintenance of labour increase much more rapidly than population."

As Marx's work showed, Ricardo's argument that rising wages lowers profitability does not exhaust the probable causes, since capital-deepening technical progress and rising capital–output ratios not sufficiently compensated by growing profit shares will also reduce profitability. In turn, falling expected profitability, the motive for accumulation, will undermine the desire to expand.

Now despite rising from its 1983 trough, US nonfinancial corporate profitability in the 1990s failed to reach the lofty levels registered in the 1960s. In this regard, Uctum and Viana (1999) highlighted "the dramatic decline over the last half century" of profit rates in all sectors of the US economy, as estimates fell from a 28 percent average in the 1960s to 20 percent in the 1990s, a decrease of nearly one third. In fact, as Uctum and Viana stressed, the profitability downturn was uneven, rates in manufacturing falling more than in the rest of the corporate sector. With manufacturing profit rates in the 1990s averaging a mere 9 percent, their decline amounted to near 60 percent from their average 22 percent in the postwar heyday between 1948 and 1960. Moreover, after the 1960s, the profitability slump extended to all areas of the economy, including finance, insurance and real estate (FIRE), although in the 1990s the recovery in FIRE surpassed that of nonfinancial corporate sectors.

Uctum and Viana estimated profitability in the nonfinancial corporate sector as the ratio of property income, defined as "gross operating surplus," over gross reproducible fixed assets. Gross operating surplus includes depreciation or capital consumption allowances, and the gross capital stock is also gross of depreciation. As Wolff (2003), in his empirical investigation of profitability trends in the 1980s and early 1990s pointed out, dividing the gross operating surplus by gross capital and not net capital stock is the best option. The Bureau of Economic Analysis, however, ended publication of gross capital stock estimates in 1994, thus preventing implementation of this principle beyond that date.

Uctum and Viana identified the decisive force behind falling profitability in non-manufacturing industries with capital-intensive technical change and its impact on "the real price of capital." Despite the capital intensity of technology being generally stronger in manufacturing than in other nonfinancial businesses (with the exception of transportation, mining and utilities), they also attributed the postwar profitability downturn in manufacturing to rising real wages. These inconsistencies did not render their theoretical perspective easily encapsulated within any well-defined tradition of classical political economy. Uctum and Viana sought to demonstrate the close long-run relationship between profitability and accumulation trends. Estimating their profit rate as the ratio of "gross operating surplus" to the nonresidential capital stock, and the accumulation rate as the ratio of gross investment to output, they argued that the cash flows tied directly to profitability shaped business accumulation plans. Measuring the percentage change of the two variables with respect to their previous values one period earlier, they showed their roughly parallel paths.

The international scope of falling profitability

Since the late 1970s new research projects undertaken by both mainstream and heterodox economists have found substantial evidence of international downward trends in profitability present in leading OECD countries. Despite their lack of comprehensive data comparable to US sources, Nordhaus' earlier expressed concern that the US rate of profit exhibited a falling trend in the postwar years now extended to other advanced capitalist countries as well. Noting that until recently the essential data on capital stocks was conspicuously unavailable for most advanced countries, Hargreaves-Heap praised Hill's (1979) research findings for the major economies in the OECD showing a decline in international profit rates from 1955 through 1976: "This work suggests that there has been a pronounced worldwide fall in the profit rate which can be attributed to the combined effect on a squeeze on the share of output going to profits and a rise in the capital-output ratio" (Hargreaves-Heap, 1980, p. 66).

Five years later Chan-Lee of the OECD Economics and Statistics Department noted that his findings on profitability trends, as shown in Figure 8.5, extended earlier claims of a "secular decline" in US rates of return to other leading capitalist economies: "In most countries and sectors, since the 1960s, there appears to have been such a decline, most pronounced in the manufacturing sector... Rates of return have declined more than profit shares, implying capital productivity is a key explanatory factor" (Chan-Lee and Sutch, 1985).

Our own estimates of profitability trends, as shown in Figures 8.6 and 8.7, confirm the international scope of falling profitability trends from the 1960s to the early 1980s. While openly critical of mainstream research efforts, heterodox

Selected OECD Nonfinancial Corporate Business Before Tax Average Profit Rates

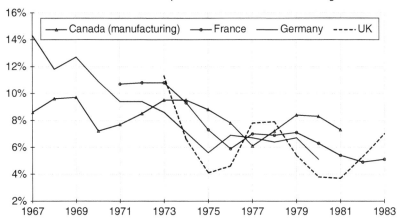

Figure 8.5 OECD data on corporate profitability, 1967–1983 (Chan-Lee and Sutch, 1985).

Figure 8.6 OECD business sector profit rates, 1951–1981.

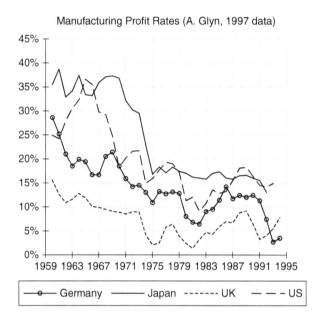

Figure 8.7 OECD manufacturing profit rates, 1959–1995.

economists Armstrong, Glyn and Harrison also found evidence of falling profitability trends, but, in contrast to the Chan-Lee study, attributed the decline to a profit squeeze brought on by the growing bargaining power of the international labor movement (Armstrong *et al.*, 1984). However, the extent to which rising wage shares may account for the decline in long-term profitability trends is questionable.

Despite their professed roots in Marxian economics, Armstrong *et al.* failed to explain precisely how rising wage shares could produce downward long-run trends in profitability: a sustained "profit squeeze" brought on by wages rising faster than labor productivity would blunt the propensity to accumulate. With lower accumulation, employment growth would fall and the "reserve army of labor" would expand. Rising unemployment would in turn weaken the bargaining position of labor, not strengthen it: a rising "reserve army of labor" would undermine workers' ability to push forward with vigorous wage claims. While recurrent business fluctuations may include temporary "profit squeeze" episodes in the last stages of the upturn just before the downturn occurs, such developments will likely fade once the reversal is underway and cannot produce well-defined long-run trends.

Moseley on Weisskopf's 1978 profitability estimates

In the mid-1980s, Moseley took issue with Weisskopf's (1979) explanation of the structural determinants behind postwar profitability trends. Weisskopf had claimed that, between 1945 and 1975, falling profitability in the nonfinancial corporate sector of the US economy resulted from a 28 percent decline in its profit share. Now Moseley wished to distinguish between the wages of productive labor, V, paid to workers that produce surplus value, and the wages of unproductive labor, U (including sales and supervisory workers), which in Marxian economics represent surplus value consumption instead. Moseley then argued that the decline in US nonfinancial profitability did not occur because the wage shares of productive workers rose but rather because the wage share of unproductive labor expanded.

Moseley pointed out that the distinction is crucial in Marxian theory because unproductive labor consumes but does not create surplus value, this being the Marxian source for money profits. The expansion of "unproductive" labor relative to productive workers would require a rising share of surplus value (gross profits in money terms), siphoned off for the maintenance of unproductive activities. Hence the ratio of "gross profits" to total wages of productive plus unproductive labor might fall, while the ratio of "gross profits" to the productive labor involved in its production rose.

Besides supervisory workers, Moseley drew attention to the fact that Marx included the portion of capital devoted to employ "circulation" labor as "unproductive" precisely because this portion of the workforce is not engaged in the production of goods and services, but rather in sales, that is turning these goods and services into money. Moseley (1985, p. 66) estimated that:

> By 1975 almost half the wage bill of capitalist enterprises in the US was paid to workers who performed unproductive labor. This analysis leads to the conclusion that the decline in the ratio of profits to wages was caused directly by the large increase in the ratio U/V.

Robert Brenner's vs. Nicholas Kaldor's "stylized facts"

Diametrically opposed views expressed by Kaldor and Brenner on the structural trends that shape the evolution of capitalism frame the recent debates on global turbulence. Nicholas Kaldor presented a growth model of capitalism at the 1957 Corfu Conference on Capital Theory which he claimed to be consistent with a set of "stylized facts" capturing the characteristic features of capitalist development. Despite his failure to produce any empirical evidence in support of his "stylized facts" and the skeptical response of various luminaries attending that conference, with the passing of time Kaldor's "stylized facts" came to be regarded by mainstream economists as self-evident truths. We may recall that Kaldor's set of "stylized facts" included, among other things, claims that profit shares, capital–output ratios, and profit rates were trendless in the long run, despite the steady rise in capital–labor ratios brought about by labor-saving technical progress.

As we showed in Chapter 2, Kaldor's historical evidence regarding most of the "stylized facts" emerging out of his steady-state growth paths is weak. We accept as valid the secular rise of capital per worker and increasing labor productivity, but we found no empirical support for Kaldor's constancies involving the profit share, the capital–output ratio, and the profit rate. We also reject his technical progress function as an artificial construct designed to achieve steady-state growth. In fact, confronted with the new evidence on secular trends emerging from the data, we may rule out the notion of steady-state growth paths in favor of changing capital accumulation trends driven by profitability.

Robert Brenner's *The Economics of Global Turbulence*, published in 1998 shortly after the crisis of the Asian tigers plunged the world economy into yet another slump, provided ample evidence of the link between falling profitability and flagging accumulation trends. As a celebrated historian, Robert Brenner's empirical findings forcefully showed that, contrary to Kaldor's "stylized facts," capital–output ratios rose and profit rates declined steadily in Germany, Japan, and the US for at least two decades after the mid-1960s (Brenner, 2006).

Brenner upheld the centrality of profitability as the chief force behind capital accumulation, thereby establishing his roots in classical political economy. The significance of Brenner's 1998 book, followed in 2002 by its sequel, *The Boom and the Bubble*, could only grow if the historical dynamics that undergirded its findings received a sounder theoretical foundation. Highlighting the contributions made by Brenner's critics to the development of an alternative theoretical framework capable of explaining the historical facts is the essential first step.

From the 1980s onward the labor share declined while the profit share rose significantly in major OECD countries (Blanchard, 1997). Our empirical findings reveal that the secular rise in labor productivity was characteristically associated with a falling output–capital ratio (neoclassical writers refer to it as "capital productivity"). We think of this output–capital ratio as the maximum rate of profit (assuming zero wages and all value-added translated into profits). Our own estimates of "stylized facts" for the leading OECD countries show a significant decline in their output–capital ratio due to rising capital intensity in production and increasing competitive pressures to lower prices. In fact, the accumulation rate did not recover much because the recovery of profitability was less than satisfactory from the perspective of the pre-1980 "golden age." The actual profit rate, however, depends on the impact of a falling maximum profit rate on capital accumulation.

The thrust of Brenner's account of global turbulence is that competitive forces, largely from German and Japanese industries, battered the profitability of the US manufacturing sector. As the contraction extended to the rest of the economy, the worst recession since the 1930s engulfed the industrialized countries. But any investigation seeking to bring out the characteristic patterns of capitalist development could not proceed without theoretical support. Thus despite acknowledging the strength of Brenner's argument concerning the historical dimensions of the profitability crisis engulfing the advanced countries, we find his theoretical perspective unsatisfactory. Brenner's identification of unbridled international competition in the manufacturing sector as the cause of falling profitability trends will not stand scrutiny. In order to preserve its persuasive character, Brenner's masterful account of the events leading up to the global crisis requires stronger theoretical underpinnings.

After careful examination of the major data sources relevant for the reconstruction of international secular trends in profitability and capital accumulation, our empirical findings confirm Brenner's results. But our theoretical account of such trends differs considerably from his. Brenner's theoretical presuppositions are compatible with those of perfect competition. We agree with Anwar Shaikh's (1978, 1980) admonitions that standard views of perfect competition are not applicable to real industrial markets; Shaikh's critique provided the theoretical framework necessary to set Brenner's historical account into a logically sound structure. Moreover, Shaikh's (1999a) detailed critique of Brenner's major work provides all the elements necessary to sort out Brenner's theoretical underpinnings of his global crisis.

Indeed, Shaikh's comprehensive analysis exposed the theoretical inconsistencies in Brenner's account and provided a sound alternative to Brenner's explanation for the falling profit rate in the US economy. The microfoundations of free competition as proposed by Shaikh and Baumol provide the launching pad for our own evaluation of Brenner's account. Free competition works as a coercive force requiring firms to expand their market shares in order to survive the challenge of market-share losses. In order to succeed in this effort, firms need to beat their competitors, offering quality products at a lower price (Baumol, 2002). Thus, victory in the competition-as-war context requires first lower total unit costs, involving investments in capital-intensive technology (including the funding of costly R&D programs), and then lower prices that undermine the market shares of technological laggards.

In the context of raging global competition, Brenner views the profitability crisis in the US economy since the late 1960s as stemming from labor productivity growth trailing behind real wage gains caused by falling manufacturing prices (Brenner, 2006, 2002). On the other hand, the contention that a profitability crisis may occur only if wage shares remain unchanged (because labor captures the gains of productivity growth) while capital–output ratios rise is not acceptable either (Foley and Michl, 1999). Brenner correctly dismissed the relevance of theories of profit squeeze in the previous two decades as determining the onset of crisis. But he went on to claim that falling manufacturing prices in the US caused by unbridled international competition resulted in excessive real wage hikes (higher product wages) that compressed profitability in US manufacturing, dragging down the economy as a whole. According to Brenner, labor's excessive wage gains (above productivity advances) did not happen due to a stronger bargaining position on the part of labor, but rather by unintended wage windfalls originating in the dynamics of international competitive wars. In addition to Shaikh work, Zacharias (2002) brought out the contradictory message imbedded in Brenner's account of the rise in wages.

Indeed, US manufacturing profit rate levels appeared to exceed those in the nonmanufacturing sector until the early 1980s. The extent of the decline in manufacturing profit rates appeared to surpass that of nonmanufacturing. Brenner read the significance of this pattern to indicate that the privileged position of manufacturing was undermined by the juggernaut of international competition on the part of German and Japanese producers, since manufacturing products make up the bulk of foreign trade. German and Japanese firms reconstructed their plants and equipment with the most advanced techniques of production, employed cheaper workforces and generally enjoyed lower unit costs than their US competitors. Hence, cheaper foreign producers gained market share in American markets and forced American manufacturers to match their lower prices. Consequently, US manufacturing profit rates felt the downward pressure exerted by the lower price of imports to a greater extent than the nonmanufacturing sector. As manufacturing profit rates fell, Brenner argued, they dragged down the profit rates of nonmanufacturing businesses because product wages, wage rates adjusted by an index of product prices, rose and profit margins declined throughout the system.

This view of a US manufacturing sector initially enjoying a privileged position supported by profit rates above those in the US nonmanufacturing corporate businesses and then forced to retrench with significantly lower profit rates does not fit the evidence. As an insightful paper by Duménil and Lévy (2002) showed, the profile of higher profitability levels in manufacturing relative to nonmanufacturing loses content once three business categories are removed from nonmanufacturing, namely, mining, transportation, and utilities. The capital–output ratio in mining, transportation, and utilities is much higher than in other nonmanufacturing industries and their profit rates much lower due to price regulations in transportation and public utilities. As our estimates in Figures 8.8 and 8.9 show, the lower

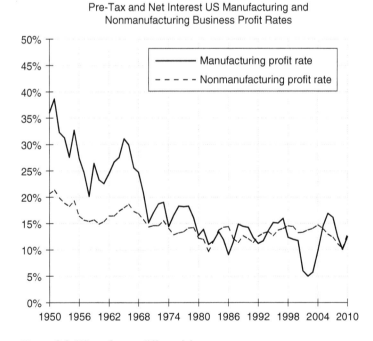

Figure 8.8 US profit-rate differentials.

Figure 8.9 US profit-rate equalization.

profitability level of nonmanufacturing is due to the presence of inordinately high capital-intensive technologies in mining, transportation, and utilities. Removing these industries from the estimates of nonmanufacturing raises its profitability to levels comparable to manufacturing. We then see that both manufacturing and nonmanufacturing enjoyed very similar trend profiles from 1949, although the manufacturing sector's profit rate exhibited wider fluctuations around its (downward) trend. Thus, international competition could not have been the cause of falling profitability in both sectors when foreign producers had not yet gained any significant ground in world trade. Figure 5.8 showed striking similarities in the manufacturing profitability trends of the three major countries vying for competitive leadership, Germany, Japan, and the US since the early 1950s. Competitive pressures would explain the tendency to even out the differences in profitability levels among the three, but not the direction of the common trend. The profitability trends would respond, rather, to the specific strategies pursued by the manufacturing sectors in Germany, Japan, and the US. For the three major contenders raising labor productivity in their respective manufacturing and business sectors via increasingly mechanized plants led to falling output–capital ratios.

The alleged bifurcation of accumulation and profitability

The prevalent view among heterodox economists regarding post-1982 profitability trends in the US and other major OECD economies is that the trend reversal of the

1980s gained momentum in the 1990s and restored profitability levels well within the reach of their previous 1960s levels. Similar developments are believed to characterize the experience of other leading OECD economies: profitability levels everywhere recovered their lost ground. Despite this rise in profitability trends, however, the consensus on accumulation trends among heterodox economists is that they continued their long-term downward drift.

In this section, we wish to challenge the claim that US profitability trends achieved in the 1990s full restoration of their lofty postwar levels. Our argument of the post-1980 continued weakness in capital accumulation takes into account the growing profitability differentials between nonfinancial and financial corporate sectors. Thus, contrary to Moseley and others, we suggest that the modest recovery of nonfinancial corporate profitability that followed the bounce-back from its trough in 1980 did not match the sharp increase in the profits of the financial sector. This lag accounts for the faster growth of financial "investments" and the continuation of the declining trend in real capital accumulation experienced since the 1960s. In our view, after the 1980s US nonfinancial corporations raised their dividend distributions and privileged buy-backs of their own equity, because financial investments returned higher yields than "real" alternatives offered. Corporate retained funds for capital accumulation did not recover after the 1980s because the prospects for nonfinancial profitability did not justify a rise in capital accumulation. The management of corporate finance reflected the higher payoffs of financial investments compared with the expected yields in nonfinancial sectors.

Traditional heterodox views regarding accumulation and profitability trends consistently stressed their direct relationship. As Bhaduri (1986, pp. 169–170) has argued, in the post-Keynesian perspective

> the level of expenditure or investment is the independent variable... it can hardly be doubted that investment is not altogether autonomous. Capitalists invest with a view to making profits. The higher are the expectations of profit... the larger is the investment that capitalists are willing to undertake.

From a different theoretical perspective, Shaikh (1992, p. 179) took for granted that "the actual rate of accumulation is roughly proportional to the actual profit rate," and Weisskopf's (1994, p. 147) assessment did not challenge the influence of profitability on accumulation:

> Capitalists are assumed to undertake capital accumulation to the extent that they expect investment to yield future profits; and expected profitability is in turn considered to be primarily a function of rates of profit actually experienced in the recent past... It follows that the overall rate of capital accumulation will depend (with a lag) on the average rate of profit.

As recently as 2005, three distinguished heterodox economists found profitability trends to be crucial for the analysis of capital accumulation, providing them with a powerful foundation for their textbook, *Understanding Capitalism*.

Clearly writing before the new heterodox consensus on profitability shaped their perception of the vicissitudes attending the overall postwar trend, these authors estimated the US corporate profit rate for 1948–2002 and showed that:

> The trend was generally downward, with corporate profits before taxes hovering at around 16 percent in the two decades following World War II and then declining to roughly half that rate, on average, in the last two decades of the century.
>
> (Bowles *et al.*, 2005, p. 233)

With regard to investment, they argued at length that:

> Businesses invest for one reason: to make money... investment is essential to enable a business to keep up in the competitive race, for only by renewing and expanding the capital goods used in production can the firm protect and enlarge its share of a market... Business owners usually decide how much they want to invest based on the expected profit rate and the rate of interest... the expected amount of profit per dollar of investment ... is one of the major determinants of the amount of investment undertaken.
>
> (Bowles *et al.*, 2005, p. 433)

Drawing chiefly on the rich data sources provided by official US agencies such as the Bureau of Economic Analysis, Figure 8.10 replicates five estimates of profit rates shown in influential papers by Cordonnier (2006, p. 101), Duménil and Lévy (2011a, p. 11; 2011b), Mohun (2006, p. 348; 2010, p. 2), and Moseley (2009, p. 315). Their efforts to challenge orthodoxy while building an alternative approach to the analysis of accumulation and profitability merit a large measure of approval. But their conclusion concerning the bifurcation of accumulation and profitability trends is untenable. Like "monopoly capital" theory of the past, these writers posit highly profitable firms eschewing accumulation for the sake of distributing dividends to shortsighted shareholders oblivious to the coercive nature of competitive forces.

The estimates produced by these leading heterodox economists seemed to confirm the claim of a roughly full restoration of US profitability levels in the 1990s. While Mohun's (2010) version follows a general course reflecting rather closely Duménil and Lévy's trend estimates, it is clear that their levels emerge separately. Obviously their calculations include different data elements. Moseley's profit rate, on the other hand, seems to bounce between them and after the early 1980s its trend rises more steeply than the other two. It is striking, however, that Mohun's (2006) profit rate version and his (2010) estimates differ so markedly. Indeed Mohun's (2006) profit rate rise after 1982 amounts to a bounce-back from its trough. While profitability appeared to climb steeply in the early 1990s, this was only the upward phase of a cycle that ended in 2001. Looking at the three complete cycles between 1982 and 2001, a sharp rise is not evident: in 2001 the profit rate at 8.1 percent did not exceed the level reached in 1988 and 1992.

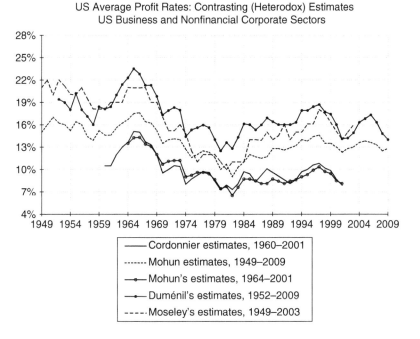

Figure 8.10 Contrasting estimates of US business profit rates.

Cordonnier's paper eloquently overturns the classical view linking capital accumulation and profitability, proclaiming in its title "Le profit sans l'accumulation: la recette du capitalisme gouverné par la finance." The apparent decoupling of (falling) accumulation and (rising) profitability trends, however, could only be explained as something of a paradigm shift in the understanding of capitalist investment behavior. We show, however, that such rupture is neither plausible nor necessary to account for the empirical evidence at our disposal.

On the other hand, three estimates of the US accumulation path replicated from Beitel (2009, p. 82), Cordonnier (2006, p. 101), and Duménil and Lévy (2011a, p. 13), shown in Figure 8.11, illustrate the agreement among heterodox economists that despite persistent cycles, the US accumulation rate trended downwards from the mid-1960s to the present. It is worth noting that while all three register a sharp climb from a low level in the early 1990s, this is only the rising half of a complete cycle that ultimately ends up lower than when it started. Indeed, this downturn, lasting into the early years of the twenty-first century, brought the accumulation rate to the lowest level of the postwar period before the Great Recession.

Moseley's contrasting estimates of profitability trends

The influential work of Robert Brenner contributed to rehabilitating the status of profitability studies as essential for the understanding of economic instability.

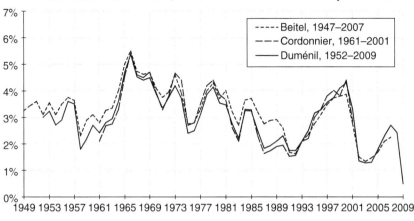

Figure 8.11 Three similar estimates of US accumulation rates.

His major works (Brenner, 2002, 2005, 2006) gained currency among critics of the mainstream on the strength of his detailed accounts of the historical transformations issuing from intensified competition among manufacturing producers in the US, Germany, and Japan. Brenner's work on economic turbulence, however, reached conclusions at odds with most heterodox research on profitability trends. His empirical estimates on profitability trends differed significantly from those produced by other leading heterodox economists, such as Moseley, and Duménil and Levy.

While Robert Brenner's analysis remained focused on manufacturing and the nonfinancial sector, Moseley's empirical work included the corporate sector as a whole, that is, both financial and nonfinancial corporations. As could be expected, Moseley's profitability estimates since the 1980s are higher than Brenner's because financial profits rose faster than profits in nonfinancial corporate industries. Mosely's (1985, 1988, 1992, 1999) sustained research program, ostensibly proceeding from a Marxian perspective, advanced an alternative account of US postwar economic crisis caused by the systemic tendency for the rate of profit to fall. Moseley's approach, however, emphasized the growth of unproductive labor activities, including the expansion of financial sectors, as the major force behind the profitability decline. From 1940s through the early 1980s, Moseley argued that falling profitability dragged down the rate of capital accumulation and ushered in the deepest recession experienced in the US since the 1930s. The long-term effects of the 1982 downturn reverberated throughout the decades that followed, up to the Great Recession of 2008:

> To understand the fundamental causes of the current crisis, we have to look back over the entire post-Second World War period. The most important cause

of the subpar performance of the US economy in recent decades is a very significant decline in the rate of profit for the economy as a whole. From 1950 to the mid-1970s the rate of profit in the US economy declined almost 50 percent, from around 22 to around 12 percent.

(Moseley, 2009, p. 297)

Moseley's summary of the major developments framing the postwar crisis high-lights changes in the rate of profit, falling from 1950 to the mid-1970s, and capital accumulation declining while unemployment rose. In response, govern-ments enacted policies to spur growth through deficit spending, reduction of business taxes, and lowering interest rates. But such fiscal stimulus failed to spur the investment spending of nonfinancial corporate businesses, which instead raised prices in order to reverse their profitability losses. As Moseley sees it, such busi-ness practices caused the unprecedented inflationary storm that brought about a prolonged phase of stagnation in the US. As a measure of protection against the perceived ravages of inflation to their profitability, "financial capitalists" in the 1980s pushed for restrictive monetary policies designed to raise interest rates: a new growth path of higher profitability and lower capital accumulation was launched. Indeed, from the vantage point of the first crisis of the twenty-first century, Moseley found that "In the US economy... the last three decades" inau-gurated a new phase of capital accumulation aiming to restore profitability "to its earlier, higher levels."

Moseley (2002) estimated that businesses managed to raise profitability lev-els above the depressed levels of the early 1980s, but Moseley (2009) hazarded that profitability had managed to climb in the 1990s to the levels achieved in the 1960s. However, he hedged his claim to full restoration of profitability with an important caveat, one that he hoped could definitely be cleared once untainted data was available:

On the other hand, these estimates do include a large and increasing percent-age of profits from the financial sector (approximately one third of total profit in recent years has been financial profit) much of which will probably turn out to be fictitious (i.e. anticipated future earnings that are "booked" in the current year, but will never actually materialize because of the crisis).

(Moseley, 2009, p. 300)

Moseley's profitability reversal claim rests on two legs. The first is the higher public deficits and lower profit taxes allowed firms to boost their prices without raising output. But if profitability was restored by price hikes on the strength of public deficits, one might question how such a policy affected the compet-itive position of the firms involved. Robert Brenner's evidence regarding the intensification of international competition in the 1970s and its impact on US manufacturing in the 1970s would be at odds with Moseley's argument. The sec-ond is the unprecedented increase in the rate of surplus value that businesses achieved at the expense of workers' living standards. What effectively brought about a higher profitability trend was "basically... the holding down of wages and consequently... the rate of surplus value has approximately doubled, from about 1.5 to around 3" (Moseley, 2008). But this claim contradicts Moseley's (2002) estimate: "the share of profit in 2001 was even lower than it was in the early 1990s; indeed it was the lowest of the entire postwar period. In the late 1960s and 1970s, the share of profit declined approximately 35 percent and has never recovered."

Moseley's claim regarding the sharp profitability reversal is questionable on the basis of the available evidence. The claim should be examined carefully in the light of all its empirical underpinnings, and this is not an issue framed in abstract claims of consistency or lack of it with classical political economy. Focusing on the correct elements that enter our estimates of profitability trends undoubtedly involves theoretical guidance in the selection of the sectors involved: corporate business; nonfinancial and financial; noncorporate business and the self-employed; before taxes or after taxes and so on. The various measures of profits to be considered include gross operating surplus, net operating surplus, corporate profits, and nonfinancial corporate profits.

Prominent heterodox economists, including Mohun, Duménil, and Lévy, share Moseley's view that the Great Recession did not issue from inadequate profitability yields, and that in fact profitability trends were more than sufficient to sustain a positive rate of accumulation if the link between them had not been severed. Between 1982 and 2009, for example, Mohun (2010) found "rising profitability, growing income and wealth inequalities, deregulation; culminating in speculative excess, implosion of money supply and credit."

On the other hand, Bruce Bartlett (2002), a leading financial analyst with a distinguished and conservative career, reminded his readers that "profits are what make the US economy run. It is why people invest, start businesses, hire workers, and take risks. Even those on the far Left admit this." But contrary to the heterodox consensus on the complete recovery of profitability from its trough in the early 1980s, Bartlett found that "all measures of corporate profitability have fallen over time" and worried that the tendency for profits to decline continued unabated. Citing a Commerce Department study, he found that gross profits declined by "about a third since the 1960s":

> Unfortunately, the rate of profit in the US economy has been trending downward for decades. According to a new report from the Commerce Department, the rate of return on corporate capital averaged better than 10% in the 1960s. But in the 1990s, it was one third lower, averaging 6.3%. Even at the height of the 1990s economic boom, profits peaked at just 7.8% in 1997. By contrast, profitability reached 12.1% in the 1960s.
>
> (Bartlett, 2002)

Because nonfinancial corporations, however, carry the lion's share of real investment and finance their spending largely out of their retained profits, focusing on their accumulation and profitability trends seems the most appropriate. Simply

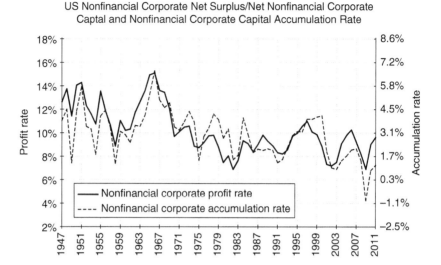

Figure 8.12 US nonfinancial corporate profitability and accumulation rates.

put, experiencing lower profitability would explain their lower accumulation rate. In our view, acknowledging that Robert Brenner's profitability estimates reflect the slower profitability recovery of nonfinancial relative to financial corporations, but subscribing to the strong profitability recovery of the past three decades, Moseley, Duménil and Lévy, and others failed to avail themselves of the simplest and most natural explanation for the lack of a "strong revival of investment." We are satisfied that Figure 8.12 supports the view that linking capital accumulation and the profit rate in the US nonfinancial corporate sector is a concept validated by empirical evidence spanning more than 50 years.

Profit rate expectations are sharply affected by current and past profit rate trends, and the influence of capacity utilization and (prime) interest rates significantly improves the estimates of future capital accumulation trends. In this light, the falling general trend of capital accumulation since the mid-1960s is perfectly in line with past and present profit rate trends, admittedly falling between the mid-1960s and the early-1980s. Following a noticeable bounce-back out of the 1982 trough, the profit rate experienced persistent fluctuations between the late 1980s and 2009 without setting on a rising trend. From each initial low point of every cycle to its ending low point starting in 1986, the end point fell lower than the previous one. The first end point brought down the profit rate in 1992 to 8.2 percent from a previous low in 1986 of 8.4 percent; the second cycle ending in 2002 lowered the profit rate to 7.2 percent down from 8.4 percent; and finally, the completed cycle in 2009 reduced the profit rate to 6.9 percent. No especial theory of accumulation seems to be required in order to account for the empirical evidence behind its long-run trend.

9 Profit-driven capital accumulation in OECD countries

Introduction

We aim to show in this chapter that accumulation trends in the business and cor-porate sectors, by and large, reflected similarly directed trends in business and corporate profitability. First, we argue here that past profitability trends played a crucial role in framing the outlook on future yields of current business investment plans. A legacy of various decades of stagnant profitability will tend to dampen expectations and therefore will produce relatively weak investment plans. In our view, then, the continuing decline of the US nonfinancial nonresidential capital accumulation rate (calculated as net investment flows in that sector relative to the current cost net capital stock with one-year lag) reflects the weak profit expecta-tions generated by a relatively flat profitability trend originating in the late 1980s. We extend this appraisal to major OECD countries as well, showing that prof-itability trends in the business sectors of major OECD countries do in fact provide reliable guides to predict the direction of actual accumulation trends.

Keynes' concept of *marginal efficiency of investment*, interpreted as referring to the expected profitability of investment, shares with classical political economy, including Marx, the view of profit-driven accumulation. While Keynes empha-sized the uncertainty surrounding future profitability prospects, however, the weight assigned to past profitability trends loomed large in classical economics, including Ricardo's and Marx's approach to the formation of profit expecta-tions. In Marx, the availability of funds as well as borrowing capacity of firms considering implementation of current investment plans clearly depends on the profitability of past investments. If, due to innumerable factors weighing in on the success of current investment plans, radical uncertainty clouds the assessment of future yields, past results are likely to play a decisive role in the final decision to implement them.

Nonfinancial corporate shares in US nonresidential investment

Fixed capital investment is largely the preserve of corporate business. Figure 9.1 shows that for around 30 years US nonfinancial corporations increased their share of nonresidential investment, despite the shrinking share of manufacturing depicted in Figure 9.2. Between 1945 and 1960 profitability and capital accumulation trends in the nonfinancial corporate sector did not display a common

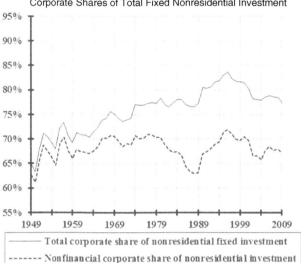

Figure 9.1 Corporate shares in fixed investment.

trend: falling profitability did not cause a falling accumulation path. This apparent anomaly, however, occurred because in the postwar years profitability levels were at their highest and expectations of future profitability had not yet weakened, as they did after the mid-1960s. In the early postwar period up to the early 1960s, not only did profits retention and accumulation remain stable, but the accumulation rate rose, pulled by high profitability levels despite its reversal at the end of that decade. Figure 9.3 shows, from the late 1940s through 2009, retained earnings as a share of nonfinancial corporate net surplus fluctuating within a narrow band between 20 and 35 percent, averaging 28 percent. But Figure 9.5 shows that in the US since the mid-1960s falling accumulation trends reflected the downward evolution of actual profitability (calculated as net operating surplus, over the respective net capital stocks in the nonfinancial corporate and business sectors at current replacement values). The profit rate after deducting net interest payments fell lower in both cases.

Business sector net operating surplus

The Bureau of Economic Analysis (2006, p. 9) defines *net operating surplus* as:

A profits-like measure that shows business income after subtracting the costs of compensation of employees, taxes on production and imports (less subsidies), and CFC from gross product (or value added), but before

US Manufacturing Shares of Net Value Added, Nonresidential Investment, and Profits in Nonfinancial Corporate Sector

Figure 9.2 Manufacturing shares in corporate net value added, investment, and profits.

subtracting financing costs (such as net interest) and business current transfer payments. Net operating surplus consists of net operating surplus of private enterprises ... and current surplus of government enterprises.

Government enterprises are defined elsewhere (Gutierrez *et al.*, 2007, p. 6) as "government agencies – such as the US Postal Service or state government-run utilities – that cover a substantial portion of their operating costs by selling goods and services to the public."

From 1960 to 2008 the nonfinancial corporate nonresidential capital accumulation rate normalized by the capital stock tracked US nonfinancial corporate retained earnings also normalized by the capital stock quite closely and exhibited considerable inertia.

Figure 9.3 shows retained earnings of nonfinancial corporations maintaining a stable share of net operating surplus, lending support to the claim of profit-led accumulation. Their internally generated funds largely covered gross fixed investment plans and budget deficits only reached depths over 40 percent after the 1980s when net acquisition of financial assets required increased borrowing. Despite the profitability recovery after the 1980s, US nonfinancial corporate profit

Figure 9.3 Retained earnings shares in corporate net surplus.

expectations did not rise sufficiently to increase the share of internal funds needed for capital accumulation path. The empirical evidence presented in Figures 9.7 and 9.8 for eight leading countries of the OECD, linking the accumulation and profitability trends, is strong enough to reach a similar conclusion.

Considering the turbulent nature of capital flows, we should expect the evolution of profitability in the financial and nonfinancial corporate sectors to follow divergent paths. But such turbulence does not preclude what Shaikh calls "tendential regulation" of dynamic systems exerted by gravitational forces dampening their explosive tendencies. Figure 9.3 underscores the fact that US profitability cycles in the financial sector exceeded those of nonfinancial corporations in length and amplitude. Figure 9.4 shows the financial share of corporate profits rising from around 7.5 percent in 1949 to over 36 percent in 2004.

Along with that surge, capital flows into the sector intensified. Indeed the share of retained profits in financial corporate net operating surplus registered major fluctuations since the late 1960s, plunging precipitously through the early 1980s and sharply bouncing back thereafter, understandably so because it reflected major profitability swings and significant capital inflows. In line with our claim that

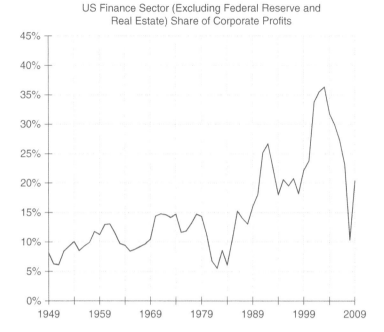

Figure 9.4 US financial sector profit shares in total corporate profits.

profitability drives the growth of business activity, the evolution of the US financial sector is highly relevant here. That finance growth led the profitability recovery in the corporate sector (and the accumulation of debt) without significantly altering the accumulation prospects of nonfinancial corporations explains the gravity of the current global slump. The bubbles associated with financialization sustained aggregate demand via the so-called "wealth effect" from the 1990s, but once they burst the debt pileup prevented a quick recovery from the slump despite the rise in profit margins.

Financialization and accumulation trends

Much of the controversy surrounding the effect of financialization on capital accumulation revolves around the degree to which corporate investment funding relies chiefly on internally generated business savings, the retained share of profits, or, as post-Keynesians argue, on new credit extended by the banking system. In the US, corporate accumulation is largely financed internally out of corporate profits. Corporate businesses set the share of after-tax available profits they wish to retain in accordance with the magnitude of their investment plans, and then decide dividend disbursements with the residual. As Figure 9.5 shows, the path followed by retained profits relative to capital stock closely mirrors, at a lower level, that of corporate profitability.

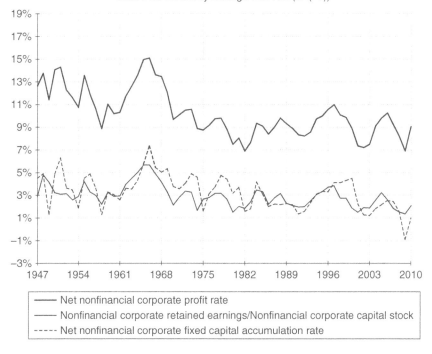

Nonfinancial Corporate Net Operating Surplust/Capital Stock(–1) and
Nonfinancial Corporate Retained Earnings (Domestic and Foreign)/
Capital Stock(–1) and Nonfinancial Corporate Fixed Capital Accumulation
Rate Plus Inventory Change with IVA (I/K(–1))

——— Net nonfinancial corporate profit rate
——— Nonfinancial corporate retained earnings/Nonfinancial corporate capital stock
----- Net nonfinancial corporate fixed capital accumulation rate

Figure 9.5 US nonfinancial corporate accumulation and retained profit rates.

When assessing the prospects for future profitability in investment plans, evaluation of past profitability trends adjusted for variations in capacity utilization
plays a major role. Moreover, deciding the appropriate share of retained profits to provide the necessary funds for the implementation of planned investments
requires balancing the pressures exerted by shareholders to distribute dividends.
Since the implementation of investment projects stretches beyond the near future,
businesses need to estimate the availability of finance throughout the full gestation
period. Changing expectations as implementation proceeds requires a considerable measure of funding flexibility. If these assumptions are true, we should expect
to find empirical evidence showing the turning points of corporate saving decisions
generally preceding those of actual investment. We believe that our empirical findings for the US nonfinancial corporate sector show cycles of retained earnings
relative to capital stock generally anticipating those of capital accumulation
rates. Because planning investment projects requires the prior allocation of
funds in real time, retained earnings persistently appear ahead of accumulation
cycles.

According to recent post-Keynesian interpretations of the impact of financial activities on profitability and accumulation, after the economy recovered from the profitability trough of 1983 a new set of "stylized facts" (somewhat reminiscent of Kaldor's earlier version) defined corporate behavior. Post-Keynesian economists argue that in the last three decades nonfinancial corporations drastically altered their growth strategies. Instead of relying on internal sources of finance to cover their fixed capital accumulation needs they increased their bank borrowing in order to purchase financial assets, including their own, while simultaneously reducing their offerings of new equity shares. These practices expanded corporate debt to unprecedented levels, forcing corporate managers to raise short-term profitability targets as revenue sources to cover higher financial obligations, and lower funds allocated for fixed capital investments (Dallery, 2009).

In recent post-Keynesian and neo-Marxian accounts of the upturn in profitability trends registered in major OECD countries since the early 1980s, the recovery path is presented as steadily rising, reaching levels in the 1990s comparable to those recorded before the troubled 1970s. The accumulation rate, however, displays a downward direction. From the perspective of classical political economy, simultaneously rising profitability and generally stagnant or falling capital accumulation rates are a somewhat puzzling development. If such findings were real, the bifurcation between profitability and capital accumulation trends would thoroughly unravel the classical notion of a feedback loop between capital expansion and profitability. Indeed a good many writers identified with post-Keynesian and neo-Marxian perspectives claim precisely that: diverging profitability and investment trends are characteristic features of neocapitalism driven by the ascendance of finance. The title of an influential French study claiming to substantiate the alleged dichotomy says it all: "Le profit sans l'accumulation: la recette du capitalism gouverné par la finance" (Cordonnier, 2006).

Numerous contributions to the heterodox literature (Tropeano, 2012), seeking to break with classical principles as outmoded vestiges of theories unsuitable for the contemporary practices of financialization, advance similar claims. Beitel (2009) recently acknowledged that "Marxian theory, as well as neoclassical economics, predicts that higher rates of expected profits should trigger a higher rate of investment." Beitel concedes that in the past the connection generally held up, since competitive firms sought market leadership, gaining cost advantages over rivals, chiefly through investments on new technologies. Through such strategies, leading industry firms achieved lower unit costs, allowing them to lower prices, gain higher market shares, and enjoy a higher profit rate than their hapless competitors. Beitel argued, however, that this nexus between profitability and accumulation no longer existed. After the 1980s, Beitel claimed that "in a mature industrial economy" rising profitability no longer spurred higher investment in new technologies because "a diminishing share of investment" is now required to finance technical progress, since the expansion of capacity leads to rising output–capital ratios:

> The result is a tendency for the system to drift towards a lower rate of investment absent the appearance of major capital-absorbing technological

innovations that drive recapitalization of existing branches of industry and spur the emergence of entirely new industrial sectors. . . In other words, the rise in the nominal output/capital ratio means that capitalists as a whole can meet any expected rate of growth of market-demand with a proportionately smaller outlay on new plants and equipment.

(Beitel, 2009, p. 83)

Contrary to the view that globalization imposes world standards in unit costs and prices on nonfinancial industries, Beitel argued that in recent decades competitive pressures weakened in intensity. In this light, the predominance of oligopolies in the US and other countries turned moot the logic of competitive price wars and justified the rejection of views assuming that corporations carried out "coerced" investments to achieve industry leadership over their competitors (Crotty, 2005).

Instead of seeing the global reach of corporate firms as adding power to their arsenal of competitive weapons, recent post-Keynesian and neo-Marxian critiques of classical theories of free competition imply that oligopolistic corporations possess the means to choose their own success strategies, undisturbed by coercive competitive pressures. Accordingly, they are free to choose technological blueprints of any capital intensity, set their price markups and curtail their growth without regard to the consequences for future market shares: in short, abrogate the coercive rules of free competition. Managers no longer face choices in the context of competitive battles. Neocapitalism and the financialization of capital, according to critics of classical views, pulled corporations out of the crisis path, transformed their practices into an engine of rising profits, fulfilled their need for higher yields and moved capital accumulation to a lower channel of corporate options. In this paradigm, the coercive force behind accumulation, so central to classical economics, recedes into oblivion.

Heterodox critiques of the classical approach to profit-led growth argue that changes in governance regimes favor the growth of financial preferences, meaning the rise of so-called "shareholder value orientation" to a ruling principle of corporate management. In this view, shareholders prefer receiving larger dividends rather than allowing firms to increase their retained profits for expansion. This inverts the order of priorities between retained earnings and dividend payouts. In the era of financialization, raising dividends paid to shareholders became the paramount goal of corporate governance, hence the decline in accumulation. Instead of seeking to attract new funds for capacity expansion through sale of new equity issues, corporate strategy switched to buying financial assets for speculative gains. As nonfinancial corporations repurchased their own shares as well as those of other corporations, they contributed to stock market booms delivering the expected financial gains. Lazonick and O'Sullivan (2000) refer to this turn in corporate governance as a new phase of capitalism characterized by policies aiming to "downsize and distribute," in contrast to previous practices designed to "retain and reinvest."

Seeking to explain the alleged dichotomy between rising profitability and falling accumulation rates in neocapitalism, post-Keynesian economists (Skott and Ryoo,

2008; Stockhammer, 2005–06; Van Treeck, 2007, 2008) face a seemingly intractable conundrum. In their view, as nonfinancial corporations lower the share of retained profits and the overall savings rate falls, the effect should lead to a higher multiplier and an expansion of aggregate demand. Through the lens of Keynesian economics, rising aggregate demand should increase capacity utilization and raise profitability, which if sustained at some point should improve expectations and motivate higher investment plans rather than lower rates of accumulation.

The actual decline in real investment growth that post-Keynesian economists observe, however, plays havoc with Keynesian theory, setting the scene for a thorough reappraisal of post-Keynesian explanations. Solving the puzzle required the introduction of *ad hoc* motivational concepts hitherto excluded from the story: the new preference for short-term earnings returns dictated by shareholders' value orientation trumped the long-term benefits of expanding capacity and getting higher profits through rising capital investments. Accordingly, nonfinancial corporations channeled a growing portion of their profits into purchases of financial assets yielding higher returns, including their own equity shares, setting in motion a virtuous circle of profitability gains without accumulation. Their own purchases boosted equity prices and helped to sustain the attraction of financial over real investments assets.

Figure 9.6 shows that, by and large, US nonfinancial corporate internal funds covered gross investment expenditures and therefore the significant rise in corporate debt was due to the net acquisition of financial assets.

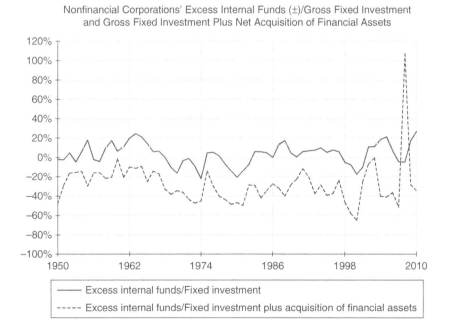

Figure 9.6 US corporate internal financing of accumulation.

Accumulation trends in major OECD countries

Contrary to claims advanced in the heterodox literature regarding the bifurcation of profitability and accumulation trends, our findings support the traditional view stressing their overall parallelism. After the mid-1960s, OECD actual profitability trends generally declined through the early 1980s, and beyond that period settled at a lower level (compared to the postwar highs). Even without adjusting for capacity utilization, profitability trends declined in most countries and net investment expenditures fell. Accordingly, US corporations lowered their corporate saving, that is, reduced the retained profits appropriated for reinvestment on nonresidential fixed capital expansion.

Regarding the primacy of corporate business savings in relation to their investment spending, US data published by the Bureau of Economic Analysis is crucial because it is more detailed than what most other OECD countries' national accounting services offer. Hence, our empirical evidence on this point relies heavily on US data. But in those OECD countries where data on retained corporate profits is not readily available, the close parallelism between business profitability and capital accumulation trends provides a strong measure of support for the classical view of profit-led growth.

Raising labor productivity and lowering total unit costs generally requires deployment of capital-intensive, labor-saving technology. We have argued all along that growth-driven firms seek to achieve larger market shares and higher profitability than their less dynamic rivals by deploying capital-intensive techniques, lowering total unit costs and reducing prices below their rivals' capabilities. Despite raising unit fixed capital costs, such techniques lower total unit costs because the reduction in unit variable (chiefly labor) costs exceeds the rise in unit fixed costs. This reduction in total unit costs sets the stage for a lower market price and leads to the expansion of market shares, casting lagging competitors into the marginal rungs of industry with lower profitability. As in all wars, industry leaders surviving the competitive struggle and gaining higher profitability pay a price in the event. Leading firms switching to a strategy involving more capital-intensive technology (with higher unit fixed costs) coupled with aggressive price-cutting (made possible by lower total unit costs) will achieve lower output–capital ratios and reduced profit rates. But, on the other hand, they will accomplish two things: a higher market share and the highest profit rate among the remaining firms surviving the industry shakeup.

The average profit rate estimates displayed in Figure 9.7 clearly show the extent to which the business sector profit rates of five major OECD countries experienced a significant decline since the 1970s, and a close view of its trends generally belies the claim of any significant restoration of profitability after the 1980s. The precipitous decline experienced in the 1970s abated, but there is no evidence indicating that OECD profitability reverted to the higher levels of earlier decades. Moreover, as Figure 9.8 shows, for seven major OECD countries nonresidential capital accumulation rates faithfully mirrored their respective profitability trends. Such parallelism suggests that even though the formulation of forward-looking

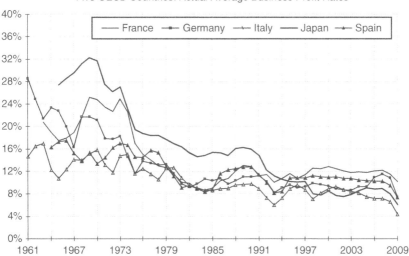

Figure 9.7 Business sector profit rates in five OECD countries, 1961–2009.

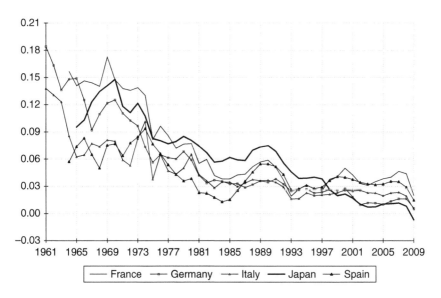

Figure 9.8 Capital accumulation rates in five OECD countries, 1961–2009.

investment plans faced the vagaries of expectations, their implementation largely reflected the long-term profitability patterns underlying their course.

Table 9.1 provides additional support for our contention regarding the leading role of profitability in the determination of accumulation trends. These are simple regressions of the accumulation rate on profitability. We added one-period lagged accumulation rates into our equations because, while profitability patterns shape the general direction of accumulation plans, multi-period completion of fixed-capital projects imparts some inertia to new investment expenditures.

Canada's case for bifurcation

The elaborate theoretical structure built up by heterodox economists to account for the alleged bifurcation of profitability and accumulation rates in OECD countries appears to stand without general empirical support except, that is, in the case of Canada from 1993 until the outbreak of the recent crisis. The anomalous behavior of these variables in Canada after 1993 contrasts sharply with the gravitational pull exerted by falling profitability upon accumulation rates for nearly half a century between 1949 and 1993. Canada's belated and rising gap between accumulation and profitability, roughly spanning over a decade, undoubtedly reflects investment plans failing to match rising rates of return. But the implications of such a singular dichotomy cannot be extended beyond the context of a small country and a few years to proclaim a new stage in the development of capitalism. Heterodox writers working within the theoretical perspective of Keynes or Marx cannot sustain claims of structural changes in the development of capitalism on such ephemeral empirical foundation.

Table 9.1 Business accumulation and profit rates: nine major OECD countries: regression results

	C	Profit rate	Profit rate(-1)	Profit rate(-2)	Profit rate(-3)	Accu. rate(-1)	R^2
Canada 1949–2009	−0.0295 (−2.63)	0.524 (9.98)	−0.396 (−6.1)			0.862 (12.79)	0.893
France 1964–2009	−0.007 (−1.28)	0.661 (7.21)	0.544 (−5.28)			0.84 (12.09)	0.964
Germany 1961–2009	−0.017 (−3.91)	0.54 (13.36)	−0.30 (−4.56)			0.723 (10.84)	0.990
Italy 1960–2009	−0.0135 (−1.92)	0.825 (9.55)	−0.558 (−4.77)			0.678 (7.66)	0.929
Japan 1965–2009	−0.005 (−2.68)	0.62 (12.26)	−0.56 (−7.954)			0.932 (14.34)	0.991
Spain 1964–2009	−0.02 (−3.34)	0.504 (6.03)	−0.184 (−1.6)			0.598 (5.5)	0.907
Sweden 1965–2009	−0.032 (−4.23)	0.60 (8.37)				0.811 (14.61)	0.934
UK* 1965–2009	−0.003 (−.45)	0.48 (4.346)		−0.315 (−2.45)		0.74 (5.47)	0.672
US 1949–2010	−0.016 (−2.35)	1.01 (10.09)	0.78 (−5.09)			0.839 (8.37)	0.873

The remarkable parallelism displayed in Figure 9.9 between the accumulation and profitability paths between 1949 and roughly 1993 (underscored by a 0.907 correlation coefficient) should count as confirmation of the classical view regarding their structural linkage. It reveals the existence of a remarkably strong gravitational pull keeping the long-run growth of fixed capital in line with the evolution of profitability.

Incremental profitability and fixed investment growth

In this section we provide evidence of the close fit between the incremental profit rate (IPR) and nonresidential investment growth rates in the same group of major OECD countries where we previously found accumulation paths largely mirroring average profit rates. The feedback loop between average profit rates and the growth of capital stocks sets the structural channel for sustaining the accumulation of total capital. The feedback between incremental profitability and investment growth, on the other hand, links the dynamics of industrial competition with the ebb and flow of short-term new investments. That profit-rate differentials guide the allocation of new investments is not a controversial principle across otherwise contending theoretical perspectives: "The idea that capital flows accelerate and decelerate in response to differential rates of return on real investment is common to all of economic theory" (Sarich and Hecht, 2010, p. 5).

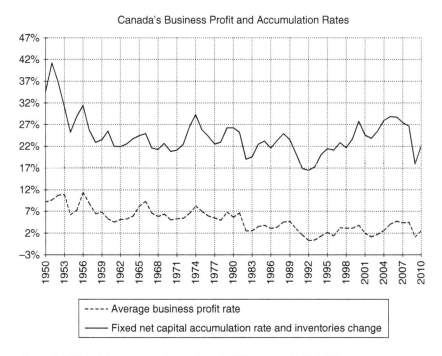

Figure 9.9 Canada's accumulation and profitability rates, 1950–2010.

It needs stressing, however, that it is incremental, not average profit rates that regulate new investment growth rates and capital flows across industries globally located. Shaikh's (2008) formulation of real competitive dynamics (Shaikh, 2008) provides the theoretical and empirical foundation for our premise exploring the connection between marginal profitability and capital flows. Shaikh's (1978, 1980, 1987) theory of competition stresses the turbulent dynamics of capital flows across industries, speeding up when higher profit rates signal favorable differentials and racing out when declines reverse the incentives.

Seeking to capture higher profit rates when market conditions favor a particular industry (or a country's industrial yields) if demand growth temporarily outpaces supply or technical change improves best-practice methods, investments flows into that sector will grow in intensity. At some point the capital rush is likely to overshoot its original target and then the profitability luster is likely to fade. Falling prices will signal the growth of excess capacity and diminishing incremental profitability, thus signaling the decline in investment growth. In the event, the unending search for higher profit rates and the exit from subpar activities sustains the crisscrossing of capital flows underlying the tendential equalization of profit rates across industries, branches, and countries. Tsoulfidis and Tsaliki (2005, p. 20) tested its predictive power in Greek manufacturing and found it to be "a fertile ground for further theoretical and empirical research."

Individual firms operate with different technologies, management systems, cost structures, and profit rates. Competitive forces in each market enforce the one-price rule, hence the coexistence of diverse unit costs in each industry confers on those firms operating with the best available technology and the lowest unit costs a position of market leadership characterized by profit rates higher than the rest. Capital investment flows across industries, located in various countries, seek to replicate or adopt the operating conditions of the highest-profitability firms in the target industry, not the lower ones or the industry's average. The fact that individual industries are scattered across various countries does not necessarily imply that each country harbors an equal number of leading firms. Leading industrial firms may actually crowd in one country, with industry laggards scattered in various other locations.

Thus it is the profitability yielded by the leading firms in each industry, using the most advanced techniques generally available, that will attract capital flows across industries scattered in various countries. Given the cost advantages of such firms and their competitive price practices, Shaikh's (1999c) term *regulating* capitals conveys the sense in which such capitals enforce best production practices and act as magnets for capital inflows. Advances in productive techniques will necessarily render the least competitive firms within each industry unprofitable, and technical change through time will recreate the dispersion of unit costs behind the diversity of profit rates. Hence, the profitability of firms with average unit costs, as well as those with the lowest, will diverge from the profitability of the leading regulating capitals in the industry.

New investments will seek to reproduce the production methods of regulating capitals yielding the highest profit rates, and their growth will depend on the extent to which these expectations are fulfilled. In any given industry the average rate of profit differs from the profit rate of the leading, *regulating* best-practice firms. Firms' total profits reflect the results of all past investment flows and their average profit rate measures the ratio of total profits to their accumulated stock of capital investments. On the other hand, their incremental profit rate relates their change in profits to their most recent investment. We can therefore write the total profits currently available to an industrial firm, Π_t, as the sum of profits yielded by the most recent investment plus the profits generated by all past investments:

$$\Pi_t = \Pi_{It} + \Pi'_t.$$

Hence the change in profits related to the most recent investment, $\Pi_{It} = \Pi'_t - \Pi_t = r_t I_{t-1} + (\Pi'_t - \Pi_{t-1})$, provides the conceptual foundation for our estimation of incremental profit rates, r_{It}. We can define such a measure of short-term capital profitability as the ratio of the change in current profits in one firm, industry or country relative to the most recent, lagged (say, by a year) current cost gross investment in that firm, industry or country. Now the difference between the profits received from all past investments and the profits generated by the most recent investment is bound to be small and can be ignored. As a guide to investment flows, the incremental rate of profit, defined as the actual change in profits brought about by the most recent gross investment will play the decisive role, $r_{It} \approx \Delta \Pi_t / I_{t-1}$.

Shaikh's theory of industrial competition expands the conceptual linkage between average profit rates and capital accumulation, identifying the ebb and flow of incremental profitability as the chief driver of gross fixed capital investment growth rates across industries and countries. Estimating incremental profit rates from National Income Accounts data does not encounter the obstacles that average profit rates calculations normally involve. Gross nonresidential investment data are readily available and the series are more reliable than capital stock estimates for most OECD countries. For our purposes, relating nonresidential gross investment growth rates to incremental profit rates in major OECD countries provides an invaluable measure of the linkage between accumulation and profitability.

Capital accumulation and profitability: the OECD evidence

We have argued that the long-run trend in average profitability plays a decisive role in shaping the long-run trend in capital accumulation. We defined the capital accumulation rate as the ratio of net investment plus inventory change in the relevant sector of the economy over the capital stock in that sector. This profitability trend encompasses the average of the yields, including those obtained in the best-performing capitals of the given industry along with the worst, that is, those lower rates associated with the use of obsolescent technologies, bad locations, etc. This relationship between capital accumulation in the industry or sector and average profitability is mediated by the trend in corporate retained earnings, generally reflecting conjectures regarding future profits formed in the light of past experience. Since a high degree of uncertainty surrounds decisions that will only prove their soundness in future developments, the weight of past experience acquires an overwhelming importance.

Empirical evidence shows that the fairly constant share of retained earnings in the net operating surplus of nonfinancial corporations behind the ratio of retained earnings to capital stock roughly tracks the rate of capital accumulation. In addition, the ratio of retained profits to capital stock typically precedes in real time the movement of the accumulation rate. We conclude from this that the long-run trend in average profitability is the dominant force behind capital accumulation. In the US the share of dividends disbursed in net operating surplus only increased recently when the yields of financial investments outperformed those of the nonfinancial sector.

As opposed to net investment in our calculations of the capital accumulation rate (net investment/capital stock), our empirical work shows the incremental (marginal) profit rate driving the growth of gross investment plus inventory change. Indeed, the growth rate of gross investment appears to be highly correlated with the fluctuations in marginal profit rates, that is, those yields associated with the most recent investments. Investment growth reflects volatile appraisals of likely short-term yields in the best available projects of industry, since below par new investment projects involving obsolescent technologies or otherwise mediocre conditions of production will be shunned, despite their availability.

The profit fluctuations resulting from such innovating investment projects are likely to exceed the fluctuations in average profitability precisely because they take place in untested conditions. Average profitability reflects the yield of established methods of production, even if they are no longer attractive as cutting-edge ports of entry for capital flows into the industry. But the fluctuations in the marginal profitability space driving new investments impact the average profitability trend directly, in so far as they affect the capital stock growth of industries or sectors of the economy. While the variance of marginal profits exceeds that of average profitability, the mean of both variables is roughly the same.

The AMECO database of the European Commission's Directorate-General for Economic and Financial Affairs (DG ECFIN) provides the time series extending from 1960 to 2010 necessary to derive empirical estimates of incremental profitability and nonresidential fixed capital investment growth rates for France, Germany, Italy, Japan, Spain, and Sweden. For these countries, profit-type measures of net economic surplus consist of the difference between factor-cost national income and employee compensation.

While the AMECO database does not explicitly include the category of nonresidential fixed capital investment as such, we derived it from the difference between the available gross fixed capital investment data and the housing investment series, adding investment in inventory changes to the final estimates. For Canada, the

UK and the US, National Accounting tables furnished the necessary time series for a longer span, extending from 1948 to 2009. For Canada our estimates of incremental profitability and nonresidential gross investment growth are for the nonresidential business sector. The UK estimates refer to the private nonfinancial corporate sector.

Figures 9.10–9.18 show our estimates of the relationship between marginal profitability and nonresidential gross investment growth in major OECD countries. In all cases and for extended periods of time we found that nonresidential gross investment growth in the nine countries under consideration tracked very closely the fluctuations of the marginal profit rate. Figure 9.19 for the US sets the average profit rate as the gravitational center for the marginal values. The graphs, however, reveal a change in the overall trajectory of both variables, with a distinct decline evident after the mid-1980s relative to the previous decades. We believe that the effect of this decline anticipated the state of financial fragility that led to the financial crash of 2008. Finally, we found the only evidence supporting the heterodox claim of rising average profit rates coupled with falling accumulation values in our profile of the business sector of the Canadian economy after 1993.

To summarize, while competition across industries brings about a rough equalization of profit rates through new investment flows attracted by regulating

Figure 9.10 France's incremental profitability and investment growth rates.

Figure 9.11 Germany's incremental profitability and investment growth rates.

capitals best-practice profitability, it also recreates the diversity of profit rates in each industry caused by the dispersion of operating unit-costs within. Moreover, since the regulating capitals of various industries may cluster in different countries, the tendential equalization of their profit rates will underpin the pattern of new investment flows across their borders. But in every industry, not necessarily circumscribed to a single country, a variety of profit rates will persist despite the constant ebb and flow of capital investments because industrial structures are not homogeneous in their technical endowments, or conditions of production.

Adjusting for capacity utilization

We now introduce the concept of capacity utilization as a tool for the (partial) adjustment and transformation of actual estimates of profitability trends into normalized tendencies of the system's evolution. A comprehensive treatment of the issues involved in the assessment of capacity utilization and the procedure followed to estimate actual measures for major OECD countries will be presented in Chapter 12. Normally, persistent declines in capacity utilization will induce firms to reduce their fixed capital investment and thus downsize their accumulation

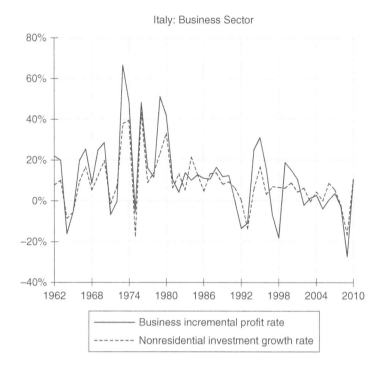

Figure 9.12 Italy's IPR and investment growth.

plans. As Shaikh's (1989) growth models show, when first confronted with falling aggregate demand, firms will respond by lowering their circulating capital expenditures, cutting down on purchases of materials, trimming their workforce and reducing working hours. Steady expansion of capacity utilization will, on the other hand, trigger operational adjustments in the opposite direction. Only when these adjustments cross a certain time threshold impacting the prevailing set of expectations will accumulation rates undergo modification.

A steady rise in capacity utilization forces firms to operate less efficient facilities otherwise left unused, signaling the need for additions to productive capacity, that is, a rise in the accumulation rate of fixed capital. On the other hand, the expansion of productive capacity may be resisted when the long-run path of profitability augurs no reversal in its downward trend and hence a weakening in the propensity to invest. Of course, in the short and medium run, the impact of fluctuations in aggregate demand will change the degree of capacity utilization, and consequently the actual output–capital ratio will register significant changes. Indeed, the actual output–capital ratio is likely to exhibit major cycles with amplitudes depending on the strength of capacity utilization changes.

The impact of capacity utilization on the estimation of output–capital ratios is significant. Output–capital ratios exhibit short- and medium-term cycles in three

Figure 9.13 Japan's IPR and investment growth.

major sectors of the US economy: the business, nonfinancial and manufacturing corporate sectors. The business sector national income of the US economy encompasses all profit-based activities of the private and public sectors and should exclude incomes imputed to resident homeowners that do not involve actual market transactions. While government administration expenditures are clearly not driven by profit constraints, government enterprises are. Thus all profit-based business activities, excluding government administration and such imputations as those related to residential ownership, are included in the business sector. Encompassing both corporate and noncorporate firms as well as the self-employed, the business sector provides the largest context for the study of profitability and capital accumulation. Within the business sector, US nonfinancial corporations account for the lion's share of nonresidential investment and remain the bellwether of the national economy. Manufacturing in turn belongs to a smaller subset of nonfinancial businesses, including both private and government enterprises.

Adjusting for sustained capacity utilization fluctuations reveals the existence of a smoother output–capital path with a distinct downward long-run trend. We ranked capacity utilization indexes in the US business, nonfinancial, and manufacturing sectors after identifying the highest value obtained as one,

Figure 9.14 IPR and investment growth, Spain.

assuming that such points represent measures of full capacity. Adjusting the output–capital ratio for capacity utilization generally uncovers capacity-capital paths, Y^*/K, characteristically exhibiting smooth, downward-sloping trends. These capacity-capital measures in the three sectors under consideration allow a partial adjustment from actual profitability subject to capacity utilization fluctuations to normal profitability reflecting long-run trends,

$$r^* = \frac{\Pi}{Y}\frac{Y^*}{K}.$$

As we show in Chapter 12, after adjusting the actual output–capital ratios for the US business and nonfinancial corporate sectors for capacity utilization, the emerging long-run trends, while negative, do not share the same rates of decline. A steadily falling capacity-capital path is likely to lower the normal profitability trend despite sporadic boosts to aggregate demand, rising capacity utilization, and increasing profits share. While short- and medium-term variations in capacity utilization (responding to fluctuations in aggregate demand) affect the movement of actual profit rates, normal profitability trends in turn, that is, actual profitability adjusted for capacity utilization, drives the long-run path of capital accumulation.

Figure 9.20 shows our estimates of the rise in capacity utilization experienced in major OECD countries after the early 1980s. We explain in Chapter 10 the

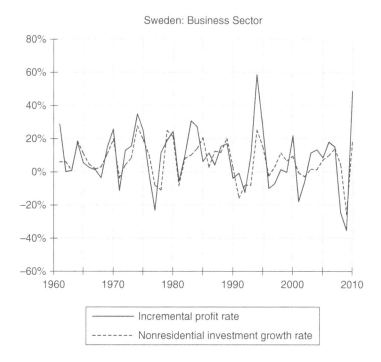

Figure 9.15 IPR and investment growth, Sweden.

procedure used to derive these estimates. Such increases alone would account for a good measure of the observed changes in profitability trends since then. But simultaneously, as we show in Chapter 12, the concerted movement toward full capacity utilization occurred with a rising trend in labor unemployment and falling wage shares in national income. Full capacity utilization does not necessarily imply full employment of labor. With rising capacity utilization and falling wage shares, the steep downturn in profitability experienced in major OECD countries after the mid-1960s was corrected, leading to relatively stable profit rates, albeit at a lower level. But despite higher levels of capacity utilization and lower wage shares, a significant recovery of business profit rates was not achieved. As Figure 9.8 shows, capital accumulation trends across these countries did not benefit from the stabilization of profit rates due to the insufficient recovery of profitability. In the absence of a vigorous recovery of profitability trends, business strategy favored squeezing more output out of existing plant and equipment rather than the expansion of capacity to meet demand pressures.

Limitations in OECD data

OECD *Economic Outlook* data allowed us to obtain empirical support for the contention that accumulation rates closely reflected the evolution of actual

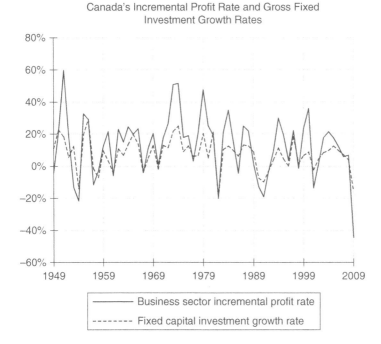

Figure 9.16 IPR and investment growth, Canada.

profitability trends between 1960 and 2006. The OECD *Economic Outlook* pro-vided the data used to calculate the nominal capital stock, average profitability, and capital accumulation in the business sector of six major OECD countries from 1960 to 2006; beyond that year, the AMECO data bank supplied the growth rates for the capital stock used to extend our estimates to 2009. In the case of Spain we used data on investment and capital stocks published by the BBVA bank from 1965 to 2007.

For the UK calculations we downloaded the relevant data series from the web-site of the Office for National Statistics. OECD *Economic Outlook* data does not include corporate retained earnings, and in any event, after 2005, this source ended publication of all time series related to the business sector. Before the OECD *Economic Outlook* discontinued publishing data on the business sector, such as business GDP and business capital stock, the term generally meant the whole economy minus general government administration. Lacking direct data, we cal-culated business sector profitability and accumulation trends that include corporate and noncorporate business, and which do not differentiate between nonfinancial and financial corporations, subtracting government variables from the relevant published series. In addition, the switch from fixed-weight to chain-type volume series implemented in some OECD countries at the end of the 1990s, and carried

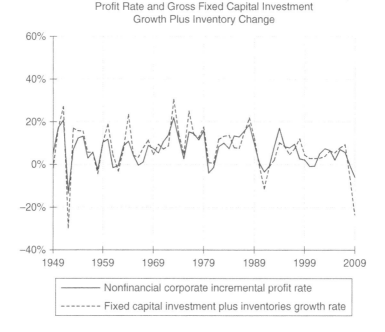

Figure 9.17 IPR and investment growth, UK.

over generally to the *Economic Outlook* volume data after 2006, set the end for direct profitability calculations using that source. GDP chain-type volume series do not add up to their constitutive components and hence do not allow for meaningful calculation of operating surplus estimates. Despite these roadblocks we obtained estimates of profitability and accumulation trends in various major OECD countries whose general characteristics between 1960 and 2009 confirm their close fit.

The core argument restated

We identify profitability in the nonfinancial corporate sector as the driving force behind capital accumulation. Despite a falling manufacturing share in US nonfinancial corporate investment, between 65 and 70 percent of all US nonresidential investment is carried out by US nonfinancial corporations. Financial corporations' investment shares rose significantly after the 1980s because the share of financial corporate profits rose substantially in the same period.

From the prosperous years of the 1950s to the eve of the Great Recession, US nonfinancial corporations largely covered their fixed capital expenditures out of their internal funds, within a sustained range of plus or minus 20 percent. Purchases of new financial assets since the 1980s drove their debt accumulation.

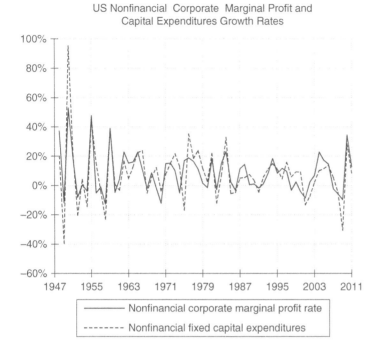

Figure 9.18 IPR and investment growth, US.

Nonfinancial corporate retained earnings fluctuated narrowly around 35 percent of their net operating surplus, so that a decline in retained earnings allocated to fixed capital expenditures merely reflected a (roughly) proportional decline in net operating surplus. On the other hand, the proportion of profits saved by financial corporations changed significantly with the more pronounced swings of the financial sector average profit rate. Contrary to the steady savings propensity of the nonfinancial corporate sector, the savings propensity of financial corporations itself rose and declined with the rise and fall of the financial sector's profitability.

In the US and eight other major OECD countries the capital accumulation path of the business sector mirrored the long-run trend of average profitability. This finding contradicts the claim advanced in the heterodox literature regarding an alleged bifurcation between rising profitability and falling accumulation trends after the 1980s. Presented as a characteristic feature of neoliberalism, this dichotomy is said to emerge due to changes in the "governance regime" of corporations and the change in shareholders priorities favoring high financial yields, high dividends, and low accumulation. Our findings suggest that the global crisis precipitated by the 2008 collapse of accumulation was not a fortuitous event. Falling incremental profitability trends after the mid-1980s provide a logical cause of the parallel declines in nonresidential gross investment growth paths. In this

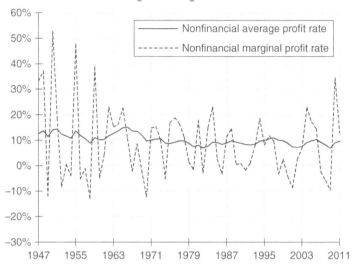

Figure 9.19 US nonfinancial corporate average and marginal profitability rates.

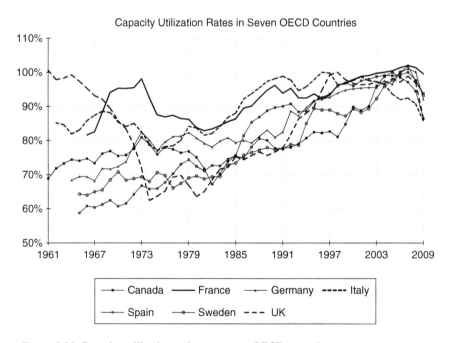

Figure 9.20 Capacity utilization estimates: seven OECD countries.

light, the alleged shift in corporate finance favoring dividend payouts instead of nonresidential fixed capital growth reflected the falling yields of new corporate investments. The beneficiary of such corporate bonanza, of course, was none other than the financial sector where those funds flowed. Outpacing the growth of household incomes and goaded by the euphoria surrounding implausible stock market and housing bubbles, debt accumulation by households and banks reached levels that at some point proved unsustainable and led to the financial collapse.

10 Nonfinancial versus financial profitability trends and capacity utilization

Introduction

We assess in this chapter the empirical evidence behind the contention that capital flows from nonfinancial to financial investments responded to profitability differentials between the two sectors. We further argue that adjusting the actual measures of nonfinancial corporate profitability for capacity utilization strengthens the view of a falling trend. It follows that the higher yields found in financial markets relative to nonfinancial corporate investments prompted the transfer of capital funds to that sector. After the mid-1980s, the falling share of value-added in US manufacturing, once the center of the nonfinancial corporate sector, extended to the nonfinancial corporate sector as a whole. Consequently, the falling share of nonfinancial corporate value-added in total corporate value-added reflected the structural changes brought on by the ascendance of finance.

Conventional accounts of the postwar economic recovery in the US such as Maddison's (1982) glossed over one of its chief characteristics: the falling trend in nonfinancial corporate profitability, running through short-term fluctuations that shaped the path of capital accumulation from 1947 to 1982. In that period, the impact of technical change and global competition first lowered manufacturing profitability trends and then spread throughout the wider nonfinancial corporate sector. Such a declining trend was symptomatic of profound structural changes caused by technical progress, undertaken by expanding firms under the pressure of international competition, to raise the capital intensity of production and so increase the growth of labor productivity. Our interpretation derives from the approach of nineteenth-century classical political economy to the centrality of profits, taken as both the goal of accumulation and its internal source of finance. Smith, Ricardo, Malthus, J. S. Mill, and Marx took for granted that profitability prospects, not effective demand or supply, powered the growth of capitalism. The recent consolidation of globalization trends not only preserved the pursuit of profits as the central object and support of capital accumulation, but also extended its domain beyond national boundaries and heightened its relevance.

From the late 1940s on the profitability path of US businesses, while punctuated by cycles of various amplitudes, took on a downward bend that stretched for thirty years before reaching its trough in the early 1980s. Thus, after business profitability rose sharply to a peak in the mid-1960s, it then plunged just as steeply through the second half of that decade. Profitability not only fell off the lofty perch attained in the mid-1960s as precipitously as it had previously climbed it, but once the downward correction ended the profit rate sank to a new trough much lower than any attained since the 1950s.

Taken as a whole, the nonfinancial corporate profitability trend initiated in 1948 fell, reached its trough in 1982, and bounced back up to a peak in 1988. After that year it failed to sustain a significant recovery trend despite major cyclical takeoffs in the 1990s. Since 1988 and up to the so-called financial meltdown of 2007, the before-tax nonfinancial corporate profitability linear trend, unadjusted for capacity utilization and gross of interest payments, while exhibiting substantial fluctuations, experienced a mild descent. In the smaller manufacturing sector, moreover, the profitability trend running through significant short-run fluctuations maintained its fall to the present albeit at various rates of decline.

To sum up, the underlying weakness in nonfinancial profitability trends and hence capital accumulation in that sector was not caused by the growth of financial activities. On the contrary, it was the falling profitability trend in nonfinancial corporate business after the 1970s that led to rising capital flows into financial assets, leading to the ascendance of finance. The declining profitability path dogging the investment prospects of US nonfinancial corporations from the late 1940s into the early 1980s briefly experienced a sharp rebound in the 1980s, but financial corporate investments led the economic recovery. This view is not new, as critics of financialization such as Crotty (2005) attributed the growth in US demand for financial products as the alternative to depressed yields in nonfinancial corporate (NFC) investments:

> Many NFCs responded to the low profits and high costs of external funds they faced in much of the 1980s and 1990s, as well as to the high returns they observed being made on financial assets and financial enterprises, in two innovative ways. First, an increasing percent of NFC investment funds were used to acquire financial assets. Second, firms created or bought financial subsidiaries, and expanded those financial subsidiaries already in existence. These widely noted developments are sometimes referred to as the "financialization" of the NFC in the neoliberal era.

As we showed in Chapter 9, the falling profitability trends of the 1970s were not limited to the US but rather common in major OECD countries, where rates of capital accumulation in nonfinancial activities generally fell before and after the early 1980s. Hence as the profitability crisis spread throughout the advanced capitalist countries, the growth of surplus capital, seeking relief from low profitability prospects at home and searching for higher returns abroad, reached levels that provided global depth to investment in financial instruments. The notion that recovery from the 1930s depression and post-World War II expansion could unravel due to the impact of declining profitability upon the rate of accumulation challenged the basic assumptions of neoclassical growth models and therefore received scant attention from mainstream economists. Various research efforts designed to track the actual course of business profitability grudgingly considered that possibility but found reasons to reject it.

Motivated by the unexpected stagnation of the once vigorous US recovery from the Great Depression, empirical work carried out by neoclassical economists in the 1970s and early 1980s detected some evidence confirming the fall in profitability trends. While the existence of falling profitability trends provided sufficient reason to explain the visible signs of declining capital accumulation, slowing economic growth, rising unemployment-cum-inflation, higher interest rates, and subpar productivity growth of the 1970s, prevailing opinion refused to draw negative implications for future growth prospects.

The prolonged downturn of the 1970s brought out in sharp relief the limitations of Keynesian economic policies and indeed undermined the survival of Keynesian economics, thus contributing to the neoclassical restoration. The confluence of stagnation and inflation in the 1970s wreaked havoc on growth prospects in advanced capitalist economies, undermining the credibility of Keynesian economics as a general interpretation of macroeconomic dynamics. As the decade came to a close, the effects of the sluggish growth on labor markets pushed the unemployment rate to unprecedented levels not known since the 1930s Depression, while rising inflation raised questions about the effectiveness of fiscal policy. Keynesian economics was simply not ready to provide a coherent explanation of the stagflation conundrum and hence it lost its influence both as sound theory and as a source of guidance for policy makers.

Declining profitability was central to Keynes' view of the Great Depression's origins. Writing on the relevance of Keynesian economics to explaining and guiding the recovery effort facing the global economy after the 2007 financial meltdown, the Swedish economist Axel Leijonhufvud (2008) argued that Keynes' motivation to write the *General Theory* responded to his conviction that:

> The background to the Great Depression in Britain, as Keynes saw it, was the declining trend in the return to investment since the end of World War I . . . The combination of a declining marginal efficiency of capital and interest rates that did not decline propelled the country into a recession that was deep even before the United States slipped into depression.

Leijonhufvud's remarkable insight, coming from an unrepentant Keynesian economist wary of modern theoretical offshoots since the 1970s, provides an invaluable historical bridge to our views on the current global crisis.

It is our contention that the rise to prominence of financial activities in the relentless search for higher corporate profits was preceded by the long downturn in the average profitability of nonfinancial corporations ending in 1982. Indeed, the overall decline extending from the late 1940s to 1982 presented a major challenge to corporate confidence in future prospects. In our view the growth of the financial sector and its profit share took off precisely at this juncture, when a way out of the profit stagnation facing nonfinancial corporations was most needed. We do not blame the expansion of financial investments for the decline in nonfinancial accumulation and its diminished profitability. On the contrary, we associate the declining trend in capital accumulation of US nonfinancial corporations from the mid-1960s to the present with falling profitability trends culminating in 1982 and since then with the relative stagnation of profitability at a historically low level.

Understanding the dynamics behind such massive flows of capital into financial assets begs a fundamental question: Were the alternative profitability options in the nonfinancial industries so patently inferior? The question applies not only to the US economy but also to other countries whose large surpluses (savings) financed the purchase of US financial assets after the 1980s. Indeed, it was such massive capital flows from various parts of the world that sustained US trade and government deficits while allowing the maintenance of low interest rates despite spiraling debts. In the US, where financial innovations proliferated so rapidly, banks built their fortunes upon a bed of toxic products incapable of withstanding their corrosive foundation. Were there no other investment options available in fast-growing China that yielded better returns than those found in US Treasury bills? Why did so much capital opt for low-yield "investments" if higher yields were available elsewhere? These questions raise obvious doubts about the nature of profitability trends not only in the US but world-wide.

Measuring corporate profitability

The corporate sector consists of nonfinancial and financial corporations. Our empirical evidence builds on NIPA files issued by the Bureau of Economic Analysis (BEA) that provide the necessary data to work out a fairly accurate picture of nonfinancial corporate profitability, subject to less ambiguity than profitability trends in the non-corporate sector. To obtain profitability estimates in the business sector as a whole requires plausible assumptions for the assessment of proprietors' equivalent wages. NIPA data on the noncorporate sector, however, does not distinguish between the income of self-employed persons and their imputed wages, and hence fuddles the division between wages and business profits shares in the proprietors category. Usually researchers assume that, on average, proprietors' wages reflect the average wage of full-time employees in the economy as a whole, but this is only a plausible conjecture. Thus empirical work derived from official data on nonfinancial corporate profitability benefits from the steady flow of standardized information for a sector lacking proprietorships, compared to the business sector, which combines corporate and noncorporate (proprietors') businesses.

Shareholders in nonfinancial corporate industry turned to financial investments as promising grounds for prospective gains, thereby forcing managers to reduce the share of retained profits in net corporate surplus earmarked to fund nonfinancial investment while raising dividends. As shareholders favored financial assets over real ones, to accommodate the demand for financial assets nonfinancial corporations expanded their dividend payments. Lower profitability and rising dividend payments were bound to alter the use of corporate funds. The expansion of the financial sector in turn required financial innovations; deregulation of financial markets; falling interest rates, and ample supplies of capital from the US and abroad. As Tobin (1965) noted:

> Keynesian difficulties, associated with divergence between warranted and natural rates of growth, arise when capital intensity is limited by the unwillingness of investors to acquire capital at unattractively low rates of return. But why should the community wish to save when rates of return are too unattractive to invest? This can be rationalized only if there are stores of value other than capital, with whose rates of return the marginal productivity of capital must compete.

Since the 1990s, rising pressures on nonfinancial corporate management to expand dividends in order to fund shareholders' growing appetite for financial assets displaced nonfinancial investment from its central role in the accumulation of capital. Low profitability in nonfinancial sectors justified equally low corporate rates of capital expansion, while rising profitability in financial sectors spurred investors to acquire financial assets in banking, insurance, and mortgage lending as superior alternatives. Total retained profits, including foreign and domestic sources, financed average net capital accumulation rates of 2.7 percent for the period 1983–2008, compared to 3.8 percent for 1948–1982. The share of interest payments in the net operating surplus of nonfinancial corporations did not rise substantially after the mid-1980s, but the share of dividends increased sharply after the early 1990s once financialization gained momentum. Figure 9.4 showed the rising shares of financial sector profits relative to total corporate values, confirming the irresistible ascendance of finance. Figure 10.1 shows the growth of financial corporate profits keeping pace with GDP and nonfinancial corporate

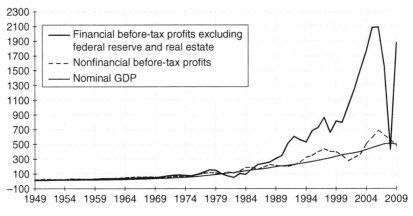

Figure 10.1 Rise of US financial sector corporate profits after the mid-1980s.

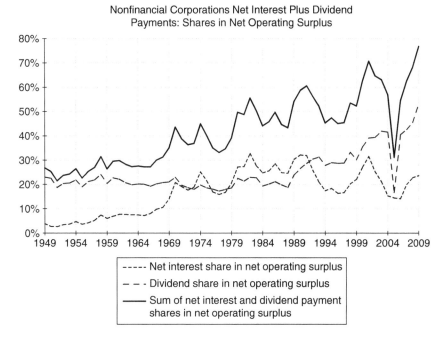

Figure 10.2 Net interest and dividend shares in nonfinancial corporate net surplus.

profits up to the mid-1980s, but rising with a distinct acceleration since then. The share of financial corporate gross value in total value-added more than trebled from 4.5 percent in 1948 to nearly 14 percent in 2007. But the share of financial profits in before tax corporate profits in the same period more than quadrupled from 8.4 percent to almost 35 percent. After 1989, coinciding with the acceleration of the "financialization" drive, as Figure 10.2 makes clear, the share of dividends in the net operating surplus of nonfinancial corporations experienced a sharp increase. Rising dividends provided owners of corporate equities greater opportunity to diversify their capital allocation away from nonfinancial sectors and into financial assets.

Alternative profitability measures

It is important to note that the distinction between NIPA corporate *net operating surplus* and domestic corporate profits hinges on the inclusion or exclusion of net interest payments in the measure. NIPA estimates of domestic corporate profits exclude corporate net interest payments, and we need to consider further whether the long-run evolution of corporate profitability differs once interest payments are subtracted from the net operating surplus of the corporate sector. The capital consumption adjustment to corporate profits converts historical (book) valuations of fixed capital consumption (capital consumption allowance) into current replacement costs of fixed capital consumption (capital consumption adjustment). Thus the NIPA before-tax corporate profit rate, $r_{CORP} = \Pi_{CORP}/K_{CORP}$, measures profits after-interest payments over current-cost net capital stock in that sector, and in the case of nonfinancial corporations the corresponding variables apply, $r_{NFC} = \Pi_{NFC}/K_{NFC}$.

With regard to inventories, the NIPA adjustments change the historical valuations of inventories to current replacement cost valuations in line with the NIPA estimates of the capital stock. In the NIPA methodology, profit gains or losses derived from the price adjustment from historical to replacement costs of inventories are counted as changes in business income. The inventory valuation adjustment involves reversing the sign of the change (Bureau of Economic Analysis, 2006, p. 5).

As we saw in Chapter 9, in contrast with the profitability trends displayed in Figure 9.5, the prevailing view among leading heterodox economists is that a pronounced upward trend in the US and other OECD countries, extending from the early 1980s to the present, ended the postwar decline. In this connection, Duménil and Lévy have persistently argued in recent papers (2011a, 2011b) that the profit rate of US nonfinancial corporations in the 1990s had fully recovered the lofty levels achieved in the 1960s. In their view, calculations of profitability *after* subtracting net interest payments possibly obscured this alleged trend reversal. Defining nonfinancial profitability as the ratio of profits before net interest payments to net nonfinancial capital stock should bring out the extent of the full recovery in profitability, while defining it after deducting net interest payments presumably veils the profitability upturn.

Figure 10.3 shows the lack of empirical evidence supporting this claim. It displays profitability trends in nonfinancial corporate sectors, $r_{NFC}^{BI} = NOS_{NFC}/K_{NFC}$, before and after the subtraction of net interest payments. Our profitability estimates are generally based on NIPA data for *net operating surplus* (see Chapter 9). Figure 10.3 shows sharp cyclical movements in before-tax nonfinancial corporate profitability punctuating a sharp downward trend extending from 1948 to 1983. The difference in procedure to calculate the average profit rate in nonfinancial and financial corporate industries stems from the nature of financial capital. Nonfinancial businesses use fixed means of production, plant, and equipment to transform materials into final products for sale. Of course this transformation is mediated by money flows at each step of the way towards the final product. But financial businesses such as banks and insurance companies do not engage in similar transformations of materials when providing credit or other services to customers. On the other hand, the nature of their business requires retention of considerable capital reserves to meet unexpected contingencies and secure the uninterrupted flow of transaction businesses.

Generally, no questions of data selection need arise when computing the profit rate of nonfinancial corporations defined as the ratio of various measures of current annual profits to current-cost fixed capital stocks: all the relevant data are found more or less ready-made in BEA publications. But in order to calculate the average

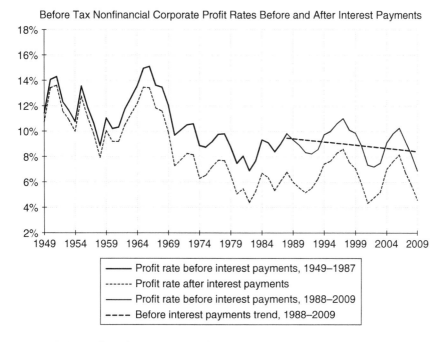

Figure 10.3 Nonfinancial corporate profit rates, before and after net interest payments.

profit rate of the financial corporate sector, the procedure to augment the fixed capital stock estimates with relevant measures of liquid reserves stocks requires careful judgment and identification in the Federal Reserve Flow of Funds data.

Duménil and Lévy have argued that rising interest payments of nonfinancial corporate balance sheets present incontrovertible evidence of the financial sector's power to siphon off a growing share of the nonfinancial corporate net operating surplus. But while the net interest share in the net operating surplus of nonfinancial corporations rose in the 1980s, it has trended downwards since the 1990s, in contrast with the trend of dividend shares that remained noticeably flat throughout the 1980s and thereafter rose substantially.

As Figure 10.3 shows, nonfinancial corporate profitability before tax and before interest payments, experienced a bounce-back from 1982 to 1988 that restored it to late 1970s levels above the trough of 1982. The profitability upturn in the second half of the 1990s seemed to validate the view that a sustained break with previous trends had materialized and the recovery of previously attained high profitability levels had been fully achieved. But the steep rise in profitability of the 1990s proved to be no more than the upward half-phase of a full cycle that, like all others before, completed its course in a sharp downturn extending through the early years of the twenty-first century; indeed, its trough in 2001 brought it within the range of the 1982 low point, the lowest level since 1948.

The financial boom and corporate profit rates

The financial sector's activities, including commercial and investment banks, insurance companies, credit unions, and security brokers, do not involve material production but the creation of financial instruments with various default risks. In order to calculate its profit rate we need to relate its profits to the combined stocks of financial reserves and fixed capital stocks underpinning its operations. The BEA issues data on fixed assets for both corporate categories, financial and nonfinancial, but offers no data on the financial capital advanced in addition to the fixed stocks. The Flow of Funds data published by the Federal Reserve, on the other hand, offers disaggregated data for the various institutions making up the financial sector. Our selection of individual financial categories follows the activities identified by Duménil and Lévy as constituents of finance. We did not follow their methodology concerning financial capital values as we opted in favor of a reasonable selection of available assets acting as capital reserves. We agree with them, however, that despite the fact that NIPA data for the financial sector includes real estate, this commercial activity does not fit well with the characteristics of finance and insurance companies proper, since real estate largely involves the rentals, actual or imputed, of household-owned residences, commercial buildings and other structures. For the purpose of tracking the profitability paths of nonfinancial and financial corporate businesses we excluded both the profits and capital held by the Federal Reserve (because it is not a private business) and real estate (because it does not involve the kind of commercial activities undertaken by financial companies).

As we have repeatedly stressed, an account of the forces that brought about these structural changes favoring the growth of financial corporations would be incomplete without including the profitability trends of nonfinancial corporations. Figure 10.4 displays the profitability path of nonfinancial corporations for comparative purposes. Matching the BEA definition for financial, net-of-interest, before-tax profits relative to the current-cost capital stock (through persistent cycles), our calculation shows a falling trend for the nonfinancial profit rate extending from the late 1940s to 1982. Bouncing back from the trough of the early 1980s and despite the so-called neoliberal regime of deregulation, wage suppression, and falling interest rates, the full extent of the recovery consists at best in the stabilization of nonfinancial corporate profit rates. Before-tax profitability estimates, after deducting net interest payments from net operating surplus, arguably reveal a rather flat trend from 1984 through 2008, averaging about 6 percent. Comparing the nonfinancial sector profit rate with the average profit rate in the US financial sector, including banks, insurance companies, and other financial institutions, brings out the long-term gravitational pull present between the two yields despite their short-term deviations.

In the post-1980 period, the recovery of the financial sector profit rate proceeded faster, outpacing the nonfinancial corporate industries. It is our contention that the growth of ostensibly lucrative financial activities drew world capital away from investment in low-profitability nonfinancial sectors and diverted it into

Figure 10.4 US average corporate profit rates, financial and nonfinancial sectors.

higher-yield financial assets. Sustained efforts on the part of the Federal Reserve to spur growth by lowering interest rates substantially contributed to possibly unintended as well as unsustainable asset bubbles. Financial asset inflation under-pinned the internet, stock market and housing bubbles behind the vaunted booms of the 1990s and early twenty-first century. As we note below, falling interest rates induced complacency in the assessment of risks associated with financial invest-ments of dubious provenance, and financial capital pursued speculative mirages with disastrous consequences. Once the housing bubble burst and the subprime mortgage debacle broke out, the financial boom collapsed, dragging the whole system with it.

The effect of falling interest rates

While the evolution of interest rates impinges on the "cost of capital," we take expected rates of return to be the decisive force behind the formation of corporate investment plans. Nominal as well as real prime interest rates fell substantially from their highs in the early 1980s, and this decline contributed to the stabiliza-tion of net profitability trends in the nonfinancial corporate sector. In the pursuit of high yields, moreover, falling interest rates muted risk aversion and spurred asset price bubbles. The problem before nonfinancial corporate businesses after the 1980s was not high interest payments but low profitability, despite effective measures to contain wage growth. In their textbook *Understanding Capitalism* (Bowles; *et al.*, 2005) three prominent heterodox economists analyzed the chief determinants of investment plans, arguing that a corporation will consider the feasibility of investment "only if it expects to earn more profits. Every firm, when

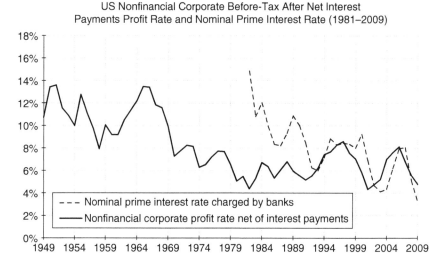

Figure 10.5 US nonfinancial corporate profit rate and prime interest rates.

considering what to do with its profits, must compare the cost of investments with the expected return from these investments" (p. 268). Now, estimating investment costs may involve two different scenarios, "a firm may borrow the necessary funds at the prevailing *interest rate* (i) from a bank... or from people who are willing to buy *bonds* from the firm . . . On the other hand, a firm may finance an investment using funds available (internally) from previous profits. In this case it must [forgo] the opportunity of lending these funds to other firms at the prevailing rate of interest (i)" (p. 269). Clearly falling interest rates will impact positively on the propensity to invest and rising interest rates will discourage the expansion of investment plans, hence "This places a significant amount of responsibility with a nation's central bank . . . because it has the power to move interest rates up or down" (p. 271). We would argue that the relevant interest rate to apply when a nonfinancial firm decides to allocate its own internal funds between financing real investment rather than lending to other firms would be the comparable prime interest rate charged by banks to their own corporate borrowers. Figure 10.5 shows that after the early 1990s the levels and movement of the profit rate and the prime interest rates were strikingly similar. In the age of financialization short-term Treasury bills would be an unlikely option for nonfinancial corporations considering where to "park" their internal funds unless the fear of impending recession cut off all other financial alternatives.

Corporate and noncorporate profitability trends

The before-tax average profit rate estimated for the business sector as a whole, including corporate (both nonfinancial and financial corporations) and noncorporate businesses (including proprietors), followed a long-run cyclical path not significantly at odds with the nonfinancial corporate rate of return. We reached this conclusion after applying the following definitions for business profits and business net capital stock.

We defined business profits gross of interest payments before income taxes, but net of indirect business taxes, as the residual after subtracting from business net domestic product (BNP), found in NIPA Table 1.9.5, the sum of employee compensation in private industry, $COMP_{PI}$, plus the wage compensation imputed to proprietors, $COMP_{PROP}$:

$$\Pi_B = BNP - (COMP_{PI} + COMP_{PROP}) - (IBT_C + IBT_{NC}).$$

To obtain proprietors' wages between 1948 and 1960 we calculated the average compensation of full-time private industry employees from NIPA Tables 6.2 and 6.5, and multiplied it by the number of proprietors, from NIPA Table 6.7. These estimates were spliced with those on proprietors imputed wages derived for the years 1960–2009 from AMECO Table 7, reflecting the difference between AMECO's US net operating surplus and AMECO's net operating surplus, including imputed wages of self-employed labor. Finally, we subtracted indirect business taxes, $IBT_C + IBT_{NC}$, renamed in NIPA Table 1.13 "taxes on production and imports less subsidies plus business transfer payments" on corporate and non-corporate businesses. For the relevant categories of capital stock in the business sector we chose the sum of nonresidential corporate and noncorporate capital values from Fixed Assets Table 4.1 plus the corporate residential capital stock of Fixed Assets Table 5.1. As Figure 10.6 shows, average profit rates in the business and nonfinancial corporate sectors share a common profile. Thus, the average profit rate in the US business sector becomes:

$$r_B = \frac{BNP - (COMP_{PI} + COMP_{PROP}) - (IBT_C + IBT_{NC})}{K_C^{NR} + K_{NC}^{NR} + K_C^{R}}.$$

Impact of capacity utilization on profitability trends

An integral part of the research project engaging the work of classical political economists was to establish the connection between the growth of demand and capacity output. Fundamentally, the growth of capacity output resulted from a capital stock expanded by net fixed capital investment. The productive capacity available at any given time determined the potential level of output, while the growth of capacity depended on the dynamics of profitability with normal capacity utilization. Classical political economists assumed the persistence of systemic growth regulated by structural forces driving the system towards levels of aggregate demand in sync with normal capacity utilization. Once attaining normal capacity utilization, shifts in demand would change the composition but not the level of aggregate supply.

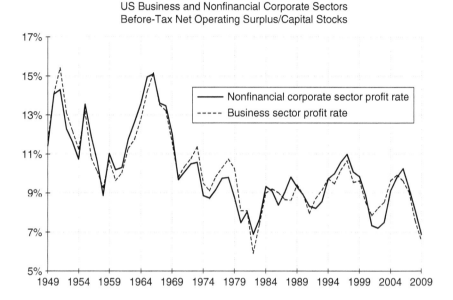

Figure 10.6 US average profit rates before taxes and interest payments, business and nonfinancial corporate sectors.

Positing the existence of such central tendencies, deriving from free market competition relentlessly driving firms to push costs to the lowest feasible levels, inter-industry free flows of capital provided the mechanism responsible for adjusting profits actually produced (in Marx, surplus value) to profit levels congruent with normal capacity utilization. In other words, classical political economists focused their analysis on the systemic forces that for the system as a whole brought produced (potential) profits to levels compatible with normal capacity utilization.

Attainment of normal capacity utilization derives from competitive pressures enforcing the use of plant and equipment at the scale where unit production costs are lowest. Competitive firms with the lower unit costs push less efficient rivals out of business. Market forces bring about these results, driving aggregate demand towards equalization with aggregate supply. Following the approach pursued in classical political economy, our long-term profitability trends emerge from a system in which capitalist enterprises strive to raise profit shares in net value-added while deploying capital-intensive technology as a general prerequisite to raising labor productivity. Adjustments of actual profitability estimates for capacity utilization prove essential to separate the effect of business fluctuations from systemic changes in the underlying capital–output trends.

When temporarily demand and sales rise faster than output in a given industry, realized profits first and then capacity utilization in that industry rise above their normal levels. The existence of profit windfalls attracts new capitals into the industry, causing an expansion of its capital stock, hence of its productive capacity and potential output. In due course, however, prices in that industry would decline dragging down its profitability. Thus the initially higher profits caused by the temporary deviation of aggregate supply and demand will not persist. The larger sales resulting in higher realized profits will increase produced profits and lead to capacity growth. But they will also attract inflows of capital into the industry and the expansion of aggregate supply will push prices down, reversing the growth in yields. As prices fall, driving down profits, output and capacity utilization will decline to their normal level once again.

Distinguishing short-run profitability cycles from long-run trends requires abstracting from fluctuations in aggregate demand causing short- and medium-run changes in capital utilization. These changes typically reflect the normal course of business cycles or the presence of systemic shocks. But such perturbations cause the actual profitability estimates to cycle around their long-run trend and occasionally obscure its real evolution. In fact, such adjustments made on actual US estimates at times revealed profitability trends running in opposite ways to the actual observations. Sharp fluctuations in aggregate demand caused by short-term booms and recessions, the longer effect on aggregate demand derived from war-time deficits, and the spillover of financial crises on the rest of the economy are likely to produce sustained changes in capacity utilization that affect actual measures of profitability. Removing these contingent elements underpinning the longer path of profitability in order to bring out the underlying trend requires effective estimates of capacity utilization.

Consistent growth and capacity utilization

In a dynamic context a constant level of (net) investment will result in a steady increase in capacity. Such an expansion is the natural consequence of the growth in the stock of fixed assets. The potential output in the economy will expand as capacity grows but not necessarily the actual level of production. This is so because sustaining rising capacity requires growing demand. Investment spending raises incomes, and depending on how such spending is financed, whether out of retained earnings as in classical political economy or bank loans as in the Keynesian framework, it may expand effective demand by a multiple of its original size.

Switching from the static framework of Keynesian economics used to derive short-run income equilibrium, with autonomous investment financed by bank credit equal to savings out of aggregate income, $S = sY = I_A$, to an endogenous growth context, we move into the domain of classical economics. In that setting, investment is largely funded out of retained profits but the conditions for balanced growth need not change: the identity of savings out of profits and *ex post* investment will be preserved. Expanding the expression for balanced growth,

$$S_t = s\Pi_t = I_t = s\frac{\Pi}{P}\frac{P}{P_n}P_n,$$

where Π_t represents profits realized in actual sales and P the produced or potential profits firms expect to realize when they bring their product to market. In order for those profit expectations that motivated the firms' investment to be fulfilled, a consistent path of capital accumulation requires market demand growth to match capacity output growth, that is, aggregate supply growth.

In the expanded expression, the ratio Π/P represents a measure of possible short-term discrepancies between aggregate demand and supply, that is, $\Pi/P = f(D/Q)$. The ratio P/P_n refers to the relationship between produced profits and normally produced profits, a parameter measuring the difference between actually produced profits and normally produced profits, defined as profits firms expect to realize when their capacity utilization and output are set at normal levels. Given its technology and a competitive environment, normal output refers to output produced at the lowest level of the firm's average cost schedule.

Hence, the $P/P_n = n(Q/Q_n)$ ratios express the possible discrepancies between firms' actual and normal output levels. The only consistent path of capital accumulation is one that allows for the growth in demand to match the growth in capacity. Once such equalization is achieved, the rate of capacity utilization, defined as the ratio of actual to potential output, need not change. Potential output should not be interpreted as engineering capacity, the maximum output possible given the physical characteristics of the existing plant and equipment. This is because such maximum outputs may entail production levels that raise unit costs of production above the minimum, and firms will not consider them as desirable. The concept refers rather to the optimal level of production in the industry given the existing technology and competitive pressures that compel firms to seek the lowest unit costs possible.

Optimal utilization levels of capacity will typically fall short of maximum output, since such expansion entails unit costs rising above normal levels of capacity utilization, not necessarily the presence of excess capacity. Capacity exceeding optimal (normal) utilization levels merely indicates the availability of reserves in order to cope with temporary discrepancies between rising demand and supply. In such cases, sustaining the required conditions for accumulation will require adjusting output to optimal levels of capacity utilization, raising or lowering the rate of accumulation, increasing or reducing capacity relative to demand.

Assuming, as in classical political economy, that all savings derive from profits, $S = s(\Pi)$, and dividing investment ($S = I$) by the capital stock, K, removes all traces of static framework and allows us to establish the conditions for a sustainable path of capital accumulation, that is, the requirements for balanced growth:

$$s\frac{\Pi}{P}\frac{P}{P_n}\frac{P_n}{K} = \frac{I}{K}.$$

We define the accumulation rate, g_K, as

$$\frac{I_t}{K_t} = \frac{\Delta K_t}{K_t} = \frac{I_t/Y_t}{K_t/Y_t} = \frac{s}{v}.$$

On the balanced growth path, the investment ratio, I_t/Y_t, must equal to the savings ratio, s, while the capital–capacity ratio, $v = K_t/Y^*$, requires maintaining a normal level of capacity utilization along that path . Indeed, for firms to operate along a consistent path of balanced growth, with aggregate demand and capacity, g_k, growing at the same rate, a normal level of capacity utilization, $u = Y_t/Y_t^* = 1$, is necessary. Then actual output will equal capacity output.

This new expression contains the basic structural elements found in the growth approach of classical political economy. In the conceptual framework of such discipline, classical economists believed that systemic forces tended to push the ratios Π/P and P/P_n to unity, so that realized profits would closely match the profits firms expected to make. Their anticipated profits, moreover, would also tend to coincide with profits consistent with normal (competitive) levels of operation. Any "unproductive expenditures" financed out of normal profits would reduce the savings propensity, s, and with it the accumulation rate. While classical economics theoretically identified normal profitability, P_n/K, as the chief driver of the sustainable rate of capital accumulation, $g_K = I/K$, in order to obtain empirical estimates of "normal" profitability reliable measures of capacity utilization are indispensable.

Measuring capacity utilization

Because engineering capacity refers to outputs requiring 24-hour operation every day of the week, with no consideration of operating costs or market demand, the concept does not provide a relevant benchmark of economic capacity. Currently the two measures of average capacity utilization in manufacturing and industry considered as the standard or official estimates are provided annually by the Institute for Supply Management (ISM) since 1989 and by the Federal Reserve Board (FRB) monthly, with indexes for manufacturing starting in 1948 and for industry as a whole since 1967. In the 1970s, however, three other measures of capacity utilization were available in addition to the estimates for manufacturing issued by the FRB, namely those offered by the Wharton School, the BEA, and the McGraw-Hill Company, which ran comprehensive surveys from 1954 to 1988.

The Wharton School methodology selected the actual production peaks at various times as cases of potential capacity output, interpreting their linear links as the effective trend of industrial capacity. One major criticism of this procedure is that such capacity measures ignored the degree of intensity with which the plant and equipment operated at peak intervals. The BEA, McGraw-Hill and FRB measures on the other hand emphasized the importance of capacity measures under "normal" conditions (Ragan, 1976).

Originally, the FRB capacity estimates were based on the McGraw-Hill survey of manufacturing capacity and capacity operating rates. Until 1988 elaboration of the FRB's indexes of capacity utilization relied heavily on information provided by the McGraw-Hill survey on operating rates, its estimates of capacity and Census Bureau deflated capital stock series. McGraw-Hill asked its respondents to provide data on production capacity under normal conditions, meaning the maximum output possible they could expect when operating plant and equipment with average intensity to produce a normal output mix. Furthermore, respondents reported what percentage of their capacity was used at year-end and how much their capacity would be expanded in the current year. But they were not given a clear-cut definition of what constituted capacity beyond their subjective judgment of normal conditions. In this regard, business downturns led plant managers to report capacity losses which frequently reflected no more than the temporary closure of marginal plants. Boom periods, on the other hand, brought on the discovery of additional capacity previously unacknowledged. The damped cyclical character of FRB estimates based on McGraw-Hill plant surveys, however, reflected not only the absence of a clear-cut definition for capacity binding respondents, but also the neoclassical view of ever present equilibrium growth paths.

Since 1974 the Census Bureau has conducted a survey of plant capacity, used by the FRB jointly with the McGraw-Hill surveys to frame its own estimates of capacity utilization. As the McGraw-Hill surveys ended in 1988, FRB estimates of capacity from 1990 on relied exclusively on data from Census Bureau sources. Funded by the FRB and Defense Department the annual survey of plant capacity provides definitions of capacity in 17,000 manufacturing companies, specifying maximum "sustainable" output. Each plant registers its production levels under (a) actual operations, (b) preferred operations, defined as output "preferred" in the sense of not involving sharply rising marginal costs, and (c) "practical capability," referring to engineering maximum capacity. A major criticism of FRB measures of capacity utilization leveled by Shapiro (1989) emphasized the damped cyclical variations that characterize the FRB indexes:

> The discussion of the Federal Reserve's data construction procedures raises serious questions about how the data should be interpreted. For many industries, capacity is based on vague survey questions. Various data are combined by complicated regression, averaging, judgmental, and interpolation procedures. Because utilization and capacity are, to borrow the term from the Chairman of the Board of Governors, elusive concepts, it is difficult to evaluate the objective of the data construction procedures. The Federal Reserve procedure, moreover, mixes engineering and economic notions of capacity, particularly in its assumption that seasonal peaks in output are unsustainable.

Shapiro pointed out that FRB's capacity indexes were constructed to reflect the notion that current output should not exceed capacity and sharply low capacity utilization rates should be avoided, hence ruling out high-amplitude cycles in capacity utilization. In response to Shapiro's critique of FRB's methods, economists at the institution pointed out that their capacity utilization indexes had their roots in survey data conveying the best practices of plant managers and their view of sustainable output and the work week of capital. FRB indexes for capacity utilization, however, required complex manipulation of such data, in order to obtain the final estimates:

> proportional to fitted values from regressions that reflect both the trend growth of capacity implied by the survey data (the growth of an industrial production index divided by a utilization rate from a survey) and the annual changes of the alternative indicator...As a result, extrapolations based on the same regressions, along with the production index, determine the Federal Reserve's capacity utilization rates since the latest survey operation.
>
> (Corrado and Mattey, 1997)

Direct measures of capacity utilization

The early studies carried out by Foss in the early 1960s to measure the full horse-power capacity of electrical motors driving machinery in US manufacturing plants in relation to their actual horse-power use produced indexes for the years 1929, 1939, and 1954. These measures proved to be consistent estimates of capacity utilization in US manufacturing. Foss needed reliable measures of capacity in order to establish his capacity utilization measures. He argued that data on installed electric motors and electric power consumption in industry as collected by the Census of Manufacturers and the Census of Mineral Industries conveyed the extent to which the available electric motor horse-power was actually utilized to run machinery. In 1929 electrical motors powered 80 percent of all mechanical operations in US industry, and that percentage rose to 88 percent in 1954. Foss' major finding highlighted the fact that in the postwar period, capacity utilization in manufacturing rose significantly relative to 1929.

Foss found that Census data for 1929, 1939, and 1954 provided information on the number of such electrical motors in place, their total amount of horse-power deployed, as well as the aggregate power consumption in kilowatt-hours per year registered in normal operations. His procedure consisted in multiplying the number of hours in a year by the amount of installed electrical motor horse-power in order to find the total amount of annual horse-power available. He then converted this figure to kilowatt-hours applying the ratio 1 hp = 0.746 kWh, dividing his result by 0.9 to account for the fact that electric motors lose 10 percent of their power when running due to heat. The final figure provided a measure of the maximum (potential) number of kilowatt-hours available. Whatever hours the electric motors ran consuming electricity matched the exact time machinery operated, hence the ratio of actual use relative to maximum potential electricity consumption yielded Foss' capacity utilization ratio. In 1954 the average piece of equipment driven by electric motors ran for 35 hours per week and his capacity utilization index for that year showed a 45 percent increase relative to 1929.

His overall estimates raised the increase in equipment utilization as high as one third to one half of the prewar rates, stressing the fact that the chosen boundaries, 1929 and the mid-1950s, qualified as periods of "high output and high relative resource utilization" (Foss, 1963). The introduction of multiple-shift work schedules was the main reason for rising capacity utilization in this period. His research showed that the production schedules associated with World War II remained largely in place in its aftermath, driving industry to higher levels of continuous operation. Foss' (1963) findings motivated Christensen and Jorgensen to seek comprehensive annual measurements for capital inputs and capacity utilization beyond the mid-1950s. They in fact produced annual indexes of capacity utilization for the period extending from 1929 to 1967, and in doing so laid the ground for the further development of longer annual time series (Christensen and Jorgensen, 1969). Nearly two decades later Foss (1981) extended his findings beyond the limits of his 1963 work.

Evidence of cyclical trends of various lengths found in Foss' indexes of capacity utilization in manufacturing industries provided a new perspective to interpret the otherwise puzzling behavior of falling capital–output ratios and rising capital intensity of production. Foss' work brought out the fact that the technical characteristics of capital-intensive methods replacing older and more labor-intensive techniques provided the conditions necessary for the introduction of multiple shifts and the practice of higher rates of capacity utilization. Foss (1963, 1985) concluded that this unprecedented jump in capacity utilization "may be a partial explanation for the observed decline in capital–output ratios from 1929 to 1955."

Shaikh's extension of capacity utilization indexes

Concerned with the structural changes derived from capital accumulation, Ricardo and Marx's focus on long-term profitability trends sought to track the evolution of capacity profits and the capital stock. Now any empirical findings purporting to trace their path required adjustments for capacity utilization, abstracting from middle- and shorter-term fluctuations in aggregate demand. Measures of long-run profitability trends derived in the spirit of classical political economy need to reflect adjustment for cyclical fluctuations in aggregate demand affecting the utilization of capital stocks. Consideration of the structural determinants of such trends brings out the distinction between actual capital–output trends and adjusted capital stock–capacity ratios.

Shaikh's (1987) early research sought to derive indexes of capacity utilization fully reflecting the hidden and turbulent path of capital accumulation with its attendant variations in effective demand. The standard procedures of the FRB methodology assumed instead that actual output did not deviate substantially from potential or capacity levels. Accordingly they produced indexes that displayed a marked anticyclical bias. Such indexes failed to reflect the impact of middle- and long-term cycles on effective demand and capacity utilization. Acknowledging the valuable precedent established by Foss' calculations provided Shaikh with a solid foundation for his extension of the capacity utilization series beyond 1963. Once Census annual surveys ceased collecting data on the quantity and power of electrical motors installed in manufacturing, the McGraw-Hill survey of business plans provided valuable information on planned capacity expansion in manufacturing industry from the early 1960s to the mid-1980s. Its survey's questions, however, did not specify whether capacity growth referred to net or gross fixed investment. Assuming that estimates of capacity expansion referred to gross additions produced indexes that coincided with Foss' 1947–1963 estimates, allowing Shaikh to splice the indexes from both sources, Foss' and McGraw-Hill's, to form a 1947–1985 long series. His results avoided the medium- and long-term anticyclical bias marring the standard versions while retaining movements in the short run similar to the FRB's measures of capacity utilization.

The cointegration proxy option

Our estimates for capacity utilization measures were produced by applying the cointegration method originally proposed in Shaikh (1999d) and extended in Shaikh and Moudud (2004). Shaikh (1999) suggested a simple cointegration procedure based on logarithmic time series of the capital stock and manufacturing output to obtain indexes of capacity utilization extended to 1996. The resulting capacity utilization estimates matched substantially Shaikh's direct estimates previously based on the Foss and McGraw-Hill industry surveys. Shaikh used two basic ratios. The first, capacity utilization, $u = Y/Y^*$, is defined as the ratio of actual to potential output. Once actual output equals capacity output, $u^* = 1$, the desired or normal utilization rate obtains but only as a transitional moment of the cyclical adjustment. Actual capacity utilization will exhibit persistent fluctuations around the normal level without necessarily settling at that level. The second, the capital-capacity ratio, $V = K/Y^*$, was expected to change on account of autonomous technical progress and the weight of embodied innovations in capital accumulation. The expression of these definitions in a simple identity gives

$$Y_t = \frac{Y}{Y^*} \frac{Y^*}{K} K.$$

Let g_V refer to the growth rate of the capital–capacity ratio, v, and g_K to the growth rate of the capital stock; let the coefficient b_1 capture the weight of autonomous technical change and b_2 that of embodied technical progress. Then the growth rate of the capital capacity ratio, $g_V = b_1 + b_2 g_K$. Shaikh's cointegration model includes three behavioral functions. The growth path of output will be reflected in the equation $\log Y_t = \log K_t - \log v_t + \log u_t$. Since random events ($e_{Ut}$) shape the path of capacity utilization deviations from the normal level, at some point actual output in the long run will coincide with capacity output, a proposition expressed in logs by the equation $\log u_t = e_{Ut}$. The final equation, also written in logs, determines the growth path of v, the capital–capacity ratio: $\log v_t = b_0 + b_{1t} + b_2 \log K_t + e_{Ut}$.

Once combined, these three equations establish the cointegration link between the logs of output and capital stock, allowing for the presence of a possible "linear deterministic trend in the actual data" (Shaikh and Moudud, 2004). Comparing our estimates of capacity utilization in US manufacturing with those of Shaikh in

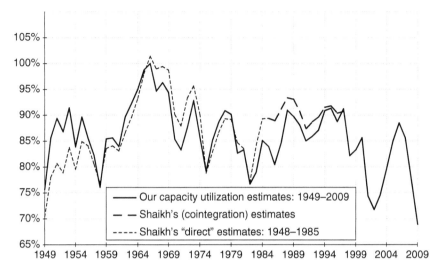

Figure 10.7 Non-FRB measures of manufacturing capacity utilization: Shaikh's data and ours.

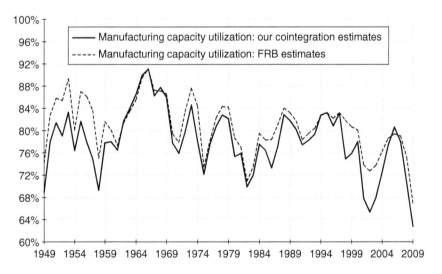

Figure 10.8 The FRB's and our estimates of manufacturing capacity utilization.

Figure 10.7, and those produced by the FRB in Figure 10.8, the following observations are in order. Our results do not deviate much from Shaikh's direct measures from the late 1940s to 1986. In the same period our estimates are not out of line with the FRB's. Beyond 1986, however, our capacity utilization time series exhibit greater amplitude than the FRB's and differ somewhat from Shaikh's, possibly

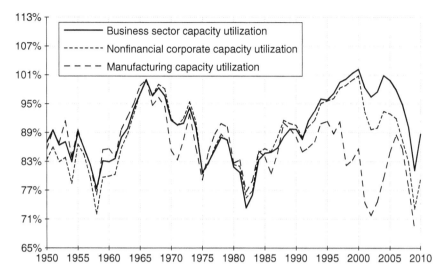

Figure 10.9 US capacity utilization in three sectors: business, nonfinancial corporate, and manufacturing.

because we used net capital stock data since BEA's publication of gross figures ended in 1994. The results of applying the same cointegration procedure to the business, nonfinancial corporate, and manufacturing sectors, shown in Figure 10.9, reveal the critical contraction in capacity utilization experienced by US manufacturing after 1997, compared to the other two, leading to a free fall briefly reversed between 2002 and 2006.

Trends after adjusting for capacity utilization

Plotting the actual output–capital ratios for the business and nonfinancial corporate sectors reveals major cycles. But adjusting for such significant waves of capacity utilization reveals a smoother long-term downward trend. This is confirmation of the fact that our capacity utilization cycles reflect major changes in effective demand caused by changes in fiscal policies. The nonfinancial corporations' lower output–capital trend, shown in Figure 10.10, reflects the higher capital intensity of production characteristic of large corporate business relative to smaller noncorporate firms. As Fox observed in the early 1960s, despite capital-intensive technical change, the resulting output–capital ratios, unadjusted for capacity utilization, in tandem with rising capacity utilization, can deceptively create the appearance of rising trends underpinning rising profitability. On the other hand, adjusting for falling capacity utilization rates during recessions reveals a temporary boost to long-term profitability estimates above their actual values.

Adjusting actual profitability trends for capacity utilization rates effectively reveals the long-run normal profitability paths in all sectors of the economy under

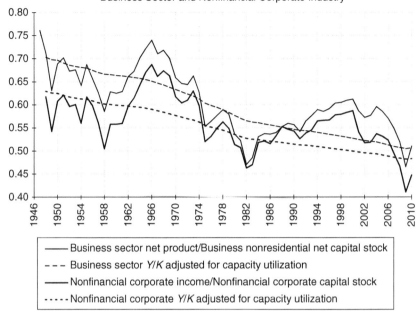

US Net Output–Net Capital Stock Ratios:
Business Sector and Nonfinancial Corporate Industry

——— Business sector net product/Business nonresidential net capital stock
– – – Business sector Y/K adjusted for capacity utilization
——— Nonfinancial corporate income/Nonfinancial corporate capital stock
· · · · · Nonfinancial corporate Y/K adjusted for capacity utilization

Figure 10.10 US output–capital ratios in business and nonfinancial corporate sectors:
actual and adjusted for capacity utilization.

US Nonfinancial Corporate Net Surplus/Nonfinancial Corporate Capital Stock
Actual and Adjusted for Capacity Utilization Profitability Trends

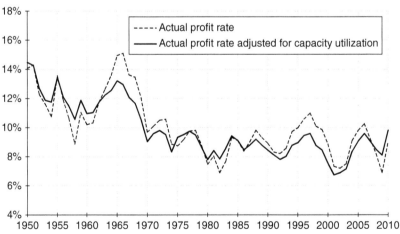

· · · · · Actual profit rate
——— Actual profit rate adjusted for capacity utilization

Figure 10.11 US nonfinancial corporate profitability: actual and adjusted for capacity
utilization.

consideration, a trajectory otherwise hidden. The division found in the unadjusted values between the two stages of the nonfinancial corporate sector profitability, the late 1940s up to 1982, and the period since, largely disappears. Instead, a steady pace of decline applies to the whole period, only distinguished by variations in the rates of that decline. All sectors' profitability paths exhibit characteristics similar to that in manufacturing. All sectors of the economy reveal a smoothed and downward sloping capacity–capital stock trend. Accordingly, explaining the falling accumulation path since the mid-1960s needs no revamping of classical principles. In Figure 10.11 a similar adjustment of profit rates for capacity utilization generates a smoother curve with a falling trend up to 2001, and a recovery in 2006 to a level no higher than its peak in 1997.

Summary

Before the ascendance of finance in the 1980s, nonfinancial corporations largely retained the funds necessary to cover their fixed capital investment, allowing any excess to provide safely for dividends to their shareholders. Financing the path of capital accumulation internally allowed nonfinancial corporations to avoid adding excessive debt. Investment trends mirrored those in corporate profitability and accumulation cycles reflected profit fluctuations as well. Financial sector expansion required nonfinancial corporations to distribute an increasing share of profits as dividends. They did so pressed by stockholders needing funds to speculate in financial markets in pursuit of higher yields. In the event, the emergence of new financial opportunities allowing corporations to reverse past profitability woes absorbed a growing share of nonfinancial corporate funds to the detriment of nonfinancial investments.

We do not interpret the decline in nonfinancial corporate accumulation, however, as being due to the rise in net interest payments or the growth of dividend disbursements, but rather as stemming from low profitability. We calculated our measures of capacity utilization in the nonfinancial corporate sector by applying the econometric procedure pioneered by Anwar Shaikh in the mid-1990s. When actual profitability paths in US nonfinancial corporate sectors are adjusted with our capacity utilization estimates, the resulting path of normal profitability emerging reveals a smoother and clear-cut trend of falling yields. Financial investments expanded precisely because the profitability of the nonfinancial corporate sector fell precipitously from 1948 to 1982 and the recovery from 1983 to the present did not raise it much above a 6 percent average. The financial expansion seemed to survive the sequential bursting of internet, stock market, and housing bubbles. In due course, however, waves of financial speculation strengthened by unsustainable increases in debt and falling interest rates tipped the scales of once profitable financial markets and triggered the deepest financial collapse since the 1930s depression.

11 Mill and Minsky on roads to speculation and crisis

Introduction

J. S. Mill and H. Minsky saw speculation and bubbles in asset prices as an intrinsic phase of the business cycle. In their view the aftermath of such episodes leads to the collapse of accumulation. But while Mill linked this development to the decline in yield prospects caused by the growth of the capital stock, Minsky focused on the inevitable transition to Ponzi finance once increasing interest rates render the further growth of debt unsustainable. For our part, we seek to explore in this chapter the extent to which the secular trends in profitability, which in the 1920s led to the stock market collapse of 1929 and the Great Depression, shared similar trajectories with those that after the late 1980s opened the way to financial fragility and triggered the Great Recession of 2008.

Scattered but traceable evidence suggests that in the 1920s and 2000s, profitability levels of nonfinancial businesses in the decade preceding the system's crisis had significantly declined. We evaluate the available evidence in light of J. S. Mill's views on the long-run tendency of profits to fall as capital accumulation progresses, and the lure of speculative investments in risky ventures as a palliative for declining yields in mature industry. Updating Mill's argument, we find capital responding to lower profitability in nonfinancial sectors privileging speculative investments in financial products offering higher yields. After the early 1980s, while falling interest rates failed to raise the accumulation of capital in nonfinancial sectors, other than housing construction and communication equipment, they facilitated the formation of internet and housing price bubbles that served as collateral for the pileup of unsustainable debts. Once the bubbles burst and debt obligations defaulted, the collapse of Ponzi finance overwhelmed the banks and the financial meltdown morphed into the Great Recession.

Pressing Ricardo's and Mill's arguments into service in the age of automation, it has been our contention that increases in the capital intensity of production, without sufficient compensating growth in the profit share, depressed the rate of return and weakened the prospects for capital accumulation in the nonfinancial corporate sector. Our view of the impact of profitability on accumulation, however, does not require a mechanical nexus between the two: capital accumulation may remain steady even when profitability is falling as long as profitability levels are historically high. But after the early 1980s, on average, profitability remained lower than in earlier decades.

Our concept of financialization refers to the rise of finance, including banking, insurance, security brokers, and dealers, to preeminence in the hierarchy of corporate activities favored by capital flows as an alternative to nonfinancial investment. Competitive pressures exerted on capital investments to cross sectors in response to profitability differentials suffice to explain the rise of finance. The more rapid growth of financial investments in response to favorable yields in financial markets simply reflected profitability differentials. Indeed, from the 1980s, financial innovations attracted capital away from the low profitability prospects of the US nonfinancial sector, offering investors not only higher returns but also the assurance of low risk. Accordingly, the enhanced image of financial markets allowed them to capture a growing share of total corporate profits (up to 40 percent in 2008), to the detriment of growth in the nonfinancial sector. We contend that such changes in the relative weights in the shares of profits accruing to US financial and nonfinancial sectors reflected the lackluster performance of nonfinancial corporate profitability in the post-1980s recovery.

Explaining the rise of finance involves both a long trend of low average yields in nonfinancial areas and an alternative field offering superior gains. We identify the profitability crisis of nonfinancial industries as a major force behind the growth of the financial sector since the early 1980s, even restricting that sector to finance and insurance activities and excluding real estate. It is clear that inflows of capital into financial sectors occurred not only because financial institutions offered a wider and more attractive array of investment products, but decidedly in response to the growing profitability gap goading capital away from accumulation in "real" nonfinancial industries. Furthermore, the underperformance of profitability in nonfinancial corporate sectors was not confined to the US economy but a symptom of global trends. We do not wish to argue, however, that low profitability in nonfinancial sectors *directly* led to the global financial crisis. But we explain the floods of international capital seeking higher yields in Wall Street products as evidence of unsatisfactory profitability in nonfinancial activities globally. And we readily accept the view, advanced by mainstream and orthodox critics, that once the internet, stock-market and housing bubbles burst, the collapse of the fragile pyramid of financial derivatives built on mountains of debt *triggered* the global financial crisis. Preceding the economic contractions of 1929 and 2008, financial booms morphed into bubbles that eventually burst because they were unsustainable, and once they cracked the economic foundations caved in. As Galbraith (1997, p. 187) noted in a survey of the economic fundamentals behind the financial crisis of the late 1920s: "Had the economy been fundamentally sound in 1929 the effect of the great stock market crash might have been small...But business in 1929 was not sound; on the contrary it was exceedingly fragile."

Contrary to the impression given by conventional accounts of business trends as the 1920s closed, nonfinancial profitability was lower than at the beginning of the decade. But in the 1920s as well as in the first decade of the twenty-first century lower profitability in the nonfinancial corporate sector as such did not trigger the immediate collapse of accumulation, only its decline. We interpret the rising capital flows into financial sectors as evidence of the dearth of profitable alternatives in industrial activities. What such low profitability instead kindled was the growth of alternative venues in financial markets, capital flows that in the event proved impossible to sustain once financial excesses could not be contained. The mini-boom in capital expenditures associated with the internet euphoria of the 1990s, for example, simply underpinned the rising half of a complete cycle whose downturn phase ended lower than the initial level of the upturn.

Interpreting these profitability differentials as drivers for inter-sector capital flows, Mullineux (1990) noted that while higher profitability prospects in financial markets typically drew capital flows seeking to derive advantage from aggressive competitive strategies, they all too often precipitate financial crises. This happens because the larger the capital flows into financial markets, the stronger the competitive pressures to lower the post-entry profit rate there. Maverick innovators will seek to gain higher profitability through financial innovations offering cheaper as well as riskier products previously unavailable. Consequently:

> Competition leads to a lowering of the quality of products and this increases the potential for crisis... Influxes of producers attracted by high profits are, therefore, potentially more serious for the banking sector than for other sectors...When a shock hits the system profitability declines and capital, which is usually run down relative to assets and risks taken in the euphoria of boom markets, proves inadequate.
>
> (Mullineux, 1990, p. 79)

Rising shares of gross operating surplus

As Figure 11.1 shows, rising gross profit shares countervailed for a time the impact of rising capital–output ratios on profitability. The early 1980s stands out as the clear divide between two stages in the development of the US and other major OECD economies. Falling profitability in US nonfinancial sectors progressively undermined the foundations of capital accumulation after the mid-1960s, plunging the US economy into a recession by the early 1980s that revived memories of the 1930s crisis. Responding to such developments, business strategies sought to reverse past trends in labor compensation while raising the growth of labor productivity, fostering deployment of technical innovations. They sought increases in the profits share in order to restore profitability and support for a higher rate of capital accumulation.

Figure 11.2 confirms the thorough implementation of such strategy, with 1982 clearly separating two distinct periods in the income distribution of the business sector. Between the mid-1940s and 1982 real wages rose roughly in tandem with labor productivity, but from that year to the present the gap between them only grew wider. Accordingly, as shown in Figure 11.2, the steady bifurcation of labor productivity and labor compensation after the early 1980s produced a marked decline in the labor share of business output. The falling share of wages was

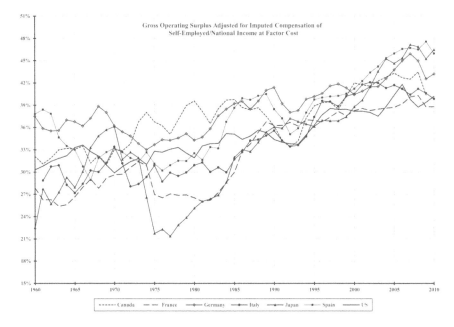

Figure 11.1 Seven countries' shares of gross operating surplus in GDP.

not confined to the US economy, but was rather a common trait of major OECD economies afflicted with falling accumulation trends.

John Stuart Mill: from low profitability to speculation

The notion that low business profitability spurred speculative activities played a central role in John Stuart Mill's analysis of business cycles and crisis. In the mid-nineteenth century Mill argued that phases of "overtrading" or unsustainable booms lowered the profitability of capital and ushered in periods of stagnation. These crises periodically occurred at the highest, not the lowest, stages of economic development:

> When a country has long possessed a large production, and a large net income to make savings from, and when, therefore, the means have long existed of making a great annual addition to capital. . .it is one of the characteristics of such a country, that the rate of profit is habitually within, as it were, a hand's breath of the minimum, and the country therefore on the very verge of the stationary state.
>
> (Mill, 1987, p. 731)

In a passage reminiscent of the financial excesses vividly portrayed by Krugman in his *New York Times* columns, Mill recounted how, motivated by the desire

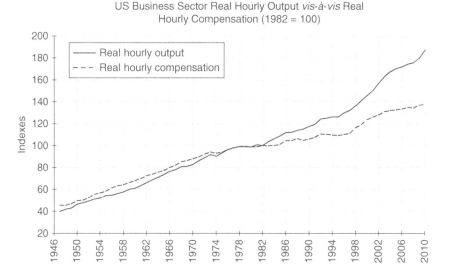

Figure 11.2 US business real hourly output and real hourly compensation.

to find profitable outlets for the accumulated capital, wishful thinking replaced realistic expectations, for:

> what would really be, not merely difficult, but impossible, would be to employ this capital without submitting to a rapid reduction in the rate of profit. . . . Mines are opened, railways or bridges made, and many other works of uncertain profit commenced, and in these enterprises much capital is sunk which yields either no return, or none adequate to the outlay. Factories are built and machinery erected beyond what the market requires, or can keep in employment. . .During the stagnation that follows. . .Establishments are shut up, or kept working without any profit, hands are discharged. . .Such are the effects of a commercial revulsion: and that such revulsions are almost periodical, is a consequence of the very tendency of profits which we are considering.
>
> (Mill, 1987, pp. 732–734)

Mill believed that memories of the devastation wrought by depressions faded all too quickly and pressures to find profitable investment outlets prompted the surviving capitals to engage in speculative activities. Mill's "speculations," however, were not restricted to financial markets since in his time finance remained tied to industrial needs for credit. In the "boom" phase of the cycle following the recovery from crisis, the deployment of massive doses of industrial capital beyond the limits of market demand typically depressed the rate of return to unacceptable levels. Furthermore, as capital accumulation in established industries failed to deliver the desired returns, the lure of shaky commercial ventures led speculators further astray into financial ruin:

> By the time a few years have passed over without a crisis, so much addi-tional capital has been accumulated, that it is no longer possible to invest it at the accustomed profit: all public securities rise to a high price, the rate of interest on the best mercantile security falls very low, and the complaint is general among persons in business that no money is to be made. Does not this demonstrate how speedily profit would be at the minimum, and the stationary condition of capital would be attained, if these accumulations went on with-out any counteracting principle? But the diminished scale of all safe gains, inclines persons to give a ready ear to any projects which hold out, though at the risk of loss, the hope of a higher rate of profit; and speculations ensue, which, with the subsequent revulsions, destroy, or transfer to foreigners, a considerable amount of capital.
>
> (Mill, 1987, p. 734)

In his view of the prospects for finding investment alternatives not suscepti-ble to the risk of falling profitability, Mill did not distinguish between financial investments and industrial accumulation. His comments regarding the rising price of public securities or their falling yield did not amount to recognition of the rela-tive autonomy achieved by financial speculation. For Mill, evidently, the financial sector's fortunes remained in the thrall of industrial success.

The centrality of profits in Keynes and Marx

Keynes' appreciation of the centrality assigned to profitability in the entrepreneurial economy stands out in Chapter 17 of his *General Theory*. Staunch Keynesians like Hyman Minsky stress the key role played by (expected) profitabil-ity in the Keynesian theory of accumulation outlined in that chapter. In line with the views of classical political economy, Keynes expected "the marginal efficiency of capital" to fall as accumulation proceeded:

> As accumulation takes place the anticipated yield on each type of produced real asset is forced, in some sequence, below the current return in kind that money yields... investment comes to a halt. Keynes argues that money rules the roost as the expected yield on real assets declines.
>
> (Minsky, 2008, p. 78)

Despite his ostensible rejection of so-called classical economics, Keynes' think-ing on the significance of profitability as the goal as well as the needed support for accumulation bore remarkable similarities to that of Smith, Ricardo, Marx, and Mill. As an authoritative interpreter of Keynesian economics, Leijonhufvud's (2009) view that Keynes attributed the loss of prosperity leading up to the

Great Depression to the falling profitability of British industry deserves serious consideration:

> The background to the Great Depression in Britain, . . . was the declining trend in the return to investment after the end of World War I . . . The combination of a declining marginal efficiency of capital and interest rates that did not decline propelled the country into a recession that was deep even before the USA slipped into depression.

Questioning the wisdom of replacing the classical view of recurrent crisis with Minsky's post-Keynesian account of the transition to financial fragility, Crotty exposed its conceptual limitations as a guide to understand recessions. In Minsky's "fully developed model," Crotty argued, a whole host of potential roadblocks fails to impact profit expectations, including the real sector's labor disputes with management; deployment of technologies raising labor productivity and the capital intensity of production; implementation of new management systems; domestic or international competitive wars for market shares; fluctuations in aggregate demand; changes in government policies; and oscillations in energy and raw materials prices. In Minsky's "seamless real-sector model":

> every possible level of investment is self-perpetuating without limit. It is only the financial fragility and rising interest rates of the mature boom that permit its demise; real sector determinants of investment profitability seen in isolation produce only perpetual growth. The ultimate or "deep" cause of capitalist instability in Minsky's world is therefore to be found in the dynamics of capitalist financial markets.
>
> (Crotty, 1986, pp. 305–306)

Upholding the classical view on the centrality of profits, Blanchard *et al.* (1993) evaluated the relationship between investment, profitability, and stock-market movements from 1900 to 1990. Despite their neoclassical orientation, their thorough empirical investigation left no doubt that profits expectations determined business investment, concluding that profitability

> explains investment better...than...the expected present value of profits... profit is highly significant...put simply, controlling for profit, there is only a marginally significant evidence of an effect of market valuation on investment behavior over the last 90 years of data... The effects of profit, however, remain large and significant and dominate investment movements
>
> (Blanchard *et al.*, 1993, pp. 124–127)

Robert Heilbroner (1985, pp. 76–77) understood the search for profits constituted the most powerful force behind the historical development of capitalism: "profit is the lifeblood of Capitalism, not merely because it is the means by which individual capitals obtain their wherewithal for expansion...In all depictions of the business system profits are the key economic variable."

In 1933, Keynes himself, in preparation for the *General Theory*, offered a rare compliment to the analytical insights of Karl Marx concerning the role of profits in entrepreneurial economies. While endeavoring to distinguish the salient difference between a cooperative economy and one dominated by entrepreneurial activities, Keynes acknowledged that:

> The distinction between a cooperative economy and an entrepreneur economy bears some relation to a pregnant observation made by Karl Marx – though the subsequent use to which he put this observation was highly illogical. He pointed out that the nature of production in the actual world is not, as economists seem often to suppose, a case of C-M-C', i.e. of exchanging commodity (or effort) for money in order to obtain another commodity (or effort). That may be the standpoint of the private consumer. But it is not the attitude of *business*, which is a case of M-C-M', i.e. of parting with money for commodity (or effort) in order to obtain more money. This is important for the following reason... An entrepreneur is interested, not in the amount of product, but in the amount of *money* which will fall to his share. He will increase his output if by so doing he expects to increase his money profit, even though this profit represents a smaller quantity of product than before.
>
> (Moggridge, 1979, pp. 81–82)

For Keynes deflation and unemployment tendencies in the entrepreneurial economy did not stem from a pre-existing excess of idle money capital, M, as claimed by Hobson, Major Douglas and others. But this recurrent excess of idle money resulted from a failure to successfully complete Marx's capital circuit, the transformation of M into M', the difference being entrepreneurial profits:

> Marx, however, was approaching the intermediate truth when he added that the continuous excess of M' would be inevitably interrupted by a series of crises, gradually increasing in intensity, or entrepreneur bankruptcy and underemployment, during which, presumably, M must be in excess.
>
> (Moggridge, 1979, p. 82)

In Marx, the transition from simple to "expanded reproduction" schemes occurred when capitalists channeled a portion of the received surplus value (profits) into accumulation instead of using it to finance their own consumption. Given the assumption of internally financed accumulation, without injections of external (bank) credit, no "output multiplier" is present in Marx's reproduction schemes. At this level of abstraction the growth rate of the system, the rate of capital accumulation, depends on profitability: the growth rate of gross profits or surplus value and the proportion that is channeled into accumulation, not capitalist consumption.

As Keynes pointed out, the circuit of productive capital starts with money capital advanced, M, to purchase commodities of different kind, labor power, L, and means of production, *MP*, needed to engage in the production of new commodities, C', for sale in money terms, M', which entrepreneurs hope will exceed the original capital advanced, M:

$$M \to C \begin{Bmatrix} L \\ MP \end{Bmatrix} \to C' \to M'.$$

$M' - M$ is the profit realized, ΔM, and r is the achieved profit rate, $\Delta M/M$. Net investment depends on the share of profits channeled into capitalist consumption, and the accumulation rate on the leakage from profitability into consumption, that is, the extent to which the profit rate is lowered by the distribution of dividends to capitalist households. Total profits, Π, rise to r^*M, but the accumulation rate will normally remain a fraction of the profit rate:

$$a_K = \alpha r, \quad \text{where } \alpha < 1.$$

In Marx, profitability trends are crucial for accumulation because profitability is essentially both the end as well as the means to keep the circuit of productive capital growing. It is, of course, *expected* profitability, what drives the expansion of capital. But since the future is uncertain, experience of past trends will influence the appraisals made. In general, falling profitability will fail to sustain for long either Keynesian "animal spirits" or the Marxian urge to accumulate.

Abstracting from technical progress, Marx presents in Chapter 25 of *Capital*, Volume I, the outline of a theory of endogenous cycles driven by the impact of accumulation on profitability via changing wage rates responding to changes in the demand for labor. These cycles do not behave explosively because every variation in the profit rate triggers a systemic response of accumulation: rising profitability leading to rising accumulation and vice versa on the downside.

If the system is bouncing back from a severe "recession" and the recovery proceeds apace away from the critical trough, business expectations improve as the pessimism rooted in the previous downturn fades: confidence grows. As the expansion enters its mature phase, profitability begins to fall because rising employment leads to higher wages; increasing demand for credit raises interest rates; higher demand for materials brings in higher input prices; expanding output weakens earlier market power to raise prices. Despite these negative developments as far as profitability is concerned, the recovery euphoria may not dissipate right away because optimism lingers, affecting investment decisions.

No better proof of the power of self-delusion exists than the recurrence of asset bubbles. On the other hand, a long-run falling profitability trend is not likely to call forth the kind of expectations necessary to raise the accumulation rate. But what if, after reaching a trough and going through relatively sharp fluctuations, profitability settled in a low holding pattern: would that suffice to spark off accumulation? Even if the profitability trend ceased falling, as long as it remained significantly lower in comparison with its previous levels, the system remains prone to collapse. In several papers published in the late 1980s (Duménil *et al.*,

1987a, 1988; Duménil and Lévy, 2011a) the authors propose the hypothesis that low profitability, not necessarily falling profitability, imparts exceptional fragility to decision making in corporate management, threatening to amplify unexpected shocks into system-wide breakdowns.

In our view, after the trough reached in the 1980s, low profitability in the nonfinancial corporate sector of the US economy prompted the flow of capital accumulation away from the real economy and into financial assets. Falling interest rates spurred banks to market high-risk financial assets and households and nonfinancial firms to accumulate debt in order to finance their purchase. After the internet mirage, born of vacuous business models devoid of profitability potential, faded, housing and the stock market moved center stage as the choice objects of speculative frenzy. The euphoria generated by asset price inflation prompted increasingly riskier practices on the part of banks and their enablers, contagion spread the rot, and after the crash the Great Recession engulfed the world. In its wake, enormous piles of debt weighed down households and banks. Banks were rescued, but consumers faced new bouts of austerity for the foreseeable future.

The first Great Depression

W. W. Rostow's (1938) study of the Great Depression of 1873–1895 provides strong evidence in support of the centrality of profits in the development of capitalism and its recurrent periods of crises. Focusing on the falling profitability of investment as a major trend behind that Great Depression, Rostow (1938, p. 139) dismissed the explanatory value of alternative monetarist arguments:

> None of the major characteristics of the Great Depression can be traced to a restricted response from the banking system. The prevailing tendencies in the short term capital market, on the contrary, were towards abundant supply…Neither the bullion shortage thesis nor more explicit propositions about the supply of loanable funds can be employed to explain the secular fall in commodity prices, interest rates, and equity prices; nor can they account for the peculiarly depressed outlook of entrepreneurs, their complaints of overproduction, or the failure of prosperity in the early 'eighties to attain full employment.

For Rostow, profit margins declined in the last two decades of the nineteenth century precisely because of rapid technological progress imposed on all viable industries by intensive global competition. While Rostow shared Bernstein's (1987, p. 211) concern with persistent "secular trends," his outlook derived from classical political economy, not the institutional approach. Focusing on "the almost continuous fall in prices" causing a "fall in industrial profit margins and in the rate of interest" (Rostow, 1938, p. 136), his argument of the developments leading to the Great Depression raised to the fore deflation effects of persistent labor-saving cost-cutting investment. That kind of technical progress raised the stocks of fixed capital across all industries and lowered their rates of return. A world-wide boom of this kind ended up undermining its own foundation:

> the expected yield on new investment would fall, dividends would drop...Fixed capital would be revalued downward. One might expect also an appearance of the bogey of overproduction... The amount of output produced under decreasing costs would increase. Should this relative growth in the proportion of fixed capital be world-wide, the atmosphere of overproduction would be accentuated.
>
> (Rostow, 1938, pp. 142–143)

The general profitability crisis encouraged further development of machinery absorbing the skills previously possessed by skilled artisans: "Machinery was sought as a means of escaping the tyranny of money wages that could not be reduced" and throughout the long depression the introduction of labor-saving devices reached all industries (Rostow, 1938, p. 150).

Raised expectations in the early 1870s encouraged entrepreneurial efforts to expand fixed capital expenditures; accommodating monetary policies provided ample finance; technical progress delivered blueprints designed to cut production costs; and intensified world-wide competition imposed these practices across all industries. In the end, "The expected marginal efficiency of capital declined" (Rostow, 1938, p. 158).

Writing in the late 1930s, Rostow's apprehensions regarding the legacy of the Great Depression extending beyond the aftermath of the Great War provide a valuable perspective to evaluate the contemporary puzzles. Comparing the business climate prevailing in the last two decades of the nineteenth century with a more recent period, Rostow (1938, p. 158) feared that:

> The irritations of the declining yield on capital which accompany intensive investment were to reach grotesque intensity in the twenty years since the war. In the Great Depression there were still outlets for enterprise that yielded a rate high enough to entice the private lender... but the lines of future development were clearly forecast. The mid-century blandishments of the profit motive had begun to lose their force.

In Rostow's view low profitability levels in the aftermath of the (First) Great Depression weakened the motivational force behind capital accumulation plans, hence the recovery of the 1920s proceeded under considerable duress. From this perspective Gordon's initial project comparing development paths in the 1920s and the 1990s allows modification to include not only investment patterns but also profitability trends.

Schumpeter on profit rates in the 1920s

Surveying the large number of industrial innovations that transformed the American economic landscape in the 1920s, Schumpeter (1946) did not fail to acknowledge both their contribution to growth and their share of responsibility for the depression that followed. Schumpeter understood that while fostering "prosperity" and initially driving market booms, they always left in their wake "a depressive undertone, a tendency for prices, profits, and interest rates to fall" (Schumpeter, 1946, p. 4). Specifically he found the "tendency of profit rates to fall, obscured as it is by the events of 1928 and 1929," of the utmost importance but requiring confirmation.

Contemporary reports on American industry fleshed out the Schumpeterian argument documenting falling profitability once the gains from industrial innovation dissipated. In *Industrial Profits in the United States*, R. C. Epstein (1934) looked at the profitability records of about 6000 corporate firms. These included 3000 larger corporations which in 1926 represented one third of total investment in US manufacturing, trade, finance, and mining and maintained their identity throughout the 1920s, plus another 3000 smaller firms which differed from the larger ones in that they included only profitable enterprises in the manufacturing and trade sectors. Between 1919 and 1928, out of a total of 73 industries, 23 of the largest corporations reported profit rates declining from 15 to 9 percent, 30 showed no trend, and the rest showed a rise. In 1928 the average corporate profitability in manufacturing reported to the Bureau of Internal Revenue fell to 8.7 percent. What Epstein (1934, p. 174) found puzzling was that from 1923 to 1928 corporations expanded their "capitalization," referring to "productive capacity," by nearly 30 percent, while sales in 1928 were 10 percent lower than in 1923.

Reviewing Epstein's book, Hollond (1936) sought to provide a plausible explanation for Epstein's findings on profitability, concluding in somewhat tortuous prose that as the decade advanced:

> the elimination of early windfall gains from innovation by the familiar process of competitive reaching out to tap lower levels of demand with consequent modifications in prices and unit costs such that earnings ratios were brought nearer to some central value(s) for industry in general.
>
> (Hollond, 1936, p. 120)

On further examination, in another review of Epstein's book, R. S. Tucker (1937) pointed out a year later that Epstein's corporate sample did not in fact accurately reflect the evolution of profitability in the industries surveyed. What marred the selection criteria was the identification requirement for large corporate firms, since only corporations with higher than average profit rates were likely to survive the market turbulence of the 1920s from beginning to end. Corporations that went out of business before the decade ended did not appear in the study. Moreover, Tucker emphasized that in addition the upward bias in profitability emerged from the measures of corporate capital stock in vogue, since for tax purposes "it is generally believed that large concerns in the decade of the twenties were inclined to understate their capital." (Tucker, 1937, p. 520).

Seeking to solve the apparent conundrum in Epstein's book regarding the reported expansion of corporate capital at rates outpacing the growth of sales in a number of industries, Tucker invoked competitive practices: successful innovators would take over rivals. The resulting growth in "capitalization" might surpass sales and lower profit rates. But the lower profitability of the winner would be preferable to the disappearance of the laggard.

On the basis of these and other empirical findings bearing on the course of innovations and profitability in the 1920s, Schumpeter's (1946) account of developments leading to depression is as relevant now as it was then. In an exhaustive study of the trends building up to the 1930s Great Depression, Duménil and Lévy (1987a) attributed the motivation for Schumpeter's waves of technical innovations in the final decades of the nineteenth century, including systemic changes in the management of business firms, to falling profitability. Lower profitability spurred the concentration and centralization of corporate business run by professional managers and their skilled staffs of salaried personnel. Corporate managers directed their efforts to solving problems of industrial production and distribution, while financial experts expanded their role in banking, the stock market and all other institutions connected with the financial solvency of their firms.

Two major available sources of pre-1929 data suitable for estimating profitability and net fixed capital accumulation trends – S. Wright's (2004b) comprehensive data set for US nonfinancial corporations and Duménil and Lévy's (1994) data set for the US private sector – offer invaluable and complementary time series spanning the twentieth century and beyond. They provide the means to assess the structural changes that lay the ground for the onset of financial meltdown. The Great Depression of the nineteenth century, 1873–1895, did not follow a stock-market crash, but that of the twentieth after 1929 and the twenty-first after 2008 certainly featured one.

Data from Wright (2004b) for the US nonfinancial corporate sector and Greasley and Madsen (2006) confirm Schumpeter's claim that the nonfinancial corporate profit rate in the 1920s fluctuated around a lower average than in the previous two decades (Greasley and Madsen, 2006, p. 401), never recovering its previous highs. The accumulation rate consistently followed the trajectory set by corporate profitability before and after the onset of the 1930s depression, remaining noticeably lower through the 1920s following the 1917 profit rate collapse.

As additional evidence of the relationship between capital accumulation and profitability trends since 1900, we refer to Figure 11.3 which shows our calculations of profit and accumulation rates derived from reliable data sources. In our historical estimates for US profitability and accumulation trends since the beginning of the twentieth century, we sought to minimize as much as possible dependence on Duménil and Lévy's (1994) comprehensive data, not because of any lack of confidence in their reliability but only to attain greater generality in our own estimates. Thus, we opted to use alternative data sources in order to strengthen the significance of the results, since such combination would likely minimize the acceptability of a single source. Accordingly, our profit rate estimates are based on estimates for the US nominal net national product published in Klein and Kosobud (1961, p. 183) for the years 1900–1928. In this period,

Figure 11.3 US business sector profitability and accumulation rates, 1900–2009.

the share of government activities in the US national income is rather small, and therefore the data overwhelmingly concerns the private economy as in Duménil and Lévy (1994). US nominal wages from 1900 to 1928 and capital stock data for 1900–1924 are from Duménil and Lévy (1994). The difference in the Duménil and Lévy data periods for nominal wages and capital stocks reflects the fact that data offered by the US Bureau of Economic Analysis (BEA) on capital stocks starts in 1925 but on wages four years later, in 1929.

Figure 11.3 shows the paths of our estimates for US business sector profitability and fixed capital accumulation for over a century. It seems clear that, for the most part, not only do the trends run parallel to each other, but also the cyclical developments are generally synchronized. In the so-called Cambridge equation (as in Marx), the accumulation rate is a function of the profit rate, $a_K = \alpha r$. Figure 11.4 shows the α values, the rate of accumulation as a share of the profit rate, a_K/r, seldom deviating from the 20–40 percent range up to 1980, but a downward trend since then.

Overinvestment as the cause of depression

Three years before the financial crash ushered in the Great Recession of the twenty-first century, Robert J. Gordon presented a paper at Duke University underlying the parallel paths tracked by the American economy in the 1920s and 1990s (Gordon, 2004a). This was in itself a courageous and stimulating research project. In his paper, Gordon argued that from the "traditional Keynesian view" the 1920s investment boom caused the 1930s depression. In his estimation, setting 1919 in line with 1990 and 1929 with 2000 revealed almost identical growth rates in real

Figure 11.4 US business capital accumulation as a percentage of business profitability.

GDP as well as real GDP per capita, employment, and labor productivity. Real growth rates of the S&P 500 index averaged 11.3 percent in the 1920s and 12.4 percent in the 1990s.

On the negative side, both the 1920s and 1990s suffered from the combined effects of "overinvestment" and stock market bubbles. Despite all the advances in economic understanding and policy made in the past half century, the decline of high-tech and telecom stocks added to the demise of dot-coms startups, providing evidence of overinvestment in the 1990s. Significant similarities between stock-market booms, bubbles, and the innovating activities of banks leading to "pyramid building" in the 1920s, and accounting frauds in the 1990s foretold of comparable outcomes. But this conclusion would be wrong, Gordon thought, because monetary policy in the twenty-first century would not let it happen.

Despite these road signs found in 2004, Gordon exuded confidence that "the evolution of the economy after 1929/2000 was entirely different, except for a short-run mirror image in the stock market collapse." Expanding monetary policy coming to the rescue in the first two years of the twenty-first century averted a repetition of the collapse experienced after 1929. It is clear that by 2004 the failure to discern the possibility of a global slump derived from the inadequate set of analytical tools deployed to assess the extent to which unsustainable practices could lead to disaster. For what could be the meaning attached to Gordon's vaunted concept of "overinvestment"?

In our view, an alternative to R. J. Gordon's expressed wish to rehabilitate the "overinvestment" hypothesis, advanced by his father, R. A. Gordon, at a conference in 1949, lies in Schumpeter's suggestion linking innovating (over)investment and profitability trends. Seeking to explain the cyclical course of the American economy in the 1920s as it trended to depression, Gordon (1951) sorted out the evidence at hand without a firm theoretical framework. In his research work, R. A. Gordon referred to the rise in "investment opportunities" associated with the growth of new industries and the development of new services as fueling the investment boom of the 1920s. Such new industries included automobiles, electric power, road building, and residential construction. Thus, once these activities reached maturity and did not need immediate replacement or expansion, the investment boom petered out and depression set in. As excess capacity developed towards the closing years of the 1920s decade, Gordon (1951, p. 212) concluded that further capital accumulation was not required or *profitable*, since all previously dynamic industries had reached maturity by then. Once they reached "maturity" and further growth no longer warranted the field of investment opportunities shrunk. The burgeoning array of investment opportunities reached its natural limits at decade's end, as excess capacity increased and stagnation reared its head.

For R. A. Gordon the linkage between "overinvestment" and the slump derived from his insight that, along with the financial excesses, "profitable" investment opportunities steadily declined in the 1920s. His summary of the developments leading to the 1929 crash drew attention to the fact that "The investment boom of the '20s resulted from a concentrated flowering of investment opportunities, created by the rapid maturing of a series of new industries and new services" (Gordon, 1951, p. 211).

In Keynes investment determines output and employment. Its level depends chiefly on the "marginal efficiency of capital" (i.e., the expected profit rate on new investment) and possibly the rate of interest, but not on preexisting business savings (NIPA's retained earnings). Fundamentally, Keynes assumed that investment finance would be available from banks, thus the "output multiplier" comes into play as a result of bank credit expansion, the growth of business debt.

It is remarkable that neither R. J. Gordon (2004a) nor R. A. Gordon (1949) found it necessary to consider the connection between overinvestment and falling profitability in the prelude to depression. While Gordon *père* legitimately complained that so many depression studies never dealt with the role of investment in the 1920s, it is remarkable that in neoclassical studies of the trends leading to that depression the impact of profitability trends on capital accumulation is effectively ignored. Most historical accounts drifting out of the neoclassical mainstream, while seeking heterodox moorings, failed to grasp the centrality of profitability trends preceding the 1920s depression.

Over three decades and a half after publication of R. A. Gordon's seminal study, Michael Bernstein's celebrated book on *The Great Depression* (1987) offered valuable insights into the nature of developments in the 1920s but provided no data on profitability trends leading to the slump. In Bernstein's view profits, profit margins, and profitability trends did not drive the accumulation of capital in the 1920s. While agreeing with Joseph Steindl's (1976, p. xv) conclusion that "oligopoly brings about a mal distribution of funds by shifting profits to those industries which are reluctant to use them," Bernstein followed R. A. Gordon's approach attributing the cause of depression to "secular developments" involving investment and consumer demand clashing with technical change and skill formation in the context of acute financial turmoil:

> What made the interim American economy so vulnerable to the business cycle was the fact that by 1929, dramatic changes were occurring in the composition of consumer demand, investment demand, technology, and employment requirements. These secular developments made previous investment patterns less capable of withstanding a cyclical downturn.
>
> (Bernstein, 1987, p. 36)

Neither R. A. Gordon's nor M. Bernstein's account of the process and product innovations that allegedly, along with changes in consumer demand, raised the fragility levels of the US 1920s economy to unsustainable levels, matched Schumpeter's theoretical account of the relevant issues involved. Schumpeter synthesized all of that into a few powerful principles that, running through the system, captured the likelihood of its downfall. These included unprecedented booms in residential construction with the attendant mortgage excesses; runaway growth of public utilities, and the stock-market mirage of 1927–1929 attracting investors disenchanted with conventional yields. Business conditions throughout the decade persuaded Schumpeter (1946, p. 7) that "the tendency of profit rates to fall" exerted a significant downward drag on business expectations in the 1920s, and despite the paroxysm of equity markets in 1928 and 1929, the overall trend culminated in collapse. Falling prices and profits overhung the business outlook, according to Schumpeter, and at some point the accumulation trends that kept the system growing unraveled. Schumpeter (1946, p. 8) discerned in the 1920s how the presence of

> certain traits[,] merely by accentuating themselves as they were bound to do, would gradually [yield] a pattern answering to our idea of depression. . .That is to say, the prevailing tendencies, such as the tendency of prices and profits to sag – quite normal for periods of the character indicated – had only to go further in order. . .to develop sectional difficulties or breakdowns from which downward "vicious spirals" attended by widespread unemployment, were increasingly likely to start.

J. Steindl's (1976, Table 36, p. 173) calculations of the US corporate profit rate on net business capital stock, derived from M. Taitel's (1941) data, showed a distinct downward trend between 1909 and 1928: profitability fell from 3.7 percent on average for the years 1909–1918 to an average 2.5 percent for 1919–1928. Schumpeter's dismissal of corporate profitability reports based on "peak" firms rather than the more comprehensive data for industry averages, which he quoted as "roughly between 2 and 3 percent," confirmed Steindl's estimates, since "a considerable share of the gross corporate business was done at a loss" (Schumpeter, 1946, p. 7).

Lower profitability and higher instability

In the conventional view, "financial excesses" occur when prolonged booms in the real economy generate euphoric expectations in capital gains and give rise to unsustainable debts:

> Another apparently systematic element was the tendency for financial excesses to develop from the buoyant expectations generated by prolonged booms, so that the depression phases of the long swings were aggravated to varying degrees by liquidity crises, bank failures, and political-monetary disturbances.
>
> (Hickman, 1963, p. 504)

We share the view expounded by Duménil *et al.* (1987a, 1987b) that the behavioral patterns associated with sound business management will be affected by an extended fall in profitability. Even after rebounding from its trough, a profitability trend that fails to achieve levels considered as normal in the past may not induce a rising wave of capital accumulation. Rational microresponses to the market signals associated with a lower profitability environment may heighten the macroeconomy's fragility threshold and give rise to unintended fluctuations in overall activity. The Great Recession of the twenty-first century did not issue from an extended boom period in the real economy. From the early 1980s financial excesses developed as a counterweight to the lackluster prospects of the nonfinancial sector. The extreme fragility that preceded the meltdown of the financial capital sector resulted from a path of debt accumulation out of sync with the expansion of profits in the real economy. The real GDP growth rates or capital accumulation trends of the real economy did not justify the euphoria behind the financial excesses of the past thirty years.

On the contrary, we extend Duménil *et al.*'s view to suggest that once the nonfinancial sector profitability trend proved incapable of regaining its previous high perch, the lure of speculative gains in the stock market proved irresistible. The buildup of unsustainable bubbles occurred in both the 1920s and 1990s, periods of relatively low industrial profitability, when rising demand for inflated housing and financial assets received seemingly boundless support from unregulated banks. While studying different theories of the Great Depression, Duménil *et al.* (1987a) focused on the impact of low profitability on managerial decisions concerning capital accumulation, arguing that, as Duménil and Lévy's earlier work anticipated:

> when the degree of response to increasing inventories (by reductions in output) and to low levels of capacity utilization (by reductions in investment) are increased, the model can display overheating, recessions, and depressions. They hypothesize that, in general, low levels of profitability induce extreme economizing behaviors which entail strong reactions to signals of disequilibrium. It follows that low rates of profit create an unstable economy vulnerable to economic perturbations.
>
> (Duménil *et al.*, 1987a, p. 33)

In a recent paper, exploring the connections between Keynesian and Marxian economics Duménil and Lévy (2011c, p. 26) reiterated the principle of instability deriving from low profitability levels:

> If the profit rate declines and remains low for more durable periods of time a "structural" propensity to instability prevails with more frequent and deeper recessions. It is not that a fluctuation downward of the profit rate, as in the example of over-accumulation above, triggers a recession, but that underlying profitability levels render the macro-economy more prone to recessions.

Post-Keynesian views on financial excesses

In our view, acknowledging the centrality of profits behind the dynamics of capital accumulation provides the key to understanding how long-term development waves unfold. In both the 1920s and the 1990s, in the wake of significant profitability declines, even after this descent was temporarily reversed, as long as profitability remained below the level previously considered normal, corporate investment strategies radically changed. In both cases, the extended periods of falling profitability increased the likelihood of economic relapse. Heightened pressures to restore corporate profitability led first to undertakings involving higher-risk investment options in the nonfinancial sector, and second to massive flows of capital channeled into financial speculation. The transition from normal accumulation to breakdown involved first the unraveling of expectations and then financial collapse.

In his collected essays portending *The Great Unraveling* of the American economy in the twenty-first Century, Paul Krugman (2005) traced its origins to the "excesses" of the 1990s, triggered by pie-in-the-sky visions of a "new economy" replacing the crisis-ridden years of an earlier decade:

> During the years of booming stock prices, which were linked to euphoria about the "new economy," businesses invested frantically, sinking vast sums into information technology. Now of course many of those businesses realize that they invested far too much. And the overhang of excess capacity is likely to keep business investment depressed for years (p. 49).

> In 1990, as in 2001, the economy went into a recession in part because of past excesses...The excesses of the 1990s dwarfed those of the 1980s (pp. 92–93).

> For corporate America as a whole, 1997 was a watershed year. According to government statistics, overall corporate profits grew rapidly between 1992 and 1997, but then stalled; after-tax profits in the third quarter of 2000 were barely higher than they were three years earlier. But the operating earnings of the S&P 500 – that is, the profits companies reported to investors – grew 46 percent over those three years...There are technical reasons that these measures of profits need not grow at exactly the same rate. So why did they suddenly diverge? Surely the main reason was that after

1997 companies made increasingly aggressive use of accounting gimmicks to create the illusion of profit growth (p. 107).

But Guttman (1994) directly linked the growth of financial activities to the tepid recovery of profit rates in the nonfinancial corporate sector. Emerging from its deep trough in the early 1980s, profitability in the corporate financial sector rebounded faster than in nonfinancial industries. Such divergence "prompted funds to move increasingly from industrial capital where the recovery of profit-rates was only moderate, into financial capital" (Guttmann, 1994, p. 297), placing the financial sector in the lead of recovery. For in the early 1990s and following the 1987 stock-market crash Guttmann (1994, p. 303) understood that:

> Financial speculation in the stock market is therefore not entirely detached from the accumulation of industrial capital in the sphere of production. In other words the autonomy of fictitious capital is only relative. Its capacity for self-expansion is ultimately limited by the performance of corporations.

Writing from a Post-Keynesian perspective, Guttmann shows that after the early 1980s the predominance of financial rewards in the US altered the structure of capital flows. In the 1980s, deregulation transformed and empowered the US credit system, while banks brought out a multiplicity of financial instruments previously unknown and ostensibly riskless. In the event, while investors with excess cash found rewarding use for their funds in the purchase of financial assets, in Guttmann's view such developments ushered in the "casino society" that Keynes had eloquently derided. For Guttmann (1994, p. 293), by the mid-1990s:

> It is surely no coincidence that the United States possesses the world's largest economy as well as its most developed capital markets. The two went hand in hand. However, the advent of the casino society has thrown the symbiotic relationship out of whack. Trading of stocks, bonds, and other kinds of securities in financial markets, amounting nowadays to several tens of trillions of dollars per year, represents mere shuffling of paper assets. This is not a productive activity and is therefore excluded from our GNP, except for brokerage commissions and service fees generated in those trades.

Indeed, as Guttmann noted, the growing volume of credit-financed acquisitions of financial assets by nonfinancial corporations revealed underlying imbalances that, if extended, would produce financial collapse. In the event the initial discrepancy in profit rates between the sectors that privileged financial investments eventually disappeared when the last housing bubble burst and financial institutions collapsed under the weight of debts and false profits:

> financial instability intensified, as entire sectors experienced debt-deflation adjustments to speculation-driven overextension of credit that was followed in each case by collapsing prices and spreading defaults.
>
> (Guttmann, 1994, p. 249)

From financial fragility to the Great Contraction

We wish to differentiate our argument regarding the path leading to the buildup of financial fragility in the US economy and then to the world-wide Great Recession by contrasting it with Hyman Minsky's views on the perils of external bank finance, as presented in one of his most recent papers. In remarks upon receiving the Veblen–Commons Award in 1996, he categorized the "current crisis of performance and confidence in the rich capitalist countries" (Minsky, 1996, p. 357) as one in which "complex corporate organizations struggle for market power in order to get an edge in the competition for profits" (p. 362) and, despite rising labor productivity, endeavor to lower real wages (pp. 364–365). While acknowledging that falling real wages signaled the deterioration of living standards for the working population, Minsky wished to argue that what really mattered for the expansion of the system was profits. For, according to him, "the economics of Keynes is not a theory for all economies. It is a theory of capitalist economies" (p. 362) and, in capitalist economies, profits drive the system's growth, because they are both "the source of the funds to validate financial instruments" and the attractor for business investment in those assets. We agree that Minsky's comments provide a solid foundation to understand "the institutional structure of capitalist economies," the chief topic discussed in his remarks.

But when he seeks to apply his interpretation of Keynesian economics to the task of theorizing the nature of the "current crisis," we find his approach questionable. In Minsky's (1996, p. 361) view, "A premise of Keynesian modeling is that the capitalist economy cannot be understood by splitting it into real and a financial or monetary sector." Whether this was one of Keynes' basic assumptions is also questionable, for Keynes considered the tendency of the "marginal efficiency of investment" in real capital assets to fall a decisive factor in the determination of the rate of investment, the level of employment, and aggregate demand. What possibly led Minsky to conflate the (nonfinancial) real and financial sectors of the capitalist economy may hinge on his view of financing sources for real investment in nonfinancial sectors. Minsky really takes for granted that: "Business investment in inventory and durable capital assets require[s] external financing from banks, other financial institutions, or the floating of bonds or shares. This need for external finance imposes a negotiating process between bankers and business people" (p. 359).

Minsky's assertion regarding the role of external finance in US corporate planning for business investment is not borne out by the available evidence. Finance for nonfinancial sector gross fixed investment in the US is largely provided out of corporate internal funds, including depreciation plus retained earnings. While bank finance of mortgages for residential housing plays a crucial role in household spending plans, external finance plays a recurrent but minor role in nonfinancial corporate real capital accumulation. Periods when internal funds exceed the requirements of business capital expenditures are interspersed with those in which deficit financing occurs. But on average, a rough balance asserts itself and retained corporate profits drive the propensity to accumulate fixed capital. On the other hand, since the early 1980s, net corporate borrowing by US nonfinancial corporations to acquire new financial assets largely accounts for the rise in nonfinancial corporate debt, although this increase was moderate compared to the debt accumulation of households and financial corporations.

Relative to GDP, US nonfinancial corporate debt rose from a little over 30 percent in the 1970s to around 50 percent in the 2000s, whereas financial corporate debts soared from about 10 percent in 1970 to 120 percent of US GDP in 2008. Next to US financial corporations, including commercial and savings banks, insurance companies, etc., household debt to GDP ratios accelerated from a near 50 percent rate in the early 1960s through the mid-1980s, reaching near 70 percent by the twenty-first century and soaring to near 100 percent in 2007. Clearly, the build-up of financial fragility was not driven by excesses in nonfinancial corporate borrowing related to fixed capital accumulation, but rather by those of households and the financial industry.

There are significant differences between Minsky's account of financial fragility and ours. Minsky's (1996) reference to "the current crisis" perhaps anticipated the gathering signs of financial fragility that eventually led to the first great depression of the twenty-first century (Shaikh, 2010a), also known as "the Second Great Contraction" (Reinhart and Rogoff, 2012). But Minsky expected instability to reach unmanageable levels due to the deterioration of nonfinancial corporate sector balance sheets brought on by excessive debts linked to capital accumulation.

Outpacing the recovery in nonfinancial corporate profitability, the 20-year bull market in equities that started in the 1980s seemed to herald a world of endless prosperity for financial investors. But all along, profitability trends in the nonfinancial corporate sector did not rise to the occasion and therefore validation of the soaring equity prices did not materialize. Once the bubble burst in 2000, the plunge in stock valuations threatened to bring about the dreaded GDP contraction that falling interest rates since the early 1980s had sought to prevent. But, from 1997 on, a new bubble in the housing market gained momentum, allowing the financial industry to expand its financial engineering globally and eventually, beyond its traditional markets, to reach insolvent clients.

According to Krugman (2010), the financial industry made its fortunes by "borrowing vast sums at low interest rates, and investing the funds in higher-yielding assets." To carry this out investment banks needed to persuade markets that their products, largely asset-backed securities, were perfectly safe and therefore merited high prices. Obviously, this assumption proved to be deceptive, but beyond the reality of misinformation, there is no question that theories of efficient asset market valuations went a long way to justify the belief that leading banking practices conformed to mainstream views, hence their products were safe (Gennaioli *et al.*, 2011).

Lavoie's (2006) view that currently "there is an extraordinary convergence among heterodox macroeconomists who are trying, through diverse means, to incorporate financial and monetary questions in the framework of models dealing with real variables" may exaggerate the degree of conceptual affinity found in those quarters. Influential post-Keynesian accounts of capitalist dynamics like those developed by Ingham and Minsky downplay the role of profitability and emphasize the role of bank credit. Calling "the supply of credit-money ... the lifeblood of the capitalist system," Ingham (2008, p. 172) goes on to assert that: "Typically, the initial phase that inaugurates the capitalist production of commodities is the raising of finance in the primary market...it is the capital market, not merely retained profits, which inaugurates and fuels the dynamic expansion of the system."

Buildup of debt and the financial crash

As Figure 11.5 shows, it is true that for half a century there is a remarkable correspondence between US net credit growth and GDP growth, with credit growth generally preceding that of GDP from the late 1940s through the early 1980s. The tight fit between the two, however, might be misinterpreted. Credit growth bridges the gap between current costs and future revenues. Periods in which credit growth in excess of profit growth fuels capital accumulation beyond the limits set by internal sources lead to deterioration of business balance sheets. Servicing the acquired debt forces cutbacks in business investments, hence a lower rate of capital accumulation. Improved balance sheets again restore business creditworthiness and allow a resumption of deficit financing.

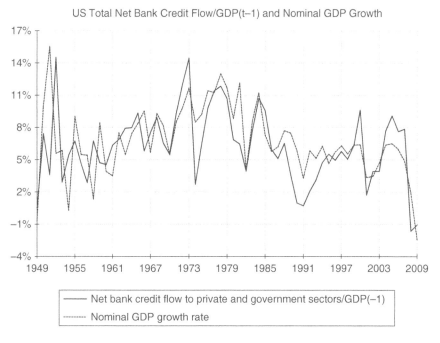

Figure 11.5 US net credit flow/GDP$_{t-1}$ and nominal GDP growth.

Thus, as shown in Figure 9.6, the path of capital accumulation unfolds cyclically punctuated by bouts of deficit financing followed by surplus budgets with lower growth, due to the repayment of business debts (Shaikh, 1989). Historically, the viability of capitalist endogenous growth driven by profitability plays a central role in Marx's analysis of expanded reproduction. As worked out in Marx's schemes of extended reproduction, the role of profits in setting the system's expansion path without external finance is meticulously demonstrated. While bank credit facilitates business transactions, the search for profit drives business investment.

When external credit is involved, as Minsky (1996, p. 366) stressed in his paper on financial fragility, all debt "has to be validated by revenues." Net revenue flows must rise sufficiently to retire debts in order to avoid ending with a Minsky crisis. Financial fragility builds up when the accumulation of debt after an extended period of deficit financing exceeds any possibility of timely repayment and new credit is sought to repay old debt. But in the nonfinancial corporate sector, the capital accumulation boom initiated in the 1990s petered out at decade's end, and the downturn ended in recession, reflecting the parallel decline in profitability.

Nonfinancial corporations suffered substantial losses when the stock market collapsed in 1987 and in the early years of the 2000s, but in that sector debt accumulation was manageable and on both occasions economic collapse was avoided. In financial sectors, Figure 11.6 clearly reveals the rise in net borrowing relative to revenues, starting in the mid-1980s. Unsustainable debts first led to the growth of financial fragility and then in 2007 triggered the credit crunch behind the collapse

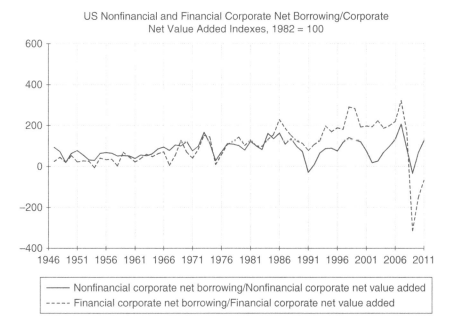

Figure 11.6 US nonfinancial and financial sector net borrowing/net value-added.

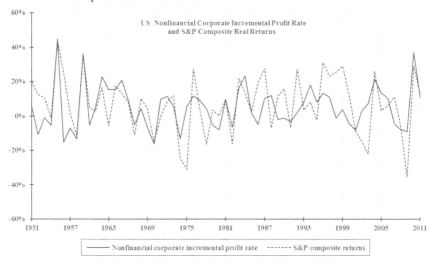

Figure 11.7 US incremental profitability in nonfinancial corporate sectors and real returns in S&P composite.

of economic activity in the economy at large. As Figure 11.7 shows, incremental rates of return in the stock market after the early 1980s exceeded those found in nonfinancial sectors and consequently attracted capital flows (and increasing debt) into equity markets.

As we showed in Figure 11.2, US real wages grew much more slowly than labor productivity from 1982 through the present. They also grew below the pace registered from the late 1940s through the late 1970s. The higher growth rate for employee compensation initiated in the late 1990s ended at the turn of the new century. The NIPA data for employee compensation skews the real trend because the high salaries and bonuses received by the financial elite are included. In the event, the growing gap between lagging household income and rising household debt would lead to the buildup of financial fragility papered over by the housing bubble.

Expenditures on housing historically averaged 30 percent of household income, but housing prices doubled from 2000 to 2007 while household income stagnated, hence the required support from revenue flows to retire debt waned. Households' growing indebtedness, enabled by financial institutions pushing loans beyond the growth of household incomes, reached unsustainable levels once housing prices crashed. It is instructive to note that historically, financial and housing bubbles also laid the path to the Great Depression of the 1930s. In the 1920s "household debt as a percentage of household wealth increased from 10.2 percent to 27.2 percent" (Gjerstad and Smith, 2009, p. 293), and from 1999 to 2008 the ratio of household liabilities to net worth rose from 15.7 percent to 26.4 percent, while the ratio of household credit market outstanding debt to disposable income rose by 32.4 percent.

12 Unemployment trends beyond the great recession

Introduction

Beyond the effect of fluctuations in aggregate demand on cyclical unemployment rates observed in major OECD economies, we attribute the rise of long-term structural unemployment since the late 1970s to the impact of labor-saving technical change on the evolution of profitability and capital accumulation trends. We argue in this chapter that labor-displacing technical progress in conjunction with falling capital accumulation trends led to persistently high structural unemployment trends.

We have shown in previous chapters that while the long-run profitability trend of US nonfinancial corporations changed course after the early 1980s, it never regained its previous high levels. We challenged the view that US nonfinancial corporate profitability trends rose beyond the mid-1990s and only fell on the eve of the Great Recession, because the troughs reached by each of the two profit-rate cycles after 1987 were lower than the previous ones. Indeed, every profitability upturn after the 1983 rebound started from a lower point than in previous cycles, and after cresting fell below its initial level. Our estimates show the recovery of nonfinancial corporate profitability after 1987 lost its vigor, following the same cyclical pattern well into the period of crisis.

Preventing the rise in unemployment caused by the labor-displacing character of technical change in advanced capitalist countries would have required strong counterbalancing pulls from the labor-absorbing force of capital accumulation. But in most cases capital accumulation trends declined. US nonfinancial capital accumulation rates in fact extended their long-run downward trend from the mid-1960s to the first decade of the twenty-first century, despite such significant upturns as the celebrated climb of the first half of the 1990s. Mounting competitive pressures continued to impose the accelerated deployment of labor-saving technology throughout the nonfinancial and financial sectors, despite a falling rate of accumulation stymieing both the prospects for the recovery of corporate profitability and the reabsorption of the displaced labor.

In previous chapters we have argued that tracking the behavior of the output–capital ratio reveals its central role in shaping the profitability and accumulation paths. Capital–output trends reflect the systemic tendencies in technical progress driving the development of industrial capitalism. The relentless effort to raise labor productivity in order to lower unit costs guides technical change in the direction of higher levels of mechanization (automation). Competitive pressures prompt dynamic firms vying for industry leadership to adopt technologies capable of raising output per unit of labor time (and so lower the engineering "throughput") in order to achieve lower unit costs. Deploying a more powerful method of production will generally require more automated machinery to process larger volumes of intermediate materials into final products per unit of time, hence higher unit fixed-capital outlays. As long as labor variable costs decline proportionately more than unit fixed costs rise, total unit costs will fall. Historically, this process is nowhere more evident than in the transformation of agriculture from a labor-intensive to a capital-intensive activity employing very few workers (Altschul and Strauss, 1937).

Rising world unemployment after the late 1970s

In nine major OECD countries, namely Canada, France, Germany, Italy, Japan, Spain, Sweden, the UK, and US, unemployment rates surged from the early 1970s through the 1980s. Despite significant fluctuations associated with effective demand cycles in the next thirty years, at the end of the rise the new averages in all of those countries except the US remained higher in the 1990s than they were before. Eatwell and Milgate (2010, p. 93) observed that "A distinct break occurred around 1970, with a sharp increase in trend levels of unemployment." As Figure 12.1 shows, despite a falling interval in the 1990s, unemployment rates in most countries failed to reach the lower values generally found in the 1950s and 1960s. In the US the 1980s upturn in average unemployment rates coincided with the structural changes in capital flows prompted by corporate pressures to reverse the previous downward trend in nonfinancial corporate profitability. The rise of financial capital flows and the decline in the weight of value-added produced in the nonfinancial sectors characterize the "financialization" stage of leading capitalist economies.

Regarding unemployment trends beyond the watershed reached in the early 1980s, the US experience is exceptional: after reaching a peak in the early 1980s unemployment rates fell throughout the decade, rose in tandem with the other countries in the early 1990s, and resumed descent through the last decade of the twentieth century, reaching levels comparable to the prosperous 1960s. The 2007 financial crisis that set off a downward spin in the global economy, however, reversed the low-unemployment phase and propelled unemployment rates everywhere to the highest levels previously observed in half a century. Besides the US sustained period of falling unemployment rates in the 1980s but in opposite ways, the unemployment growth of three other countries, Japan, Sweden and Spain, sets them apart in magnitude from the other six. Japan's experience of very low unemployment rates from the 1950s to the mid-1970s ended abruptly, not to be matched again. Rising in relatively mild waves after the mid-1970s, unemployment rates in Japan rose every decade to levels never experienced before. In Sweden, with

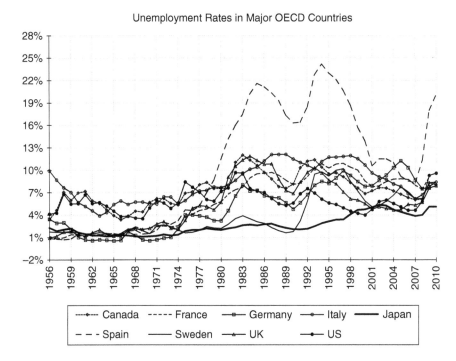

Figure 12.1 Unemployment rates in major OECD countries, 1956–2010.

unemployment rates in the 1950s and 1960s slightly higher than Japan's, the big upsurge in unemployment occurred in the early 1990s, moving from the 2 percent to the 10 percent level for several years and not falling to the 5 percent level again until 2001. While Sweden's 5 percent unemployment rate in 2001 compared favorably with labor-market conditions in most other countries, except the UK and the US, the country's unemployment rate was then twice as high as it was in 1980.

Spain's case remains unique within the OECD group of developed economies. Identifying the structural forces in the Spanish economy that pushed the unemployment rate into the 20 percent range every twenty-odd years or so (mid-1980s, mid-1990s and 2010) is a daunting task that cannot be pursued here. But just pondering the recurrence of such trends in an economy belonging to the European Union ought to raise questions about the nature of its development path. Indeed, breaking the rural–urban balance of low-single-digit unemployment rates sustained by massive emigration from the 1960s up to the mid-1970s, the breakdown of employment levels experienced from the mid-1980s to the mid-1990s pushed the unemployment rate onto levels associated with full-blown depressions anywhere else. Absent any consideration of a depression context, the argument that such outcomes were simply temporary episodes of collateral damage caused by the "restructuration" of the economy is not credible.

Figure 12.2 Real unit labor costs (labor income shares) in major OECD countries.

With credit supplied by the European Central Bank at rates well below the rate of inflation in Spain, the expansion of the housing bubble significantly raised the demand for labor in the construction trades despite low and declining productivity levels (Bielsa and Duarte, 2011). But like other previous episodes of transitory bonanzas, such as the massive inflows of emigrant workers' remittances of the 1960s and the large foreign-currency inflows associated with tourism of the 1970s, once the housing and financial bubbles burst the employment levels plunged. The notion of transient adjustments to such employment equilibria cannot gloss over the fact that, once the housing bubble fueling the economic bonanza of the past decade faded, unemployment rates quickly reverted to depression levels. But as Figure 12.2 shows, rising levels of unemployment drove down the real unit labor costs throughout the economy and hence realigned the income distribution in favor of business operating surpluses.

Long-run accumulation trends after the mid-1960s

In previous chapters we identified falling profit rates after the mid-1960s as the structural force weighing down the long-run trend of nonfinancial corporate capital from that time until the early 1980s. From the beginning of the 1980s, a relatively lower average profitability trend, unadjusted for capacity utilization, similarly exerted downward pressure on accumulation. In the immediate postwar period capital accumulation rates increased from the late 1940s to the mid-1960s despite a stagnant if not falling profit-rate trend because the initial levels from which profitability changed were relatively high. Underpinning the internet and stock-market bubbles of the 1990s, accumulation rates rose significantly, reaching a peak at decade's end. But that movement describes only the ascending half of a full cycle which on the downside reached in 2003 the lowest trough since 1958.

For half a century after the mid-1960s, cyclical movements driven by fluctuations in aggregate demand and capacity utilization punctuated the long-run trend of capital accumulation. Big swings in effective demand led to significant changes in the degree of capacity utilization, producing major cyclical movements spanning several decades. When adjusted for capacity utilization to smooth out these fluctuations, the output–capital ratio exhibited a long-run decline inversely related to the long-run rise in labor productivity. Thus, the downward overall trend of the adjusted output–capital ratio exerting a roughly equivalent drag on average business profitability provided the systemic force behind the long-run decline in capital accumulation.

Achieving the steady rise in labor productivity required acceptance of technical progress in order to build up additional capacity. The fall of the long-run output–capital coefficient, caused by more capital-intensive and labor-displacing innovations, is a consequence of the aims pursued by business enterprise. The crucial link under consideration centers on the issue of how innovations impact business profitability, since business expansion is not driven by engineering sophistication as such but by the search for higher market shares. Indeed, business innovations do not emerge out of the engineering workshops in isolation from the exigencies derived from waging competitive wars successfully, and rising unemployment is not simply the effect of the engineering quest for more powerful production techniques.

In our conceptual framework, (a) the accumulation trend mirrors that of profitability, which is driven in the long-run by output–capital trends (the maximum profit rate) once adjustment for capacity utilization is made; (b) capacity utilization variations reflecting changes in effective demand produce accumulation cycles around that trend; (c) technological progress gives rise to long-run capital–output trends, while short- and medium-run capital–output cycles emerge from capacity utilization fluctuations. Specifically, we contend that rising capital–output trends (after adjustment for capacity utilization) exert the dominant force behind the falling and low profitability trends of the US nonfinancial corporate sector. At one remove, moreover, they also shaped the falling capital accumulation trends and therefore stand behind rising unemployment rates.

Most heterodox economists have argued that profitability trends since the early 1980s achieved or approached their postwar high levels in the 1990s. We find it difficult to reconcile this view with the widely held perception in the heterodox literature that business fixed capital accumulation rates across major OECD economies trended downwards in the same period. Surely the driving force behind the expansion of capitalist firms is profits; if profitability was rising, why would it not rev up the accumulation engine? Did global competition not intensify in the last decades of the twentieth century and beyond? With flagging accumulation rates, could the rising path of profitability be sustained? For us the acknowledged decline in fixed capital accumulation rates attests to a conceptual bifurcation of the profitability and accumulation trends. On the face of it, systemic strategies for increasing labor productivity designed to undercut the market share of industrial rivals in the context of rising global competition should favor the growing capitalization of production in all branches of the economy from manufacturing to banking. And for that reason, the choice of capital-using, labor-saving technologies would dominate the evolution of profitability trends everywhere.

With regard to the causes or structural roots of such decline in accumulation trends, however, the accord ends. Influential economists, building on Keynesian theoretical foundations, tend to reject explanations of falling accumulation rates in line with declining or low long-run profitability trends: most will argue that no such trends are discernible. For their part, those sharing Marx's views on the centrality of profits acknowledge the significance of Keynes' stress on the volatility of investment and the marginal efficiency of capital. But they would challenge the sanguine view of leading post-Keynesian economists regarding their long-run trends. Endorsing Kaldor's claims for his "stylized facts," Pasinetti (1983, p. 79), for example, simply asserts as unequivocally established that in the US between 1880 and 1980, "variables like ... the rate of profit have undergone considerable variations... But the important point is that such dispersion... has done so around a roughly constant trend." However, our findings in Figure 11.3 suggest instead the presence of significant downward profitability trends for over a century and a half. At least one prominent post-Keynesian theorist has argued that Keynes recognized "the declining trend in the return to investment after the end of World War I" as the main factor driving the British economy to Depression in the 1930s (Leijonhufvud, 2009, p. 742). Clearly, beyond the theoretical divide between heterodoxy and the neoclassical mainstream, or between Keynes and Marx, the lack of consensus characterizes each of the two major heterodox perspectives as well.

The natural rate of unemployment

The conceptual structure informing the views of neoclassical economists does not allow involuntary unemployment to have any real meaning. Pressing the assumption of perfect competition to labor market dynamics with its underlying concept of flexible wages and independently formed supply and demand schedules, neoclassical economics simply discards the significance of involuntary labor unemployment. Perfect knowledge of future conditions as well as unimpeded mobility of factors conceived as perfectly substitutable, divisible and homogeneous, clinches the anticipated outcome of general market equilibrium, including the labor market. Money and uncertainty play no role in the system's adjustment, contributing nothing to the achievement of equilibrium levels in real output and employment.

In the neoclassical version of general equilibrium, interest rate movements govern saving and investment decisions in opposite ways. The existing capital stock accumulated from past investments and the equilibrium level of employment jointly set the level of real output. In product markets, the quantity of money independently decided by the monetary authority, along with its institutional turnover, simply affect the price level, not the real output level. With the demand for labor given by the falling marginal physical product and a rising labor supply schedule, prices set in the monetary sector simply produce the level of real wage rates necessary to reach full employment equilibrium simultaneously in all markets.

In the neoclassical perspective workers unwilling to accept the wage rate emerging from the general equilibrium adjustment of product and labor markets should not be considered as involuntarily unemployed. Choosing not to accept the equilibrium wage rate to which labor markets naturally gravitate, such workers bear responsibility for the consequences and therefore, Milton Friedman concluded, they are voluntarily unemployed: they opt for leisure instead of work. Accordingly, any evidence of involuntary unemployment attests to the presence of unwarranted interference with the flexible adjustment mechanism of the system. Such extra systemic obstruction is generally attributed to labor union pressures to raise wages above the marginal product of labor and/or minimum-wage legislation reflecting misguided government policies to circumvent the results ground out by the equilibrating tendencies of the labor market.

Full employment is achieved in the labor market when the demand for labor, reflecting a falling marginal labor productivity schedule, confronts an independently formed rising supply of workers, mechanically increasing their search for jobs when wage rates rise. Since the appearance of excess labor supply signals above equilibrium wage rates, the cause of the excess labor supply derives from an expected rise in workers' search for employment. Such response occurs despite the fact that the theory endows workers with perfect knowledge of all market conditions. Assuming homogeneous labor and perfect knowledge, however, workers should be able to foretell that peers' response would match their behavior when they increase their job searches, hence they should conclude that current high wages will not outlast the avalanche of job seekers: they should not be deceived by the mirage of "high wages" to expand their job search.

Milton Friedman's acknowledgement that the neoclassical concept of general equilibrium is compatible with a persistent measure of unemployment allowed neoclassical theory to resolve a glaring conflict between theory and reality. Addressing the American Economic Association in 1967, he said:

> At any moment of time, there is some level of unemployment which has the property that it is consistent with equilibrium in the structure of real wage rates. At that level of unemployment, real wage rates are tending on the average to rise at a "normal" secular rate, i.e., at a rate that can be indefinitely maintained so long as capital formation, technological improvements,

etc., remain on their long-run trends. A lower level of unemployment is an indication that there is an excess demand for labor that will produce upward pressure on real wage rates. A higher level of unemployment is an indication that there is an excess supply of labor that will produce downward pressure on real wage rates. The "natural rate of unemployment," in other words, is the level that would be ground out by the Walrasian system of general equilibrium equations, provided there is imbedded in them the actual structural characteristics of the labor and commodity markets, including market imperfections, stochastic variability in demands and supplies, the cost of gathering information about job vacancies and labor availabilities, the costs of mobility, and so on.

(Friedman, 1968, p. 8)

Friedman's acceptance of a "natural rate of unemployment" provided a much needed dialectical solution to the neoclassical conundrum. Confronting the reality of persistent unemployment that appeared to contradict the conclusions derived from the general equilibrium approach of neoclassical economics, Friedman developed a more nuanced concept of full employment which, in theory, resolved the contradiction. The unemployment reality challenging the integrity of neoclassical concepts lost its theoretical import once Friedman's new concept of full employment absorbed it as one of its structural elements, thereby denying its negative significance:

Let me emphasize that by using the term "natural" rate of unemployment, I do not mean to suggest that it is immutable and unchangeable. On the contrary, many of the market characteristics that determine its level are man-made and policy-made... legal minimum wage rates... the strength of labor unions all make the natural rate of unemployment higher than it would otherwise be . . . I use the term "natural" for the same reason Wicksell did - to try to separate the real forces from monetary forces.

(Friedman, 1968, p. 9)

Malinvaud on market disequilibrium

Neoclassical theories of unemployment, whether framed in general equilibrium models or not, may contribute partial insights into the problem but fail to provide a comprehensive explanation of its growing importance. According to Malinvaud's recast of unemployment theory along "Keynesian" lines, mass unemployment signaled the persistence of market disequilibrium. Despite the growth of mass unemployment experienced in OECD countries since the 1970s, Malinvaud (1985) did not offer any policy guidelines to solve the problem. Instead, he conceived his task as reaching the lofty goal of integrating "Keynesian theory" with the conceptual structure of neoclassical general equilibrium. Succinctly put, for Malivaud the emergence of mass unemployment proved the existence of disequilibrium in the system and its persistence attested to a malfunctioning economy: a malady remediable as long as markets freely are allowed to reach their natural balances but not otherwise. By definition, once general equilibrium is reached full employment should follow. But Malinvaud's concept of "Keynesian unemployment," by his own admission, is fictitious and not derived from Keynes': it only appears in sanitized versions advanced by Keynes' neoclassical "disciples" (Malivaud, 1985, p. xiii). Accordingly, we have an unemployment concept of dubious origins:

> Keynesian unemployment occurs when prices are too high in comparison with the nominal assets. . .of consumers and given the volume of autonomous demand. Classical unemployment, on the other hand, is typical of a situation in which real wages are too high, so that firms do not find it profitable to employ all the labor force.
>
> (Malinvaud, 1985, p. 90)

Without acknowledging that the conceptual framework of the Walrasian theory of successive equilibria offered no guidance for the empirical investigation of mass unemployment, Malinvaud argued that the wayward character of capital accumulation explained the failure of productive capacity to grow sufficiently to provide full employment. This position led to glaring inconsistencies of judgment. On the one hand, inadequate growth of productive capacity underlay the simultaneous appearance of excess labor and excess demand in product markets. From his general equilibrium analysis standpoint, Malinvaud saw the rise in mass unemployment as a sign of disequilibria in product and labor markets. Now, insufficient capacity to support a high level of employment would lead to inadequate levels of effective demand reflecting mass unemployment. But insufficient capacity would also produce excess demand if deflation followed the growth of unemployment. Straddling the classical world of insufficient capacity due to low profitability and high real wages, and the Keynesian view of insufficient capacity and low effective demand, Malinvaud settled for his original "Keynesian" claim, attributing the cause of mass unemployment to "under-consumption" (Malinvaud, 1985, p. 118).

Malinvaud's more empirically oriented study in *Mass Unemployment* (1986) however, addressed exclusively the problem of "classical" unemployment, eschewing his previous conflation of Keynesian and general equilibrium perspectives. Insisting that unemployment persisted due to inadequate capacity expansion, Malinvaud argued that despite high rates of gross investment in the 1960s and 1970s, equally high rates of obsolescence rendered the net expansionary effect on capacity quite small. This was so because after the 1970s in France and other European countries rising product wages and higher unit labor costs lowered profitability, inducing firms to accelerate scrapping of older plants and equipment. Malinvaud wished to argue that low profitability "in some sectors" undermined capital accumulation in the economy at large and blocked employment growth. Along with neoclassic theory, Malinvaud blamed rising real wage rates for the rise in unemployment, since they caused net accumulation rates to fall and therefore brought about the parallel decline in labor productivity.

Anticipating interest rate trends after the 1980s, Malinvaud argued in favor of the neoclassical concept of "pure" profit rates as the "most relevant" measure of profitability. Claiming that the relevant measure "is not the business profit rate as such, but the amount by which this rate exceeds the real interest rate," Malinvaud pinned his hopes for full employment on falling interest rates. Despite the fact that the standard profit rate estimates for nonfinancial corporations declined to 2.5 percent in 1979 from their 5 percent level in the 1960s and plunged to zero in the early 1980s, he hoped that falling real interest rates would eventually cushion the decline of the "pure profit rate, namely the excess of the real profit rate earned on productive operations over the real interest rate earned on finance capital" (Malinvaud, 1986, pp. 49–50, 89) and thus bring on higher accumulation rates.

For his part, Assar Lindbeck, the Swedish economist and member of the Committee for the Nobel Prize in Economic Science, 1969–1994 (chairman 1980–1994), also sought to formulate a theory of macroeconomic unemployment within a general equilibrium framework. Lindbeck (1993) drew attention to the fact that unemployed workers failed to bid down market wage rates and consequently the labor market did not clear. Observing that unemployed labor in Western Europe persisted through the 1970s and well into the 1980s, along with "more liberal" programs of unemployment relief, he concluded that unemployed labor failed to find employment precisely because the available unemployment benefits sapped its resolve to seek employment (Lindbeck, 1993, pp. 132–133). In Lindbeck the neoclassical view of labor unions as the chief impediment to full employment features achieves prominence. Indeed, Lindbeck warned of the dire consequences issuing from allowing labor unions to extort undeserved benefits from liberal governments. Stressing the dangers inherent in "centralized bargaining" between governments and labor unions Lindbeck (1993, pp. 167–168) argued that, "In such a system, the central union leadership can exert political blackmail over the government by asking for political favors for themselves as a requirement for their willingness to accept wage moderation."

The persistence of technological unemployment

Early in the twentieth century the prevailing consensus "by practically all students of the problem" (Leiserson, 1916, p. 19) in the US and Britain regarding the inevitable occurrence of permanent labor unemployment derived its strength from close study of the historical record. The consensus bound followers of Adam Smith arguing that since competitive markets led to optimal resource allocation the emergence of unemployment was a bearable dead weight in the process, with socialist critics of capitalism who thought otherwise. Both sides agreed that unemployment was a permanent feature of competitive capitalism but disagreed on its social merit. For free enterprise supporters, unemployment was merely an "incidental evil" of a good system, while for socialists it proclaimed the antisocial nature of capitalism. Prevailing views rejected the possibility of eliminating unemployment as long as capitalism remained undisturbed, "for if industrial progress proceeds in cycles of prosperity and depression...then a reserve of unemployed labor must ever be present to allow for the extension of industrial enterprises" (Leiserson, 1916, p. 19).

As the twentieth century ended the concern expressed in the 1930s and 1940s by economists at the Graduate Faculty of the New School for Social Research in New York City that technological progress caused labor displacement and increased unemployment acquired wider recognition outside the neoclassical mainstream. In the early 1930s, Emil Lederer argued that profit-seeking enterprises would support technical progress in three forms: (a) technologies that lowered unit labor costs because they reduce the man-hours normally necessary to produce a given output; (b) technical change that results in the replacement of old models with new ones of superior quality; (c) innovating technologies turning out entirely new products hitherto unknown. For Lederer types (a) and (b) caused labor displacement and expanded the unemployment pool, whereas type (c) fueled the employment growth of the nineteenth-century industrial revolution that led to projections of excessive optimism (Lederer, 1933, pp. 1–6).

In a world where the innovating urge dominated business growth strategies and technological change was continuous, the timely occurrence of countervailing forces aiming to absorb displaced workers was not guaranteed: "Capital invested with a view to economizing labor in existing industries cannot be the source of a fresh demand for labor, even in the most favorable case" (Lederer, 1933, p. 14). Since for Lederer the feasibility of adopting innovations depended on long-term profitability criteria, the decline in wages caused by growing unemployment might not enhance profit expectations, thus failing to spur investment. Anticipating the Keynesian conundrum, Lederer (1933, p. 25) believed that the strength of investment plans depended on long-term prospects being unaffected by declining wage costs, since such a turn might instead pull down current prices and weaken effective demand.

Two years later Alfred Kahler (1935, p. 439) recalled that "Socialist theory in Germany before the World War was for decades closely bound up with the concept that mechanization of production must permanently increase unemployment." On the other hand, the sanguine view of mechanization's impact on the reabsorption of labor held that whatever funds technical progress released from lower labor costs would reappear as higher profits or due to falling prices larger consumer purchases. In both cases effective demand would rise sufficiently to provide the necessary re-employment of the displaced workers. But Kahler objected that higher fixed capital investments did generally precede increases in labor productivity, burdening the innovating firms with higher interest liabilities that would depress their future investment plans.

Joining Lederer in the spirit of the yet-to-come Keynesian assault on Say's law, Kahler disparaged earlier views concerning the "unlimited desire to consume." Once Ricardo acknowledged the impact of mechanization on wages and labor employment in the third edition of his *Principles of Political Economy*, the theoretical views on the possibilities for future full employment changed. Marx's view of capitalist development fostering the growth of fixed relative to variable capital shared with Bohm-Bowerk's theory of the increasing roundabout character of modern technology Ricardo's concern with technological unemployment. In both cases the replacement of circulating with fixed capital caused unemployment to rise and wage shares to decline. Accepting Schumpeter's theory of creative destruction, Kahler pointed out that technical progress did not just add new productive capacity to the existing stock but also rendered older techniques unprofitable to operate. In periods of business upturns, the price increases derived from an expanding market might preserve the profitability of marginal firms unable to upgrade, but once the downturn occurred the fall in prices brought them down. As a counter-tendency cushioning the labor-saving character of mechanization, the falling share of wages created expanding opportunities for employment in the area of "personal services" where technical innovations did not predominate. In addition, sales and trade-related labor activities were likely to expand in response to the growing discrepancy between the growth capacity of the system and the underlying consumption limitations of the market. Because such activities are less capital-intensive than the productive branches of traditional industry, they could provide alternative employment opportunities without large investments.

But for Kahler the historical record provided ample statistical evidence to support the labor-displacement theory of technical progress. The crucial issue hinged on the legitimacy of linking the appearance of high unemployment in a crisis period with the waves of technological progress sustaining the boom preceding the slump. Kahler (1935) argued that "This is easy to do if the explanation of present unemployment is not limited to the increase in productivity in the period since 1929." He could show that in the 1920s technical progress eliminated jobs in "agriculture, manufacturing, mining." The fact that unemployment did not rise substantially at the end of that decade reflected the strength of compensatory labor-market balances in personal services, trade, construction, and transportation in the years of expansion. In the 1930s, the reserve pool of unemployed workers increased once the compensatory forces active in the previous decade failed to countervail the direct effects of mechanization. In the 1930s depression, on the other hand, unemployment swelled not only because new technologies required less labor per unit of output, or the decline in profit income curtailed expenditures on personal services or housing construction, but also because firms operating with old equipment went out of business.

Seven years after Kahler sought to statistically verify the contention that technical change sustained a permanent pool of unemployed labor, Hans Neisser (1942, p. 70) credited Marx with "consistently expounding the paramount ideas of the Ricardian system" and interpreting "the capitalistic process as a race between displacement of labor through technical progress and reabsorption of labor through accumulation." In Neisser's view "permanent" technological unemployment of labor was unavoidable in a system persistently buffeted by labor-saving waves of innovations and where labor reabsorption hinged on the strength of fixed capital accumulation. Technological progress issued from advances in science, technology, and managerial know-how. The decisions shaping the accumulation trend, however, derived from profit expectations independently formed through the filters of past business experience and confidence in future profitability. The upshot of such conjectures determined the growth parameters governing the demand for labor, not the frequency or strength of the innovation swarms (Neisser, 1942, p. 71).

Is labor unemployment irrational or functional?

Despite the mounting evidence linking unemployment to the relentless growth of labor-saving technological progress, progressive opinion in this as well as other matters remains divided. Post-Keynesians like Eatwell and Milgate remain unconvinced that the persistence of high levels of unemployment on a world scale in the late twentieth century derived from labor-saving technological change. In a recent study investigating the growth of world unemployment, they denied validity to the "common view," held since Ricardo's treatment of this issue, "that technological change is a threat to jobs." Thus, Eatwell and Milgate doubted that the growth of automation in the 1950s and 1960s laid the foundation for growing unemployment in the 1970s, and they challenged the 1970s and 1980s perception that information technologies destroyed jobs. On the contrary, Eatwell and Milgate (2010, p. 95) are sure that technological change had absolutely nothing to do with the unemployment surge witnessed in the 1980s:

> there is no evidence that the speed of technological change was behind the growth of unemployment throughout the G7. If it were, then there should have been an acceleration of productivity growth in the 1980s and 1990s as new techniques sharply reduced the labor input required per unit output.

But since labor unemployment trends did exhibit a tendency to rise, the question whether unemployment should be viewed as an irrational excess, albeit a "normal feature of capitalist economies" (Forstater, 2001, 2002), or a necessary lever preventing wage increases from outpacing productivity growth poses a dilemma for post-Keynesian economists straddling the theoretical legacies of Marx and Keynes (Lange, 1935, pp. 198–199; Kalecki, 1971; Forstater, 2001, 2002; Pollin, 1998; Stockhammer, 2008).

Forstater (2001) observed that Marx's views on accumulation and endogenous technical change played minor roles in the post-Keynesian theory of unemployment. One major exception was Goodwin's research program. Richard Goodwin's (1972) celebrated formalization of Marx's growth cycle outlined in Chapter 25 of *Capital*, Vol. I, led him to expand his formulation of dynamic models integrating Keynesian concepts of effective demand with profit-led accumulation cycles. These growth models reflect the nonlinear dynamics involving cyclical fluctuations in accumulation, changing profit shares caused by wage changes and unemployment movements. But they also show the effect of fluctuations in effective demand derived from changing accumulation rates giving rise to irregular long-run output cycles. All cyclical changes in employment, however, occur around a persistent pool of unemployed labor: full employment is never present.

Forstater (2002) also expressed concern with the fact that recent post-Keynesian theory largely failed to integrate the analysis of money and effective demand with "structural and technological change," ignoring the vast reservoir of knowledge compiled in the 1930s by German researchers of the Kiel School, including Emil Lederer, Alfred Kahler, and Hans Neisser. Their research showed that unemployment was not an excrescence of the system, but rather one of its structural components: it served a purpose. Maintaining a pool of unemployed workers weakened the bargaining position of labor and kept wages from rising beyond productivity growth, the critical level needed to maintain profit margins and allow capital accumulation to proceed.

Writing in 1943, Kalecki (1971, p. 141) acknowledged that "profits would be higher under a regime of full employment" than they are when the system maintains a reserve of unemployed workers, but "'discipline in the factories' and 'political stability' are more appreciated by the business leaders than profits." According to Robert Pollin (1999) the specific size of the reserve pool of unemployment, and hence the lever that regulates the bounds of wage rates, "depends on how the inherent conflicts between workers and capitalists are resolved." This proposition concerns the effect of unemployment on wages and falls short of Kalecki and Lange's views of unemployment as a structural component of the system. Nonetheless, Pollin (1999, p. 105) concluded that Friedman's "natural rate theory actually contains a legitimate foundation of truth."

Bypassing the effect of accumulation rates on unemployment fluctuations, Felipe's (2002) sophisticated econometrics conclusively showed the direct link between profitability and unemployment fluctuations in the case of Spain's economy. Focusing on profitability as the driving force behind unemployment allowed Felipe's remarkable study to overcome the artificial notion "that economies can be either profit-led or wage-led" (Storm and Naastepad, 2012, p. 20), thus enriching the post-Keynesian research program with central concepts of classical political economy.

Krugman on technological progress and unemployment

Writing in the *Wilson Quarterly*, Krugman (1994) raised again the question "Is it really possible for technological progress to harm large numbers of people?" and concluded "It is and it has been." In his view, the persistent displacement of labor from existing jobs ensures the permanence of a reserve pool of unemployment and its periodic growth acts as a lever pressuring wages downward. Krugman identified labor-saving technical change as the main force behind the rise of European unemployment as well as the decline in the share of compensation for most workers in the US. Thus, the upturn in unemployment rates across the advanced economies of our OECD sample registered since the 1980s would underlie the falling labor compensation shares or real unit labor costs characteristic of the past thirty years.

In Krugman's view, from the nineteenth-century industrial revolution to the present, technical progress

> encouraged industrialists to use less labor and to invest more capital to produce a given amount of output. The result then was a fall in the demand for labor that kept real wages stagnant for perhaps 50 years, even as the incomes of England's propertied classes soared...Economists more or less agree that the same thing is happening to the Western world today.

Now, however, new technology favored "symbolic analysts" endowed with the necessary skills to use it, ranging "from data processing to physicians," or more significantly, "lawyers, doctors, and, above all, corporate executives." The new technological advances in the twentieth century, according to Krugman, did not result in higher business profits, instead "the benefits of biased technological change are flowing not to capital but to the highly skilled" (Krugman, 1994). Despite his characterization of modern technology as definitely biased against low-skilled labor, Krugman's confidence that in the not too distant future "the current era of growing inequality and the devaluation of ordinary work will turn out to be only a temporary phase...I predict that the current age of inequality will give way to a golden age of equality," in hindsight, appears to be groundless. It is true that computer software appropriated many skills possessed by privileged professionals and lowered their market value in a manner reminiscent of machinery incorporating the skills of former artisans. But, contrary to Krugman's beguiling link between technical skills and high pay, the unraveling financial crisis brought home the incongruous association between exorbitant bonuses and the reckless behavior of banking "experts," suggesting instead a warped structure of rewards.

While critics of globalization since the mid-1990s raised the specter of shrinking employment in the advanced economies, Jagdish Bhagwati repeatedly denied globalization's responsibility in lowering US employment and wages, arguing that "there are good theoretical and empirical reasons why trade did not cause the adverse impact one might fear, and that the case therefore for the overwhelming role of technical change...in explaining the misfortune of the unskilled is very strong" (Bhagwati, 1995, p. 42). Instead, in his influential book on globalization in the twenty-first century, still fending off charges lodged by critics of globalization about the deterioration of US wages, Bhagwati (2007, pp. 126–127) identified technological change as the driving force diminishing the share of labor income in developed economies: "the problem for real wages of the unskilled workers comes from labor-saving technical change."

Robert Reich (2010, p. 6), former Secretary of Labor in the Clinton Administration, recently traced the origin of the relentless deterioration in "middle class" living standards to "around 1980, when the American middle class started being hit by the double whammy of global competition and labor-replacing technologies." Reflecting on three decades of falling labor income shares, Reich argued that the effects of technological unemployment extended beyond the lack of demand for unskilled workers to the employment prospects and wages for all workers. The effects of labor saving technologies reached more markets than ever before and consequently no job was safe:

> The problem was not simply the loss of good jobs to workers in foreign nations but also automation. New technologies such as computerized machine tools could do the same work people did at a fraction of the cost. Even factories remaining in the United States shed workers as they automated...Remember bank tellers? Telephone operators? The fleets of airline workers behind counters who issued tickets? Service station attendants? These and millions of other jobs weren't lost to globalization; they were lost to automation.
>
> (Reich, 2010, pp. 52–53)

Capital–output and unemployment trends

Fear that the technical progress underlying the growth of capitalist enterprises could lead to rising capital–output ratios and thus lower their profitability trends was never exorcised from the lore of political economy. Heterodox economists did not flinch from considering its impact on the accumulation drive. In her introduction to Rosa Luxemburg's *Accumulation of Capital*, Joan Robinson allowed that if labor productivity increased in branches producing machinery matching similar gains in consumer goods sectors, and if capital-saving methods on balance appeared alongside labor-saving technology, the labor value of capital per worker might not rise. "However, we can easily get out of this difficulty by postulating that as a matter of fact technical progress is mainly labor-saving, or, a better term, capital using, so that capital per man is rising through time" (Robinson, 2003, p. XXXI).

Searching for the conceptual roots of biased technical progress in classical political economy, H. Kurz identified Ricardo's third edition of his *Principles* as the decisive source. Building on Ricardo's insights in this regard, H. Kurz analyzed the development of technology within the framework of income distribution. Linking Marx's views to Ricardo's breakthrough, when formulating his theory of induced technical change, Kurz found the roots of a systemic bias towards more capital-intensive and labor-saving methods of production in the capitalist drive to contain rising wage costs. Aiming to increase labor productivity by reducing the dispersion of labor compliance with production norms, capitalists relentlessly sought out technologies to displace labor from production. The time-honored strategy to accomplish these goals favored the mechanization of production: replacing labor inputs with larger stocks of fixed capital.

Kurz (2009) concurred with Ricardo's view that such technical change responds to the "antagonism between capital and wage labor" and reflects the class struggle over the distribution of output. "Inspired by Piero Sraffa's studies in his hitherto unpublished papers," Kurz argued that "the progressive replacement of labor by fixed capital is a characteristic feature of modern economic development" and that not Marx but Ricardo "was one of the first authors to deal with the emerging trend of a growing fixed capital intensity of production and its implications." Thus skewing the composition of total capital towards techniques employing less labor and more fixed capital inputs resulted in higher (fixed) capital–output ratios, a proxy for the Marxian concept of organic composition:

> Ricardo focused attention on the process of the mechanization of production, whereby labor power was successfully replaced by machine power. This form implied a rise in labor productivity but at the same time a fall in the maximum rate of profit, that is, a rise in the capital-to-output ratio, expressing an increased fixed capital intensity of production.
>
> (Kurz, 2009, p. 34)

Our findings support the view that long-term trends of the maximum rate of profit set the underlying path for the cyclical movements of the actual rate, reflecting changes in capacity utilization. Once adjusted for capacity utilization, the medium-term cyclical fluctuations of the output–capital ratio reveal the underlying path of the (falling) maximum profit rate. This trend then causes the accumulation rate to fall and the unemployment rate to rise. A declining maximum rate of profit weighs down the actual profit rate once capital-using, labor-saving technical change is so advanced that despite further gains in labor productivity and successful efforts to lower wage shares ("unit labor costs"), the mass of profits fails to grow sufficiently to compensate for the increase in the fixed capital stock. Technical innovations typically seek to lower real unit labor costs proportionately more than the parallel increase in capital–output ratios and in fact real unit labor costs in the US sustained a marked decline from the early 1980s to the present.

Kurz contends that Ricardo's technical change raised labor productivity but also displaced labor in sufficient measure to depress wages and expand the profits share. It follows then that the path of long-run unemployment trends hinges on the strength of two interrelated tendencies studied by Ricardo and Marx. One is the rising capital–output ratio, the inverse of the maximum rate of profit, reflecting a capital-intensive bias in technical change. This is the decisive force behind falling unit labor costs and higher profit shares. The other is the strength of fixed capital accumulation, causing the expansion of productive capacity and the extent to which displaced labor will be reemployed. But this capacity growth is contingent on expected profitability. Indeed, the tempo of accumulation reflects the expectations derived from past profitability trends as well as the constraints imposed by current levels of capacity utilization. A low or falling profitability trend will likely induce an equally low or falling accumulation rate, one insufficient to prevent unemployment from rising.

Again, the larger fixed capital requirements per unit output of the successful innovators will lower total unit costs if the variable unit costs, largely tied to employment, are more than proportionately reduced. Thus, the rapid spread of capital-intensive technologies will generally need optimistic expectations of a sustained boom, as happened in the 1960s. Whether unemployment levels rise or fall depends on the strength of compensatory mechanisms set in motion by the accumulation of capital. Successful innovations are likely to drive marginal firms out of business and the full effects of technological change on real unit labor costs and employment need not appear simultaneously. For technologically dynamic economies like the US, France, Germany, and Japan, we found a relatively close relationship between capital–output and unemployment rates.

Figure 12.3 shows the (capacity utilization) adjusted long-term capital–output trend in the private sector of the US economy rising since the late 1940s to the present, although not at constant rates. Cyclical fluctuations of the actual capital–output ratio around that trend reflected strong changes in capacity utilization caused by fluctuations in effective demand. Unadjusted capital–output ratios rose substantially in the US between the mid-1960s and 1982. Growth rates of capital–output ratios and unemployment are remarkably correlated, as Figure 12.4 shows. The empirical evidence in the US confirms the growth of unemployment for more than a decade after the mid-1960s following the rise of capital–output ratios in the same period. In most G7 economies, capital–output ratios increased in the 1970s as well, while unit labor costs declined markedly in the 1980s.

Starting from a near capacity position but high unemployment, rising industry utilization levels will lower the unemployment rate as firms expand output

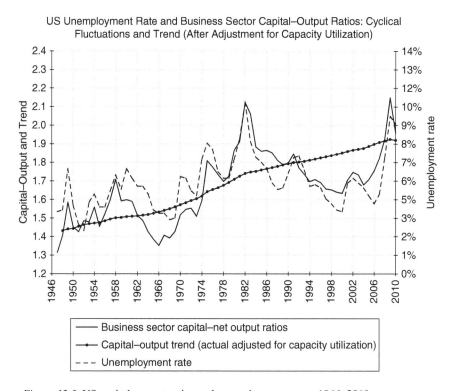

Figure 12.3 US capital–output ratios and unemployment rates, 1946–2010.

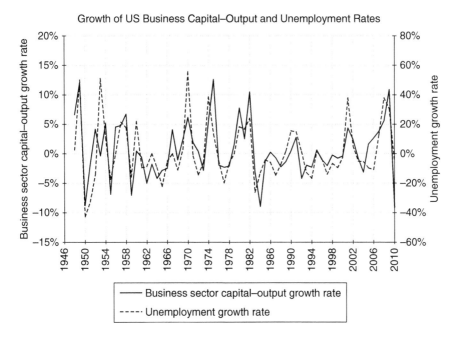

Figure 12.4 US capital–output growth ratios and unemployment growth rate.

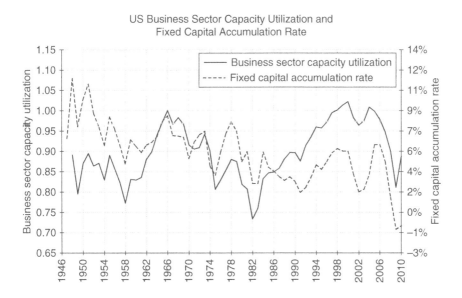

Figure 12.5 US capacity utilization and capital accumulation rates.

in order to maintain competitive cost effectiveness. As Figure 12.5 shows, from 1948 to 2010 in the US the only exception to the parallelism between the rate of accumulation and capacity utilization occurred between 1984 and 1988. Following the deep recession of the early 1980s that pushed the unemployment rate to a peak, capacity utilization increased and the unemployment rate fell from 1984 to 1989, but the accumulation rate did not recover. The anomalous behavior of falling accumulation rates for nearly half a decade, eluding the upward pull of rising capacity utilization, stemmed from the fact that profitability trends shaped the path of capital accumulation in those years. Indeed, after 1987, despite falling capital–output ratios and rising capacity utilization, shown in Figure 12.6, the profitability trend of nonfinancial corporations at best remained rather flat for the next twenty years. The relative stagnation of business profitability in that period stifled the effects of rising capacity utilization, dragging down the accumulation rate from 1985 into the next decade. From then on the movements of accumulation and capacity utilization resumed their normal synchronization.

Innovators may occasionally counter their labor-saving plans with an expansion of production and will in consequence avoid job destruction. With the intensity of competitive pressures regulating the strength of labor-displacing technological change, declining wages may expand compensatory employment in activities requiring low fixed capital investments, such as personal services and residential construction. As Kahler observed in the mid-1930s, despite falling employment in traditional industrial sectors in the years before the 1929 crash, the unemployment rate did not reflect those losses because in labor activities where the capital–output ratio was low, such as personal services and residential construction, the

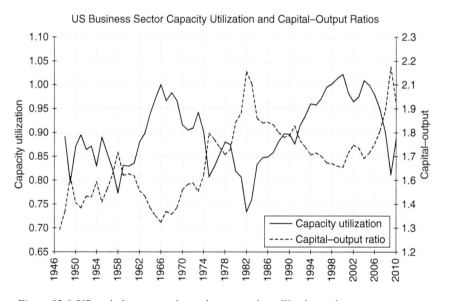

Figure 12.6 US capital–output ratios and our capacity utilization estimates.

growing share of profit-income induced wealthy employers to hire displaced workers (Kahler, 1935, p. 457).

Labor-saving technology and capital–output trends

Figure 12.7 offers the empirical evidence linking capital–output trends as a proxy for the labor-saving characteristics of technological progress and unemployment rates in three advanced capitalist economies. In technologically advanced countries such as France, Germany, Japan, and the US the impact of technological change on unemployment trends appears to be stronger than in lagging OECD economies. But since capital–output ratios adjusted for capacity utilization trended upwards and accumulation rates trended downwards in the majority of cases, unemployment trends rose everywhere. Figure 12.8 shows the nonlinear trends and high correlation linking unemployment and accumulation rates in major OECD countries between 1960 and 2010.

Summary of the main points

The technological transformations that upgraded industrial production in OECD countries for several decades before the Great Recession laid the ground for the surge in structural unemployment that followed once the housing and financial bubbles burst and credit flows collapsed. In the aftermath of the Great Recession, barring a sustained recovery of profitability and accumulation trends, the prospects

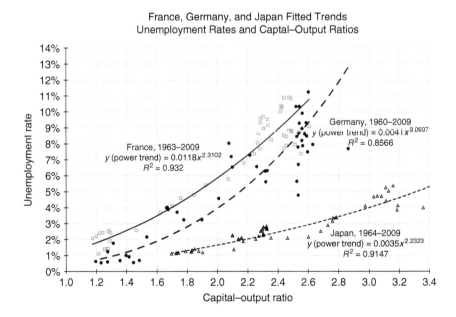

Figure 12.7 Unemployment and capital–output ratios in three OECD countries.

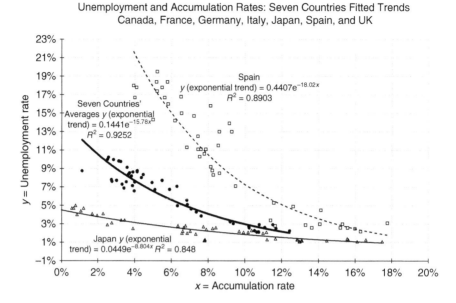

Figure 12.8 Unemployment and accumulation rates in seven OECD countries.

for the return to high employment levels remain poor. Simply focusing on the static mismatch between workers' skills and the know-how required to operate advanced technology as the chief cause of growing structural unemployment overlooks the destructive impact of technical change on skill formation. Historically, the development of machinery facilitated the transfer of skills from labor to the equipment itself.

We take the evolution of capital–output ratios as a measurable proxy for technological change, roughly tracking the movement of unemployment trends. This conclusion derives from our view of competitive behavior by firms seeking to expand market shares. We explained the rise in capital–output ratios by the exigencies of competition-as-war. In that context, aggressive firms seeking improvements in labor productivity, aiming to lower unit labor costs, deploy capital-intensive, labor-saving technology as competitive weapons to defeat rivals. In these competitive battles for higher market shares such expensive technology proves its worth by driving rivals out of business.

Despite the innovators gaining sales and securing market leadership, however, higher fixed costs per unit of output lower their profitability. Once the market losers are driven off, the rising capital–output trend associated with best-practice technology directly leads to a relatively smaller demand for labor. The potential displacement of labor will become effective once accumulation rates fail to rise in compensation, that is, once the displaced labor can no longer find employment in technologically advanced industry. Since the strength of accumulation reflects the evolution of profitability, when rising capital–output ratios are no longer matched by higher profit shares and profitability falls, unemployment rates increase because the accumulation rate falls. But leading firms enjoy the highest profit rates in the industry, and yet their relative demand for labor has declined. Consequently, the bifurcation of (rising) capital–output and (falling or trendless) profitability trends leads to (falling) accumulation and (rising) unemployment trends for the industry as a whole. We show that for six decades preceding the Great Recession, the unemployment rate in the US economy followed a path closely linked to cyclical movements in aggregate capital–output ratios. Indeed, in the advanced capitalist countries of the OECD such as France, Germany, Japan and the US, our empirical estimates for unadjusted capital–output ratios (unadjusted for capacity utilization) directly track the cyclical rise of labor unemployment rates.

Sources and methods

1 Introduction

Figure 1.1

US nonfinancial corporate profitability, a broad measure of profitability, calculated as net operating surplus of nonfinancial corporations, both private and government, quarterly estimates, NIPA Table 1.14, divided over the quarterly data comprising capital stocks of both corporate nonfinancial corporations and government enterprises. The capital stock of nonfinancial corporations is the sum of nonresidential corporate equipment and software, Flow of Funds FL105013265Q, and structures, Flow of Funds FL105013665Q, plus corporate nonfinancial, residential equipment, Flow of Funds FL105012265Q, and structures, Flow of Funds FL105012665Q, plus the capital stock of government enterprises, Fixed Assets Tables 7.1A and 7.1B (see http://www.bea.gov/iTable/index_FA.cfm).

The nonfinancial corporate capital accumulation rate is calculated as nonfinancial corporate gross fixed capital investment, Flow of Funds FA105019005Q, plus investment of government sponsored enterprises, Flow of Funds FA405013865Q, plus nonfinancial corporate business capital consumption (CC) adjustment, Flow of Funds FA106310005Q, and business inventories with inventory valuation adjustment (IVA), Flow of Funds FA105020005Q, minus CC allowances of both government sponsored enterprises, Flow of Funds FA406330005Q, and nonfinancial corporate business, Flow of Funds FA106300015Q, over the current cost capital stock of both corporate nonfinancial corporations and government enterprises as defined above.

Figure 1.2

Data for our measure of quarterly estimates of undistributed profits with inventory and CC adjustments in NIPA Table 1.14 divided over the capital stock of nonfinancial corporations as in Figure 1.1, without government enterprises. Accumulation rate as in Figure 1.1.

Figure 1.3

Three indexes (1983Q4 = 100): the nonfinancial corporate stock of financial assets, derived from Flow of Funds FL104090005Q, the nonfinancial corporate net operating surplus, derived from NIPA Table 1.14, and the nonfinancial corporate fixed capital stock, the sum of nonresidential corporate equipment and software, Flow of Funds FL105013265Q, and structures, Flow of Funds FL105013665Q, plus residential corporate equipment, Flow of Funds FL105012265Q, and structures, Flow of Funds FL105012665Q.

Figure 1.4

Indexes of debt/income calculated as total debt, including nonfinancial domestic liabilities from households, nonfinancial businesses, and state, local, and federal governments, Flow of Funds LA384104005Q, plus financial business liabilities, Flow of Funds LA794104005Q, over national income, Flow of Funds FA086010005Q (1980Q1 = 100). Indexes of financial profits/income calculated as financial domestic corporate profits with IVA and CC adjustments, NIPA Tables 6.16B, C and D over national income, Flow of Funds FA086010005Q (1980Q1 = 100).

2 Kaldor's "stylized facts": real or merely convenient?

Figure 2.1

Capital–output ratios in France (1951–1991), Germany (1951–1991), Japan (1890–1991), and United Kingdom (1890–1991) derived from capital stock data in Maddison (1995). GDP data in Maddison (2010).

4 Mechanization and price/quality competition

Figure 4.1

Relative real unit labor costs in manufacturing, national currency basis, UK/Germany and UK/Japan, 1961–2009. Real unit labor costs in manufacturing for each country calculated as unit labor cost, Bureau of Labor Statistics (BLS), 19 countries, 1950–2009, Table 9, divided by the producer price index in IMF International Financial Statistics, 2002 = 100.

5 Capital intensity and profitability: dissenting views

Figure 5.6

UK average profit rates for private nonfinancial corporate and manufacturing industries. Private nonfinancial corporate average profit rate, 1949–2009, calculated as private nonfinancial corporate gross trading profit, 2009 Statistical Release, UK Office for National Statistics, code CAGKAU, minus private nonfinancial corporate CC, 2009 Statistical Release, UK Office for National Statistics, code BGXZAU, over private nonfinancial corporate net capital stock, 2009 Statistical Release, UK Office for National Statistics, code CIXHAU. The UK's manufacturing average profit rate, 1960–2009, calculated as manufacturing private nonfinancial corporate operating surplus, 1960–1969, UK's National Accounts, Volume 2 and 1970–2009, 2009 Statistical Release, UK Office for National Statistics, code LRXSAU, over manufacturing nominal net capital stock, 2009 Statistical Release, UK Office for National Statistics, code GSRFAU.

Figure 5.7

UK hourly labor productivity, BLS International Comparisons of Manufacturing Productivity and Unit Labor Cost Trends, Table 1, and UK real hourly compensation, Table 13, 1980 = 100.

Figure 5.8

Manufacturing profitability trends in Germany, Japan, and the United States. The German profit rate replicated from Brenner (2005, Figure 9.4, p. 208). The Japanese profit rate calculated as operating profits over year-end fixed assets minus land data from the Ministry of Finance Policy Research Institute, Japan. The US manufacturing profit rate before interest payments measures domestic corporate profits with IVA and CC adjustments, NIPA Tables 6.16ABC, plus net interest, NIPA Tables 6.15BCD, over current-cost manufacturing net capital stock, Fixed Assets Table 4.1.

7 Capital–output ratios in retrospect

Figure 7.1

Two output–capital ratio estimates: from 1870 to 1934, taken from Mayor (1968, Figure 1, p. 496). The output–capital ratio from 1900 to 1934 calculated using Klein's US net national product data in Klein and Kosobud (1961, Table III, p. 183), and Goldsmith's (1952) capital stock data.

Figure 7.2

Two alternative measures of real output–capital ratios: Gordon's nonfarm real output/Gordon's adjusted real capital stock data translated from Gordon (2004b, Figure 2.9, p. 78). The second real output–capital ratio calculated on the basis of data provided by Duménil and Lévy's (1994) real GNP, over Gordon's adjusted real capital stock as described above.

Figure 7.3

Two measures of US capacity utilization for the business sector: Duménil and Lévy's capacity utilization comes from their database, August 1994. Our capacity utilization is calculated following the method suggested by Shaikh and Moudud (2004). The cointegrating coefficients were derived in EViews using the Johansen cointegration test, assuming no deterministic trend and no lags in first differences of logarithmic series for the net national product and net capital stock. The source for the net national product from 1900 to 1928 is Klein and Kosobud (1961, p. 183) and from 1929 to 2010 is data from the Bureau of Economic Analysis, Table 1.9.5. Capital stock data from 1900 to 1924 from Duménil and Lévy (1994). From 1925 to 2010 data from the Bureau of Economic Analysis, Table 4.1.

Figure 7.4

US actual output–capital ratios for the business sector before and after adjustments for capacity utilization, from 1880 to 2010 derived as follows: Private net domestic product, 1880–1928 from Duménil and Lévy (1994); business sector net domestic product, 1929–2010 data from NIPA, Table 1.9.5. The business sector capital stock, 1880–1924, from Dumeni and Lévy (1994); for the period 1925–2010, NIPA Table 4.1. The adjusted capital–output ratio calculated as the actual values divided by capacity utilization, estimated as in Figure 7.3.

8 Profitability trends after the "golden age"

Figure 8.1

Share of corporate profits plus net interest in GDP data from Okun and Perry (1970, Table 1, p. 468).

Figure 8.2

Feldstein and Summers' US nonfinancial corporations' profit rate on capital and its corresponding linear trend, $\Pi = 0.1278 - 0.0014t$. US nonfinancial corporations' profit rate on capital, including land, calculated by Feldstein and Summers (1977, Table 1, p. 216).

Figure 8.3

Manufacturing profit rates in six OECD countries, Canada, France, Germany, Italy, United Kingdom, and the United States, 1951–1986 data in Weisskopf (1992).

Figure 8.4

Four estimates of US profitability: 1948–1976, Feldstein and Summers (1977, Table 1, p. 216); 1948–1979, Feldstein and Poterba (1981, Table 2, p. 10); 1953–1985, Aschauer (1988, Figure 1, p. 12); 1959–1996, Poterba (1998, Table 1, p. 219).

Figure 8.5

Chan-Lee's OECD data on nonfinancial corporate business before-tax average profit rates for Canada, France, Germany, and UK, 1967–1983, in Chan-Lee (1986, Table 2, p. 11).

Figure 8.6

Armstrong, Glyn, and Harrison's data of business sector before-tax average profit rates for Canada, France, Germany, Italy, and UK, 1951–1981, in Armstrong *et al.* (1984, Table A.2, p. 465), Fontana.

Figure 8.7

Glyn's data on manufacturing profit rates in Germany, Japan, UK, and US, 1960–1994, in Glyn (1997, Table A.7, p. 618).

Figure 8.8

Comparing US manufacturing and nonmanufacturing profit rates: manufacturing profit rates estimated as manufacturing profits with IVA and CC adjustment, NIPA Tables 6.16ABC, plus manufacturing net interest, NIPA Tables 6.15BCDP, over manufacturing net capital stock, Fixed Assets Table 4.1. Nonmanufacturing profit rates derived from private industry surplus minus manufacturing surplus data over the nonresidential, nonmanufacturing, private capital stock. The private industry surplus estimated as business net value added, NIPA Table 1.9.5, *minus* compensation of employees of private industries, NIPA Tables 6.2ABCD, *minus* proprietors' wages [total proprietors NIPA, Table 6.l7, × (compensation of employees of private industries over total employees of private industries)], NIPA Tables 6.5BCD, *minus* taxes on production and imports, NIPA, Table 3.5. The manufacturing surplus calculated as manufacturing national income without CC adjustment, NIPA Tables 6.1BCD, *minus* compensation of manufacturing employees, 1948–1987 (SIC); 1988–2010 (NAICS), *minus* manufacturing proprietors' wages [total self-employees in manufacturing, NIPA Tables 6.7BCD, × (compensation of manufacturing employees over total manufacturing employees)], 1948–1997 (NAICS); and 1998–2010, NIPA, Table 6.5D, *minus* taxes on production and imports, 1948–1987 (SIC); 1988–2010 (NAICS). The nonresidential, nonmanufacturing private capital stock is the private nonresidential corporate and non-corporate net capital stock minus the manufacturing private net capital stock, both data sets from Fixed Assets Table 4.1.

Figure 8.9

Manufacturing profit rate sources and methods as described in Figure 8.8; non-manufacturing profit rates excluding mining, transportation, and utilities calculated as nonmanufacturing profits excluding profits in mining, transportation, and utilities over the nonresidential, nonmanufacturing, private capital stock minus the capital stock in mining and transportation and public utilities, Fixed Assets Tables 4.1 and 3.1ES. Nonmanufacturing profits excluding profits in mining, transportation, and utilities calculated as private industry surplus minus manufacturing surplus, as in Figure 10.9, excluding mining, transportation, and public utilities surplus. The mining surplus is equal to mining value added in BEA GDP by industry, minus mining employees compensation, NIPA Tables 6.2BCD, minus mining proprietors' wages [mining total proprietors, NIPA Table 6.7, × (mining employees compensation, NIPA Tables 6.2BCD, over total employees in mining, NIPA Tables 6.5BD)] minus taxes,1948–1987 (SIC) and 1988–2010 (NAICS).

The transportation plus public utilities surplus is equal to the total value added in transportation, excluding warehousing, and public utilities, BEA GDP by industry, minus transportation and public utilities employees compensation, 1948–1987, NIPA Tables 6.2BC; 1988–2010 (NAICS), minus transportation and public utilities proprietors' wages [transportation and utilities total proprietors, NIPA Tables 6.7BCD, × (transportation and public utilities employees compensation, 1948–1987, NIPA, Tables 6.2BC; 1988–2010 (NAICS), over total employees in transportation, excluding warehousing, and public utilities, NIPA Tables 6.5BCD)] minus taxes on transportation and public utilities,1948–1987 (SIC) and 1988–2010 (NAICS).

Figure 8.10

Five different estimates of US average profit rates for the business and nonfinancial corporate sectors: Cordonnier's estimates of the US average profit rate in Cordonnier (2006, p. 102); Duménil and Lévy's estimates in Duménil, G. and Lévy, D. (2011a, Figure 4, p. 8); Mohun's two estimates, 1949–2009 in Mohun (2010) and 1964–2001 in Mohun (2006, Figure 1, p. 348); and Moseley's US average profit rate in Moseley (2004, p. 81).

Figure 8.11

Three similar estimates of the U.S. accumulation rate, including Beitel (2009, Figure 7, p. 82), Cordonnier (2006, p. 101) and Duménil and Lévy (2011a, Figure 4, p. 8).

Figure 8.12

The US profit rate calculated as net operating surplus of nonfinancial corporate business, NIPA Table 1.14, over the current cost net stock of private fixed assets of nonfinancial corporations, Fixed Assets Table 6.1; plus government enterprise fixed assets, Fixed Assets Tables 7.1AB. Business capital accumulation rates estimated as net fixed investment over nonfinancial capital stock. Net fixed investment equals fixed investment of nonfinancial corporations, Fixed Assets Table 4.7, minus capital expenditures of nonproduced nonfinancial assets, Flow of Funds Table F.102, minus depreciation of private fixed assets of nonfinancial corporations, Fixed Assets Table 4.4, plus inventory change with IVA Flow of Funds Table F.102. Current cost nonfinancial capital stock includes the net stock of private fixed assets of nonfinancial corporations, Fixed Assets Table 6.1, plus that of government enterprise fixed assets, Fixed Assets Tables 7.1AB.

9 Profit-driven capital accumulation in OECD countries

Figure 9.1

Nonfinancial corporate shares in total nonresidential fixed investment calculated as financial corporate nonresidential fixed investment plus nonfinancial private corporate nonresidential fixed investment, Fixed Assets Table 4.7, over total nonresidential fixed investment, NIPA Table 1.1.5. Nonfinancial corporate share in total nonresidential fixed investment calculated as nonfinancial private corporate nonresidential fixed investment, Fixed Assets Table 4.7, over total nonresidential fixed investment, NIPA Table 1.1.5.

Figure 9.2

Manufacturing shares of profits, net value-added, and nonresidential investment in the nonfinancial corporate sector calculated as manufacturing domestic corporate profits with inventory valuation adjustment, NIPA Tables 6.16ABCD, and manufacturing corporate CC allowance, NIPA Tables 6.22ABCD. The manufacturing share of net value-added estimated as manufacturing income without CC adjustment, NIPA Tables 6.1BCD, and manufacturing net interest, NIPA Tables 6.15BCD. Finally, the share of nonresidential investment is calculated as manufacturing investment, NIPA Table 4.7, relative to nonfarm, nonfinancial corporate fixed investment, Flow of Funds F.102.

Figure 9.3

The share of retained earnings in net surplus for the financial sector equals the financial sector retained profits over the domestic financial net operating surplus. Retained earnings in the financial sector calculated as corporate retained profits with IVA and CC adjustments, NIPA Table 1.16, minus the nonfinancial domestic and foreign corporate retained profits with IVA and CC adjustments, NIPA Table 1.14, and Federal Reserve System, Flow of Funds Accounts, F.102, for nonfinancial corporate business.

Figure 9.4

US financial sector profit shares in corporate profits calculated as financial domestic corporate profits before tax, excluding the profits of the federal reserve banks and real estate (including rental and leasing from 1998 to 2009) with IVA and CC adjustments, NIPA Tables 6.16ABCD and Tables 6.17ABCD, over corporate profits before tax with IVA and CC adjustments, NIPA Table 1.14.

Figure 9.5

The nonfinancial corporate profit rate calculated as net operating surplus of nonfinancial corporate business, NIPA Table 1.14, over net stock of the private fixed assets of nonfinancial corporations, Fixed Assets Table 6.1, plus government enterprises' fixed assets, Fixed Assets Accounts Tables 7.1AB. Nonfinancial corporate retained earnings including undistributed domestic profits with IVA and CC adjustments, NIPA Table 1.14 plus foreign earnings retained abroad, Flow of Funds Table F.102, divided over the nonfinancial corporate capital stock from Fixed Assets Table 6.1, plus government enterprises fixed assets from Fixed Assets Tables 7.1AB. The business capital accumulation rate refers to net fixed investment over nonfinancial capital stocks. Net fixed investment equals nonresidential fixed investment of nonfinancial corporations, Fixed Assets Table 4.7, minus capital expenditures of nonproduced nonfinancial assets of nonfinancial corporate business, Flow of Funds Table F.102, minus depreciation of private nonresidential fixed assets of nonfinancial corporations, Fixed Assets Table 4.4, plus inventory change with IVA of nonfinancial corporate business, Flow of Funds Table F.102.

Figure 9.6

Calculation of percentages pertaining to nonfinancial corporations' excess internal funds, relative to both gross fixed investment and gross fixed investment plus net acquisition of financial assets, uses data from the Flow of Funds Table F.102.

Figure 9.7

Nominal profit rates for five countries. The problem here consists of finding reliable extensions for the business sector capital stock of OECD countries outside Canada, the UK and US beyond 2006, since the major source for this information largely disappeared after that year, when the OECD *Economic Outlook* both moved to publish data series in chained mode and simultaneously ended all reference to the business sector estimates. In order to extend our estimates beyond that year we followed a similar procedure in most cases. We made extended use of AMECO capital stock data (http://ec.europa.eu/economy_finance/db_indicators/ameco/index_en.htm) to fill the gap, for while the AMECO series for capital stock do not fit directly our requirements for estimation of business sector capital accumulation, updates are published every 6 months and provide some data on growth rates.

France profit rate, 1963–2009, calculated as domestic income at factor costs, AMECO Table 6, minus the administration value-added, Institut National de la Statistique et des Etudes Economiques (INSEE), series code 884394, minus the sum of employee compensation, AMECO Table 7, and imputed self-employed compensation, AMECO Table 7, to derive gross operating surplus. Profitability estimated as the resulting surplus over nominal capital stock, estimated as real capital stock in Outlook 78 for the period 1963–2006, times the deflator for nonresidential business investment, 1963–2006. After Outlook 81 in 2006, the *Economic Outlook* published capital stock data only in chained series precluding any calculation of the nominal capital stock beyond this year. Between 2007 and 2009, our business capital stock estimates apply the growth rate of nominal business capital stocks calculated as year-end fixed net capital stock, in INSEE series code 2603, subtracting residential housing, INSEE 2603, but retaining the nonfinancial business residential capital stock, INSEE 2656, to extend our capital stock series.

Nominal profit rate for Germany's business sector, 1961–2009, calculated by subtracting from domestic income at factor costs, AMECO Table 6, government wages in *Economic Outlook* 78, 1961–1990, and from *Economic Outlook* 90, 1991–2009 (as a proxy for general administration expenses); then subtracting total employee compensation, AMECO Table 7, after adjusting again for government wages with one-year lag minus imputed self-employed compensation, AMECO Table 7, over nominal capital stock. The nominal capital stock, 1961–2000, equals the real capital stock in Outlook 76 times the deflator for nonresidential business investment in Outlook 76, for the period 1961–1990; then from Outlook 77 for the period 1991–2000. Finally, from 2001 to 2009 data for our capital stock estimates taken from the Federal Statistics Office, National Accounts, Fixed Assets Table by Sector: capital stock at current prices equals gross total fixed assets, including government machinery and equipment, minus the total fixed assets of the government minus households and non-profit institutions serving households minus intangible fixed assets for the total economy.

Italy's nominal profit for the period 1961–2009 calculated in steps from domestic income at factor costs, AMECO Table 6, deducting government wages in Outlook 78 with one-year lag, for the years 1961–1969; For 1970–2009, government wages data in Outlook 90, minus total employee compensation, AMECO Table 7, adjusted for government wages with one-year lag minus imputed self-employed compensation, AMECO Table 7. Thus profit rates measure gross operating surplus adjusted for imputed compensation of self-employed with one-year lag, over the nominal capital stock calculated as the real capital stock in Outlook 78, 1961–2006 times the total fixed investment deflator, 1961–2006, in Outlook 78. For the period 2007–2009, the expanded nominal capital stock reflects the growth rate of the nominal total capital stock in AMECO data, obtained after multiplying the total real capital stock, AMECO Table 8, times the gross fixed capital formation deflator, AMECO Table 3.

Japan's business sector profit rate, 1965–2009, estimated after subtracting from domestic income at factor costs, AMECO Table 6, government wages data with one-year lag in Outlook 89, then total employee compensation, AMECO Table 7, adjusted for government wages with one-year lag and dividing over the nominal capital stock, calculated as the real capital stock, 1965–2006 in Outlook 76, times the deflator for private nonresidential investment, for the same period, in Outlook 89. For the years 2007–2009 the nominal capital stock reflected the growth rate of the nominal capital stock in AMECO Table 8, that is, total real capital stock, times the gross fixed investment deflator, AMECO Table 3.

Spain's business sector profit rate, 1964–2009, derived from domestic income at factor costs, AMECO Table 6, minus government wages in Outlook 79 for 1964–1969 and Outlook 90 for 1970–2009, after subtracting the sum of employee compensation, AMECO Table 7, and the imputed compensation of self-employed, AMECO Table 7. Thus gross operating surplus adjusted for imputed compensation of self-employed with one-year lag minus government wages divided over the nominal capital stock provided by Fundación BBVA.

Figure 9.8

Capital accumulation rates in five OECD countries. In all five OECD countries capital accumulation defined as nominal net nonresidential fixed capital investment plus inventory change over the corresponding stock of capital.

France, 1964–2009, private net nonresidential investment, gross total fixed investment, AMECO Table 3, minus gross fixed residential investment in Outlook 78 for the period 1964–1969, and AMECO Table 3, for the years 1970–2009, plus changes in inventories, AMECO Table 3, minus private and government fixed CC in AMECO Table 3, 1964–1977, plus Outlook 81 for the years 1978–2009 over the nominal capital stock calculated as in Figure 9.7.

For Germany, 1961–2009, gross private nonresidential investment in Outlook 89, adjusted for changes in inventories and CC, AMECO Table 3, over the nominal capital stock calculated as in Figure 9.7.

Italy, 1961–2009, private nonresidential investment, gross total fixed investment, AMECO Table 3, minus gross fixed residential investment in Outlook 78, for the period 1961–1969 and AMECO Table 3, for the years 1970–2009 adjusted for changes in inventories, AMECO Table 3, over the nominal capital stock calculated as in Figure 9.7.

Japan, 1965–2009 gross total fixed investment minus gross fixed residential investment, both in AMECO Table 3, plus changes in inventories, AMECO Table 3, over the nominal capital stock calculated as in Figure 9.7.

Spain, 1964–2009, nonresidential gross fixed investment, gross total fixed investment, AMECO Table 3, minus gross fixed residential investment, 1964–1969, in Outlook 77 and AMECO Table 3, for 1970–2009 adjusted for changes in inventories, AMECO Table 3, minus consumption of fixed capital, AMECO Table 3, minus government consumption of fixed capital, AMECO Table 3, over the nominal capital stock calculated as in Figure 9.7.

Figure 9.9

The nominal profit is the net national income at factor cost minus employee compensation with one-year lag, 1950–1959, in Robert B. Crozier, "Section F: Gross National Product, the Capital Stock, and Productivity," Conference Board of Canada, Series F1–13, http://www.statcan.gc.ca/pub/11–516-x/pdf/5500096-eng.pdf and AMECO Tables 6 and 7, extending to 1960–2009. The nominal capital stock between 1950 and 1960 derived from the private sector real net capital stock, Series F183–192, multiplied by the gross fixed capital formation deflator (gross fixed capital formation, Series F14–32, over gross fixed capital formation in 1971 Canadian dollars, Series F33–55). Between 1961 and 2009 the nominal capital stock downloaded from Statistics Canada, "Table 031–0003: Flows and stocks of fixed non-residential capital, NAICS and assets, Canada;

Canada; Current prices; Business sector," http://www5.statcan.gc.ca/cansim/pick-choisir?lang=eng&searchTypeByValue=1&id=0310003.

The accumulation rate is the business gross fixed capital formation, 1950–1960 in Crozier, Series F14–32; and 1961–2009 in AMECO Table 3; minus consumption allowances, 1950–1960 in Crozier, Series F1–13; and 1961–2009 in AMECO Table 3; plus change in inventories, 1950–1960 in Crozier, Series F14–32 and 1961–2009 in AMECO Table 3; then divided over the nominal capital stock.

Figures 9.10–9.16

Our estimates of incremental profitability for France, Germany, Italy, Japan, Spain, Sweden, Canada, UK and US share a common methodology. All except the UK and US draw on AMECO data for the relevant calculations as described in previous entries. Incremental profit rates reflect our estimates of nominal net operating surplus and data on nominal gross investment plus inventory changes. They are defined as the change in net operating surplus divided by gross fixed investment plus inventory change in the previous year.

Figure 9.17

Our UK incremental profitability and investment growth rate estimates derive from data downloaded from the Office of National Statistics. The incremental profit rate is the change in the private NFC gross trading corporate profits, UK Office of National Statistics, code CAGKAU, over total gross fixed investment of the previous year, code NPQXAU. The investment growth rate is the rate of growth of total gross fixed investment, code NPQXAU, plus private NFC inventories, code DLQXAU. See http://www.ons.gov.uk/ons/search/index.html?content-type=Dataset&nscl=Economy&pubdateRangeType=allDates&newquery=data&pageSize=50&applyFilters=true

Figure 9.18

US incremental profit and investment growth rates at current prices calculated as the change in domestic nonfinacial corporations' net operating surplus, NIPA Table 1.14, over the total gross fixed investment of the previous year, after deducting from capital expenditures nonproduced nonfinancial assets, Flow of Funds Table F.102. The investement growth rate is the rate of growth of total gross fixed investment as defined above.

Figure 9.19

Comparing our US nonfinancial corporate incremental profit rate and the non-financial corporate average profit rate reveals the sharper fluctuations of the incremental measure around the average.

10 Nonfinancial versus financial profitability trends and capacity utilization

Figure 10.1

Indexes of before-tax financial domestic corporate profits with IVA and CC adjustment, excluding Federal Reserve and Real Estate, 1980 = 100, derived from NIPA financial domestic corporate profits with IVA and CC Adjustment Tables 6.16BCD after subtracting Federal Reserve profits plus real estate profits, including rental and leasing from Tables 6.17BCD. Indexes of before-tax nonfinancial corporate profits derived from NIPA Table 1.14, 1980 = 100. Nominal GDP indexes, 1980 = 100, derived from NIPA Table 1.5.5.

Figure 10.2

Estimates of net interest and dividend shares in net operating surplus of nonfinancial corporations derived from nonfinancial corporate net dividends and net interest payments, NIPA Table 1.14, divided over nonfinancial net operating surplus also in NIPA Table 1.14.

Figure 10.3

The nonfinancial corporate profit rate in NIPA Table 1.14 measures the domestic nonfinancial corporate net operating surplus business income derived after subtracting the costs of employee compensation, taxes on production and imports, less subsidies, and consumption of fixed capital, but before subtracting financing costs such as net interest and business transfer payments. The Bureau of Economic Analysis (2006 p. 9) defines NIPA's "net operating surplus" as the net operating surplus of nonfinancial corporations plus the "current surplus" of government enterprises. Thus we have in net operating surplus a broad measure of corporate gross profits which divided over the capital stock of nonfinancial corporations (Fixed Assets Table 6.1) jointly with the capital stock of government enterprises in Fixed Assets Tables 7.1A and 7.1B, provides our results.

NIPA estimates domestic nonfinancial corporate profits after subtracting net interest payments from net operating surplus in Table 1.14. Thus this ratio over the nonfinancial capital stock of private nonfinancial corporations and government enterprises, with one-year lag since capital stock estimates are taken at year's end, shows a lower level measure of profitability and a less pronounced downward trend after 1988 than the previous one, mainly because the bounceback from the 1982 trough was weaker.

Figure 10.4

Our financial corporate sector profit rate refers to financial activities initially identified in Duménil and Lévy (2004, Table A1, p. 106). Our estimates relate NIPA's domestic financial profits with IVA and CC adjustment from Tables 6.16ABCD, after subtracting the profits from the Federal Reserve found in the same tables as well as profits of real estate companies in NIPA Tables 6.17ABCD, divided over total financial capital stock, including fixed capital equipment and structures, plus financial capital, that is, reserves and available liquid assets.

Fixed Asset Table 3.1ES provided the current cost of our fixed assets in finance and insurance after subtracting from the total the fixed assets of Federal Reserve and real estate companies listed in the table. Since the calculation involves financial capital, however, we added to the total fixed capital stock our estimates of the liquid assets held as reserve capital in financial institutions. The assets counted as available business capital in this group include (a) from Flow of Funds L-110, commercial banks' vault cash and reserves at the Federal Reserve plus (b) commercial banks' agency and government sponsored entity (gse) backed securities; (c) Flow of Funds L-114, saving institutions' time and saving deposits, (d) saving institutions' reserves with the Federal Reserve, (e) saving institutions' agency and gse-backed securities; (f) Flow of Funds L-115, credit unions' checkable deposits and currency, (g) credit unions' time and saving deposits, (h) credit unions' agency and gse-backed securities; (i) Flow of Funds L-116, property-casualty insurance companies' checkable deposits and currency, (j) property-casualty insurance companies' agency and gse-backed securities; (k) Flow of Funds L-117, life insurance companies' checkable deposits and currency; (l) Flow of Funds L-127, finance companies' checkable deposits and currency, (m) Flow of Funds L-127, finance companies' time and saving deposits; (n) Flow of Funds L-129, security brokers and dealers' checkable deposits and currency, (o) Flow of Funds L-129, security brokers and dealers' agency and gse-backed securities.

Figure 10.5

Nonfinancial corporate profit rate from NIPA Table 1.14, nonfinancial corporate profits with CC and IVA adjustments, divided over nonfinancial corporate net private capital stock from Fixed Assets Table 6.1 plus the capital stock of government enterprises in Fixed Asset Tables 7.1AB; prime interest rate charged by banks from Table B-73, Economic Report of the President.

Figure 10.6

Nonfinancial corporate profit rate calculated as the ratio of nonfinancial corporate net operating surplus from NIPA Table 1.14 divided over the sum of nonfinancial corporate net private capital stock from Fixed Assets Table 6.1 plus the capital stock of government enterprises in Fixed Asset Tables 7.1AB. Business sector average profit rate estimated as the ratio of business net operating surplus, calculated as business net domestic product from NIPA Table 1.9.5 minus the sum of private industries employee compensation and self-employed imputed compensation, equivalent compensation of full-time employees, minus domestic corporate taxes on production and imports less subsidies plus business transfers, divided over private nonresidential net capital stock from Fixed Assets Table 4.1 plus net capital stock of government enterprises in Fixed Asset Tables 7.1AB.

Figure 10.7

Compares Shaikh's 1947–1985 direct estimates of US manufacturing capacity utilization with our results from cointegration, using series of the natural logarithms of manufacturing national income, NIPA Tables 6.1BCD, and manufacturing private net capital stock from Fixed Assets Table 4.1 plus the net stocks of government industrial structures in Fixed Assets Tables 7.1AB, 1949–2009. Shaikh's extended cointegration estimates for the years 1986–1997 are also shown to be about 10 percent lower than ours. The correlation coefficient between Shaikh's direct measures, labeled UMHF, for 1948–1985, and our cointegration results is 0.896; the coefficient between Shaikh's direct measures and his cointegration results for the same period is 0.899.

Figure 10.8

Contrasts our cointegration estimates of US manufacturing capacity utilization with those made by the Federal Reserve Board (FRB), taken from *The Economic Report of the President*, Table B-54, showing greater amplitude than the FRB's estimates, particularly before 1960 and since the late 1980s.

Figure 10.9

These are our capacity utilization estimates emerging from our cointegration procedure for three sectors, manufacturing, nonfinancial corporate business and the business sector in general (comprising the previous two plus the noncorporate business activities). In each case we ran a cointegraton regression of net value, business net product, that is, from Table 1.9.5; nonfinancial net value-added from Table 1.14 and manufacturing income from Table 6.1BCD, series in natural logarithms on the relevant measures of net capital stock expressed in natural logarithms. After obtaining the equation for potential income from our cointegrating procedure, capacity utilization reflected the ratio of actual to potential income.

Figure 10.10

Shows actual net product or value-added relative to net capital stocks in the US business and nonfinancial corporate sectors. While the overall trends of the actual ratios show a cyclically downward bend, adjusting for capacity utilization as in Figure 12.8 clearly brings out the overall downward linear trend around which the cycles occurred.

Figure 10.11

Highlights the impact of capacity utilization adjustment on the gross profit rate of the nonfinancial corporate sector, that is, the ratio of net operating surplus, before subtracting net interest payments and the total net capital stock of nonfinancial corporations including government enterprises as in Figure 10.3. The trough reached by the profit rate in 1982 is not as deep as it appears after adjusting for capacity utilization. But contrary to Kaldor's vaunted historical "constancies", which included the profit rate at their core, the capacity utilization adjustment sharpens the image of a downward trend in profitability taking hold in nonfinancial corporate sectors across the years preceding the Great Recession. Clearly after the late 1980s such downward trend culminated in the 2001 crash, all intervening cycles between those dates ended at lower levels than they started.

11 Mill and Minsky on roads to speculation and crisis

Figure 11.1

Gross operating surplus adjusted for imputed compensation of self-employed, AMECO Table 7, over domestic income at factor cost, AMECO Table 6.

Figure 11.2

Real hourly compensation and real business output per hour, BLS, code PRS84006153, 1982 = 100.

Figure 11.3

Business sector profitability and accumulation rates, 1900–2009. The business sector profit rate is equal to nominal profits before tax over nominal nonresidential net capital stock. Nominal profits equal the net national product minus total wages. The source for the net national product from 1900 to 1928 is Klein and Kosobud (1961, p. 183); from 1929 to 2010 data from the Bureau of Economic Analysis, Table 1.9.5. Total wages from 1900 to 1928 equal hours worked times hourly wages: data from database built by Gerard Duménil and Dominique Lévy, August 1994; from 1929 to 2010 total wages equal total employee compensation, NIPA Table 1.12 plus self-employed imputed wages (private industry employee compensation, NIPA Tables 6.2ABCD, over full time private industry employees, NIPA Tables 6.5ABCD, times self-employed, NIPA Table 6.7ABCD, minus government employee compensation, NIPA Table 3.10.5). Net capital stock from 1900 to 1924 downloaded from Duménil and Lévy's website; from 1925 to 2010, NIPA Table 4.1. Capital stock equals the private non-residential capital stock minus nonprofit institutions' and households' fixed assets.

The accumulation rate is private net nonresidential fixed investment over nominal capital stock. From 1900 to 1928 private nonresidential fixed investment equals total private fixed investment minus nonprofit institutions and households, NIPA Table 6.7, minus private fixed CC, NIPA Table 7.5, plus change in private inventory plus nonfarm inventory valuation adjustment, NIPA Tables 5.6.5AB. The net capital stock is calculated as above.

Figure 11.4

US accumulation rate as in Figure 11.3, divided over the profit rate.

Figure 11.5

US net credit flow is the change in claims on central government by monetary authorities, IMF, IFS 11112A.ZF, plus claims on central government by banking institutions, IFS 11122A.ZF, minus central government deposits made by commercial banks, IFS 11126D.ZF, plus claims on state and local government by commercial banks, IFS 11122B.ZF, plus claims on private sector by commercial banks, IFS 11122D.ZF plus total trade payable, Flow of Funds L.223. The source for GDP is NIPA Table 1.5.5.

Figure 11.6

Data for the US nonfinancial and financial corporate business net borrowing from Flow of Funds F.1. Data for the net value-added of financial corporate business equals net value-added of corporate business minus net value-added of nonfinancial corporate business, in NIPA Table 1.14.

Figure 11.7

The real US incremental profitability in nonfinancial corporate sectors is the change in real nonfinancial corporate operating surplus over the real nonfinancial corporate business gross investment of the previous year. The real nonfinancial corporate operating surplus is the nominal domestic operating surplus, NIPA Table 1.14, divided by the nonresidential gross private domestic investment implicit deflator, NIPA Table 1.1.9. The real nonfinancial corporate business gross investment is equal to the nonfinancial corporations' capital expenditures, fixed investment plus inventory change with IVA, minus nonfinancial corporate nonproduced nonfinancial assets, Flow of Funds F.102. The real marginal returns in the S&P composite are the change in capital gain plus dividends in real terms over the stock price of the previous year. Robert Shiller, online data, http://www.econ.yale.edu/~shiller/data.htm.

12 Unemployment trends beyond the great recession

Figure 12.1

Data downloaded from ALFS Summary tables, OECD. Stat: *Rate of Unemployment as a percentage of the Civilian Labor Force*.

Figure 12.2

Data downloaded from AMECO Tables: *labor share* equals 1 minus "gross operating surplus adjusted for the labor income imputed to self-employed labor," Table 7, and national income at factor cost, Table 6.

Figure 12.3

US data derived from NIPA and Fixed Asset Tables: Business sector capital–output ratio $= K_B/Y_B$, where $K_B =$ private current cost net stock of fixed assets, Fixed Assets Table 6.1, minus private residential net stock of households, Fixed Asset Table 5.1, minus private net stock of nonprofit institutions, Fixed Assets Table 6.1, plus current cost net stock of government enterprises, Fixed Assets Tables 7.1A and 7.1B; $Y_B =$ business net product, NIPA Table 1.9.5. US unemployment rate downloaded from the BLS seasonally adjusted estimates, Table LNS14000000.

The capital–output trend $= K_B/Y_B u$, the actual capital–output ratio in the business sector adjusted for capacity utilization, u, defined as actual income over potential income $= Y_B/Y_B^*$; actual income in business net domestic product, NIPA Table 1.9.5; potential income derived from cointegrating, using EViews 7, the logarithmic series for business income and the business capital stock. The resulting cointegrating equation, $0.3719 + 0.921 \ln K$, provided the basis to calculate potential net product, Y_B^*.

Figure 12.4

Combines data used to estimate US business sector capital–output ratios and unemployment growth rates.

Figure 12.5

Showing the impact of US capacity utilization in the business sector on US capital accumulation rates as previously defined.

Figure 12.6

Plotting data on the relationship between actual US capital–output and capacity utilization ratios.

Figure 12.7

Capital output ratios and unemployment rates in three major OECD economies.

France's nominal business capital stock derived from OECD *Economic Outlook* 78 unchained business capital stock volume series, multiplied by the *Economic Outlook* nonresidential investment, 1963–2006 expanded to 2009, applying the growth rate of INSEE 8.201 capital stock data from *Comptes de patrimoine de l'économie nationale*, S1, comprising private nonresidential capital stocks, downloaded from: http://www.insee.fr/fr/themes/theme.asp?theme=16&sous_theme=5.4.2.

France's business nominal business income derived from France's national income at factor cost from AMECO Table 6, minus France's government administration value added, code 000884397, 1949–2009, downloaded from INSEE: http://www.bdm.insee.fr/bdm2/choixCriteres.action?codeGroupe=1198.

Germany's domestic income at factor cost, data extracted from AMECO Table 6. Germany's nominal business capital stock in OECD *Economic Outlook* 77 volume series, multiplied by the nonresidential fixed investment deflator from Outlook 77 until 2000, and extended from 2001 through 2009 with data downloaded from German National Accounts current cost Fixed Assets data: http://www.destatis.de/jetspeed/portal/cms/Sites/destatis/Internet/DE/Content/Publikationen/Fachveroeffentlichungen/VolkswirtschaftlicheGesamt rechnungen/Vermoegensrechnung/AnlagevermoegenSektoren,templateId=render Print.psml.

Japan's business domestic income at factor cost extracted from AMECO Table 6. Japan's business gross capital stock derived from OECD *Economic Outlook* 76 unchained business capital stock volume series, multiplied by the nonresidential investment deflator in Outlook 89 from 1965 to 2003 and expanded to 2004–2009 with data from Japan's National Accounts downloaded from: http://www.stat.go.jp/english/data/nenkan/1431–03.htm.

Figure 12.8

We defined capital accumulation rates as net nonresidential (business) investment plus inventory change relative to net business capital stock lagged one period, $I_B + \Delta I_{Inv}, / K_{B,-1}$

Canada's data for nonresidential fixed capital formation derived from gross fixed investment minus gross housing investment plus inventories change, all found in AMECO Table 3, divided over private business nonresidential net capital stock, downloaded from Statistics Canada: http://www5.statcan.gc.ca/cansim/pick-choisir?lang=eng&searchTypeByValue=1&id=0310003

France's gross nonresidential investment minus CC allowances plus inventories change extracted from AMECO Table 3. France's business capital stock for the business sector, defined as the nonresidential capital stock of nonfinancial business, derived from the OECD *Economic Outlook* 78 edition volume series, which remained unchained through 2006, multiplied by the nonresidential investment deflator; then expanded to 2009 with INSEE data as in Figure 12.8.

Germany's gross private nonresidential investment in OECD *Economic Outlook* 89 minus private CC allowances, minus government CC in Outlook 89, plus inventory change, AMECO Table 3, adjusted for the ratio of private nonresidential investment to total fixed investment.

Italy's gross private nonresidential investment from *Economic Outlook* 78, unchained nominal series, minus private fixed CC, subtracting government CC, adjusted for the ratio of nonresidential investment to total fixed investment plus inventory change.

Japan's industrial investment in plant and equipment minus annual depreciation of industrial fixed assets plus inventories change, divided over year-end total industrial fixed assets less land calculated on an annual basis in quarterly data downloaded from Japan's Policy Research Institute, Ministry of Finance website: http://www.mof.go.jp/english/pri/reference/ssc/historical.htm

Spain's private gross nonresidential investment in AMECO Table 3 minus gross fixed housing investment, in *Economic Outlook* 77, 1960–1969, then extended with nonresidential investment data from AMECO Table 3 from 1970 to 2009; inventory change in AMECO Table 3; net nonresidential private investment calculated as gross minus fixed CC in AMECO Table 3 minus government CC in Outlook 78 and Outlook 86. Nonresidential capital stock data estimated as total minus dwellings, from Fundación BBVA-Ivie: http://www. fbbva.es/TLFU/microsites/stock08/fbbva_stock08_index.html

UK data in Blue Book 2009, including private nonfinancial corporate gross fixed investment, code DBGPAU, minus private nonfinancial corporate CC, code BGXZAU, plus change in private corporate inventories, first difference of inventories series, code DLQXAU, divided over net private nonfinancial corporate capital stock, code CIXHAU. All data downloaded from: http://www.ons. gov.uk/ons/datasets-and-tables/search/index.html?content-type=Dataset

Bibliography

Abramovitz, M. and David, P. A. (1973) Reinterpreting economic growth: Parables and reality, *American Economic Review*, 63 (2), 428–439.

Aiginger, K. (1997) The use of unit values to discriminate between price and quality competition, *Cambridge Journal of Economics*, 21, 571–592.

Altschul, E. and Strauss, F. (1937) *Technical Progress and Agricultural Depression*. Bulletin 67. National Bureau of Economic Research.

Amato, L. and Wilder, R. P. (1985) The effects of firm size on profit rates in U.S. manufacturing, *Southern Economic Journal*, 52 (1), 181–190.

Ames, E. and Rosenberg, N. (1965) The progressive division and specialization of industries, *Journal of Development Studies*, 1 (4), 363–383.

Anderson, P. (1961) The apparent decline in capital-output ratios, *Quarterly Journal of Economics*, 75 (4), 615–634.

Armstrong, P., Glyn, A. and Harrison, J. (1984), *Capitalism Since World War II*. London: Fontana.

Aschauer, D. (1988) Government spending and the "falling rate of profit", *Economic Perspectives*, Federal Reserve Bank of Chicago, May–June.

Atack, J., Bateman, F. and Margo, R. A. (2003) Capital deepening in American manufacturing: 1850–1880. Working Paper 9923, National Bureau of Economic Research, Cambridge, MA.

Auerbach, P. (1989) *Competition, The Economics of Industrial Change*. Cambridge, MA: Basil Blackwell.

Barrère, A. (1965) Capital intensity and the combination of factors of production. In F. A. Lutz and D. C. Hague (eds), *The Theory of Capital*. New York: St Martin's Press.

Bartlett, B. (2002) Are companies earning their keep? *National Review Financial*, October 21. http://www.nationalreview.com/nrof_bartlett/bartlett102102.asp.

Baumol, W. J. (1990) Entrepreneurship, productive, unproductive, and destructive, *Journal of Political Economy*, 98 (5), 893–921.

Baumol, W. J. (2002) *The Free-Market Innovation Machine*. Princeton, NJ: Princeton University Press.

Baumol, W., Blinder, A. and Wolff, E. (2003) *Downsizing in America*. New York: Russel Sage Foundation.

Baumol, W., Litan, R. and Schramm, C. (2007) *Good Capitalism, Bad Capitalism*. New Haven, CT: Yale University Press.

Beitel, K. (2009) The rate of profit and the problem of stagnant investment: A structural analysis of barriers to accumulation and the spectre of protracted crisis, *Historical Materialism*, 17, 66–100.

Bernanke, B. (2005) The global saving glut and the U.S. current account deficit. Federal Reserve Board, March 10.

Bernstein, M. (1987) *The Great Depression*. New York: Cambridge University Press.

Bhaduri, A. (1986) *Macro-Economics: The Dynamics of Commodity Production*. Armonk, NY: M.E. Sharpe.

Bhagwati, J. (1995) Trade and wages: Choosing among alternative explanations, *Economic Policy Review*, Federal Reserve Bank of New York, 42–47.

Bhagwati, J. (2007) Technology, not globalization, is driving wages down, *Financial Times*, January 4.

Bielsa, J. and Duarte, R. (2011) Size and linkages of the Spanish construction industry: Key sector or deformation of the economy? *Cambridge Journal of Economics*, 35, 317–334.

Blanchard, O. (1997) The medium run, *Brookings Papers on Economic Activity*, 2. 89–158.

Blanchard, O., Rhee, C. and Summers, L. (1993) The stock market, profit, and investment, *Quarterly Journal of Economics*, 108, 115–136.

Blaug, M. (1963) A survey of the theory of process-innovations, *Economica*, 30 (117), 13–32.

Blaug, M. (1989) Nicholas Kaldor, 1908–86. In D. Greenaway, and J. R. Presley (eds), *Pioneers of Modern Economics in Britain*. New York: St Martin's Press.

Boddy, R. and Crotty, J. (1974) Class conflict, Keynesian policies, and the business cycle, *Monthly Review*, 26 (5).

Bohm-Bawerk, E. (1896) The positive theory of capital and its critics III, *Quarterly Journal of Economics*, 10 (2), 121–155.

Bosworth, B. (1993) *Saving and Investment in a Global Economy*. Washington, DC: Brookings Institution.

Bosworth, B. P., Solow, R. M. and Summers, L. H. (1982) Capital formation and economic policy, *Brookings Papers on Economic Activity*, 13 (2), 273–326.

Bowles, S., Edwards, R. and Roosevelt, F. (2005) *Understanding Capitalism: Competition, Command, and Change*. New York: Oxford University Press.

Brenner, R. (2002) *The Boom and the Bubble*. London: Verso.

Brenner, R. (2005) After boom, bubble and bust. In M. Miller (ed.), *Worlds of Capitalism*. London: Routledge.

Brenner, R. (2006) *Economics of Global Turbulence*. London: Verso.

Bricker, J., Kennickell, A. B., Moore, K. B. and Sabelhaus, J. (2012) Changes in U.S. family finances from 2007 to 2010: Evidence from the survey of consumer finances, *Federal Reserve Bulletin*, 98 (2).

Bronfenbrenner, M. (1971) *Income Distribution Theory*. Chicago: Aldine.

Bronfenbrenner, M. (1989) Schumpeter and Keynes as "rich man's Karl Marxes". In H. Wagener and J. Drukker (eds), *The Economic Law of Motion of Modern Society*. Cambridge: Cambridge University Press.

Brozen, Y. (1957) The economics of automation, *American Economic Review*, 47 (2), 339–350.

Bureau of Economic Analysis (2006) *A Guide to the National Income and Product Accounts of the United States*. http://www.bea.gov/national/pdf/nipaguid.pdf.

Cassidy, J. (1997) The return of Karl Marx, *The New Yorker*, October 20 and 27.

Chan-Lee, J. (1986) Pure profit rates and Tobin's *q* in nine OECD countries. Working Paper No. 34, OECD Department of Economics and Statistics.

Chan-Lee, J. and Sutch, H. (1985) Profits and rates of return in OECD countries. Working Paper 20, OECD Economics and Statistics Department.

Christensen, L. R. and Jorgensen, D. W. (1969) The measurement of U.S. real capital input, 1929–1967. *Review of Income and Wealth*, 15 (4), 293–320.

Clifton, J. A. (1977) Competition and the evolution of the capitalist mode of production, *Cambridge Journal of Economics*, 1 (2), 137–151.

Clifton, J. A. (1983) Administered prices in the context of capitalist development, *Contributions to Political Economy*, 2, 23–38.

Coen, R. (1980), Alternative measures of capital and its rate of return in United States manufacturing. In D. Usher (ed.), *The Measurement of Capital*, pp. 121–152. Chicago: University of Chicago Press.

Cordonnier, L. (2006) Le profit sans l'accumulation: La recette du capitalisme gouverné par la finance, *Innovations*, 23, 79–108.

Corrado, C. and Mattey, J. (1997) Capacity utilization, *Journal of Economic Perspectives*, 11 (1), 151–167.

Creamer, D. (1958) Postwar trends in the relation of capital to output in manufactures, *American Economic Review*, 48 (2), 249–259.

Crotty, J. (1986) Marx, Keynes and Minsky on the instability of the capitalist growth process and the nature of government policy. In S. Helburn and D. Bramhall (eds), *Marx, Schumpeter, Keynes: A Centenary Celebration of Dissent*. Armonk, NY: M. E. Sharpe.

Crotty, J. (2005) The neoliberal paradox: The impact of destructive product market competition. In G Epstein (ed.), *Financialization and the World Economy*. Cheltenham: Edward Elgar.

Dallery, T. (2009) Post-Keynesian theories of the firm under financialization, *Review of Radical Political Economics*, 41, 492–515.

David, P. A. (2004) Innovation and accumulation in the first two centuries of U.S. economic growth. SIEPR Discussion Paper 03-24, Stanford Institute for Economic Policy Research, Stanford University.

Denison, E. F. (1993) Robert J. Gordon's concept of capital, *Review of Income and Wealth*, 39 (1), 89–102.

Domar, E. (1965) The capital-output ratio in the United States: Its variation and stability. In F. A. Lutz and D. C. Hague (eds), *The Theory of Capital*. New York: St Martin's Press.

Dos Santos, P. (2009) On the content of banking in contemporary capitalism, *Historical Materialism*, 17, 180–213.

Duca, J. V. (1997) Has long-run profitability risen in the 1990s? *Federal Reserve Bank of Dallas Economic Review*, Fourth Quarter, 2–14.

Duménil, G. and Lévy, D. (1990). Continuity and ruptures in the process of technological change. Working paper, CEPREMAP, August.

Duménil, G. and Lévy, D. (1994) The US economy since the Civil War: Sources and construction of the series. http://www.cepremap.cnrs.fr/~levy/uslt4.txt.

Duménil, G. and Lévy, D. (2002) Manufacturing and global turbulence: Brenner's misinterpretation of profit rate differentials, *Review of Radical Political Economy*, 34(1), 45–48.

Duménil, G. and Lévy, D. (2004) The real and financial components of profitability (United States, 1952–2000), *Review of Radical Political Economics*, 36 (1), 82–110.

Duménil, G. and Lévy, D. (2011a) The crisis of the early 21st century: A critical review of alternative interpretations (preliminary draft). http://www.jourdan.ens.fr/levy/

Duménil, G. and Lévy, D. (2011b) The crisis of the early 21st century: General interpretation, recent developments, and perspectives. http://www.jourdan.ens.fr/levy/

Duménil, G. and Lévy, D. (2011c) Keynesian and Marxian macroeconomics: Toward a synthesis. http://www.jourdan.ens.fr/levy/

Dumenil, G., Glick, M. and Rangel, J. (1987a) Theories of the Great Depression: Why did profitability matter? *Review of Radical Political Economics*, 19 (2) 16–40.

Dumenil, G. Glick, M. and Rangel, J. (1987b) The rate of profit in the United States, *Cambridge Journal of Economics*, 11, 331–351.

Dumenil, G., Glick, M. and Levy, D. (1988) Long-term trends in profitability: The recovery of World War II. Working Paper 10, Jerome Levy Economics Institute, Annandale-on-Hudson, NY.

Eatwell, J. and Milgate, M. (2010) *The Fall and Rise of Keynesian Economics*. New York: Oxford University Press.

Eltis, W. (1971) The determination of the rate of technical progress, *Economic Journal*, 81 (323), 502–524.

Eltis, W. (1985) Ricardo on machinery and technological unemployment. In G. Caravale (ed.), *The Legacy of Ricardo*. New York: Blackwell.

Eltis, W. (1996) How low profitability and weak innovativeness undermined UK industrial growth, *Economic Journal*, 106 (434), 184–195.

Engerman, S. L. and Gallman, R. E. (eds) (1986) *Long-Term Factors in American Economic Growth*. Chicago: University of Chicago Press.

Epstein, R. C. (1934) *Industrial Profits in the United State*. New York: National Bureau of Economic Research.

Fagerberg, J. (1996) Technology and competitiveness, *Oxford Review of Economic Policy*, 12 (3), 39–51.

Faunce, W. (1965) Automation and the division of labor, *Social Problems*, 13 (2), 149–160.

Feldstein, M. (ed.) (1991) *The Risk of Economic Crisis*. Chicago: University of Chicago Press.

Feldstein, M. and Foot, D. (1971) The other half of gross investment: Replacement and modernization expenditures, *Review of Economics and Statistics*, 53, 49–58.

Feldstein, M. and Poterba, J. (1981) The effective tax rate and the pretax rate of return. Working Paper 740, National Bureau of Economic Research, Cambridge, MA.

Feldstein, M. and Rothschild, M. (1974) Towards an economic theory of investment replacement, *Econometrica*, 42 (3), 393–424.

Feldstein, M. and Summers, L. (1977) Is the rate of profit falling? *Brookings Papers on Economic Activity*, 1, 211–227.

Felipe, J. (2002) Unemployment and profitability. In P. Davidson (ed.), *A Post Keynesian Perspective on 21st Century Economic Problems*. Cheltenham: Edward Elgar.

Felipe, J. and McCombie, J. S. L. (2006) The tyranny of the identity: Growth accounting revisited, *International Review of Applied Economics*, 20 (3), 283–299.

Fisher, I. (2011) *Booms and Depressions*, Michael Schemmann: Lexington, KY

Foley, D. (1986) *Understanding Capital*. Cambridge, MA: Harvard University Press.

Foley, D. and Marquetti, A. (1997) Economic growth from a classical perspective. In J. Teixeira (ed.), *Money, Growth, Distribution and Structural Change: Contemporaneous Analysis*. Brasilia: University of Brasilia Press.

Foley, D. and Michl, T. (1999) *Growth and Distribution*. Cambridge, MA: Harvard University Press.

Ford, M. (2009) *The Lights in the Tunnel: Automation, Accelerating Technology and the Economy of the Future*. Acculant Publishing.

Forstater, M. (2001) Unemployment in capitalist economies: A history of thought. Working Paper 16, Center for Full Employment and Price Stability. http://www.cfeps.org/pubs/wp-pdf/WP16-Forstater.pdf

Forstater, M. (2002) Full employment policies must consider effective demand and structural and technological change: A prime point of Pasinetti's political economy. In P. Davidson (ed.), *A Post Keynesian Perspective on 21st Century Economic Problems*. Cheltenham: Edward Elgar.

Foss, M. (1963) The utilization of capital equipment, *Survey of Current Business*, 43 (6), 8–16

Foss, M. (1981) Long-run changes in the workweek of fixed capital. *American Economic Review*, 71 (2), 58–63.

Foss, M. (1985) Changing utilization of fixed capital: An element in long-term growth, *Monthly Labor Review*, May, 3–8.

Fox, J. (2010) The real story behind those "record" corporate profits, *Harvard Business Review*, November 24. http://blogs.hbr.org/fox/2010/11/the-real-story-behind-those-re.html

Freeman, C. (1982) *The Economics of Industrial Innovation*. Cambridge, MA: MIT Press.

Friedman, M. (1968) The role of monetary policy, *American Economic Review*, 58 (1), 1–17.

Galbraith, J. K. (1997) *The Great Crash*. New York: Houghton Mifflin.

Gallman, R. E. (1986) The United States capital stock in the nineteenth century. In S. L. Engerman and R. E. Gallman (eds), *Long-Term Factors in American Economic Growth*. Chicago: University of Chicago Press.

Gennaioli, N., Shleifer, A. and Vishny, R. (2011) Neglected risks, financial innovation, and financial fragility, *Journal of Financial Innovations*, May 27.

Ghemawat, P. and Caves, R. (1986) Capital commitment and profitability: An empirical investigation, *Oxford Economic Papers*, 38, 94–110.

Gjerstad, S. and Smith, V. (2009) Monetary policy, credit extension and housing bubbles: 2008 and 1929, *Critical Review*, 21 (2–3), 269–300.

Glyn, A. (1997) Does aggregate profitability really matter? *Cambridge Journal of Economics*, 21, 593–619.

Glyn, A., Hughes, A., Lipietz, A. and Singh, A. (1991) The rise and fall of the Golden Age. In S. Marglin, and J. Schor (eds), *The Golden Age of Capitalism*. Oxford: Clarendon Press.

Goldsmith, R. (1952) The growth of reproducible wealth of the United States of America from 1805 to 1950. In S. Kuznets (ed.), *Income and Wealth of the United States: Trends and Structure*. Cambridge: Bowes & Bowes.

Goodwin, R. M. (1972) A growth cycle. In E. K. Hunt and J. G. Schwartz (eds), *A Critique of Economic Theory*, pp. 442–449. Harmondsworth: Penguin.

Gordon, D. M. (1991) Kaldor's macro system: Too much cumulation, too few contradictions. In E. Nell and W. Semmler (eds), *Nicholas Kaldor and Mainstream Economics*. New York: St Martin's Press.

Gordon, R. A. (1949) Business cycles in the interwar period: The quantitative-historical approach, *American Economic Review*, 39 (3), 47–63.

Gordon, R. A. (1951) Cyclical experience in the interwar period: The investment boom of the twenties. In *Conference on Business Cycles*, pp. 163–224. New York: National Bureau of Economic Research.

Gordon, R. J. (1967) Problems in the measurement of real investment in the U.S. private economy. PhD dissertation, Massachusetts Institute of Technology.

Gordon, R. J. (1969) $45 billion of U.S. private investment has been mislaid, *American Economic Review*, 59 (3), 221–238.

Gordon, R. J. (1990) *The Measurement of Durable Goods Prices*. Chicago: University of Chicago Press.

Gordon, R. J. (1993) Reply: The concept of capital, *Review of Income and Wealth*, 39 (1), 103–110.

Gordon, R. J. (2004a) The 1920s and the 1990s in mutual reflection. Paper presented to *Understanding the 1990s: The Long-term Perspective*, Economic History Conference, Duke University, March 26–27.

Gordon, R. J. (2004b) Interpreting the 'one big wave' in U.S. long-term productivity growth. In *Productivity Growth, Inflation and Unemployment, The Collected Essays of Robert J. Gordon*. New York: Cambridge University Press.

Greasley, D. and Madsen, J. (2006) Investment and uncertainty: Precipitating the Great Depression in the United States, *Economica*, 73, 393–412.

Gutierrez, C. M., Glassman, C.A., Landefeld, J. S. and Marcuss, R. D. (2007) *Measuring the Economy*. Bureau of Economic Analysis, US Department of Commerce. http://www.bea.gov/national/pdf/nipa_primer.pdf.

Guttmann, R. (1994) *How Credit-Money Shapes the Economy*. Armonk, NY: M. E. Sharpe.

Haldi, J. and Whitcomb, D. (1967) Economies of scale in industrial plants, *Journal of Political Economy*, 75 (4), 373–385.

Hansen, A. (1951) Schumpeter's contribution to business cycle theory, *Review of Economics and Statistics*, 33 (2), 129–132.

Harcourt, G. C. (1982) A critique of Mr Kaldor's model of income distribution and economic growth. In P. Kerr (ed.), *The Social Science Imperialists*. London: Routledge & Kegan Paul.

Hargreaves-Heap, S. (1980) World profitability crisis in the 1970s: Some empirical evidence, *Capital and Class*, 12, 66–84.

Harrison, A. (2005) Has globalization eroded labor's share? MPRA Paper 39649. http://mpra.ub.uni-muenchen.de/39649/

Heilbroner, R. (1985) *The Nature and Logic of Capitalism*. New York: W. W. Norton.

Hickman, B. (1963) The postwar retardation: Another long swing in the rate of growth? *American Economic Review*, 53 (2), 490–507.

Hicks, J. R. (1963) *The Theory of Wages*, 2nd edition. London: Macmillan.

Hill, P. T. (1979) *Profits and Rates of Return.*. Paris: OECD.

Hill, P. T. (1998) Gross, productive and net capital stock. *Camberra Group on Capital Stock Statistics*, Agenda Item 5, Document 10. Paris: OECD.

Hobsbawm, E. J. (1969) *Industry and Empire from 1750 to the Present Day*. Harmondsworth: Penguin, 1969.

Holland, D. M. and Myers, D. (1978) Trends in corporate profitability and capital costs. Working Paper #999–78, Sloan School of Management, MIT.

Hollond, M. T. (1936) Review: Industrial profits in the United States, *Economic Journal*, 46, 181, 117–120.

Hunt, S. and Morgan, R. (1995) The comparative advantage theory of competition, *Journal of Marketing*, 59 (2), 1–15.

Ingham, G. (2008) *Capitalism: With a New Postscript on the Financial Crisis and Its Aftermath*. Cambridge: Polity Press.

Jovanovic, B. (1982) Selection and the evolution of industry, *Econometrica*, 50, 649–670.

Kahler, A. (1935) The problem of verifying the theory of technological unemployment, *Social Research*, 2, 439–460.

Kaldor, N. (1965) Capital accumulation and economic growth. In F. A. Lutz and D. C. Hague (eds), *The Theory of Capital*. New York: St Martin's Press.

Kaldor, N. (1968) Productivity and growth in manufacturing: A reply, *Economica*, 35 (140), 385–391.

Kaldor, N. (1972) The irrelevance of equilibrium economics, *Economic Journal*, 82 (328), 1237–1255.

Kaldor, N. (1975) Economic growth and the Verdoorn law – a comment on Mr. Rowthorn's article, *Economic Journal*, 85 (340), 891–896.

Kaldor, N. (1978a) *Further Essays on Economic Theory*. New York: Holmes & Meier.

Kaldor, N. (1978b) The effect of devaluations on trade in manufactures. In *Further Essays on Applied Economics*. New York: Holmes & Meier.

Kaldor, N. (1986) Limits on growth. *Oxford Economic Papers*, 38, 187–198.

Kaldor, N. (1939) Capital intensity and the trade cycle, *Economica*, 6, 40–66.

Kalecki, M. (1971) Political aspects of full employment. In *Selected Essays on the Dynamics of the Capitalist Economy, 1933–1970*. London: Cambridge University Press.

Kaplinsky, R. (1985) Electronics-based automation technologies and the onset of systemofacture: Implications for Third World industrialization, *World Development*, 13 (3), 423–439.

Kaplinsky, R. and Santos-Paulino, A. (2005) Innovation and competitiveness: Trends in unit prices in global trade, *Oxford Development Studies*, 33, 333–354.

Kaplinsky, R. and Santos-Paulino, A. (2006) A disaggregated analysis of EU imports: The implications for the study of patterns of trade and technology, *Cambridge Journal of Economics*: 30, 587–611.

Kendrick, J. W. (1961) *Productivity Trends in the United States*. Princeton, NJ: Princeton University Press.

Kitson, M. and Michie, J. (1996) Britain's industrial performance since 1960: Underinvestment and relative decline, *Economic Journal*, 106 (434), 196–212.

Klein, L. R. and Kosobud, R. F. (1961) Some econometrics of growth: Great ratios of economics, *Quarterly Journal of Economics*, 75 (2), 173–198.

Knight, F. (1946) Immutable law in economics: Its reality and limitations, *American Economic Review*, 36 (2), 93–111.

Kregel, J. A. (1971) *Rate of Profit, Distribution and Growth, Two Views*. New York: Aldine.

Krugman, P. (1994) Technology's revenge, *The Wilson Quarterly*, Fall.

Krugman, P. (2005) *The Great Unraveling*. New York: W. W. Norton.

Krugman, P. (2010) Pesos, Ponzi, and financial sector profits, *New York Times*, April 23.

Krugman, P. (2012) *End This Depression Now*. New York: W. W. Norton.

Kurz, H. (2006) Schumpeter on innovations and profits. *"Economics from all Sides" Seminar*, University of Amsterdam. http://www.lib.hit-u.ac.jp/service/tenji/amjas/Kurz.pdf.

Kurz, H. (2009) Technical progress, capital accumulation and income distribution in classical economics: Adam Smith, David Ricardo and Karl Marx. Paper presented to *ESHET 2009 Conference*. www.uni-graz.at/schumpeter.centre/download/summerschool09/Literature/Kurz/

Kuznets, S. (1940) Schumpeter's business cycles, *American Economic Review*, 30 (2), 257–271.

Kuznets, S. (1952) Long-term changes in the national income of the United States of America since 1870, *Review of Income and Wealth*, 2 (1), 29–241.

Kuznets, S. (1961) *Capital in the American Economy: Its Formation and Financing*, Princeton, NJ: Princeton University Press for NBER.

Lange, O. (1935) Marxian economics and modern economic theory, *Review of Economic Studies*, 2 (3), 189–201.

Lange, O. (1943) A note on innovations, *Review of Economic Statistics*, 25 (1), 19–25.

Lavoie, M. (2006) Do heterodox theories have anything in common? A post-Keynesian point of view, *Intervention Journal of Economics*, 3 (1), 87–112.

Lavoie, M. (2008) Neoclassical empirical evidence on employment and production. Robinson Working Paper 08-09. http://aix1.uottawa.ca/~robinson.

Lazonick, W. and O'Sullivan, M. (2000) Maximizing shareholder value: A new ideology for corporate governance, *Economy and Society*, 29, 13–35.

Lederer, E. (1933) Technical progress and unemployment, *International Labour Review*, XXVIII (1), 1–25.

Leijonhufvud, A. (2008) Between Keynes and Sraffa: Pasinetti on the Cambridge School, *European Journal of the History of Economic Thought*, 15 (3), 529–538.

Leijonhufvud, A. (2009) Out of the corridor: Keynes and the crisis, *Cambridge Journal of Economics*, 33, 741–757.

Leiserson, W. M. (1916) The problem of unemployment today, *Political Science Quarterly*, 31 (1), 1–24.

Liebling, H. (1980) *US Corporate Profitability and Capital Formation: Are Rates of Return Sufficient?* New York: Pergamon Press.

Lindbeck, A. (1993) *Unemployment and Macroeconomics*. Cambridge, MA: MIT Press.

Lovel, M. (1978) The profit picture: Trend and cycles, *Brookings Papers on Economic Activity*, 3, 769–789.

Lutz, F. A. and Hague, D. C. (eds) (1965) *The Theory of Capital*. New York: St Martin's Press.

Maddison, A. (1982) *Phases of Capitalist Development*. New York: Oxford University Press.

Maddison, A. (1991) *Dynamic Forces in Capitalist Development*. Oxford: Oxford University Press.

Maddison, A. (1995) Standardized estimates of fixed capital stocks: A six country comparison. In *Explaining the Economic Performance of Nations*. Aldershot: Edward Elgar.

Maddison, A. (2010) Historical statistics of the world economy: 1–2008AD. http://www.ggdc.net/maddison/Historical_Statistics/horizontal-file_02-2010.xls.

Magnus, G. (2011) Give Karl Marx a chance to save the world economy. http://www. bloomberg. com/ news/ print/ 2011-08-29/ give-marx-a-chance-to-save-the-world-economy-commentary-by-george-magnus.html.

Malinvaud, E. (1985) *The Theory of Unemployment Reconsidered*. New York: Basil Blackwell.

Malinvaud, E. (1986) *Mass Unemployment*. New York: Basil Blackwell.

Marquetti, A. (2003) Analyzing historical and regional patterns of technical change from a classical-Marxian perspective, *Journal of Economic Behavior and Organization*, 52, 191–200.

Marquetti, A. and Mendoza, G. (2010) An analysis of the stylized facts of economic growth for good and bad outputs. Sixth International Marx Congress. http://actuelmarx.u-paris10.fr/cm6/index6.htm.

Marx, K. (1976) *Capital*, Volume I. Harmondsworth: Penguin.

Marx, K. (1982) *Selected Correspondence*. Moscow: Progress.

Marx, K. (1993) *Grundrisse*. Harmondsworth: Penguin.

Matthews, R. C., Feinstein, C. H. and Odling-Smee, J. C. (1982) *British Economic Growth: 1856–1973*. Stanford, CA: Stanford University Press.

Mayor, T. (1968) The decline in the United States capital/output ratio, *Economic Development and Cultural Change*, 16 (4), 495–516.

McNulty, P. J. (1968) Economic theory and the meaning of competition, *Quarterly Journal of Economics*, 82 (4), 639–656.

Meek, R. L. (1964) Ideal and reality in the choice between alternative techniques, *Oxford Economic Papers*, 16 (3), 333–354.

Meeks, G. and Meeks, J. G. (2005) Ever bigger firms?, *European Economy*, 13 (4), 511–523.

Metcalfe, J. S. (1981) Impulse and diffusion in the study of technical change, *Futures*, 13 (5), 347–359.

Metcalfe, J. S. (1999) Competitiveness and comparative advantage: Notes toward an evolutionary approach to growth and foreign trade. ESRC Centre for Research on Innovation and Competition, University of Manchester.

Metcalfe, J. S. (2004) The entrepreneur and the style of modern economics, *Journal of Evolutionary Economics*, 14, 157–175.

Milberg, W. (2005) The high road and the low road to international competitiveness: Extending the neo-Schumpeterian trade model beyond technology, *International Review of Applied Economics*, 19 (2), 137–162.

Milberg, W. (2006) Pricing and profits under globalized competition: A post Keynesian perspective on U.S. economic hegemony. SCEPA Working Paper 2006-5, Schwartz Center for Economic Policy Analysis, New York.

Mill, J. S. (1987) *Principles of Political Economy*. New York: Augustus M. Kelley. First published 1848.

Minsky, H. (1996) Uncertainty and the institutional structure of capitalist economies, *Journal of Economic Issues*, XXX (2), 357–367.

Minsky, H. (2008) *John Maynard Keynes*. New York: McGraw-Hill. First published 1975.

Moggridge, D. (ed.) (1979) *John Maynard Keynes, The General Theory and After: A Supplement* (*The Collected Writings of John Maynard Keynes*, Vol. 29). Cambridge: Cambridge University Press.

Mohun, S. (2006) Distributive shares in the US economy, 1964–2001, *Cambridge Journal of Economics*, 30, 347–370.

Mohun, S. (2010) The present crisis in historical perspective. Historical Materialism 7th Annual Conference, 11–14 November.

Moos, S. (1957) The scope of automation, *Economic Journal*, 67, 26–39.

Moseley, F. (1985) The rate of surplus value in the postwar U.S. economy: A critique of Weisskopf estimates, *Cambridge Journal of Economics*, 9, 57–79.

Moseley, F. (1988) The rate of surplus value, the organic composition, and the general rate of profit in the U.S. economy, 1947–67: A critique and update of Wolff's estimates, *American Economic Review*, 78 (1), 298–303.

Moseley, F. (1992) Unproductive labor and the rate of profit in postwar US economy. In F. Moseley and E. Wolff, *International Perspectives on Profitability and Accumulation*. Fairfield, VT: Edward Elgar.

Moseley, F. (1999) The decline of the rate of profit in the post-war United States: Due to increased competition or increased unproductive labor? *Historical Materialism*, 4, 131–148.

Moseley, F. (2002) Goldilocks meets a bear: How bad will the U.S. recession be? *Monthly Review*, April, 1–12.

Moseley, F. (2004) Marxian crisis theory and the current US economy. International Conference, Gyeongsang National University, May 21–22.

Moseley, F. (2008) The long trends of profits. http://www.workersliberty.org/story/2008/03/19/marxists-capitalist-crisis-1-fred-moseley-long-trends-profit

Moseley, F. (2009) The U.S. economic crisis: Causes and solutions. *Marxism 21*, 13, 296–316. http://nongae.gsnu.ac.kr/~issmarx/eng/article/13/vol13_uscrisis.pdf.

Moseley, F. and Wolff, E. (1992) *International Perspectives on Profitability and Accumulation*. Fairfield, VT: Edward Elgar.

Mullineux, A. W. (1990) *Business Cycles and Financial Crises*. London: Harvester Wheatsheaf.

Munley, F. (1981) Wages, salaries, and the profit share: A reassessment of the evidence, *Cambridge Journal of Economics*, 5, 159–173.

Negishi, T. (1989) *History of Economic Theory*. New York: North-Holland.

Negishi, T. (1998) Marx, economies of scale, and the falling rate of profit, *Japan and the World Economy*, 10, 253–263.

Neisser, H. (1942) "Permanent" technological unemployment: "Demand for commodities is not demand for labor", *American Economic Review*, 32 (1), 50–71.

Nickell, S. (1996) Competition and corporate performance, *Journal of Political Economy*, 104 (4), 724–746.

Nordhaus, W. D. (1974) The falling share of profits, *Brookings Papers on Economic Activity*, 1, 169–208.

Okun, A. and Perry, G. (1970) Notes and Numbers on the Profit Squeeze, *Brookings Papers on Economic Activity*, 3, 466–473.

Pasinetti, L. (1983) *Structural Change and Economic Growth*. New York: Cambridge University Press.

Pavitt, K. (1980) *Technical Innovation in British Economic Performance*. London: Macmillan.

Pollin, R. (1998) The "reserve army of labor" and the "natural rate of unemployment": Can Marx, Kalecki, Friedman, and Wall Street all be wrong? *Review of Radical Political Economics*, 38 (1), 1–13.

Pollin, R. (1999) Class conflict and the "natural rate of unemployment", *Challenge*, 42, 6, 103–111.

Poterba, J. (1998) The rate of return to corporate capital and factor shares: New estimates using revised National Income Accounts and capital stock data, *Carnegie-Rochester Conference Series on Public Policy*, 48, 211–246.

Pratten, C. (1971) Economies of scale for machine tool production, *Journal of Industrial Economics*, 19 (2), 148–165.

Pratten, C. (1972) The reasons for the slow economic progress of the British economy, *Oxford Economic Papers*, 24 (2), 180–196.

Pratten, C. (1980) The manufacture of pins, *Journal of Economic Literature*, 18, 1, 93–96.

Ragan, J. (1976) Measuring capacity utilization in manufacturing, *Federal Reserve Bank of New York Quarterly Review*, Winter, 13–20.

Reich, R. (2010) *Aftershock*. New York: Alfred A. Knopf.

Reinhart, C. and Rogoff, K. (2012) U.S. recoveries really aren't different. http://www. bloomberg. com/ news/ print/ 2012-10-15/ sorry-u-s-recoveries-really-aren-t-different. html.

Ricardo, D. (1981) *On the Principles of Political Economy and Taxation*, Cambridge University Press: Cambridge, UK.

Richardson, G. B. (1965) Ideal and Reality in the Choice of Techniques, *Oxford Economic Papers*, 17, 2, 291–298.

Robinson, J. (1937) *Essays in the Theory of Employment*, New York: Macmillan.

Robinson, J. (2003) Introduction. In R. Luxemburg, *The Accumulation of Capital*. New York: Routledge.

Rostow, W. (1938) Investment and the Great Depression, *Economic History Review*, 8 (2), 136–158.

Roubini, N. (2011) Is capitalism doomed? http://www.economonitor.com/nouriel/2011/08/ 15/is-capitalism-doomed/

Rowthorn, R. (1975) What remains of Kaldor's law? *Economic Journal*, 85 (337), 10–19.

Samuelson, P. (1943) Dynamics, statics, and the stationary state, *Review of Economic Statistics*, 25 (1), 58–68.

Sarich, J. and Hecht, J. (2010) Competition and international equity returns: Some empirical tests of "turbulent arbitrage", *Review of Radical Political Economics*: 42(1), 5–31.

Schoenberger, E. (1989) Some dilemmas of automation: Strategic and operational aspects of technological change in production, *Economic Geography*, 65 (3), 232–247.

Schumpeter, J. (1928) The instability of capitalism, *Economic Journal*, 38, 151, 361–386.

Schumpeter, J. (1946) The decade of the twenties, *American Economic Review*, 36, 2, 1–10.

Shaikh, A. (1978) Political economy and capitalism: Notes on Dobb's theory of crisis, *Cambridge Journal of Economics*, 2, 233–251.

Shaikh, A. (1980) Marxian competition versus perfect competition: Further comments on the so-called choice of techniques, *Cambridge Journal of Economics*, 4, 75–83.

Shaikh, A. (1987) The falling rate of profit and the economic crisis in the U.S. In R. Cherry *et al*. (eds), *The Imperiled Economy*. New York: Union for Radical Political Economics.

Shaikh, A. (1989) Accumulation, finance, and effective demand. In W. Semmler (ed.), *Financial Dynamics and Business Cycles*. Armonk, NY: M.E. Sharpe.

Shaikh, A. (1991) Wandering around the warranted path: Dynamic non-linear solutions to the Harrodian knife-edge. In E. J. Nell and W. Semmler (eds) *Nicholas Kaldor and Mainstream Economics*, pp. 320–334. London: Macmillan.

Shaikh, A. (1992) The falling rate of profit as the cause of long waves: Theory and empirical evidence. In A. Kleinknecht, E. Mandel and I. Wallerstein (eds), *New Findings in Long Wave Research*. London: Macmillan Press.

Shaikh, A. (1999a) Explaining the global economic crisis, *Historical Materialism*, 5, 103–144.

Shaikh, A. (1999b) Explaining inflation and unemployment: An alternative to neoliberal economic theory. In A. Vachlou (ed.), *Contemporary Economic Theory*. London: Macmillan.

Shaikh, A. (1999c) Real exchange rates and the international mobility of capital. Working Paper 265, New School University, New York.

Shaikh, A. (1999d) Notes on capacity utilization measures. Mimeo, New School University.

Shaikh, A. (2003) Labor market dynamics within rival macroeconomic frameworks. In G. Argyrous, G. Mongiovi and M. Forstater (eds), *Growth, Distribution and Effective Demand: Alternatives to Economic Orthodoxy.* Armonk, NY: M.E. Sharpe.

Shaikh, A. (2004) The power of profit, *Social Research*, 71 (2), 371–382.

Shaikh, A. (2005) Nonlinear dynamics and pseudo-production functions, *Eastern Economic Journal*, 31 (3), 347–366.

Shaikh, A. (2008) Competition and industrial rates of return. In P. Arestis and J. Eatwell (eds), *Issues in Finance and Industry*. Basingstoke: Palgrave Macmillan.

Shaikh, A. (2009) Economic policy in a growth context: A classical synthesis of Keynes and Harrod, *Metroeconomica*, 60 (3), 455–494.

Shaikh, A. (2010a) The first Great Depression of the 21st century. In L. Panitch, G. Albo and V. Chibber (eds), *Socialist Register 2011*. London.

Shaikh, A. (2010b) Crisis and distribution, *New School Economic Review*, 4(1), 72–76.

Shaikh, A. and Moudud J. (2004) Measuring capacity utilization in OECD countries: A cointegration method. Working Paper 415, Levy Economics Institute of Bard College, Annandale-on-Hudson, NY.

Shapiro, M. D. (1989) Assessing the Federal Reserve's measures of capacity and utilization, *Brookings Papers on Economic Activity*, 1, 181–241.

Sharpe, A. (2002) Angus Maddison rewrites economic history again, *Challenge*: 45 (4), 20–40.

Sheshinski, E., Strom, R. and Baumol, W. (2007) *Entrepreneurship, Innovation, and the Growth Mechanism of the Free Enterprise Economies.* Princeton, NJ: Princeton University Press.

Sidgwick, H. (1883) *The Principles of Political Economy*. London: Macmillan & Co.

Skott, P. and Ryoo, S. (2008) Macroeconomic Implications of Financialisation, *Cambridge Journal of Economics*, 32, 827–862.

Smith, A. (1965) *The Wealth of Nations*. New York: The Modern Library (Random House).

Smith, T. (2010) Technological changes in capitalism: Some Marxian themes, *Cambridge Journal of Economics*, 34, 203–212.

Smith, V. (1962) The theory of capital, *American Economic Review*, 52, 3, 481–491.

Smulders, S. (ed.) (2001) Introduction. In *Growth Theory in Historical Perspective*. Cheltenham: Edward Elgar.

Snyder, C. (1936) The capital supply and national well-being, *American Economic Review*, 26, 195–224.

Snyder, C. (1940) *Capitalism the Creator*. New York: Macmillan.

Solow, R. M. (1987) *Growth Theory, an Exposition*. New York: Oxford University Press.

Spence, M. (1984) Cost reduction, competition, and industry performance, *Econometrica*, 52 (1), 101–122.

Sraffa, P. (1963) *Production of Commodities by Means of Other Commodities*. Cambridge: Cambridge University Press.

Steindl, J. (1976) *Maturity and Stagnation in American Capitalism*. New York: Monthly Review Press.

Stern, E. (1945) Capital requirements in progressive economics, *Economica*, 12 (47), 163–171.

Stiglitz, J. (2010) The non-existent hand, *London Review of Books*, 32 (May 22), 17–18. http://www.lrb.co.uk/v32/n08/joseph-stiglitz/the-non-existent-hand.

Stiglitz, J. (2011) To cure the economy, *Project Syndicate*, October 3. http://www.project-syndicate.org/commentary/stiglitz143/English.

Stiglitz, J. (2012) The Book of Jobs, *Vanity Fair*, January. http://www.vanityfair.com/politics/2012/01/stiglitz-depression-201201.

Stockhammer, E. (2005–06) Shareholder value orientation and the investment–profit puzzle, *Journal of Post Keynesian Economics*, 28 (2), 193–215.

Stockhammer, E. (2008) Is the NAIRU a monetarist, new Keynesian, post Keynesian or a Marxist theory? *Metroeconomica*, 39 (3), 479–510.

Stoneman, P. and Kwon, M. J. (1996) Technology adoption and firm profitability, *Economic Journal*, 106 (437), 952–962.

Storm, S. and Naastepad, C. (2012) *Macroeconomics Beyond the NAIRU*. Cambridge, MA: Harvard University Press.

Summers, L. (2011) We have to do better on inequality, *Financial Times*, November 20.

Summers, L. (2012) Current woes call for smart reinvention not destruction, *Financial Times*, January 8.

Sweezy, P. (1943) Professor Schumpeter's theory of innovation, *Review of Economics and Statistics*, 25 (1), 93–96.

Taitel, M. (1941) *Profits, Productive Activities and New Investment*. Temporary National Committee Monograph 12. Washington, DC: US Government Printing Office.

Taussig, F. W. (1896) *Wages and Capital*. New York: Appleton.

Tice, H. S. (1967). Depreciation, obsolescence, and the measurement of the aggregate capital stock of the United States, *Review of Income and Wealth*, 13, 119–154.

Tobin, J. (1965) Money and economic growth, *Econometrica*, 33 (4), 671–684.

Toporowski, J. (2010) *Why the World Economy Needs a Financial Crash*. London: Anthem Press.

Torrini, R. (2005) Profit shares and returns on capital stock in Italy: The role of privatizations behind the rise of the 1990s. Centre for Economic Performance, London School of Economics.

Tropeano, D. (2012) Income distribution, growth and financialization: The Italian case. In C. Gnos, L.-P. Rochon and D. Tropeano (eds), *Employment, Growth and Development, A Post-Keynesian Approach*. Cheltenham: Edward Elgar.

Tsoulfidis, L. (2010) Economic theory in historical perspective. Discussion Paper No. 15/2010, Department of Economics, University of Macedonia.

Tsoulfidis, L. (2011) Classical vs. neoclassical conceptions of competition. Discussion Paper No. 11/2011, Department of Economics, University of Macedonia.

Tsoulfidis, L. and Tsaliki, P. (2005) Marxian theory of competition and the concept of regulating capital: Evidence from Greek manufacturing, *Review of Radical Political Economics*, 37 (1), 5–22.

Tucker, R. S. (1937) Is there a tendency for profits to equalize? *American Economic Review*, 27 (1), 519–524.

Uctum, M. (1998) Why have profits declined? An international comparison, *Review of International Economics*, 6(2), 234–251.

Uctum, M. and Viana, S. (1999) Decline in the US profit rate: A sectoral analysis, *Applied Economics*, 31, 1641–1652.

Van Treeck, T. (2007) Reconsidering the investment-profit nexus in finance-led economies. Working Paper 1/2007, Institut für Makroökonomie und Konjukturforschung, Düsseldorf.

Van Treeck, T. (2008) The political economy debate on 'financialization': A macroeconomic perspective. Working Paper 1/2008, Institut für Makroökonomie und Konjukturforschung, Düsseldorf.

Vickers, J. (1995) Concepts of competition, *Oxford Economic Papers*, 47, 1–23.

Wade, R. (2011) The economy has not solved its problems, *Challenge*, 54 (2), 5–41.

Wagener, H. J, and Drukker, J. W. (eds) (1989) *The Economic Law of Motion of Modern Society*. Cambridge: Cambridge University Press.

Weber, B. and Handfield-Jones, S. J. (1954) Variations in the rate of economic growth in the USA, 1869–1939, *Oxford Economic Papers*, 6 (2), 101–131.

Weiss, L. W. (1973) Economies of scale in manufacturing industry, *Journal of Business*, 46 (3), 454–455.

Weisskopf, T. E. (1979) Marxian crisis theory and the rate of profit in the U.S. economy, *Cambridge Journal of Economics*, 3, 341–378.

Weisskopf, T. E. (1981) Wages, salaries and the profit share: A rejoinder, *Cambridge Journal of Economics*, 5, 175–182.

Weisskopf, T. E. (1985) The rate of surplus value in the postwar U.S. economy: A response to Moseley's critique, *Cambridge Journal of Economics*, 9, 81–84.

Weisskopf, T. E. (1992) A comparative analysis of profitability trends in the advanced capitalist economies. In F. Moseley and E. Wolff, *International Perspectives on Profitability and Accumulation*. Brookfield, VT: Edward Elgar.

Weisskopf, T. E. (1994) Alternative social structures of accumulation approaches to the analysis of capitalist booms and crisis. In D. Kotz, T. McDonough and M. Reich (eds), *Social Structures of Accumulation*. Cambridge: Cambridge University Press.

Weston, J. F. and Brigham, E. F. (1993) *Essentials of Managerial Finance*, 10th edition. New York: Dryden Press.

Wolfe, J. N. (1968) Productivity and growth in manufacturing industry: Some reflections on Professor Kaldor's inaugural lecture, *Economica*, 35 (138), 117–126.

Wolff, E. N. (1979). The rate of surplus value, the organic composition, and the general rate of profit in the U.S. economy, 1947–67, *American Economic Review*, 69 (3), 329–341.

Wolff, E. N. (1988). The rate of surplus value, the organic composition, and the general rate of profit in the U.S. economy, 1947–67: Reply, *American Economic Review*, 78 (1), 304–306.

Wolff, E. N. (2003). What's behind the rise in profitability in the U.S. in the 1980s and 1990s? *Cambridge Journal of Economics*, 27, 479–499.

Wood, A. (1993) *A Theory of Profits*. Fairfield, NJ: Augustus M. Kelley Publishers.

Wright, G. (1990) The origins of american industrial success: 1879–1940, *American Economic Review*, 80 (4), 651–668.

Wright, S. (2004a) Measures of stock market value and returns for the U.S. nonfinancial corporate sector, 1900–2002, *Review of Income and Wealth*, 50 (4), 561–584.

Wright, S. (2004b) Dataset. http://www.ems.bbk.ac.uk/faculty/wright/

Zacharias, A. (2002) Competition and profitability: A critique of Robert Brenner, *Review of Radical Political Economics*: 34, 19–34.

Index

For Product Safety Concerns and Information please contact our EU
representative GPSR@taylorandfrancis.com
Taylor & Francis Verlag GmbH, Kaufingerstraße 24, 80331 München, Germany

www.ingramcontent.com/pod-product-compliance
Ingram Content Group UK Ltd.
Pitfield, Milton Keynes, MK11 3LW, UK
UKHW021839240425
457818UK00007B/241